GW00630555

# Information science
# in transition

# Information science in transition

Edited by
**Alan Gilchrist**

| SURREY LIBRARIES | |
| --- | --- |
| | |
| **Askews** | 07-Aug-2009 |
| 025.1  LIT | £44.95 |
| | |

**f** facet publishing

© CILIP: the Chartered Institute of Library and Information Professionals, 2009

Published by Facet Publishing,
7 Ridgmount Street, London WC1E 7AE
www.facetpublishing.co.uk

Facet Publishing is wholly owned by CILIP: the Chartered Institute of Library and Information Professionals.

Except as otherwise permitted under the Copyright, Designs and Patents Act 1988 this publication may only be reproduced, stored or transmitted in any form or by any means, with the prior permission of the publisher, or, in the case of reprographic reproduction, in accordance with the terms of a licence issued by The Copyright Licensing Agency. Enquiries concerning reproduction outside those terms should be sent to Facet Publishing, 7 Ridgmount Street, London WC1E 7AE.

*British Library Cataloguing in Publication Data*
A catalogue record for this book is available from the British Library.

ISBN 978-1-85604-693-0

First published 2009

Text printed on PEFC accredited material. The policy of Facet Publishing is to use papers that are natural, renewable and recyclable products, made from wood grown in sustainable forests. In the manufacturing process of our books, and to further our policy, preference is given to printers that have FSC and PEFC Chain of Custody certification. The FSC and/or PEFC logos will appear on those books where full certification has been granted to the printer concerned.

PEFC/16-33-111
CATG-PEFC-052
www.pefc.org

Typeset by Facet Publishing Production in 10.5/14pt Aldine 401 and Nimbus Sans.
Printed and made in Great Britain by MPG Books Ltd, Bodmin, Cornwall.

# Contents

# Contributors

## Peter A. Bath

Peter Bath is a Senior Lecturer in Health Informatics in the Department of Information Studies at the University of Sheffield. Having completed his PhD in the Department in 1994, he was appointed Research Fellow, then Lecturer, in the Sheffield Institute for Studies on Ageing (SISA). In 2000, Peter returned to the Department of Information Studies to become Co-ordinator of the new MSc Health Informatics programme. He is Head of the Health Informatics Research Group in the Department and is Director of the Centre for Health Information Management Research (CHIMR). Peter has published over 50 full research articles in refereed journals and over 40 papers/abstracts in refereed conference proceedings, and has edited six Conference Proceedings. He is currently leading the development of the new MSc Health Informatics programmes.

Contact Peter at: p.a.bath@sheffield.ac.uk.

## David Bawden

David Bawden is Professor of Information Science at City University, in London, and director of the Information Science Centre within the University's Department of Information Science, arguably the 'home' of British Information Science. Originally coming into information science via a degree in organic chemistry, and an interest in chemical information systems, he holds masters and doctoral degrees from Sheffield University, and worked in pharmaceutical research information services before joining City University. David has a particular interest in overlaps between concepts of information in the physical, biological and information sciences. He is editor of the *Journal of Documentation*.

Contact David at: dbawden@soi.city.ac.uk.

## Blaise Cronin

Blaise Cronin is the Rudy Professor of Information Science at Indiana University, where he has been Dean for 17 years. He was educated at Trinity College Dublin (MA) and the Queen's University of Belfast (PhD, DSSc). He held the Chair of Information Science at the University of Strathclyde from 1985 to 1991, and has been a visiting professor at City University, London; Brighton University; Manchester Metropolitan University; and Napier University, Edinburgh. He was awarded an honorary DLitt in 1997 by Queen Margaret University, Edinburgh. In 2006, he received the Award of Merit from the American Society for Information Science and Technology, the Society's highest honour. Blaise has been Editor of the *Annual Review of Information Science and Technology* since 2000, and from 2009 Editor of the *Journal of the American Society of Information Science and Technology*.

Contact Blaise at: bcronin@indiana.edu.

## Elisabeth Davenport

Elisabeth Davenport is Emeritus Professor of Information Management in the School of Computing at Napier University (www.soc.napier.ac.uk). She was educated at the University of Edinburgh (MA Hons; MLitt), Strathclyde University (MSc; PhD) and has a BSc from the Open University. She has been a Visiting Scholar in the School of Library and Information Science at Indiana University at Bloomington since 1994. Her involvement with Social Informatics dates from 1987, when she read the (1982) 'Web of Computing' article by Kling and Scacchi, and she has undertaken a number of empirical and theoretical studies that have drawn on SI methods and lines of thinking. Her current research interests include knowledge trajectories, collaborative work, digital genres, and ethnographic methods.

Contact Elisabeth at: E.Davenport@napier.ac.uk

## Stella G. Dextre Clarke

Stella Dextre Clarke is an independent consultant, specializing in the design and implementation of thesauri and other knowledge organization structures. She is also Convenor of the Working Group responsible for the British Standard for structured vocabularies, and Leader of the Project to adopt these as International Standards. Stella is widely known for her work on behalf of the UK Cabinet Office, as principal architect of the IPSV (Integrated Public

Sector Vocabulary), a key component of the e-Government Metadata Standard. In 2006 she won the Tony Kent Strix Award for outstanding achievement in information retrieval, in recognition of the impact this work has had on information sharing in the public sector.

Contact Stella at: stella.lukehouse.org.

## Peter Enser

Peter Enser is Emeritus Professor of Information Science at the University of Brighton. He has extensive teaching and management experience in Higher Education, together with long standing research interests in visual information retrieval. His publications and conference presentations have addressed international communities in library & information science, computer science, and cultural heritage, and he has directed a number of externally-funded research projects in this field. He has also held an Honorary Visiting Professorship within the Department of Information Science at City University.

Among a variety of professional roles, Peter was President of the Institute of Information Scientists from 2000 to 2002, and long-standing Chair of the Accreditation Board of the Chartered Institute of Library & Information Professionals (CILIP). He is a member of the Arts & Humanities Research Council Peer Review College, and also serves on a number of editorial and advisory committees.

Contact Peter at: peter.enser@btinternet.com.

## Eugene Garfield

Eugene Garfield is a pioneer in information retrieval systems and founder of Current Contents, Index Chemicus, Science Citation Index, Social Sciences Citation Index, Arts & Humanities Citation Index, Journal Citation Reports, Citation Classics and The Scientist Magazine. He has authored over 1,000 publications, available for free at www.eugenegarfield.org.

His early interest in using citations to generate historiographs algorithmically recently culminated in the release of the HistCite software, which creates chronological trees of research topics based on searches of the Web of Science database. Thus, he combined his training in chemistry, linguistics, and information science to create information retrieval systems that anticipated online citation linked search engines.

Contact Eugene at: Garfield@codex.cis.upenn.edu.

## Alan Gilchrist

Alan Gilchrist started his information science career in industry, moving after four years to Aslib, to work in the Research Department. He then helped to establish the consultancy function, before leaving in 1977 to set up his own practice, undertaking consultancy projects in the private and public sectors and for international organisations. He has published widely and is co-author of the extensively used manual *Thesaurus Construction and Use*, now in its fourth edition. He was awarded an Honorary Doctorate by the University of Brighton in 2006, is a Fellow of the Institute of Management Consultancy, a Certified Management Consultant, and an Honorary Fellow of the Chartered Institute of Librarians and Information Professionals. He is an active member of the Advisory Board of Ibersid, the annual International Conference on Information and Documentation Systems, organised by the University of Zaragoza. He was the Founding Editor, and is now Editor Emeritus, of the *Journal of Information Science* and also serves on several editorial boards and advisory committees.

Contact Alan at: cura@fastnet.co.uk.

## Barry Mahon

Barry Mahon holds a Masters Degree in Information Science. He ran an information service for industrial users in Ireland before being seconded to the European Union in 1978 to manage the first telecommunications network dedicated to online information. From 1985 to 1991, he set up and managed one of the first email services in Europe, and supervised EU research projects. From 1991 to 1996 he was Executive Director of Eusidic, the European Association of Information Services.

Following two years as a volunteer development worker in West Africa in 1997/98, he became the Executive Director of Paris based ICSTI, the International Council for Scientific and Technical Information. He relinquished the post in 2005.

He has published widely and made presentations on information related topics throughout the world. He has worked as a consultant for the EU, the UN, the Arab League and other public and private organisations.

Contact Barry at: barry.mahon@iol.ie.

## Jack Meadows

Jack Meadows obtained a first degree in physics from Oxford, followed by postgraduate qualifications in astronomy (also from Oxford) and the history and philosophy of science (from UCL). More recently, he has received an honorary DSc in information science from City University. He moved to Leicester University in the mid-1960s, subsequently serving as head of the Departments of Astronomy and the History of Science, and as Dean. He moved to Loughborough University in the mid-1980s, serving as head of the Department of Information Science, Dean, and Pro-Vice-Chancellor. He retired at the beginning of the present century, and is now Emeritus Professor.

Contact Jack at: a.j.meadows@lboro.ac.uk.

## Charles Oppenheim

Charles Oppenheim has been Professor of Information Science at Loughborough University since 1998. He became Head of the Department of Information Science in 2006. Previously, he had held a variety of posts in academia and the electronic publishing industry, working at various times for International Thomson, Pergamon, and Reuters.

Charles is an Honorary Fellow of the Chartered Institute of Library and Information Professionals. He is one of only three people in the world to have been awarded a higher doctorate in Information Science. He is a member of the Legal Advisory Board of the European Commission. He is a regular contributor to conferences and to the professional and scholarly literature, and is on the editorial board of several professional and learned journals, and of *Annual Review of Information Science and Technology*.

Contact Charles at: c.oppenheim@lboro.ac.uk.

## Elizabeth (Liz) Orna

Liz Orna's career began in technical-book and magazine journalism; she went on to set up and manage information services for organizations and edit their publications. Studying information science at UCL with B. C. Brookes in the early 1970s brought all these strands together and set the course of her future work.

She became an independent information consultant, writer, and lecturer in the year when the *Journal of Information Science* was launched. An assignment in 1981 gave her the opportunity to develop an information policy for an organization, and she became identified with the subject in the 1990s through *Practical Information Policies* (1990 and 1999) and *Information Strategy in Practice* (2004). Collaboration from the 1960s onwards with information designer Graham Stevens led, in the 1990s, to her doctoral research on how organizations create their information products, and to *Making Knowledge Visible* (2005). The experience of working with first-time researchers, as a visiting teacher in the UK, Australia and the US, resulted in *Managing Information for Research* (Orna and Stevens, 1995; new edition to be published 2008).

Contact Liz at: lo@orna.co.uk.

## Stephen Robertson

Stephen Robertson is a researcher at the Microsoft Research Laboratory in Cambridge, UK. He retains a part-time professorship in the Department of Information Science at the City University. He worked full-time at City University from 1978 to 1998, and started the Centre for Interactive Systems Research. His research interests are in theories and models for information retrieval and the design and evaluation of IR systems. In 1976, he was the author (with Karen Sparck Jones) of a moderately influential probabilistic theory of relevance weighting; further work (with Stephen Walker, on the Okapi system) led to the BM25 function for term weighting and document scoring, now used by many other groups. He is a Fellow of Girton College, Cambridge, and was awarded the Tony Kent Strix award in 1998 and the Gerard Salton award in 2000.

Contact Stephen at: ser@microsoft.com.

## Mike Thelwall

Mike Thelwall is Professor of Information Science and leader of the Statistical Cybermetrics Research Group at the University of Wolverhampton, UK. He is also visiting fellow of the Amsterdam Virtual Knowledge Studio, a Docent of the Department of Information Studies at Åbo Akademi University in Finland, and a research associate at the Oxford Internet Institute. He has developed tools for downloading and analysing web sites, blogs and social networking sites, including the research web crawler SocSciBot and software for statistical and topological analyses of site structures (through links) and site content (through text). He has published 134 refereed journal articles and the book *Link Analysis: An Information Science Approach*.

Contact Mike at: m.thelwall@wlv.ac.uk.

## Brian Vickery

Brian Vickery was born in Sydney, Australia, in 1918. After completing a chemistry degree at Oxford, he was directed to an explosives factory during World War 2, and then became librarian at ICI Akers Research Laboratories. In 1952, he helped to form the Classification Research Group. In 1960, he became deputy to Donald Urquhart at the NLLST (now British Library Document Supply Centre). After a spell as Librarian of the University of Manchester Institute of Science and Technology, he became Research Director at Aslib in 1966. Seven years later, he moved to University College London, as Director of the School of Library, Archive and Information Studies. Retired in 1983 as Professor Emeritus, and has worked as a consultant with the Institution of Mechanical Engineers, NIREX, and Tome Associates. More information at http://www.lucis.me.uk.

Contact Brian at: briancvickery@yahoo.co.uk.

## Wendy A. Warr

Wendy Warr has MA and DPhil degrees in chemistry from the University of Oxford. She is a Chartered Chemist, a Fellow of the Royal Society of Chemistry and a Fellow of the Chartered Institute of Library and Information Professionals. She has over 40 years experience in cheminformatics, including nearly 20 years in the pharmaceutical industry. Before founding Wendy Warr & Associates in January 1992, she was Manager of Information Services for ICI Pharmaceuticals. Wendy Warr & Associates offer consultancy services in cheminformatics, drug discovery, and electronic publishing. Clients include pharmaceutical companies and their partners, software companies, publishers, and scientific database producers. Wendy is active in the Chemical Information Division of the American Chemical Society (ACS) and has served on many international scientific committees. She has been an Editor of the *ACS Journal of Chemical Information and Modeling* (formerly *Journal of Chemical Information and Computer Sciences*) since 1989. She writes a news and business column for the *Journal of Computer-Aided Molecular Design* and an online column for *QSARWorld.com*.

Contact Wendy at: wendy@warr.com.

## Peter Willett

Following a first degree in Chemistry from Oxford, Peter Willett obtained MSc and PhD degrees in Information Science from the Department of Information Studies at the University of Sheffield. He joined the faculty of the Department in 1979, and was awarded a Personal Chair in 1991 and a DSc in 1997. Peter is included in *Who's Who*, is a member of the editorial boards of four international journals, and has over 480 publications describing novel computational techniques for the processing of chemical, biological and textual information. His many awards include the 1993 Skolnik Award of the American Chemical Society, the 2001 Kent Strix Award of the Institute of Information Scientists, and the 2005 American Chemical Society Award for Computers in Chemical and Pharmaceutical Research.

Contact Peter at: p.willett@sheffield.ac.uk.

## Tom Wilson

Tom Wilson has worked in the information sector since 1951, holding positions in the public sector, industry, colleges, and universities. He has been a visiting professor at the Universities of Maryland and North Carolina in the USA, at McGill University in Canada, Curtin University in Perth, Western Australia, and at Tallin Pedagogical University in Estonia. He was Head of the Department of Information Studies at the University of Sheffield for fifteen years, and in 2000 was awarded the ALISE Professional Contribution Award for services to education. Following his retirement he was awarded the title of Professor Emeritus and is now a Visiting Professor at Leeds University Business School and at the Swedish School of Library and Information Science, Högskolan i Borås, Sweden. He is also Professor Catedrático Convidado in the Faculty of Engineering at the University of Porto, Portugal. He is Publisher and Editor in Chief of the e-journal, *Information Research*. He founded and edited *Social Science Information Studies* and *The International Journal of Information Management*. He was awarded an honorary doctorate by Gothenburg University in 2005.

Contact Tom at: wilsontd@gmail.com.

# Preface

Why publish a monograph of papers that have already appeared in journal format? There are two answers to that question: the first is that the previous publication, which constituted a special issue of the *Journal of Information Science*, was so well received that it was thought to be both useful and permissible to broadcast the contents to a wider readership; and second, but less importantly, those libraries that already subscribe to the *Journal* may find it convenient to be able to shelve the monograph separately.

The special issue was first published in 2008 to commemorate the founding of the UK Institute of Information Scientists fifty years previously. Its aim was to review a wide range of topics under the broad banner of information science, showing how the core concepts had evolved to the point where, as Jack Meadows says in his paper, '...information science activities developed over the past 50 years have triumphed, but information science as a separate activity may be on the wane. If so, its final epitaph might well be that of Sir Christopher Wren in St Paul's Cathedral: "If you want a monument, look around you"'. In fact, as traditional information science increasingly merges with information technology, the word 'informatics' is coming back into fashion and 'information sciences' are referred to in the plural. Institutions come and go, but even as the web-dominated information world evolves there is still much to be learnt from the past.

*Information Science in Transition* is an exact reproduction of the original papers, and there is only one minor correction to be made. The Editorial stated that Jason Farradane, co-founder of the Institute, was a Polish immigrant. In fact, it was his father who emigrated to England, and Jason was born in Hampstead.

I should like to record my thanks to Facet Publishing and Helen Carley for producing this publication.

Alan Gilchrist

# Editorial

ALAN GILCHRIST

It is difficult to be precise about the acorn that gave rise to this oak of an issue, but it seems to have been sown in the Strix Committee,[1] which is why that Committee is also the Editorial Board of this special issue. A regret was voiced at one of the meetings of this Committee that so little had been done to formally capture the history of information science in the UK. 'History is more or less bunk', as the automobile magnate Henry Ford notoriously said. On the other hand, the Spanish philosopher George Santayana proposed that 'Those who cannot remember the past are condemned to repeat it'. Reflecting on these thoughts last year, it was remembered that 2008 was the 50th Anniversary of the founding of the Institute of Information Scientists in the UK, and that many of the ideas of the earlier information scientists are not only still valid today, but became the foundations upon which later generations have built. Consequently, feeling that it might be worth the effort to capture some insights into advances made in the last 50 years, a number of pre-eminent information scientists were commissioned to write articles on a range of topics reflecting many facets of information science. This issue does not purport to be a history of information science, nor a comprehensive review of each topic. The authors were given only broad guidelines and encouraged to choose their approach and style within them. All the contributions were read by the Editorial Board and, as is usual, all were refereed by peer professionals.

Hopes of consulting an Institute archive for this editorial were dented when it was discovered that the bulk of the material had been pulped when the Institute merged with The Library Association. Whatever may remain appears to be stored at two sites, and is not readily accessible. (This is not the only interesting archive to have gone missing: it seems that all the minutes, correspondence and copies of publications of about 40 years of hugely important work of the Classification Research Group was also lost in a separate misadventure). It may thus be that the only publicly available records of the Institute are to be found in its journals. The first of these was the *Bulletin of the Institute of Information Scientists*, succeeded in 1967 by *The Information Scientist*, a slim publication in an A5 format, and in 1979 by the *Journal of Information Science*. One of the outstanding names in the history of information science in the UK was Jason Farradane, a Polish immigrant who changed his name to an amalgam of those of two of his scientist heroes – Faraday and Haldane – and who became the prime mover in establishing both the Institute and the first course in information science in the world, at what is now the Department of Information Science at The City University in London. Fittingly, it was Farradane himself who recorded these initiatives in an early issue of *The Information Scientist*, which makes interesting reading today [1]. Farradane starts by paying tribute to Benjamin Fullman, who worked at the British Non-Ferrous Metals Research Association, and who he says may be regarded as being the first information officer. In 1923, Fullman and a Professor Hutton organized an informal meeting to seek new ways of tackling what they recognized as a growing information problem. The Library Association was invited to send representatives, but declined to do so. A second meeting in 1924 saw the establishment of the Association of Special Libraries and Information Bureaux (Aslib), which grew steadily, with some government support. Now came the long struggle to get information science on the map. To quote Farradane:

> By 1948 it was apparent that information problems were now urgent ... At Aslib's Annual Conference in 1948, Fullman presented proposals for a syllabus of education to meet the new needs, which librarianship had failed to appreciate ... however, there was strong opposition from librarians who were members of Aslib.

Farradane returned to the attack at the 1950 Conference, and was invited to submit his ideas more fully and to arrange for them to be elaborated by a working party. When the new proposals were submitted to the Aslib Council in 1952, as Farradane reported, 'a note of alarm was sounded amongst librarians, and increasingly organized opposition became evident during the next five years' and 'it became increasingly obvious that nothing would be done ... the proposals were finally defeated at the Aslib Annual Conference in 1957'. From these frustrations, the Institute was born. Farradane, and a few colleagues, convened a meeting at the Institution of Electrical Engineers (since renamed The Institution of Engineering and Technology) on 23 January 1958, at which the following motion was debated:

> that a professional body be, and is hereby, set up to promote and maintain high standards in scientific and technical information work and to establish qualifications for those engaged in the profession.

The motion was carried almost unanimously. By March 1959, the membership was 150, increasing to a figure of 750 by the time Farradane's article was published in 1970. In April 1959, the first issue of the *Bulletin of the Institute of Information Scientists* appeared: seven pages of duplicated material, written and printed by Farradane himself. In 1961, the first course in information science, under the title 'Collecting and communicating scientific knowledge' was offered at what was then the Northampton College of Advanced Technology. (An obituary of Jason Farradane appeared in a special issue of the *Journal of Information Science*, dedicated to his memory [2], and a history of the Department of Information Science at the City University appeared in the same title in 1986 [3].)

*Homo sapiens* has existed for some half a million years. The first alphabet is thought to have developed around 4000 years ago. Gutenberg produced his printing press in 1439, and Alexander Graham Bell patented the first working telephone in 1876. The ENIAC computer was launched in 1946, and in the 1970s the internet, from which the world wide web grew in the 1990s, began; it has been growing exponentially ever since. Fifty years ago, information scientists were getting to grips with the possibilities of IBM punched card machinery, and now they are concerning themselves with Web 2.0 and the possibilities of the Semantic Web. Information technology is in the ascendant, and nobody knows what the outcome will be or how people will adapt to what finally begins to look like the much vaunted 'information revolution'. Nearly 2500 years ago, Socrates is reputed to have said: 'Young people now love luxury, they have bad manners, contempt for authority; they have become tyrants in the household. They contradict their parents and tyrannise their teachers'. Two years ago, Baroness Greenfield, speaking in a debate on education in the UK House of Lords, drew on the results of a study of 8–18 year-olds which had shown that they were now spending an average of 6½ hours a day using electronic media and which went on to conclude that:

screen culture is a world of constant flux, of endless sound bites, quick cuts and half-baked ideas. It is a flow of gossip tidbits, news headlines and floating first impressions. Notions don't stand alone but are massively interlinked to everything else; truth is not delivered by authors and authorities but is assembled by the audience [4].

What resonates between these two quotations is the old cliché 'Kids will be kids', albeit that the later group are armed with gadgets whose facilities and use by 'kids' perplex many adults. But Socrates was followed by Aristotle, and other clever people, and one may assume that many of today's 'kids' will develop into enquiring descendants of *Homo sapiens*, and will be assisted in their endeavours by all those working in the information sciences in their broadest sense.

## Note

1    The Strix Award is given each year in memory of Tony Kent, a stalwart of the Institute of Information Scientists, in recognition of an outstanding contribution to the field of information retrieval.

## References

[1]    J.E.L. Farradane, The Institute: the first twelve years, *The Information Scientist* 4(4) (1970) 143–151.

[2]    P. Yates-Mercer, Guest editorial: an appreciation of Jason Farradane, *Journal of Information Science* 15(6) (1989) 305–6.

[3]    J.S. Rennie, A history of the Department of Information Science of The City University, *Journal of Information Science* 12(1/2) (1986) 3–13.

[4]    Available at: http://www.publications.parliament.uk/pa/ld199697/ldhansrd/ pdvn/lds06/text/60420-18.htm (accessed 7 April 2008).

# Guest Editorial: Meeting the challenge

BRIAN VICKERY

## Introduction

It is a great privilege to be asked to contribute some comments to this special issue of JIS.

I have enjoyed reading these papers, and seeing how much our field has moved on since the *Journal of Documentation* attempted a similar historical survey in 1994 [1], just as the internet was 'taking off'.

My first thoughts were of Jason Farradane, who played such a big part in founding the Institute of Information Scientists in 1958. The IIS has now disappeared within CILIP, and Jason would have been very dismayed at this development.

I first encountered him at the Royal Society Scientific Information Conference of 1948, where he spoke on 'the scientific approach to documentation'. In 1952 he was one of the founder members of the Classification Research Group, where he was often defending a minority position, connected to his own ideas of relations between topics, to which Stella Dextre Clarke refers in her paper. He was a serious man, but the more I talked with him, and disagreed with him over many things, the more I liked him.

In 1955, we were invited together to a meeting of the Aslib Aeronautical Group, at which Cyril Cleverdon spoke about his plans for retrieval evaluation (Cranfield1), which Stephen Robertson discusses in his paper. We spoke about faceted classification, and Cyril challenged us to prepare a scheme for aeronautics, that he could use in his test. With inordinate bravado, we accepted the challenge, and – after much advice from Cyril and his team – managed to produce one. In retrospect – given that it was compiled by two chemists – we were amazed that it performed at all.

What else was happening around about 1958? There were printed publications of every kind. There were libraries – public, national, government, academic, institutional, industrial – and they were classified and had catalogues. We were much concerned with interlibrary loan, and Donald Urquhart had recently been told to drop all other work and start to plan a new national science lending library for the UK. There were printed indexing and abstracting periodicals, and bibliographies. An industrial firm might have, as well as a technical library, a centre for internal reports, a section dealing with patents, an 'intelligence' unit for commercial information, and a correspondence registry. Some of us were playing around with punched or edge-notched cards for 'mechanized retrieval'. There were reported to be 1000 electronic computers in the USA, and 160 in Europe. Some firms were building structured computer files searched by 'database management' software.

An International Conference on Scientific Information was held in Washington in 1958 (ICSI [2]). Coming as it did near the beginning of the impact of the computer on information provision, it to some degree charted the future. In the titles of its papers were many of the concepts we still have today: users' requirements, evaluation, effectiveness, efficiency, cost analysis, quantitative survey, international cooperation, codes, computers, mechanical translation, linguistics, machine searching, semantics, information retrieval. An inventive IBM engineer, Peter Luhn, distributed a computer-based 'keywords-in-context' index to the titles of the pre-published conference papers. For some participants this was their first encounter with a computer-based information product.

## What is information activity?

I like to think of an analogy. There is a social activity known as medical practice, aiming to help people to become more healthy. Medical science seeks principles and methods that will improve medical practice. The practice, broadly speaking, consists of two activities: diagnosis and treatment. Diagnosis is identifying what is the most probable cause of a particular state of ill health. Treatment is deciding what action is most likely to counteract the cause. Medical science seeks to understand what are the potential causes of ill health; to develop methods of correct diagnosis; to understand and expand the range of possible treatments; and to develop methods of deciding what treatment is most likely to be effective in a particular case.

Information practice, again broadly speaking, consists of two activities that we may call diagnosis and provision. Diagnosis is identifying what is the most probable information need of a user in a particular state of information want.

Provision is deciding what action is most likely to meet that need. Information science seeks to understand the potential range of user situations giving rise to information want and need; to develop methods of identifying the actual information needed; to understand and expand the range of possible ways of satisfying information need; and to develop methods of deciding what way is most likely to be effective in a particular case.

So information practice is concerned with facilitating the interaction between knowledge seekers – through channels – with knowledge (personal and recorded). Stepping back from practice, we may see the role of the science as exploring the characteristics of people and their 'information behaviour', the features of knowledge records of every kind, the variety of channels (oral, written, printed, graphic, digital) that may be used to transmit information, and how the three elements interact. Science and technology are now so closely linked that analysis and experiment lead quickly on to invention, to the introduction of new channels (and documents).

In the beginning, the role of 'information science' was to study the activities of the information practitioner – what he or she did, and how it might be done better. But the science indicated above goes far beyond the practitioner, to explore all the elements of the process of 'becoming informed'. These elements are of interest to investigators other than 'information scientists'. There are, for example, the psychologists and sociologists who study people's behaviour in general; there are those who devise and produce communication channels (from ink-on-paper to the internet); there are those concerned with the symbolism of knowledge representation (linguists); and those concerned with the knowledge content within 'documents' (e.g. data mining, geographic information systems, Peter Willett's chemoinformatics). The totality of activity related to information is today necessarily a multidisciplinary exercise, and the information practitioner, trying to 'do better', may draw insights from any of these areas of investigation. His particular concern is with the process as a whole – the interaction between the three elements that leads to people becoming informed.

## The computer

It has taken some time for the full potential of the digital computer to be realized. It was at first used for numerical 'computing', representing numbers in a binary code. But this code could be used to represent any symbol, so the computer came to be seen as a tool for 'symbol manipulation' in general.

Eventually, it was shown that any representation – numbers, text, sound, music, images, 'movies', 'data' of every kind – could be recorded in binary code. How could it be manipulated? As Ada Lovelace said of Charles Babbage's Analytical Engine, the computer 'can do whatever we know how to order it to perform'.

Ordering a computer to perform (programming) was a skilled and at first very laborious task. Getting the program instructions and the coded data into the computer (via punched cards) was equally laborious. The space inside for storage and manipulation was at first very limited. Computer 'printout' was very clumsy. It would be some time before computers could 'talk' to each other via telecommunications. And all this was quite outside the experience of the library/information profession. How could we make use of the computer for our purposes?

This was the challenge that faced, and still faces, the profession. And it has been continually changing. We have been through computer-aided production of abstracts journals; their tapes offered for current awareness search; citation indexes ('how we learnt to love the Yanks'); fast-response online searching; remote telecommunication access to computers; bibliographic databases with machine-readable records; online search intermediaries and interfaces; OPACs; the internet; the www protocol; an enormous expansion of websites; graphical interface browsers; search engines; and much more.

Ever since the advent of the digital computer, there has been a continual drive to see, as Robert Fairthorne put it in 1961 [3], 'how far we can go by using ritual in place of understanding'. Robert lived to see the arrival of our current universal digital automaton, the internet. Given an electronic connection, the user can now search an ever-growing slice of the world's documents from his own desktop. (I use the word 'documents' as shorthand for every type of record.) At every step of the way, there is nothing but mechanisms 'making physical responses to physical signals', as Fairthorne put it, untouched by human hand or mind. If we want the 'reality' of a Gutenberg Bible or a Leonardo painting we have still to go to the trouble of visiting the place that houses them. But reproductions of them, and of live events around the world, can be brought into our homes. The world has been reduced to a vast unified information store, which we can browse from our desks.

Writing further of automation, Fairthorne noted that 'a clerical system seeks to replace as far as possible semantic activities by manipulations of marked objects according to unambiguous rules. Semantics must enter at output and input at least, else the system would be merely a game, but intermediate operations should involve only the internal semantics of the system; that is, recognition of the marks and what actions they should lead to'. On the internet, semantics at input comprises the intellectual effort that has been put into writing texts, creating images, composing music and so on. Semantics at output comprises the intellectual effort of stating a query that represents what you want and of comprehending the response. The internal semantics are the 'unambiguous rules' that the computer has been given in its program.

## What has the internet become?

At first we thought of the internet as a new way to store and access recorded knowledge. We thought we knew how to deal with it – classify it, like the Yahoo! or BUBL directories. It was an information activity that we were familiar with, but using a new medium. But the internet has become vastly more than that. First, of course, it was from the beginning a new form of person-to-person telecommunication, challenging letter mail and the telephone. Second, it has added a mass of 'documents', such as images and detailed 'raw' data, with which the information practitioner finds it difficult to deal. Third, it has become a medium for chatter (sorry, social networking) about every topic, public or personal, under the sun. Fourth, and most important, it has been seized upon by commerce, and has become a market place for every kind of consumer goods and services, reputable and disreputable. Information providers have to compete for attention in that market. There are, no doubt, still other functions, present or to come. The internet as a whole is therefore wholly beyond the library/information profession's experience and control.

The internet – that includes a fair percentage of everything being recorded in the world – has an uncontrolled and ever-growing vocabulary. On the user side, it has opened up the practice of information search to people of every occupation and of none. Many of their searches do not arise from structured intellectual environments; consequently the semantic relations important to them are unpredictable and variable. There has come about a separation of the 'visible' web (that is, visible to search engines) from the 'deep' web that lies beyond it on the internet, even though the latter is very much richer in content (BrightPlanet [4]).

Much current recorded knowledge has migrated to the internet (or intranets) – not only public knowledge, but also the private knowledge of industrial firms, government agencies and other institutions. If the internet becomes the primary source of recorded knowledge, and access to it is directly available to the user, in what sense will the information practitioner be an intermediary, 'between' knowledge and seeker? In the library, even if he was not acting as a reference librarian or information officer, he controlled and guided access to recorded knowledge by his acquisition policy, his classification, his catalogues, his loan policy. What role can he continue to play?

There is surely still a task for information practitioners to perform – guiding access to recorded knowledge by incorporating our understanding (of the records, and of user needs) into the ritual performed by the computer, to improve its performance in handling information. Recent books (e.g. Lambe [5]; White [6]) emphasize the importance of detailed understanding of the information behaviour of users, and of the types of document used, in designing taxonomies and choosing computer search systems for corporate enterprises.

## New tasks, new skills

Our problem is that this new task – of giving understanding to the computer – calls for new skills. The information profession believed that it was concerned with organizing recorded knowledge so that people could find their way around it. There was a structure to knowledge, which we sought to embody in classified arrangement, facets, thesaural relations, so that people could navigate within it. 'The core of arguments [in favour of one knowledge structure or another] was generally, not empirical, but philosophical', writes Stephen Robertson in his paper in this issue. 'There was resistance to a strictly functional view of such schemes'. Cleverdon's Cranfield project, already mentioned, 'tackled the philosophical divisions in the field head-on'.

The approach to retrieval used by web search engines has been to explore how far ritual could go based strictly on analysis of the occurrence of words in texts, taking into account their frequencies in a document and in the collection, their positions in the document, the document length, and so on, as well as the occurrence of links to other documents. More recently, techniques such as 'latent semantic analysis' have been introduced, which seek to deduce semantic links between words based on analysis of their co-occurrence in documents. Since the meanings of the words are ignored, the structure of knowledge plays no part.

The real structure of knowledge is immensely complex. But if people are to navigate a 'knowledge organization system' (KOS), they must become familiar with it, it must be relatively limited and simple to understand. Consequently the KOS we construct can only depict a small part of the whole, and the choice of what to depict should, as Stephen Robertson emphasizes, be 'functional' – i.e. based on tests as to whether it is useful in manipulating information. The structural tools developed by the profession – hierarchical classification, facets, thesaural relations, topical maps, the predicates used in ontology – will still be of use, provided that they can in each case pass a test of utility.

The information profession will continue to need its skills in acquiring knowledge of users and of recorded knowledge, but needs to develop its understanding of how to incorporate this knowledge into computer ritual. This is much more complex than incorporating it into clerical ritual – as in a static card catalogue – because the computer is dynamic, and can manipulate texts, graphics and data at our command, as well as bibliographic records.

Traditionally, the producers of documents (publishers in the widest sense) have been a profession separate from the information profession. But the computer is still a relatively new environment for both professions. Elizabeth Orna's idea [7] is a good one: that information designers and information managers should interact and collaborate in the development of computer-based information systems. In this way, documents can be designed from the start to make retrieval and use more effective.

## Looking ahead

I sense an unease, an uncertainty about the future, in a number of the contributions in this issue. Barry Mahon concludes, 'It remains to be seen if the current professional bodies recognize the benefits to be gained by embracing the ideas created by the newcomers to the information sector'. Tom Wilson writes that 'some may already believe that the position has been reached that professional education and research are irrelevant to practice'. David Bawden, speaking of information science theory, suggests, 'We have not fully worked through the insights of the founders of the discipline, let alone replaced them with entirely new insights'. Speaking of developments in practice, Stella Dextre Clarke feels that 'the greatest part of the credit [...] goes to enhanced information technology rather than fundamental new thinking in knowledge organization'. I took Stephen Robertson's advice and followed up a recommended reference, and found our greatly missed Karen Spärck Jones [8] urging the need to 'rethink TREC from the bottom up [...] on some principled view of what information management is, should be'. And Jack

Meadows concludes that 'information science activities developed over the past 50 years have triumphed, but information science as a separate entity may be on the wane'.

The uncertainties arise in various contexts, but perhaps an underlying cause in some cases is, as Jack suggests, the apprehension that information science may become 'submerged' in the larger field of computer science. Authors more directly associated with computer developments (such as Peter Enser and Peter Willett) are markedly more confident of the future.

Is it possible that we are at a moment of pause or turn in digital information? The expansion of the internet was unprecedented. Search engines dealt with it in the only way possible – scan as much as they could and throw it all into an inverted index. TREC helped to establish a search algorithm that performed as well as any alternative tested, though performance could be improved by relevance feedback (to amend the query terms). Online database search – now with nearly 40 years' experience – was pushed into the background. Yet, wrote Karen Sparck Jones, the difficulty of obtaining appropriate literature test sets has meant that it is still impossible to make comparisons between natural language approaches and the use of controlled language indexing (the 'Boolean thesaurus' model).

Now, the search engines are beginning to experiment with ways to help the searcher amend a query. Attempts are being made to include the deep web in searching. Corporate information systems, much more aware of their problems than a general search engine can be, have been spending much effort on taxonomies. Facet analysis, on a small scale, is making a come-back (Vickery [9]). The Semantic Web, though still very experimental, is demonstrating how much more can be done with a computer if you give it enough knowledge. It seems that we are in for a period of experimental development that may lead to new steps forward in information handling.

## References

[1]  B.C. Vickery (ed.), *Fifty Years of Information Progress* (Aslib, London, 1994).

[2]  ICSI, *Proceedings*. Available at: www.nap.edu/catalog.php?record_id=10866 (accessed 5 April 2008).

[3]  R.A. Fairthorne, *Towards Information Retrieval* (Butterworths, London, 1961).

[4]  BrightPlanet, *The Deep Web* (2000–2008). Available at www.brightplanet.com/resources/details/deepweb.html (accessed 5 April 2008).

[5]  P. Lambe, *Organising Knowledge* (Chandos, Oxford, 2007).

[6]     M. White, *Making Search Work* (Facet, London, 2007).

[7]     E. Orna, Collaboration between LIS and information design disciplines, *Information Research* 12(4) (2007) CoLIS 6 conference proceedings supplement. Available at: http://informationr.net/ir/12-4/colis/colis02.html (accessed 5 April 2008).

[8]     K. Sparck Jones, Metareflections on TREC. In E.M. Voorhees and D.K. Harman (eds), *TREC* (MIT Press, Cambridge, MA, 2005).

[9]     B.C. Vickery, Faceted classification for the web, *Axiomathes* 18(2) (2008).

# 1

# Fifty years of UK research in information science

JACK MEADOWS

## Abstract

An attempt is made to discern the main research themes in British information science over the past half-century. Within these themes, emphasis is placed on research in the UK that has had some impact on the international information science community. The major factors that have influenced information science research in the UK are also briefly considered.

## Introduction

Research that clearly falls under the 'information science' heading was already being carried out in the UK in the first half of the twentieth century, though the volume of such research was small. It was in the second half of the century that systematic research in this field – and, indeed, the name itself – became fully established, and that the amount of research began to grow rapidly. Today, information science has matured to the stage where even the study of its history has become a legitimate topic for research [1]. A definition of information science acceptable to everyone has always proved difficult to find, from the early days right up to the present. There has, however, been greater agreement on what are the important topics that information scientists should study: most of the topics mentioned in the early days are still regarded as important today, though relative emphases have changed. The development of information science research – as with most science and social science subjects – is reflected reasonably well by the changing nature of the research papers published in its leading journals. So I have used these as my main guide to UK research over the past half century.

The UK is fortunate in possessing a number of internationally recognized journals that cover library and information science research. These, and especially the *Journal of Information Science* and the *Journal of Documentation*, have published a wide variety of research by British information scientists over the past 50 years. The contents of the *Journal of Information Science* cover all areas of the field and little that is not relevant, but it only started publication in 1979. The *Journal of Documentation* gives better time coverage, since it goes back beyond the beginning of the period discussed here. It, too, covers all areas of information science, but also includes other topics, more especially relating to libraries. Both journals have always been held in high regard by researchers in the field of information science. Consequently, an analysis of the two together probably provides a reasonable picture of the range of information research in the UK and how it has developed with time (though the papers published by these journals are not, of course, restricted to UK authors only). In examining these journals (along with reading a number of historical reviews and reminiscences), I have tried to look mainly for themes, rather than for individual articles or authors. Correspondingly, the references cited mainly represent examples of a theme, rather than constituting the sole essential reading in that area. In other words, different papers and different authors could often have been cited to illustrate the research theme under discussion. There is one proviso. For research to be labelled as important, it must be recognized as such internationally. I have therefore primarily quoted UK research that has been well cited abroad as well as at home.

## Major topics in information science

What, then, have been the significant themes? A survey of 40 LIS journals published over the period 1965–85 found that information retrieval – defined in fairly broad terms – dominated their coverage as measured in terms of number of articles published [2]. This was followed fairly closely by studies of library and information services. Between them, these two topics accounted for over half of all the research reported throughout the whole period: no other area breached the 10 percent barrier in terms of relative contribution. It is interesting to examine the coverage of topics in the *Journal of Information Science* from its birth to the present day, and to compare it with these figures using the same kind of categorization. The dominant theme is again information retrieval. But now it is closely followed by research in the general area of information seeking. Research on library and information services is much less important. (The difference is mainly due to the inclusion in the earlier survey of a large number of library journals.) Behind the two main themes – but still representing significant coverage – come studies in the fields of bibliometrics and communication. Bibliometrics has been a regular topic from the start, but articles on communication studies have increased with time. A comparison with the contents of the *Journal of Documentation*, including the period before the *Journal of Information Science* appeared, suggests that these four themes – information retrieval, information seeking, communication, and bibliometrics – provide a reasonable basis for looking at how UK research in information science has developed over the past 50 years.

## Information retrieval

The present issue contains other contributions that deal with aspects of information retrieval in more detail. The discussion here simply aims at noting developments in the UK that have been important outside the country, as well as within. One that undoubtedly falls into this category occurred right at the beginning of our 50-year period. This was the series of Cranfield experiments that began in the late 1950s. The first set of experiments evaluated and compared retrieval of information from different kinds of database. The second looked at the use of alternative indexing languages [3]. These studies emphasized recall and precision as important parameters in such evaluation, since they allowed numerical comparison of the different systems under assessment. This pioneering work naturally led to the idea of improved experiments, especially as electronic data handling became more sophisticated. In the UK, there was considerable discussion of the need for improved test collections for use in a new range of experiments [4]. In the event, this development did not occur until the early 1990s, when the TREC (Text REtrieval Conference) exercise was initiated in the USA. The emphasis here was on large-scale retrieval using a vast collection of documents. In typical American style, teams of specialists in information retrieval have competed against each other to see who can obtain the best retrieval results. The exercise has had a major impact, since it has been repeated year by year and the results widely disseminated. Although the bulk of the teams are American, a range of other countries have been involved and the UK contribution has been significant [5].

Methods of retrieving information have typically been discussed by specialists in the field long before they have been implemented in practice. It is only in recent years that the world at large has caught up in terms of day-to-day application. At the theoretical level, the input by UK researchers has been particularly significant. One reflection of this can be found in the widely read texts that they have produced [6–8]. The idea of using Boolean operators for searching had already been mentioned by Bradford in his pioneering text on documentation [9]. It was commented on again by Fairthorne in 1962 in the context of the developing use of computers [10]. But it has the drawback that the retrieved documents are all regarded as being of equal relevance (they are usually presented to users simply in terms of date of publication). One way round this has been to give the various search terms different weightings. An important step forward here was the introduction of an automatic weighting scheme based on 'inverse document frequency' [11], which subsequently became a standard approach. It depended on an understanding of the likely frequencies of different words in the documents concerned. A computer using this system could now output a list of references in order of likely relevance to the user. Another significant step forward in the early 1970s was the demonstration that automatic clustering of documents could be implemented as part of the search process in order to improve the relevance of the items retrieved [12]. A few years later came the demonstration that ranking based on probable relevance was the optimum way of ordering the results of retrieval [13].

The word 'relevance' constantly appears in information retrieval, but its interpretation has been a continual matter of dispute. In principle, retrieved information is relevant if the user who posed the query says that it is. One problem with the Cranfield experiments was that relevance assessments were not made by genuine end-users, so there has since been an increasing interest in involving users directly in the evaluation of retrieved information. Such relevance feedback can be obtained in various ways (e.g. by asking the user to select the most relevant documents, and using these as the basis for another round of retrieval). One of the most successful developments of such an interactive approach is the Okapi project, which began in the early 1980s, moving to the City University in 1989 [14]. The design has been improved over the years, and has proved highly successful in the TREC competition. Some of the improvements have been widely copied. The growing interest in interaction with users has led to an increasing cross-fertilization between research in information retrieval and in information seeking [15]. The actual approach followed in information retrieval obviously depends in part on the type of information involved. The TREC experiments, for example, included retrieval of graphics as another track alongside text. One specialized area of information retrieval to which the UK has made a significant contribution relates to chemical compounds. Work on retrieval of chemical information began at Sheffield in the 1960s, and has expanded in subsequent decades. The work there on the computer-based retrieval of chemical structures has been especially valuable. It has helped provide a basis for the now rapidly expanding field of chemoinformatics (with subsequent input to the even larger field of bioinformatics) [16].

The definition of information retrieval used in [2] includes cataloguing, classification, indexing and database creation along with the information retrieval activity itself. These different retrieval aids have varied in their relative importance over the past 50 years, but it has always been clear that they are linked together. The Okapi project, for example, was originally designed as an online public access catalogue (OPAC) which was later developed to search scientific abstracts. One spin-off from the post-war concern with information, in part stimulated by the Royal Society's interest, was the formation of a Classification Research Group in 1952. The group was therefore already going strong at the start of our 50-year period, and its interest in classification covered all types of information. Its members were, for example, concerned with the major post-war advances in biomedical classification. It was evident from the start that classification and information retrieval were interlinked – indeed, future prospects for the two were discussed at length in a conference on 'Classification for information retrieval' held at Dorking 50 years ago. Similarly, the construction of thesauri was accepted from early on as a standard part of retrieval [17]. The year before the Institute of Information Scientists (IIS) was founded saw the origin of the Society of Indexers – another reflection of the growing interest in different methods of indexing. So all the retrieval components were there from the start, but they tended initially to be developed in their own ways – perhaps because the interest of information scientists and librarians in these topics often differed in emphasis. The rapid growth in computer-based handling of information over the past two decades has seen an increased level of linkage between the various activities: not least because the growth of internet browsing by end-users has meant a change of emphasis in terms of information retrieval. Nowadays, a web search engine is likely to include anything from the most recent work on information retrieval to an input from recent ideas about classification and thesauri. The ever-growing emphasis on all kinds of information retrieval means that the whole field has now become a mainline research topic. From being a characteristic component of information science, it has also become a widely investigated research topic in computer studies and related fields. As a consequence, it is becoming increasingly difficult to determine what particular input to information retrieval comes from researchers in information science.

## Information seeking

The second major category of information research noted above was information seeking, including the whole field of user studies. As with information retrieval, the topic is covered elsewhere in this issue, so I will again concentrate on work that has evoked international, as well as national interest. Surveys of users had been carried out in library contexts before they became an important feature of information studies. In the latter area, the application of such surveys in the UK was stimulated by the work of Bernal and Urquhart on users of science information in the early post-war years. The work of both investigators was reported at the famous conference on scientific information organized by the Royal Society in 1948. The Royal Society interest in information continued, leading on to an in-depth survey of researchers' activities across the sciences in the early 1980s [18]. The results indicated an interesting dichotomy – British scientists were typically conservative in terms of usage patterns, yet seemed to welcome increased automation of information seeking. This survey was relatively widely targeted. Most user studies – and there have been many of them over the past 50 years – have been aimed at more specific groups or environments. Though science, technology and medicine (STM) has been a favoured area for user studies, most other fields have been the subject of some investigation. For example, information use in the social sciences received attention from the beginning [19], and was the subject of one of the largest-scale studies carried out in the earlier years [20]. A further major study at the end of the 1970s reflected a general trend in survey work that has emerged over the past few decades – a growing emphasis on a qualitative, rather than a quantitative approach [21]. Most user studies have been on a smaller scale and, though the results may be of potentially wider application, they have sometimes been limited by the relatively small number of respondents involved. In more recent years, usage studies have particularly concentrated on the use of electronic resources. One great advantage of these is that the characteristics of the usage – if not always of the user – can be derived from statistics provided by the system itself. Consequently, the activities and habits of large numbers of users can be examined simultaneously [22].

If usage is one side of the coin for information scientists, information management is the obverse. This has been accepted as a basic component of information science from the start, though originally it often came under the heading of 'records management'. The growth of information technology during the 1970s expanded the possibilities for the more efficient management of information, and technological change has continued to have an impact ever since. By the end of the 1980s, information management had been identified in the UK as an important growth area in information science [23], with a consequent increase in the research attention that it received. The UK was obviously not unique in this. Nevertheless, a survey of information research in Western Europe in the 1990s showed that the UK was in the lead in terms of information management research [24]. With the growth of computerization, research into the management of libraries and the broader management of information sources increasingly overlapped. For example, studies of how to evaluate systems and organizations and how to implement performance measures developed in parallel for both. Information management has now become a regular part of institutional activities, as indicated, for example, by the action of the Joint Information Systems Committee (JISC) in its recent launch of an online information management kit as a standard package for use in higher and further education institutions. The appearance of knowledge management in the 1990s engendered rather more controversy. In part, this was due to the varying definitions of what knowledge management was about, since it often seemed that what was being managed was information, rather than knowledge. Indeed, views on this matter among British information scientists have ranged from considerable doubts concerning its validity [25] to the construction of lengthy textbooks on the topic [26].

As noted above, studies of information needs and usage have evolved with the passage of time. The initial emphasis was on surveys involving quantitative or semi-quantitative approaches (and these are still commonplace). In recent decades, qualitative approaches have become increasingly popular. There has been a similar shift in emphasis in the social sciences as a whole. The two trends are related in the sense that the methodologies used in information science have often been adopted or adapted from those developed for investigations in sociology and related subjects. An example is soft systems methodology – an approach devised originally for business studies in the UK – which has been used in a number of information science projects [27]. There has also been a shift from looking at the usage itself to looking at the methods whereby users actually seek for information. In this area, there have again been valuable contributions by UK practitioners. One model, in particular, which looks at the links between information needs and information-seeking behaviour, has been widely used, both in its original form and with subsequent updating [28].

Research interest in recent decades has concentrated especially on information-seeking aspects, so adding greater sophistication to the relatively simple approach taken in classical information retrieval. A proper understanding of human information seeking and retrieval is now seen as involving an examination of cognitive factors. For example, one early model – which attracted considerable attention – hinged on the point that the actual information needs of potential users are not necessarily known [29]. What can be ascertained are the users' perceptions of where they have an information problem: retrieval entailed studying these 'anomalous states of knowledge'. Since perceptions can change as retrieval progresses, the implication of such models is that retrieval systems must allow a high level of interactive input from the information seeker. The detailed characteristics of the information-seeking process will, of course, depend partly on the characteristics and background of the end-user concerned. However, comparative studies of information seeking by scientists and social scientists have revealed considerable similarities in the basic activities involved, though these may be affected by the limitations of the information system used [30]. The growing desire for flexibility in handling retrieval problems soon suggested the possibility of employing techniques from the developing world of artificial intelligence. This has led to the construction of a number of intelligent interfaces for use in online searching, including valuable work in the UK [31]. As yet, most of the systems that have been devised have remained experimental.

The rapidly expanding part played by computers in information handling has meant that information science research has come increasingly to overlap with work in computer science, particularly in the area of human – computer interaction (HCI). This marriage has been evident, for example, in the search for new approaches to training in information skills and in the production of user-friendly interfaces. In looking for understanding of these topics, information science researchers in British universities have often targeted their own students. In part, this is because the students provide an easy, and relatively docile, target group to examine; but it is also, in part, because an important motivation for such research has been the question of how best to provide computer-based and computer-assisted learning for the student population [32]. At the same time as this rapprochement between computer scientists and information scientists has been occurring, the computerization of libraries has led to a new confluence of interest between library researchers and information scientists. This is reflected most obviously in the development of OPACs, where information science concerns with retrieval have equally become central to the activities of traditional libraries. Online catalogues began to supplement card catalogues in the 1970s. By the 1980s, their capabilities had expanded to the extent that they could enhance the range of functions of a card catalogue. But it took time, and improved design, before OPACs became popular [33]. In fact, research on OPACs underlined the point made above – the need for greater flexibility and feedback when systems are being used by novices (in terms of information seeking). The overlap between information science interests and library interests has grown as libraries have moved away from their traditional role as guardians of the printed heritage to the handling of a hybrid mixture of printed and electronic information. Indeed, discussions of libraries of the future now typically concentrate on the role of the digital library with traditional aspects relegated to a subordinate role [34]. It is reasonable to expect that the overlap of interests that has occurred between information science and libraries in recent years will continue to grow in the future.

## Other themes

The growth in information science research over the past 50 years has been paralleled by the growth of research into communication studies. Information research usually revolves round some pool of information: the questions asked tend to be about how the contents of the pool should be handled. The information in the pool often consists of formal sources – more often than not articles in journals. Communication research is more often concerned with the interactive exchange of information, and the information involved may well be transmitted informally – for example, via conversations. As this suggests, the gap between the two research fields is not vast, and information scientists have often strayed into research on communication. Thus, a number of studies were carried out during the 1960s and 1970s – some in the UK – into the importance of informal communication as a method of acquiring additional information alongside that available from formal sources [35]. Communication research has actually ranged widely in terms of scope. An influential text on the topic was published by a British author right at the beginning of our 50-year period, and it covered everything from philosophy to electrical engineering [36]. A number of the ideas developed in studies of communication have proved valuable in information science research. One such is insight into how information diffuses through a community; another is the concept of the 'invisible college' [37]. The growth of computer-based communication, especially email, has both increased the importance of informal communication over the past two decades and made the borderline between formal and informal communication less easy to define. Consequently, the distinction between information and communication studies has also become increasingly blurred.

Traditionally, the communication chain for formal publications has been visualized as a sequence that starts with the author, continues through the publisher and the library (or information centre), and ends with the reader (or information user). The primary concern of information scientists has been with the last two steps in this chain. However, in terms of information content, this division is not always clear cut. To paraphrase a Tom Lehrer song, flows of information may be compared with the flow in a sewage system – what comes out at the end depends on what is put in at the start. Consequently, some studies of information handling by publishers and authors have been carried out by information scientists from the beginning. Since the researchers' interest has usually focused on R&D work, it is journal publishing that has been examined in most detail. One common characteristic of such journals is that they rely on some kind of quality control mechanism to decide on their content. The activities involved, especially the process of refereeing, have been the subject of numerous studies, including some important ones carried out in the UK [38]. The questions examined have ranged from subject differences in refereeing to the existence of bias in referees' assessments. The overall result has been to confirm the value of quality control for journal contents while also emphasizing its limitations [39, pp. 177–99].

The growth of the digital world has made it necessary to re-examine the workings of the information chain. Over the last two decades, electronic journals have moved from the experimental stage to a major branch of publishing. The first successful experiment was actually carried out in the UK in the early 1980s – the BLEND (Birmingham and Loughborough Electronic Network Development) programme [40]. It was established by HCI researchers, rather than information scientists, and provided a further stimulus for the latter to use HCI methodology as one of their tools. It was apparent from the start that electronic journals created problems for the operation of the traditional communication chain; or, to put it in more general terms, the challenge was to evaluate all the impacts on information handling that a move from a print medium to an electronic medium might entail. The main early concern in information science was with the future of journals, and this has led to a range of surveys and experiments in the last two decades [41], but interest is now broadening to cover almost any type of information source. Uncertainty regarding the future roles of both publishers and libraries has emphasized the need for information scientists to consider the whole of the publication chain. An obvious example, which has involved a number of information scientists, has been the debate – often controversial – over the provision of open access (OA) to researchers' publications. All parts of the chain – authors, publishers, librarians and users – have been involved in this discussion. The original simple idea was that researchers should put up the papers they had written on their websites, as well as publish them in printed form; but this has been considerably elaborated over the past 10 years. In consequence, a growing number of studies have been looking at both the methods of implementing OA and its consequent impact [42]. The UK has been an important focus for the OA debate, since the main proponent of OA and the website he runs have been sited at Southampton University [43]. One essential aspect of the OA debate has been the role of copyright. For example, who should claim the copyright in research papers, and so have the right to circulate them via the internet – authors, their institutions, or publishers [44]? Interest nowadays has broadened from copyright to intellectual property law as a whole. In the UK, the latter has come to the fore because EU legislation in this area – which differs from the traditional British approach – has been developing. The question now is how such legislation might affect the electronic circulation of information [45].

The fourth theme that appears regularly in information science journals involves the general area of theoretical and quantitative studies. In the earlier decades of our period, a number of attempts were made – not least in the UK – to devise a general framework for the understanding of information science [46]. Much of this work was based on the hope that quantitative studies of information flow would help provide generalizations of use to information scientists [47]. One of the terms that came to be used for such studies – bibliometrics – was actually coined in the UK [48], though it has now been partly superseded by terms seen as having broader applicability, such as scientometrics. An obvious example of a quantitative law – described first in the UK – is Bradford's law of scattering, which originated well before our 50-year period [49]. Much of the early running in the field of bibliometrics was made in the USA, and that country has remained the main focus of such work ever since (though the Soviet Union made important early contributions, and bibliometric research now has a world-wide basis). Within the UK, interest in bibliometric studies grew during the 1960s and 1970s, but then diminished, only to grow again in recent years. One area where the UK made a useful contribution in the earlier period was in the discussion of how usage of literature declined with its age, how the change might best be measured, and the implications for librarians and information scientists [50]. More recently, the emphasis in the UK has been on how to measure the relative importance of different authors, papers, or journals. A major driving force for this has been the wish to shift comparisons in the Research Assessment Exercise (RAE) towards a metrics-based approach. This has led to a number of innovative studies, with a particular interest in research which looks at ways of ensuring that different authors or subjects are compared equitably [51]. Amongst all this activity, researchers have, of course, cast a beady eye on the RAE and the metrics of information science, itself [52].

## Factors affecting information science research in the UK

One obvious influence on the development of information science research, in the UK as elsewhere, has been the availability of funding. When the Department of Scientific and Industrial Research (DSIR) was split up in the mid-1960s, one of the new bodies formed from it was the Office for Scientific and Technical Information (OSTI). Senior scientists at the time were worried by the ever-expanding flood of scientific information, and saw the need for centrally funded support to study the problems that it caused. This sort of question was, of course, meat and drink to the newly named group of information scientists, and some soon obtained grants from the new body. OSTI, itself, recognized that the research community at which they aimed was limited in its numbers. This led them, on the one hand, to encourage new researchers and, on the other, to map out their own view of what topics were of prime importance. They recognized early on that computer-based handling of information was going to be a vital area for research, and, by the 1970s, had extended this to include networking. In the mid-1970s, OSTI was absorbed into the newly formed British Library, and its name was changed to the British

Library Research and Development Department (BLRDD). OSTI had always supported some library research and also some research in the social sciences. In its new guise, the funding agency covered all subjects, including the humanities.

But the research community remained small. The Department complained in the 1970s that new teams of researchers were slow to appear – much of the work was being done by people who had already been involved in the 1960s. This changed over the next two decades, though several of the early comers continued to figure prominently in the grants list. The Department's contribution to supporting research was essential. For example, an analysis of the period 1978–85 found that nearly half of the funding for research in library and information science in the UK came from BLRDD [53, p. 151]. The Department always took a proactive approach to funding, in part because of the limited number of researchers in the field, and many of the projects it supported had a practical orientation. Over the past 25 years, government policy has been increasingly to emphasize both these aspects for all research. By the 1990s, this was reflected in BLRDD support for research. The Department had always been willing both to consider projects proposed from outside, and to support work with no near-future application. Such dispensations now became rarer. At the same time, projects became shorter in duration. Earlier grants might be awarded for periods of 2–3 years to allow in-depth exploration. Now projects might last for only half a year. In 1996, BLRDD suffered a name change and subsequently underwent a confusing series of transformations [54]. The overall result was that the amount of funding for information science research went down, and the degree of central direction of the research went up.

Though bodies such as the Arts and Humanities Research Council have provided some funds for research of interest to information science, their scope has often been limited. Of more general interest has been the Joint Information Systems Committee (JISC), which was established in 1993 to deal with networking and specialist information services for further and higher education in the UK. To this end, it developed a series of strategies, and commissioned research to support these. JISC has the virtue of good financial backing: the drawbacks are that it decides what projects are to be done, and, as the frequent use of the word 'deliverables' implies, the research is targeted at applicable results. Perhaps for this reason, JISC funding is typically excluded from the research monies submitted for the RAE. The overall outcome has been that, though funding for information science in the UK has risen again in recent years, it is now allocated via a more top-down approach than in earlier years. One spin-off from the emphasis on strategy has been a growth of activity in information policy research. This is now a matter of continuing interest in British information research [55]. For some years past, the European Commission has funded projects of interest to information scientists (initially via DG XIII), and these, too, have often emphasized policy matters. As with JISC, the nature of such projects is decided on by the Commission, but, in this case, cooperation with colleagues within the European Community is an especially important factor. Despite their limitations, both JISC and EC projects have produced research whose value is not restricted solely to immediate applications.

Research in information science in the UK has particularly thrived in universities. BLRDD research grants to institutions of higher education usually exceeded both in number and amount the grants that it allocated to all other bodies put together. Information science was one area where the old polytechnics could compete with the traditional universities, but, prior to their re-establishment as new universities in the 1990s, they mainly concentrated on teaching. Though this has now changed – not least as a result of the RAE – it is probably fair to say that the major research centres for information science have always been situated predominantly in the older universities. The impact of the RAE on research in information science at the universities has been a matter for continuing comment [56]. It is generally felt that the process has increased the emphasis on research in departments, but has also increased the time wasted on bureaucracy. The hope must be that the former can be retained, while the latter can be decreased in future such exercises. But basic questions remain unanswered. For example, will departments that receive little or no income as a result of the RAE eventually give up on research, or will it stimulate them to enhance their research efforts? As part of their research activities, departments have, for many years, established research centres to deal with particular areas of information science. One major centre, however, lay outside the university network. For three decades from 1959 onwards the Aslib Research and Consultancy Department was a major contributor to the development of research in the subject both nationally and internationally. Its main interests lay in the evaluation of operations, user studies and automation [57], and a number of the research projects carried out were of long-term interest. For example, a survey of the information-gathering habits of scientists carried out first in the 1960s was repeated in the 1980s and showed that significant changes had occurred [58]. At the other end of the spectrum, the Department was closely involved in the introduction of teletext – in the form of Prestel – in the UK. The final closure of the Department by Aslib was therefore a blow for UK research, even though, by that time, the consultancy side had begun to dominate the research side. The growth of tendering for specified projects that has developed over the past two decades has certainly encouraged consultancy work: an area in which the UK previously lagged well behind the USA. For smaller consultancy teams, JISC is the more important target for funds. The European Commission requires both continuing contact and the cooperation of institutions in different member states. This, along with the much higher level of bureaucracy, tends to favour larger teams. From the research viewpoint, consultancy work has the drawback that the results may not be published via the usual quality-controlled channels.

The Aslib Research and Consultancy Department led the field in another way – the creation of research centres covering particular areas of information science. Most of the centres created over the past few decades have been situated in universities, and have typically reflected the interests of leading researchers in the departments concerned. Such centres have the virtue not only of providing a national focus for particular kinds of research, but also of providing an element of continuity over a period of years. On the down side, centres tend to have up-and-down careers as project heads leave, sponsors switch their funding, and, not least, the research specialism itself changes. For example, a programme of catalogue research was set up at Bath University towards the end of the 1970s, which subsequently transmuted into a centre for such research. In the 1980s, mainly due to the impact of information technology, this was renamed the Centre for Bibliographic Management. At the end of the 1980s, a UK Office for Library Networking was also set up at Bath, and, in the 1990s, the two merged to form a new centre – the UK Office for Library and Information Networking (UKOLN). Another example is the Centre for Library and Information Management (CLAIM). Originally at Cambridge University (under a different name), it moved to Loughborough University in the mid-1970s. It was decided to disband it in the mid-1980s, but one part of its activities – statistics – had proved particularly valuable both at home and abroad. After representations, not least from the American Library Association (ALA), it was decided to continue this work by establishing a smaller centre at Loughborough, entitled the Library and Information Statistics Unit (LISU), which still exists. As the last story suggests, one of the virtues of setting up research centres is that they often receive attention from outside the UK as well as from within.

Interaction with information scientists in other countries has always been important. Membership of the EC has been valuable in promoting greater contact within Europe. But the yardstick for measuring research excellence in information science has always been the USA. Comparison of developments in the UK and the USA is difficult because of the differing sizes of the research communities and of the amount of funding available. It does seem, however, that the organizational arrangements in the UK have sometimes been more beneficial than those in the USA. An obvious example relates to the provision of funding. The USA has never had a funding body comparable with BLRDD (nor, indeed, has any other country). Instead, US information scientists have had to seek funds from a range of sources. The National Science Foundation (NSF), for example, has concerned itself with scientific information and with its computer-based handling over the past half-century. But the NSF has blown hot and cold on the topic during this time, producing corresponding ups and downs in the research it supports. Overall, BLRDD managed to provide a higher level of consistency and continuity in its funding provision. Or, to take a different example – the relationship between the information science world and the library world in the two countries. An important factor in the creation of the Institute of Information Scientists (IIS) was disagreement with the Library Association (LA) over training needs. Yet, in subsequent decades, the LA proved increasingly flexible in accepting greater amounts of information science into the curricula that they validated. The result has been a reasonably harmonious development of library and information teaching and research in the UK. The end result of this growing together was the combination of the IIS and the LA into the Chartered Institute of Library and Information Professionals (CILIP). In the USA, the American Library Association was for some time considerably less inclined to accept large amounts of information science into the curriculum. This made the development of curricula more difficult, and, with the decline in the number of US university library departments, also affected research. But, although the organization of information science in the UK may have had some advantages, the greater amount of funding and greater number of personnel in the USA have ensured that research in information science carried out there has been of dominant importance throughout the world over the past 50 years.

In discussing research themes, I mentioned international recognition as an important selection factor. The simplest way of assessing such influence is via citation studies, not least in terms of citations of UK research papers by authors in the USA. A citation study carried out at the end of the 1990s produced a map of what, it was suggested, were the most significant 75 names in information research over the period 1972–1995 [59]. Most – as might be expected – were North American, but 12 were British (and another four carried out their earlier work in the UK). In view of the difference in the sizes of the research communities in the USA and the UK, this suggests that British research in information science has pulled its weight in the past 50 years. British involvement was, perhaps, particularly important early on, since 'information science' was accepted as a designation in the UK before it became generally accepted in the USA. Thus the American Documentation Institute changed its name to the American Society for Information Science in 1968 – 10 years after the formation of the IIS in the UK.

Looking back over the past 50 years, one conclusion must be that past research in information science is now paying off. Activities that were relatively marginal decades ago – such as automated information retrieval – are now at the heart of major growth industries. Although this has attracted greater funding support, projects nowadays are often more narrowly focused than in the past. 'Blue skies' research may actually be more difficult to sustain now. This tendency is emphasized by the pressures on researchers in universities to give more attention to applicable research. The widening interest in information science research has also brought in researchers from other disciplines – not least computer specialists. The growing influence of these latter can readily be traced in information science jargon. For example, 'metadata' was a rare term in the subject 20 years ago, but now it is universal. Nor are computer specialists alone in spreading into traditional areas of information science: business and management researchers are also becoming increasingly involved. Both computer studies and business studies are much larger than information science in terms of number of researchers and of financial support. Consequently, this merging of interests is also, to some extent, a submerging, as can be seen in some of the departmental reorganizations at universities in the UK. The term 'informatics' – formerly regarded with suspicion in the UK – is now coming into favour as a description of this blending. The overall result is that the information science activities developed over the past 50 years have triumphed, but information science as a separate entity may be on the wane. If so, its final epitaph might well be that of Sir Christopher Wren in St Paul's Cathedral – 'If you want a monument, look around you'.

## Acknowledgements

My thanks go to Brian Vickery for his comments on this article, and to John Martyn for supplying information. I would also like to thank the referees for their suggestions.

## References

[1]    A. Black, D. Muddiman and H. Plant, *Information Management in Britain before the Computer* (Ashgate, Aldershot, 2007).

[2]    K. Jarvelin and P. Vakkari, The evolution of information science 1965–1985: a content analysis of journal articles. In: P. Vakkari and B. Cronin (eds), *Conceptions of library and information science* (Taylor Graham, London, 1992).

[3]    C.W. Cleverdon, *The Effect of Variations in Relevance Assessments in Comparative Experimental Tests of Index Languages* (Cranfield Institute of Technology, Cranfield, 1970).

[4]    K. Sparck Jones and C.J. van Rijsbergen, Information retrieval test collections, *Journal of Documentation* 32(1) (1976) 59–75.

[5]    A.F. Smeaton and D. Harman, The TREC experiments and their impact on Europe, *Journal of Information Science* 23(2) (1997) 169–74.

[6]    B.C.Vickery, *Retrieval System Theory* (Butterworths, London; 1961).

[7]    K. Sparck Jones, *Automatic Keyword Classification for Information Retrieval* (Butterworths, London, 1971).

[8]    C.J. van Rijsbergen, *Information Retrieval* (Butterworths, London, 1979).

[9]    S.C. Bradford, *Documentation* (Crosby Lockwood, London, 1948).

[10]   R.A. Fairthorne, Book review, *Journal of Documentation* 18(4) (1962) 196–8.

[11]   K. Sparck Jones, A statistical interpretation of term specificity and its application to retrieval, *Journal of Documentation* 28(1) (1972) 11–21.

[12]   N. Jardine and C.J. van Rijsbergen, The use of hierarchic clustering in information retrieval, *Information Storage and Retrieval* 7(5) (1971) 217–40.

[13]   S.E. Robertson, The probability ranking principle in IR, *Journal of Documentation* 33(4) (1977) 294–304.

[14]   S.E. Robertson, Overview of the Okapi projects, *Journal of Documentation* 53(1) (1997) 3–7.

[15]   M. Beaulieu, Interaction in information searching and retrieval, *Journal of Documentation* 56(4) (2000) 431–9.

[16]   N. Bishop, V.J. Gillet, J.D. Holiday and P. Willett, Chemoinformatics research at the University of Sheffield: a history and citation analysis, *Journal of Information Science* 29(4) (2003) 249–67.

[17]   A. Gilchrist, *The Thesaurus in Retrieval* (Aslib, London, 1971).

[18]   J.F.B. Rowland, The scientist's view of his information system, *Journal of Documentation* 38 (1982) 38–42.

[19]   J.M. Brittain, *Information and its Users* (Bath University Press, Bath, 1970).

[20]   M.B. Line, The information uses and needs of social scientists: an overview of INFROSS, *Aslib Proceedings* 23(8) (1971) 412–34.

[21]   D.R. Streatfield and T.D. Wilson, Information innovations in social services: a third report on project INISS, *Journal of Documentation* 38(4) (1982) 273–81.

[22]   D. Nicholas, P. Huntington and A. Watkinson, Scholarly journal usage: the results of deep log analysis, *Journal of Documentation* 61(2) (2005) 248–80.

[23]   N. Moore, Developing the use of a neglected resource: the growth of information management, *Journal of Information Science* 15(2) (1989) 67–70.

[24]   K.A. Stroetmann, Information research in Europe: an investigation, *Journal of Information Science* 19(2) (1993) 149–54.

[25]   T.D. Wilson, The nonsense of knowledge management, *Information Research* 8, Paper No. 144 (2002). Available at: http://informationr.net/ir/8–1/paper144.html (consulted 5 March 2008).

[26]   A. Jashapara *Knowledge Management: an Integrated Approach* (Pearson Education, Harlow, 2004).

[27]   P.B. Checkland and J.Scholes, *Soft Systems Methodology in Action* (Wiley, Chichester, 1990).

[28]   T.D. Wilson, On user studies and information needs, *Journal of Documentation* 37(1) (1981) 3–15.

[29]   N.J. Belkin, R.N. Oddy and H.M. Brooks, ASK for information retrieval, *Journal of Documentation* 38(2 and 3) (1982) 61–71 and 145–64.

[30]   D. Ellis, A behavioural model for information retrieval system design, *Journal of Information Science* 15(4/5) (1989) 237–47.

[31]   B.C. Vickery and A. Vickery, Online search interface design, *Journal of Documentation* 49(2) (1993) 103–87.

[32]   F. Wood, N. Ford, D. Miller, G. Sobczyk and R. Duffin, Information skills, searching behaviour and cognitive styles for student-centred learning: a computer-assisted learning approach, *Journal of Information Science* 22(2) (1996) 79–92.

[33]   M. Beaulieu and C.L. Borgman, A new era for OPAC research: introduction to special topic issue on current research in online public access systems *Journal of the American Society for Information Science* 47(7) (1996) 491–2.

[34]   C.L. Borgman, Digital libraries and the continuum of scholarly communication, *Journal of Documentation* 56(4) (2000) 412–30.

[35]   A.J. Meadows, *Communication in Science* (Butterworths, London, 1974).

[36]   C. Cherry, *On Human Communication* (MIT Press, Cambridge, MA, 1957).

[37]   B. Cronin, Invisible colleges and information transfer, *Journal of Documentation* 38(3) (1982) 212–36.

[38]   M.D. Gordon, The roles of referees in scientific communication. In: J. Hartley (ed.) *Technology and Writing: Readings in the Psychology of Written Communication* (Jessica Kingsley, London, 1992) 263–75.

[39]   A.J. Meadows *Communicating Research* (Academic Press, San Diego, 1998).

[40]   B. Shackel, D.J. Pullinger, T.I. Maude and W.P. Dodd, The BLEND-LINC Project on 'electronic journals' after two years, *Computer Journal* 26(3) (1983) 247–54.

[41]   F. Rowland, C. McKnight and J. Meadows *Project ELVYN: an Experiment in Electronic Journal Delivery* (Bowker Saur, London, 1995).

[42]   D. Nicholas, P. Huntington and H.R. Jamali, The impact of open access publishing (and other access initiatives) on use and users of digital scholarly journals, *Learned Publishing* 20(1) (2007) 11–15.

[43]   University of Southampton, Intelligence, Agents, Multimedia Group. Available at: www.ecs.soton.ac.uk/~harnad/ (consulted 3 March 2008).

[44]   E. Gadd, C. Oppenheim and S. Probets, RoMEO studies 1: the impact of copyright ownership on academic author self-archiving, *Journal of Documentation* 59(3) (2003) 243–77.

[45]   C. Oppenheim, Does copyright have any future on the internet? *Journal of Documentation* 56(3) (2000) 279–96.

[46]   B.C. Brookes, The foundations of information science: Part I, *Journal of Information Science* 2(3/4) (1980) 125–33.

[47]   R.A. Fairthorne, Empirical hyperbolic distributions (Bradford-Zipf-Mandelbrot) for bibliometric description and prediction, *Journal of Documentation* 25(4) (1969) 319–43.

[48]   A. Pritchard, Statistical bibliography or bibliometrics, *Journal of Documentation* 25(4) (1969) 348–9.

[49]   B.C. Vickery, Bradford's law of scattering, *Journal of Documentation* 4(3) (1948) 198–203.

[50]   M.B. Line and A. Sandison, Practical interpretation of citation and library use studies, *College and Research Libraries* 36(5) (1975) 393–6.

[51]   I. Rowlands, Journal diffusion factors: a new approach to measuring research influence, *Aslib Proceedings* 54(2) (2002) 77–84.

[52]   A. Holmes and C. Oppenheim, Use of citation analysis to predict the outcome of the 2001 RAE for Unit of Assessment 61: Library and Information Management,

*Information Research* 6(2) (2001). Available at: http://informationr.net/ir/6-2/paper103.html (consulted 5 March 2008).

[53]   J. Meadows, *Innovation in Information: Twenty Years of the British Library Research and Development Department* (Bowker Saur, London, 1994).

[54]   A. Goulding, Searching for a research agenda for the library and information science community, *Journal of Librarianship and Information Science* 39(3) (2007) 123–5.

[55]   I. Rowlands (ed.), *Understanding Information Policy* (Bowker Saur, London; 1997).

[56]   J. Elkin and D. Law, The 1996 Research Assessment Exercise: the Library and Information Management Panel, *Journal of Librarianship and Information Science* 29(3) (1997) 131–41.

[57]   A. Gilchrist, J. Martyn and P. Vickers, Jumping through skylights: recollections of the Aslib Research and Consultancy Department, *Managing information* 6(December) (1999) 31.

[58]   J. Martyn, *Literature Searching Habits and Attitudes of Research Scientists: British Library Research Paper No. 14* (British Library, London; 1986).

[59]   H.D. White and K.W. McCain, Visualizing a discipline: an author co-citation analysis of information science 1972–1995, *Journal of the American Society for Information Science* 49(4) (1998) 327–55.

# 2

# Smoother pebbles and the shoulders of giants: the developing foundations of information science

DAVID BAWDEN

## Abstract

Some developments in the information science discipline over a period of 30 years are discussed, by selecting topics covered in the early issues of *Journal of Information Science*, and tracing their influence on subsequent developments, largely though by no means exclusively through *JIS* papers. Five main themes are covered: the information discipline per se; the foundations of that discipline; the nature of information; relations between discipline and profession; and education for information science. The continuing resonance of the writings of Farradane and Brookes is noted.

## Introduction

The *Journal of Information Science* (*JIS*) was first published in 1979, replacing *The Information Scientist* (*TIS*) which – though described as the 'journal of the Institute of Information Scientists' – was not generally regarded as a true academic/professional journal. The intervening period of nearly 30 years, a time span commonly taken as equivalent to a 'generation', gives the opportunity to consider the issues covered in the early issues of *JIS*, to set them into the context of the development of the information science discipline over time, and to assess the significance of some of the main contributions and contributors.

This is done by focusing on some of the articles and editorials published in the first two volumes of *JIS*, covering the years 1979 and 1980, tracing some of the preceding treatment of the issues, and following later developments, particularly – though not exclusively – through the pages of *TIS* and *JIS*. The set of literature cited is selected to show the origins and development of the issues, and is in no way intended to be comprehensive.

The discussion is focused around five main, albeit overlapping, themes. An initial consideration of the *information science discipline* itself leads fairly naturally to thoughts on the *foundations of the discipline*, and that in turn to the central question of the *nature of information*. There follows a consideration of the *relation between discipline and profession*, and in particular the role of research, and the closely associated question of the most appropriate form of *education for information science*. As we shall see, all of these themes are represented in the first issues of *JIS*, and all have remained 'live' topics[1] to the present day.

## The information science discipline

The emergence of an information science discipline was recognized, albeit with the caveats and uncertainties which have bedevilled discussions ever since, by Alan Gilchrist, the first editor of *JIS*, in an editorial on the first page of the first issue of the first volume of the new journal. Gilchrist [1] wrote tentatively:

> a profession, and possibly a science or discipline, is being increasingly recognized

and more definitely:

> If there is such a discipline as information science (and we believe there is) then it is time that an international consensus was established as to its definitions and the area in which it should fruitfully be applied.

The cynic might say that we are still waiting for this, nearly 30 years later.

The nature of the subject had, of course, been discussed previously (and rather inconclusively), particularly in the pages of *JIS*'s predecessor. For example, Saunders [2] argued that, although the field had originated with scientific information, its methods were equally applicable to other subject areas. Farradane [3] urged that a 'true information science' should be a science in its own right, an 'academic and applied study' and 'not an applied multidisciplinary art'; this would require an application of rigorous scientific method, and a careful re-examination of basic concepts. He developed this view of information science modelled on the physical sciences, and based on experimental studies of carefully defined physical information entities in two subsequent papers [4, 5].

As noted below, Brookes [6] developed a somewhat similar view of information science, on the basis of a much more detailed analysis of the foundations of the subject. There was 'a very important role for a science of information, a role as yet unclaimed by any other discipline, and which is a logical and natural extension of the interests and activities of those who currently claim to be information scientists'. Like Farradane, Brookes attempted to envisage information science by analogy with the physical sciences, based on quantitative analysis of objective and publicly observable phenomena. Unlike Farradane, he regarded its central concept of interest, information, as a non-physical entity.

A different, and with hindsight perhaps more realistic, view of the nature of the discipline, through the lens of a prediction of the future was made by Charles Meadow [7] in the fourth issue of *JIS*. Meadow, like several authors in *JIS* papers at that period, looked to the year 2001 to consider the status of information science and scientists. He considered three groups: information science practitioners; information system designers; and information scientists *per se*. His predictions in general seem rather more prescient than most others of the time, given the dangers of any such attempt (Bawden [8]). He foresaw that most information would be available online and fully searchable, and that 'almost all people, in whatever area, will be more conscious of the existence of information systems', although, like all commentators of the time, he saw this in terms of professional and educational activities; no-one imagined the internet, the home computer, or social networking. His view of the future information practitioner, and the organizations in which they work, was that primarily of a counsellor/advisor. His vision here has come to pass to some extent, though – again like most other commentators – he exaggerated the imminent death of the book, and the capability of machines to act as search assistants.

His vision for the 'science of information' is rather less definitive than others of the time – Farradane for one – and with hindsight may seem more realistic. 'There is not really much of a science of information today', Meadow wrote, 'but this, I believe, will change significantly by 2001'. However, his vision of this future information science was that of an 'integrating science', since information is of concern to many other disciplines: he named computer science, mathematics, economics, psychology, electrical engineering, communication theory, linguistics, sociology, and others. The distinction is not in content, but in outlook: information science will focus on human behaviour, of both groups and individuals, in interacting with information and the systems which deliver it. Therefore:

> information science [...] may never evolve into a body of knowledge and methodology distinguishable from other sciences [... it] will be concerned with the integration of the contributions of other sciences, much as ecologists are today [... there is] evidence that information science will remain only an integrating science, never a basic one. [I have to say I do not understand the 'only' in the last sentence. It seems an unnecessary self-belittling expression.]

This idea of the 'integrating science' seems a compelling one today, after nearly three decades of seeing information science try, and fail, to claim particular areas of expertise or practice as its own, from online searching to text retrieval to internet portal creation. As Jack Meadows [9] points out, information science seems to be more sensitive than other disciplines about exchanges with other areas.

Various ideas have been put forward as to how the information science discipline may be understood: Webber [10] summarizes a variety, and two more recent examples are given by Zins [11] and by Zhang and Benjamin [12]. Several have followed Meadow's general approach, of regarding it as a multidisciplinary or interdisciplinary area, focusing on the concept of information or some aspect of it, as two examples almost 30 years apart will show:

> an interdisciplinary science that investigates the properties and behaviour of information, the forces that govern the flow and use of information, and the techniques, both manual and mechanical, of processing information for optimal storage, retrieval and dissemination. (Borko [13])

> a multidisciplinary field of study, involving several forms of knowledge, given coherence by a focus on the central concept of human, recorded information, and underpinning several practical disciplines (Bawden [14])

The idea of information science as a borrowing or integrating science has attractions, apart from its seeming to be realistic: but against this must be set the viewpoint that a constant input of ideas, and people, from other disciplines may militate against the development of a cohesiveness, and consequent lack of an ability to develop any specifically information science theory base (Robertson, [15]; Weller and Haider [16]). Conversely, while we may like to find evidence that information science ideas, and people, filter into and enrich other disciplines, 'such expansions of our horizons make no sense unless we have some academically coherent core which relates the disparate activities' (Robertson [15]).

It would be wrong to conclude this section without acknowledging that some commentators in the early twenty-first century held the view that the optimism about the developing discipline which was exhibited by the writers in the early *JIS* has proved ill-founded: that, as Webber [10] reports it:

> the sapling which Farradane and Brookes had such hopes for in 1980 has, unnoticed by many, shot up, but become tangled in the undergrowth of more robust disciplines and is now weakened, perhaps beyond saving.

I certainly do not accept such a view. On the contrary, I have argued [14, 17] that the validity and strength of the information science discipline may only show itself in the future, by the adoption of concepts from that discipline by the physical and biological sciences, in contrast to the usual 'intellectual flow'. This would be a more fundamental adoption of concepts and perspectives, rather than a more superficial adoption of techniques and algorithms, as in the chemoinformatics and bioinformatics specialisms. I think that the *JIS* writers of 1980 would like that idea.

## Foundations of the discipline

Considering the significant number of papers written over the years dealing with information science as a discipline and profession, there have been relatively few attempts to spell out in detail what the foundations, or underlying philosophical or conceptual bases, of such a discipline might be.

One such attempt, arguably the most ambitious to date, was provided by Bertie Brookes, in a series of four papers in the first three issues of *JIS*, preceded by his 1976 article in *TIS*. The first, and arguably the most fundamental, deals with 'philosophical aspects' [18]. It argues for Popper's 'three worlds' ontology as a suitable foundation for the discipline, and presents a 'fundamental equation' for information science: an approach very much in line with Farradane's desire for an equivalence with the physical sciences, and building on Brookes' earlier thought [19]. The next two papers [20, 21] deal with quantitative aspects: mainly with the need for rank-frequency statistics and 'logarithmic laws' in analysing social, including informational matters, and in providing a mathematical description of information spaces, again building on earlier studies by Brookes [22–24]. The final paper in the series [6] discusses the 'changing paradigm' of information science. In this, Brookes brings together the arguments of the previous three papers, to show, both in outline and in specifics, what an information science based on his ideas would be like. The specifics are essentially those of bibliometric analysis, of the use of rank-frequency logarithmic plots to analyse any example of the communication of information, and of the construction of concept maps based on these. In more abstract disciplinary terms, Brookes claims that his four papers, in showing the need for a science of information noted above, also show that such a science would be based on several foundational principles:

- its main role would be 'the exploration and organization of Popper's World III of objective knowledge';
- it would be scientific, in that all the data studied would be 'publicly observable and the whole approach objective';
- it would require a recognition that information and knowledge were not physical, but 'extra-physical entities which exist only in cognitive (mental or information) spaces';
- quantitative analysis would be paramount, using techniques from the physical sciences, adapted to cognitive spaces.

Brookes' series of papers has been highly influential and widely cited, and continues to be cited to the present day, with varying degrees of attention given over time to their different aspects; for an assessment of his influence, see a biography and bibliography in an issue of *JIS* dedicated to him (Shaw [25]).

His bibliometric principles have been generally accepted into the mainstream, particularly his emphasis on methods based on measurement of ranks rather than sizes (Tague-Sutcliffe [26]). Nonetheless, the situation described by Shaw in 1990 [25] is still the case: his early bibliometric works are still more highly cited in total than his philosophical propositions.

He is generally accepted as the originator of the highly influential 'cognitive approach' to information science, and to information retrieval in particular (Ingwersen and Järvelin [27]).[2] Belkin [28] wrote that not only was he one of the earliest proponents of this view, but he personally influenced many of those others who have also espoused it […] he is one of those who have succeeded in using the cognitive view to develop a strong and influential theory for information science. Although this is only one facet of Brookes' contribution to information science, it is a significant one.

Brookes' proposal of Popper's three worlds ontology as a suitable philosophical basis for information science, however, is arguably his most distinctive, and certainly longest lasting, contribution, since, as noted above, his bibliometric writings, though initially highly cited, have now been 'absorbed' into the mainstream, and are not so strongly associated with his name. (Central to Popper's analysis of objective, i.e. communicable, knowledge is the idea of three 'worlds': World 1 of physical items – books, computers etc.; World 2 of subjective mental state and 'personal knowledge'; and World 3 of communicable information – the 'contents' of books, databases, etc.) Whilst others (for example, Swanson [29]) independently commended the relevance of Popper's epistemology to librarianship and information science, Brookes made it the basis of a well-developed meta-theory. Neill [30] provided a critical and detailed, though generally supportive, analysis of Brookes' series of papers, soon after their publication, in agreeing that

> there is a very real place for Popper's philosophy in library and information science

and that:

> Brookes has been very astute in recognizing the relevance of Popper to information science. Indeed, it is not for his logarithmic law of information that he [i.e. Brookes] will be remembered, but for this discovery of Popper's three worlds. When Brookes teaches quantitative methods, it is his discussion of Popper that excites the students, not his logarithms: for Popper's is clearly a working epistemology for librarians and for information scientists.

It seems that Neill was correct, for Brookes' views have been widely cited and generally supported (see, for example, Neill [31], Abbott [32, 33], Bawden [34], Spink and Cole [35], Ingwersen and Järvelin [27], and Zins [11]), though some have dissented (see, for example, Rudd [36] and Capurro [37]), and some have used the concepts of information spaces and Popper's worlds without reference to Brookes (see, for example, Boisot [38]).

It is perhaps ironic that the validity and value of Popper's three worlds viewpoint have gained greater acceptance in the information science area than in philosophy itself. As Notturno [39], a proponent of Popperian viewpoints, puts it:

> many contemporary philosophers regard World 3 as an unfortunate product of Popper's old age: as incoherent, irrelevant and perhaps, if the truth be told, a bit ridiculous.

It would be nice to think mere information scientists have something to teach the philosophers.

In the first paper of Brookes' series, alongside his Popperian viewpoint, and intrinsically connected to it, was presented his 'fundamental equation of information science'. This widely quoted equation takes the form:

$$K[S] + \Delta I = K[S + \Delta S]$$

A knowledge structure $K[S]$ is changed by the addition of an increment of information $\Delta I$ to a new knowledge structure, the change in structure denoted by $\Delta S$. Brookes noted that this equation is stated only in general terms; the terms are ill-defined, and dependent upon one another, so that the equation cannot be used for calculation or prediction. But it is central to the cognitive approach to information science, and Brookes argued that the interpretation of this fundamental equation was the basic research task of information science.

Although this equation has been much quoted, relatively little has been achieved in applying it in any practical way, or even in understanding it better. Todd [40] has proposed how this might be done, and examples have been given by Cole [41] and Todd [42] For the most part, however, the equation remains as a rather reproachful reminder of how far we are from fulfilling Brookes' research programme.

It is notable that there has been no other example of such an ambitious attempt to set out the foundations of the subject since Brookes' series of papers. Perhaps the nearest is Hjørland's socio-cognitive theoretical perspective, with its associated domain analysis approaches providing an understanding of the unique competences of information scientists [43–45].

## The nature of information

The first issue of *JIS* included an article by Jason Farradane [4] in which he set out a definition of 'information' which could form the basis for a 'true science of information', based on ideas alluded to in his earlier *TIS* paper [3]. This pair of papers may be considered the first to discuss in detail the nature of information as understood in information science, although Wersig and Neveling [46] had outlined a variety of possible ways of understanding the term, and Belkin [47] almost simultaneously presented alternative views.

Farradane's view was that information must be understood as a physical thing: 'any physical form of representation, or surrogate, of knowledge, or of a particular thought, used for communication'. (In this, he foreshadows the now commonly made distinction between knowledge as the personal and subjective understanding possessed by individuals, and information as the objective means by which it is communicated.) This, for Farradane, is the only sort of understanding of information which can support the development of information as an 'experimental science'. He eschews philosophical speculation and mathematical modelling; what matters is the obtaining of experimental data for analysis and predication, echoing the concepts and methods of the physical sciences. Farradane's ideas and their practical consequences have been developed in detail by Davenport [48], among others.

As noted above, Brookes [6] took a very different view of information, arguing that it was not physical, but existing only in cognitive space, which he identified with Popper's World III of objective knowledge. For Brookes, information was 'fragmented knowledge', while knowledge was 'coherent structures of information'.

In these early *JIS* papers, we already see the genesis of two principal models (using the term in its most general form, to mean a simple picturing of concepts to aid understanding) which have been used to explain the distinction between information and knowledge. Farradane's view, noted above, of information as a communicable surrogate for knowledge points to a view of knowledge as the personal and subjective understanding possessed by individuals, and information as the objective means by which it is communicated (see, for example, Orna and Pettitt [49]). Brooke's view of knowledge and information as essentially the same 'essence', distinguished by the degree of coherence, points to the commonly quoted 'information hierarchy', with data–information–knowledge–wisdom arranged on a line, or in the form of a pyramid, sometimes with other elements such as 'capta' ('interesting data') added (see, for example, Checkland and Holwell [50] and Rowley [51]).

Despite this early elucidation of two helpful ways of understanding the concept of information, there has subsequently been little agreement on the best way of defining or explaining it with any precision: an unfortunate state of affairs, given the necessity, as noted by Farradane, for such a definition to act as a basis for the explication of the discipline (see, for example, Meadow and Yuan [52], Bawden [53], Cornelius [54], Capurro [55], and Floridi [56]).

A current point at issue strikes an interesting echo from the past. As noted earlier in this paper, one approach to the nature of information sees information as intrinsically physical, or at least having roots as an entity in the physical universe (see, for example, Stonier [57], Bates [58, 59], and Bawden [14, 17, 60, 61]). The other sees it as non-physical, a purely human and socially constructed entity (see, for example, Hjørland [62]). It may not be too fanciful to see the origins of both in the early *JIS* debates, the former following Farradane's insistence on the basically physical nature of information, the latter drawing largely from Brookes' cognitive stance.

## Relation between discipline and profession

The relation between discipline and profession, and – almost equivalently – between theory (or research) and practice, has been a difficult issue for as long as long as either has existed.

Farradane's disapproval of a 'multidisciplinary art', and corresponding approval of an academic discipline, has already been noted. Brookes [63], in the same issue of *TIS*, gave a more positive assessment, drawing an analogy with the industrial revolution. The scientific laws of thermodynamics were only elucidated many years after steam engines were in widespread use: similarly, the laws of information science may emerge only after the practice of information handling is well developed. Meadows [9] makes a similar point, that:

> the simplest picture is to see information science as a wide-ranging subject in which various sectors develop a theoretical foundation, as and when they are ready to do so.

All these authors are very clear that a theoretical basis for the discipline should emerge at some point.

Brookes' analogy was referred to by Gilchrist [1] in the first *JIS* editorial, who argued that there should be a 'clear connection' between theory and practice, and that not only were practical applications worth discussing in themselves, but that 'the "science" will be advanced by rigorous examination and analysis of the practice'.

Sadly, this positive vision has not been fully realized: it has been more common to find information researchers criticizing practitioners for failing to value research, and practitioners charging researchers with conducting studies of little relevance to practice. This controversy appeared clearly in the second volume of *JIS*, with Stephen Robertson [64] suggesting that book reviews in a previous issue had:

> betray[ed] a feeling that much previous and present [information retrieval] research is misdirected or irrelevant [...] This feeling seems to me to be quite widespread in the profession, and I regret that good and useful research work may be ignored as a result.

The argument has continued ever since, despite goodwill on both sides: see, for example, Blick [65], Webber [10], Haddow and Klobbas [66], McNicol [67] and Weller and Haider [16].

Gilchrist's first editorial also emphasized the idea that information technology should never be paramount in the profession: the study of users and their needs, and of the social and organizational roles of information should be emphasized. This has been a continual, and understandable theme throughout the decades since. The last issues of *TIS* and the first of *JIS* carried a number of articles and letters dealing with a major concern of the day: the relative effectiveness and cost-effectiveness of searching printed indexes and computerized files. The proceedings of the London International Online Information Meetings for 1979 and 1980 show some other main concerns of the day: again, the relative merits of online and 'manual' searching; whether, and how, to train 'end users'; new technologies such as teletex, videodiscs, 'non-bibliographic' databases, and minicomputers; the possible uses of computer graphics; the exciting possibility of every library having a computer, and what might be done with it; and so on. Even for those of us who were there, it is difficult to remember what some of these issues were about; for a new generation, it will be impossible to imagine that it was seriously suggested that the nature of the discipline and profession could be dictated by them. Yet the same happened with the more recent technologies mentioned above, and is happening again with Web 2.0 and social networking. The only antidote is a disciplinary core of basic – perhaps theoretical is the wrong word – concepts, invariant to technology changes, so that it will be easier to evaluate and exploit whatever new technologies may emerge; exactly as Alan Gilchrist told us in 1979.

When speaking of 'profession', in this context, it is not always clear what is meant. At the time of the establishment of *JIS*, there was a very clear information science profession in the United Kingdom, with its own Institute, and an equivalent in the USA with its own Society. Since that time, both have lost their unique identity albeit in different ways: in the UK by a merger with the librarians to form CILIP, and in the USA by the explicit incorporation of information technology, to form ASIS&T [10]. Whether it is still meaningful to speak of an information science profession is therefore a moot point. However, this is not as new a situation as it might seem: Gilchrist [1] spoke of the new *JIS* serving 'allied fields', such as the management and communication sciences, and today we could name many other allied fields. It seems a remarkable waste of time and effort to worry about setting up disciplinary boundaries, and debating who is in and who is out. I have suggested [14] that it is feasible to make a distinction, on theoretical grounds from a Popperian analysis, between information science *per se*, dealing with individual information behaviour seeking and use, and related 'collection sciences' – librarianship, records management, etc. [It may not be too far-fetched to see in this an echo of an informally stated distinction, made many years ago: 'the information scientist is primarily a scientist who is approaching the literature and other sources of information from the research standpoint, while the librarian, even though he may have studied science, is trained to approach the literature from the standpoint of a custodian' (Dyson and Farradane [68]).

The important matter is to create and disseminate a body of information science theory and principles, to inform reflective practice in all the professional activities centred around information. I believe this to be the natural extension of the work of the *JIS* pioneers, in the changed environment of today.

## Education for information science

The subject of the appropriate form of education for the new discipline of information science was discussed in a paper in the first issue of *JIS* (Simpson

[69]). This is largely a detailed description of the origins of information courses at UK universities, and hence mainly of historical interest, but some issues still have resonance today. Simpson notes that information science at its outset was almost entirely concerned with the handling of scientific information, and courses were therefore largely involved with specific training for this work, sometimes with the study of scientific subjects included.[3] Hence the focus in the earliest curriculum for information science education: 'The emphasis of the syllabus throughout is that the information scientist is primarily a scientist and will obtain, organize, and disseminate information from the standpoint of one as well versed as may be possible in knowledge of the subjects dealt with' (Dyson and Farradane, [68]).

However, a broadening, under the influence of commentators such as Saunders (noted above) was already underway. He also notes that some early courses in information science had 'emphasis placed on information science as a science of information, and not simply a question of information of science'. This revisits questions of the intrinsic nature of the discipline noted above. Simpson also raised a question still being discussed today, when he stated that 'postgraduate courses in information science seem to have a greater chance of success [than undergraduate courses]'; a point later re-emphasized by Bottle [70].

He emphasized the then important role of the Institute of Information Scientists in specifying the 'Criteria for Information Science', essentially the required content of any information science course; for the origins of the Criteria, see Dyson and Farradane [68], for later development, see Oppenheim [71], and for a review of their context, see McGarry [72]. Six topics were regarded as essential, at the time Simpson wrote: knowledge and its communication; sources of information; organization of information; retrieval of information; dissemination of information; and management of information. Six other topics were regarded as of value: data processing; research methods; mathematics; linguistics; foreign languages; and advanced information theory and practice. The core topics still have a remarkably current feel, perhaps with data processing, which would now be described as IT applications, promoted to the core, at the expense of the editorial and document reproduction aspects of dissemination. The 'of value' topics, with the exception of research methods, are now too peripheral – and perhaps too demanding – to be accepted as a part of modern information education. The criteria were later modified several times, largely in the ways suggested above, before being absorbed, on the demise of the IIS into the 'virtually equivalent' CILIP criteria (Webber, [10]).

There continues to be much debate about the appropriate curriculum for 'library and information studies' or 'library and information management'; these being the two most usual terms for the subject area encompassing information science, and within which curriculum discussions tend to take place.[4] The report of a recent European curriculum development project shows the variety of views and the wide spread of subjects and their treatment in the current curriculum (Kajberg and Lørring, [73]), as do the papers in an Educational Forum at the 2007 CoLIS conference (Bawden [60]). The issues raised have a familiar ring: is there a 'core' of material for the subject, or at least a list of recommended topics, from which a curriculum might be constructed?; what should be the central 'mode of thought' for library/information education?; what is the best balance between research-based and theoretical material, and skills-based and practical issues? (and one is here reminded of Brookes' [74] concern that information should not be regarded as 'a collection of practical skills without underlying theoretical coherence'); what are the appropriate links with other subject areas?; what are the relative merits of specialized and generalist courses?; and what is the appropriate balance between first degree and postgraduate study in this area? (as noted above, an issue long debated). All of these topics were being discussed in the early issues of *JIS*, and it is difficult to know whether it is comforting or disconcerting to see them still live issues; accompanied, of course, by newer concerns, such as the validity of the I-School concept, and the place of Web 2.0 in information education (Bawden et al. [75]).

The question of a 'core' for information science education is closely associated with the idea of the discipline itself, for the educational 'core' must surely comprise those topics which are both central and unique to the discipline. As we have seen, there has been little agreement on the exact nature of the discipline, or even whether it exists, and accordingly some commentators doubt whether the concept of core is a useful one (see, for example, Raju [76]). There does, however, seem to be a reasonably consistent view through time. In 1986, Gilchrist [77] argued that the unique set of skills of the information scientist relied on knowledge and understanding of: information sources, particularly formal ones; needs and behaviour of users of information; knowledge structures, including epistemology, classification and retrieval languages; formulation of objectives and appropriate organizational structures. Now, 20 years on, it has been argued that information seeking and information retrieval, including relevant aspects of human information behaviour and also including information resources and knowledge organization, may form the realistic core of information education (Bawden, [61]). These topics approximate to the first three of Gilchrist's topics, showing a remarkable stability over time, and suggesting that this idea may have some validity. The last of Gilchrist's topics approximates to the 'information management' area, which tends to be necessarily rather mutable and contingent on circumstances and technologies of the time (Wilson [78]). This stability over time is noted by Jack Meadows in an article in this issue [79], in which he notes that there is greater agreement on what information scientists should study than on how information science should be defined.

## Conclusions

'Brookes', wrote Stephen Robertson in 1990, 'had [...] a vision of a discipline of information science, on the edges of which we have been hovering for a good 20 years.' [15] Perhaps we are still hovering there.

It is all too easy in reflecting on the significance of past events or writings to make facile or false analogies: to say that things are 'the same', while the seeming similarity is actually superficial, or due to a change in the way that terms are used. This risk must be acknowledged in an article such as this, which draws attention to apparent similarities between issues, views and visions of 30 years ago, and those of the present day. I believe, however, that these similarities are real: that the insights of Brookes, Farradane and other writers of the late 1970s and early 1980s are still valid, and that they raised issues which are still relevant, and problems which are still to be solved.

This is not to suggest that no progress has been made, which would indeed be a dismal view. This article has focused on foundations, concepts and philosophies, and these are notoriously slow to change, and tend to see the same issues re-emerging over time. A focus on the technical and operational issues within information science would have seen a different story told; of problems solved, confusions clarified, systems designed and built, and so on, though not necessarily associated with the information science 'brand'. As Meadows puts it, 'the information science activities developed over the past 50 years have triumphed, but information science as a separate entity may be on the wane' [79].

Nor is the story of the discipline and profession a negative one. Both have survived (despite some predictions during the early *JIS* years that they would not), despite the totally unanticipated changes in networked ICTs which have brought information and its communication to the forefront of professional, social, and economic life in a way which could not have been conceived 30 years ago. That, in itself, is no mean achievement.

As a result, much – arguably far too much – of the time of both academic and practising information scientists has had to be spent simply coping with the practical consequences of change, rather than reflecting on fundamentals, and reconsidering the discipline's foundations. It has at least helped to verify that it is essential to focus on basic information principles and on invariant issues of information behaviour, rather than being sucked into a concentration of the details of the technology du jour. As a result, we have not fully worked through the insights of the founders of the discipline, let alone replaced them with entirely new insights. Or, to put it more positively, of the newer theories and concepts which have been developed – and they are many – those which have built directly on the insights of the Brookes – Farradane generation have had most impact, and seem to have the potential to be developed further.

Perhaps most excitingly, we are now in a situation where the concept of information has entered the vocabulary of the physical and biological sciences, as a fundamental concept in an entirely novel way. I have suggested [14, 17] that this may be a unique opportunity for the insights of information science to be 'exported' to these other disciplines. This may be seen as a more positive prospect than a continued search for more 'information science substance'. For those in the information science discipline who came to it from the natural sciences – Farradane and Brookes among many others, including myself – it would surely be an exciting prospect.[5]

## Notes

1    It was noted that when the *Journal of Documentation* recently reprinted a series of classic papers, chosen by currently active experts, the late 1960s and early 1970s was chosen as a particularly significant time for innovations in information research. It seems that the same may be true of the late 1970s and early 1980s for conceptual thinking on the discipline. It is intriguing to speculate on the reasons for both.

2    Ingwersen and Järvelin remind us that De Mey was the first to use the term, although Brookes had already outlined the characteristics of the approach.

3    I can recall being asked at my first job interview whether I thought of myself as an 'information scientist' or a 'scientific informationist', a residuum of this distinction.

4    The Department of Information Science at City University London runs a master's course in information science. The names of the department and course have remained unchanged since their inception; the only case in the UK for which either is the case.

5    They would also recognize the references to pebbles and giants in the title as taken from the writings of Sir Isaac Newton: 'If I have seen further, it is by standing on the shoulders of giants' and 'I do not know what I may appear to the world, but to myself I seem to have been only like a boy playing on the sea-shore, and diverting myself in now and then finding a smoother pebble or a prettier shell than ordinary, while the great ocean of truth lay all undiscovered before me.'

## References

[1]    A. Gilchrist, Editorial, *Journal of Information Science* 1(1) (1979) 1–2.

[2]    W.L. Saunders, The nature of information science, *The Information Scientist* 8(2) (1974) 57–70.

[3]    J. Farradane, Towards a true information science, *The Information Scientist* 10(3) (1976) 91–101.

[4]    J. Farradane, The nature of information, *Journal of Information Science* 1(1) (1979) 13–17.

[5]    J. Farradane, Knowledge, information and information science, *Journal of Information Science* 2(2) (1980) 75–80.

[6]    B.C. Brookes, The foundations of information science, Part IV. Information science: the changing paradigm, *Journal of Information Science* 3(1) (1981) 3–12.

[7]    C.T. Meadow, Information science and scientists in 2001, *Journal of Information Science* 1(4) (1979) 214–22.

[8]    D. Bawden, The nature of prediction and the information future: Arthur C. Clarke's Odyssey vision, *Aslib Proceedings*, 49(3) (1997) 57–60.

[9]    A.J. Meadows, Theory in information science, *Journal of Information Science* 16(1) (1990) 59–63.

[10]    S. Webber, Information science in 2003: a critique, *Journal of Information Science* 29(4) (2003) 311–30.

[11]    C. Zins, Redefining information science: from 'information science' to 'knowledge science', *Journal of Documentation* 62(4) (2006) 447–61.

[12]    P. Zhang, and R.I. Benjamin, Understanding information related fields: a conceptual framework, *Journal of the American Society for Information Science and Technology* 58(13) (2007) 1934–47.

[13]   H. Borko, Information science: what is it?, *American Documentation* 19(1) (1968) 3–5.

[14]   D. Bawden, Organised complexity, meaning and understanding: an approach to a unified view of information for information science, *Aslib Proceedings* 59(4/5) (2007) 307–27.

[15]   S.E. Robertson, B.C. Brookes and information science education: a personal note, *Journal of Information Science* 16(1) (1990) 9–10.

[16]   T. Weller and J. Haider, Where do we go from here? An opinion on the future of LIS as an academic discipline in the UK, *Aslib Proceedings* 59(4/5) (2007) 475–82.

[17]   D. Bawden, Information as self-organised complexity: a unifying viewpoint, *Information Research* (2007) 12(4), paper colis31. Available at: http://informationr.net/ir/12-4/colis/colis31.html (accessed 20 December 2007).

[18]   B.C. Brookes, The foundations of information science, Part I: philosophical aspects, *Journal of Information Science* 2(3/4) (1980) 125–33.

[19]   B.C.Brookes, Robert Fairthorne and the scope of information science, *Journal of Documentation* 30(2) (1974) 139–52.

[20]   B.C. Brookes, The foundations of information science, Part II. Quantitative aspects: classes of things and the challenge of human individuality, *Journal of Information Science* 2(5) (1980) 209–21.

[21]   B.C. Brookes, The foundations of information science, Part III. Quantitative aspects: objective maps and subjective landscapes, *Journal of Information Science* 2(6) (1980) 269–75.

[22]   B.C. Brookes, The growth, utility and obsolescence of scientific periodical literature, *Journal of Documentation* 26(4) (1970) 282–94.

[23]   B.C. Brookes, Theories of the Bradford law, *Journal of Documentation* 33(3) (1977) 180–209.

[24]   B.C.Brookes, Measurement in information space: objective and subjective metrical spaces, *Journal of the American Society for Information Science* 31(4) (1980) 248–55.

[25]   A. Shaw, B.C. Brookes and the development of information science: a bibliography, *Journal of Information Science* 16(1) (1990) 3–7.

[26]   J. Tague-Sutcliffe, Quantitative methods in documentation. In B.C. Vickery (ed.), *Fifty Years of Information Progress: a Journal of Documentation Review* (Aslib, London, 1994) 147–88.

[27]   P. Ingwersen and K. Järvelin, *The Turn: Integration of Information Seeking and Retrieval in Context* (Springer, Dordrecht, 2005).

[28]   N.J. Belkin, The cognitive viewpoint in information science, *Journal of Information Science* 16(1) (1990) 11–15.

[29]   D.R. Swanson, Libraries and the growth of knowledge, *Library Quarterly* 50(1) (1980) 112–34.

[30]   S.D. Neill, Brookes, Popper and objective knowledge, *Journal of Information Science* 4(1) (1982) 33–9.

[31]   S.D. Neill, The dilemma of the subjective, *Journal of Documentation* 43(3) (1987) 193–211.

[32]   R. Abbott, Information transfer and cognitive mismatch: a Popperian model for studies of public understanding, *Journal of Information Science* 23(2) (1997) 129–37.

[33]   R. Abbott, Subjectivity as a concern for information science: a Popperian perspective, *Journal of Information Science* 30(2) (2004) 95–106.

[34]   D. Bawden, The three worlds of health information, *Journal of Information Science* 28(1) (2002) 51–62.

[35]   A. Spink and C. Cole, A human information behavior approach to a philosophy of information, *Library Trends* 52(3) (2004) 617–28.

[36]   D. Rudd, Do we really need World III? Information science with or without Popper, *Journal of Information Science* 7(3) (1983) 99–105.

[37]   R. Capurro, What is information science for? A philosophical reflection. In: P. Vakkari and B. Cronin (eds), *Conceptions of Library and Information Science* (Taylor Graham, London, 1992) 82–96.

[38]   M.H. Boisot, *Information Space* (Routledge, London, 1995).

[39]   M.A. Notturno, *Science and the Open Society: the Future of Karl Popper's Philosophy* (Central European University Press, Budapest, 2000).

[40]   R.J. Todd, Back to our beginnings: information utilization, Bertram Brookes and the fundamental equation of information science, *Information Processing and Management* 35(6) (1999) 851–70.

[41]   C. Cole, Calculating the information content of an information process for a domain expert using Shannon's mathematical theory of communication: a preliminary analysis, *Information Processing and Management* 33(6) (1997) 715–26.

[42]   R.J. Todd, Utilization of heroin information by adolescent girls in Australia: a cognitive analysis, *Journal of the American Society for Information Science* 50(1) (1999) 10–23.

[43]   B. Hjørland, Theory and meta-theory of information science: a new interpretation, *Journal of Documentation* 54(5) (1998) 606–21.

[44]   B. Hjørland, Epistemology and the socio-cognitive perspective in information science, *Journal of the American Society for Information Science and Technology* 53(4) (2002) 257–70.

[45]   B. Hjørland, Domain analysis in information science: eleven approaches – traditional as well as innovative, *Journal of Documentation* 58(4) (2002) 422–62.

[46]    G. Wersig, and U. Neveling, The phenomena of interest to information science, *The Information Scientist* 9(4) (1975) 127–40.

[47]    N. Belkin, Information concepts for information *science, Journal of Documentation* 34(1) (1978) 55–8.

[48]    E. Davenport, What do we look at when we do information science? In: P. Vakkari and B. Cronin (eds), *Conceptions of Library and Information Science* (Taylor Graham, London, 1992) 286–98.

[49]    E. Orna and C. Pettitt, *Information Management in Museums*, 2nd Edition (Gower, Aldershot, 1998).

[50]    P. Checkland and S. Holwell, *Information, Systems and Information Systems: Making Sense of the Field* (Wiley, Chichester, 1998).

[51]    J. Rowley, The wisdom hierarchy: representations of the DIKW hierarchy, *Journal of Information Science* 33(2) (2007) 163–80.

[52]    C.T. Meadow and W. Yuan, Measuring the impact of information: defining the concepts, *Information Processing and Management* 33(6) (1997) 697–714.

[53]    D. Bawden, The shifting terminologies of information, *Aslib Proceedings* 53(3) (2001) 93–8.

[54]    I. Cornelius, Theorising information for information science, *Annual Review of Information Science and Technology* 36 (2002) 393–425.

[55]    R. Capurro, The concept of information, *Annual Review of Information Science and Technology* 37 (2003)   343–411.

[56]    L. Floridi, Two approaches to the philosophy of information, *Minds and Machines* (2003) 459–69.

[57]    T. Stonier, Towards a new theory of information, *Journal of Information Science* 17(5) (1991) 257–63.

[58]    M.J. Bates, Information and knowledge: an evolutionary framework, *Information Research* 10(4) (2005). Available at: http://informationr.net/ir/10-4/paper239.html (accessed 20 December 2007).

[59]    M.J. Bates, Fundamental forms of information, *Journal of the American Society for Information Science and Technology* 57(8) (2006) 1033–45.

[60]    D. Bawden, Facing the educational future, *Information Research* 12(4) (2007), paper colise01. Available at: http://informationr.net/ir/12-4/colis/colise01.html (accessed 20 December 2007).

[61]    D. Bawden, Information seeking and information retrieval: the core of the information curriculum? *Journal of Education for Library and Information Science* 48(2) (2007) 125–38.

[62]    B. Hjørland, Information: objective or subjective/situational? *Journal of the American Society for Information Science and Technology* 58(10) (2007) 1448–56.

[63]   B.C. Brookes, A new paradigm for information science, *The Information Scientist* 10(3) (1976) 103–12.

[64]   S. Robertson, The value of research, *Journal of Information Science* 2(2) (1980) 116.

[65]   A.R. Blick, Information science research versus the practitioner, *Nachrichten für Dokumentation* 34(6) (1983) 261–65.

[66]   G. Haddow and J.E. Klobbas, Communication of research to practice in library and information science, *Library and Information Science Research* 26(1) (2004) 29–43.

[67]   S. McNicol, Is research an untapped resource in the library and information profession? *Journal of Librarianship and Information Science* 36(3) (2004) 119–26.

[68]   G.M. Dyson and J.E.L. Farradane, Education in information work: the syllabus and present curriculum of the Institute of Information Scientists Ltd., *Journal of Chemical Documentation* 2(2) (1962) 74–6. Reprinted in *Journal of Information Science* 28(1) (2002) 79–81.

[69]   I.S. Simpson, Education for information science, 1: the United Kingdom, *Journal of Information Science* 1(1) (1979) 49–58.

[70]   R.T. Bottle, Education for IS or IT: is there a difference? *Journal of Information Science* 8(4) (1984) 167–70.

[71]   C. Oppenheim, The Institute's new criteria for information science, *Journal of Information Science* 4(5) (1982) 229–34.

[72]   K. McGarry, Education for librarianship and information science: a retrospect and revaluation, *Journal of Documentation* 39(2) (1983) 95–122.

[73]   L. Kajberg and L. Lørring, *European Curriculum: Reflections on Library and Information Science Education* (Royal School of Library and Information Science, Copenhagen, 2005).

[74]   B.C. Brookes, Personal transferable skills for the modern information professional, *Journal of Information Science* 15(2) (1989) 115–17.

[75]   D. Bawden, L. Robinson, T. Anderson, J. Bates, U. Rutkauskiene and P. Vilar, Towards Curriculum 2.0: library/information education for a Web 2.0 world, *Library and Information Research* 31(99) (2007) 14–25.

[76]   J. Raju, The 'core' in library and/or information science education and training, *Education for Information* 21(4) (2003) 229–42.

[77]   A. Gilchrist, What the information scientist has to offer, *Journal of Information Science* 12(6) (1986) 273–80.

[78]   T. Wilson, Towards an information management curriculum, *Journal of Information Science* 15(4/5) (1989) 203–9.

[79]   J. Meadows, Fifty years of UK research in information science, *Journal of Information Science* 34(4) (2008) [this issue].

# 3

# The last 50 years of knowledge organization: a journey through my personal archives

STELLA G. DEXTRE CLARKE

## Abstract

At the time when the Institute of Information Scientists was launched, well established principles of classification, especially faceted classification, provided an excellent springboard for developments in knowledge organization thereafter. The principles of thesaurus construction and use were worked out during the first two decades of the Institute's existence. Up until the end of the 1980s, most practical systems to exploit any of these vocabularies were held on cards, some of them highly ingenious. The subsequent arrival of the desktop computer, soon followed by the growth of networks providing access to an almost unimaginable quantity and variety of resources, has stimulated evolution of the knowledge organization schemes to exploit the technology available. Anecdotes of events and practical applications of controlled vocabularies illustrate this account of developments over the period.

## Introduction

The last 50 years is just a blip in the history of knowledge organization, if you take the story back to the Library of Alexandria in the third century BC, with its shelf arrangement designed by Callimachus and probably inspired by Aristotle [1]. However, the period from 1958 onwards has seen a major shift in the focus of interest, and more than one transformation in the practicalities of how we apply the principles.

A systematic review of developments would be too ambitious for this article. Instead it juxtaposes an account of some milestone advances in the period, together with anecdotes illustrating how it felt to work in those times.

'Principles and practice', the byline of the *Journal of Information Science*, seems a fair summary of the approach.

## The run-up to 1958, or, the rise and rise of classification

By the time the Institute of Information Scientists was launched, the theory and pioneering development of classification schemes had seen their heyday.

The problems of an enumerative scheme such as the Dewey Decimal Classification Scheme were well known. (See Berwick Sayers in 1956 [1]: 'The curious fact remains that more and more libraries throughout the world continue to use it [...] somehow it works. We should fail [...] if we did not say that a scheme which has survived for eighty years in ever-growing currency in spite of merited criticism must have virtues which in practice outweigh our theoretical objections.') The Dewey scheme may have been widely disparaged in academic circles, but it was even more widely used in the libraries of the day.

UDC had had its great flowering, but by this time was beginning to struggle financially, as it has done ever since. (See, for example, McIlwaine [2] in 2000: 'The death of UDC has been foretold for the past forty years [...]'.)

Ranganathan and Bliss had made their revolutionary contributions to classification theory, in developing the ideas of 'faceted classification' [3].

The Classification Research Group (CRG) had taken up these ideas, and begun work on the second edition of the Bliss Classification (BC2). The year 1957 had seen publication of its memorandum, *The need for faceted classification as the basis of all methods of information retrieval* [4].

In 1960 Vickery's slim book on faceted classification [5] summed up the advances in a practical guide on how to develop a faceted classification for your organization's own special collection.

A great deal of classification research and development has continued since then, notably on adapting practice to new technology. But rarely has it yielded developments in the fundamental theory on the scale of earlier advances.

In contrast the development of thesauri was only just beginning. The vocabulary developed in 1959 for information retrieval at E.I. Dupont de Nemours and Company by B. E. Holm was the first fully operational thesaurus [6, 7], soon to be followed by many more.

Thesaurus developments then came thick and fast. They became a continuing theme in my own career, and provide the main background for this article.

My involvement in this field began only in 1970, when I took the MSc course in information science that had been developed and launched by that great pioneer and founding father of the Institute of Information Scientists, Jason Farradane. Farradane was enormously enthusiastic about faceted classification, as well as his own pet project at the time, 'relational indexing'. The aim of the latter was to capture, not just the key concepts appearing in a document, but also their inter-relationships as described in the document. The document was summarized in one or more 'analets' – strings of terms or codes representing concepts interconnected with relationship symbols. In theory the analets should enable the searcher to retrieve very precisely the subject of his query. In practice, sadly, the idea never had much take-up. Back, therefore, to the history of the thesaurus.

## The 1960s and 1970s: the time of the thesaurus has come

Although the Dupont thesaurus was never published, it led to a period of intense innovation. The Armed Services Technical Information Agency (ASTIA) and American Institute of Chemical Engineers (AICE) brought out thesauri in 1960 and 1961 respectively. The Engineers Joint Council (EJC) *Thesaurus of Engineering Terms* followed in 1964. In 1967 came joint publication by the EJC and the US Department of Defense of the influential *Thesaurus of Engineering and Scientific Terms (TEST)*[8]. According to Aitchison and Dextre Clarke [9] *TEST* embodied most of the standard features visible in alphabetically organized thesauri for the next 30 years. Although quite a few years passed before publication of the first edition of ISO 2788 *Documentation – guidelines for the establishment and development of monolingual thesauri* [10] in 1974, its content was largely built on the same rules and conventions set out in Appendix 1 of *TEST*.

The ideas had been catching on in Europe. Jean Viet, for example, authored a string of thesauri including the OECD's *Macrothesaurus* [11], which soon found applications worldwide. In the UK the deliberations of the CRG became another important influence. One of its members, Jean Aitchison, was the pioneer who saw the opportunity for combining facet analytical techniques with thesaurus construction. She had developed a faceted classification for the English Electric Library, and went on to supplement it with a thesaurus that exploited the facet structure to generate thesaural relationships. In the resulting 1969 publication, *Thesaurofacet* [12], the classification and the thesaurus were managed and presented as an integrated whole. A most important insight behind this development was that working in alphabetical order is no way to build a good strong conceptual scheme. The thesaurus developer needs to sort the terms collected into a systematic conceptual framework in order to detect overlaps and omissions, and build sound hierarchical relationships.

Aitchison went on to compile a series of thesauri built on the same principle, up to and beyond the end of the century. Another vital early contribution was her *Thesaurus Construction: a Practical Manual*, of which the first edition [13] published in 1972 was co-authored with Alan Gilchrist. The 2000 edition [14] is still the standard text for workers in the field.

## Thesauri in action in those early years

At the City University in 1970–71, I recall very little mention of the thesaurus. We learned about some of the precursors, such as the system of uniterms devised by Mortimer Taube, and Zatocoding, the brain-child of Calvin Mooers. One new member of staff had just come back from a tour in the USA, and spoke enthusiastically about *Medical Subject Headings (MeSH)* [15], the vocabulary used by an amazing computerized information retrieval service from the National Library of Medicine (NLM) called MEDLARS. The first edition of *MeSH* was published in 1960, for use with the printed *Index Medicus*, and the online service MEDLARS was launched in 1971. Having evolved from a scheme of subject headings *MeSH* never adopted the rules set out in *TEST*, but nonetheless is still fundamental to the operation of today's Pubmed (at www.ncbi.nlm.nih.gov/sites/entrez) and other NLM products and services.

In 1971 I remember visiting some information centres in the UK which used keywords rather than classification schemes for their information retrieval (IR) systems, but few of the keyword vocabularies had taken on board the structure and rules set out in *TEST*. For example the British Non-Ferrous Metals Research Association used a vocabulary of around 1500 terms in a flat alphabetical list, with no relationships other than a few 'See' references from synonyms to the corresponding preferred terms.

Computerized systems were, frankly, new-fangled things attracting enthusiasm from a tiny minority of pioneers, scepticism from the old guard (who sniffed at the lack of intellectual input into the content analysis and indexing of each document), and just a sigh of budgetary envy from the managers of most information centres. In 1967 Wilfred Ashworth [16] realistically advised, 'Computer time is usually shared among many departments of an organization, and generally the library will have low priority. It will be wise therefore not to develop any system which requires immediate access to the computer before a question can be answered.' Most practical IR systems ran on cards [16, 17]. And there were all sorts of cards.

The range extended from simple catalogue cards at the bottom end of the market to machine-sorted punched cards at the top. In between, the best known types were uniterm cards, edge-punched cards and optical coincidence cards. A key distinction in the mode of operation was between 'item cards' and 'feature cards'. With the former type, the basic principle was to create a card for each document or other type of item in the collection; these cards could then be sorted manually or by machine to find all that matched a given query. Feature cards, also known as term cards, turned this principle upside down, and indeed they demonstrated the 'inverted index' which underpins most information retrieval systems today. A card was created for every 'feature' that might be useful in a search, such as a term or keyword, and on the card was marked a pointer (such as a reference number) for every item possessing the feature in question. At the time of search, you got out the cards for the terms you sought, and used the reference numbers to find the documents. For example, if you were looking for information about the 'pruning' of 'roses' you would compare the cards for these two terms to see which reference numbers they had in common, and then use these numbers to find the items on the shelf.

It sounds so laborious now! But at the time these card systems represented huge progress and delivered real efficiency gains. The optical coincidence cards, which used the 'feature card' principle, were rather fun and their guardians were well placed in the pecking order. They were large strong cards, sometimes about 2 foot square, i.e. as big as you could comfortably handle. On each card was printed a grid of dots, sometimes as many as 100 dots in each row and column. That gave you the capacity to handle a collection of 10,000 documents. Using precision equipment, each time you added a document to the collection (say number 7682) you picked out all the cards for its index terms (say 'whisky' 'customs duty' 'inflation', etc., with no limit on the number of terms), and in each of them you drilled or punched a tiny hole in dot position 7682. At the time of search, you picked out the cards for your query terms and placed them on top of each other on a light box. The light shone through the holes wherever a document matched all the terms, giving you the numbers on the shelf. The equipment was inexpensive. It was easy to use. And it taught you the meaning of Boolean logic in a very practical way!

Alternatively you could spend a large budget on mechanized card sorters. These typically used 80-column cards, also known as IBM cards, which from memory were about $4 \times 8$ inches. They too had to be punched, but they were item cards not feature cards. Since each card represented a document, the 80 $\times$ 10 hole capacity on them had to be used economically. Either you were limited to an indexing vocabulary of just 800 terms, or you would have to apply an additional coding system along the lines of Zatocoding [16], to represent each index term with a combination of holes. 'Random superimposed coding' as it was sometimes known, would inevitably yield a percentage of false drops. Another disadvantage of the machine sorting method was the time needed to pass the complete set of cards (one for every document in the collection) through the machine for each query term in turn. The method embodied brute force rather than elegance.

The card system in the Central Electricity Generating Board (yes, the glorious era before privatization) where I worked in 1971 was less sophisticated than either of those, relying on a lengthy bank of cabinets with drawers of 4 x 6 inch catalogue cards. Each card carried the abstract and reference details of an article or other such item selected by a team of information scientists scanning hard copies of all the journals, reports, etc. (In those days 'scanning' was done by human eyes, not a machine.) The team also indexed the items using a large, well structured thesaurus. The cards were then filed in alphabetical order of the index terms, one (or a combination) of which was written in the top left corner of the card. Thus if six index terms had been assigned to one item, at least six copies of the body of the card were needed, and more if you provided for combinations in different orders.

In contrast, the CEGB's thesaurus was sophisticated. It had been prepared on the back of the renowned *TEST*, just by removing unwanted terms, adding extra ones and exorcising the American spellings. The rich network of inter-term relationships made it easy to select appropriate terms for searching and indexing. Thus a vocabulary finely tuned for postcoordinate retrieval found itself married to a primitive card system that could barely cope with precoordination – what a mismatch! By the time I left the CEGB in 1972, the tide towards computerization was beginning to turn and my boss was entranced by ASSASSIN, a system developed by ICI and one of the earliest examples of commercially available software for generating (via mainframe computers, of course) SDI services from magnetic tapes.

My own career, however, had taken a different turn. In late 1972 I found myself in Latin America. 'Information science' had been hard enough to explain in the UK. Selling my professional services in Peru and Ecuador, in Spanish, was an altogether bigger challenge. But there were a few precedents. In Chile, for example, production of a Spanish version of the OECD's *Macrothesaurus* was already in hand in an organization called CLADES, the Latin American Centre for Economic and Social Documentation.

In several of these countries businessmen were getting very fed up with their traditional reliance on 'experts' and 'advisers' from developed countries. Especially irksome was the need to pay extortionate licence fees for the use of patented technology. In a very few enlightened quarters the penny was just beginning to drop that a more appropriate unpatented technology could often be identified and adopted just by reading the literature – if only you could get hold of it [18]. (There was no hope of finding a copy in the country – you had to know how to order it from overseas.) And so I found a useful role funded by UNIDO to help CENDES, an Ecuadorian 'Centre for Development' which offered a free information service to small enterprises. CENDES was assembling a collection of well chosen articles, books and reports, and had already acquired a set of optical coincidence cards, but was struggling to index the material with its vestigial vocabulary of keywords. Armed with the invaluable manual by Aitchison and Gilchrist [13], we soon put together CENDES's *Tesauro técnico de palabras claves*, possibly the first Spanish language thesaurus to be assembled independently of any other, and fully compliant with the newly published ISO 2788 [10].

The capability to retrieve information enabled CENDES to help hundreds of small firms address technical problems, from reducing the occurrence of defective glazing on ceramic tiles, to combating an outbreak of disease at a shrimp fishery. The benefits of knowledge organization were manifest. The CENDES vocabulary served as a model for similar thesauri backing industrial information services in Peru and in Central America. By 1979, all were successfully implemented and in at least one country, Costa Rica, a minicomputer was used for the information retrieval system. For computers were now firmly in the ascendancy, and not just in the most developed countries.

During the 1970s two American companies, the Lockheed Corporation and System Development Corporation (SDC) had launched public online services for access to a range of databases, available worldwide over the telephone. (The Lockheed service is still around today, known as Dialog, from

Thomson Scientific.) Even in countries like Peru, where telephone lines were of unreliable quality and the costs staggering, the temptation to search online became irresistible for some large corporations. By the end of 1979 when I returned to the UK, 'online' was the excitement lived and breathed by the information science community. However, the incredible power of the computer to search every word of a text brought into relief a long-standing argument about whether you could prove the worth of a thesaurus, or a classification scheme, or any form of knowledge organization scheme.

## Doubts about the efficacy of controlled vocabularies

As long ago as 1961 H. P. Luhn [19] had pointed out one of the fundamental limitations of a controlled vocabulary, namely the mindset of the compiler and of the indexer when selecting index terms at a fixed point in time. If the controlled vocabulary is the only means of subject access to the document collection, 'Aspects of documents which might prove important in the light of future inquiry are therefore liable to be made inaccessible,' he objected. But at this time opinions were generally in favour of controlled vocabularies.

Between 1959 and 1964 the Aslib-Cranfield Research Project [20–22], under the direction of Cyril Cleverdon and Jack Mills, ran a ground-breaking series of tests on 'indexing languages', including the UDC, a faceted classification, an alphabetical subject catalogue and the uniterm system. The first round of tests showed little significant difference in performance between these four. One conclusion was that there were too many variables at play: each indexing language was its own amalgam of recall devices (designed to increase the number of relevant items retrieved) and precision devices (designed to decrease the number of irrelevant items retrieved). The objective of the second round of tests was to isolate some of these devices and analyse their effects on performance. This time the documents were indexed in three different ways:

- key concepts, humanly selected and recorded as phrases occurring naturally in abstracts of the documents;
- those same concept phrases, separated into single natural language words;
- main 'themes', derived by combining the concepts in various ways.

The broad conclusion, to most people's surprise, was that single natural language words did best, controlled term languages in the middle range, and natural language phrases the worst. The only devices that significantly improved on single words were synonym control and a form of stemming.

Argument has raged ever since. Perhaps the Cranfield set-up was too far removed from operational reality; perhaps the controlled language (not a fully-fledged thesaurus) was not as good as it might be, maybe the document abstracts bore little resemblance to full text natural language, etc. But proving which retrieval techniques and vocabularies work best is not easy. There are just too many variables, starting with the subjectivity of the user. As Svenonius [23] subsequently remarked, 'An experiment sophisticated and large enough to control all of the above variables [concerning effectiveness of controlled vocabularies] has never been conducted and probably never will.'

To this day our profession divides into two faiths: the believers and the unbelievers in systems of vocabulary control. In between are a great many experienced searchers [24–30], who agree that *both* free-text and controlled index terms are needed. Different types of query benefit from a different mix of search techniques [23, 31]. As noted by Rowley [32], their views are based as much on experience and case studies as on conclusive evidence.

To go back to the 1970s and early 1980s, the availability of online databases did not extinguish the demand for thesauri. For example DIALOG uploaded the INSPEC thesaurus alongside the bibliographic database, to enhance the quality of search. A substantial community still had the gut feel that word-based searching benefits from two key thesaurus capabilities: conflation of synonyms and disambiguation of homographs.

One more observation before we move on from the 1970s. Up until then, all the information retrieval applications look small when viewed from the perspective of 2008. Some of them were tiny. In the absence of the internet, there was little pressure for scalability and we were able to live with small-scale technology. Not only that, but a lot of innovative effort was specifically targeted at keeping down the size of the knowledge organization schemes. Both uniterms (which rejected compound terms in favour of single-word terms) and Zatocoding had been designed to keep things small and manageable. Even the mighty IBM (and remember the acronym stood for International Business Machines without mention of computers) was selling high-priced punched card systems that began to creak with a vocabulary of more than 800 terms. Until computers on our desks came to lift the scale constraints, our creativity was often focused on keeping things under control rather than reaching out for the stars. In 1945 Vannevar Bush [33] had dreamed of the 'memex', a device 'in which an individual stores all his books, records, and communications, and which is mechanized so that it may be consulted with exceeding speed and flexibility. It is an enlarged intimate supplement to his memory.' Few of us in the 1970s and well beyond had the vision to turn that dream into reality.

## The 1990s: arrival of the personal computer, then the taxonomy

Why skip over the 1980s? While undoubtedly plenty of good knowledge organization was in progress, I do not recall any step changes comparable with those in the decades before and after. The publication in 1985 of ISO 5964 [34] dealing with multilingual thesauri was important, but it did not change the principles already established in ISO 2788 for monolingual thesauri. The computer was on the scene, but in the background because it was rarely in-house. Typically it was a mainframe or minicomputer, needing trained programmers to do almost anything beyond physically mounting the magnetic tapes. Information professionals used it (over the telephone) for access to external information; end-users relied on these intermediaries to manipulate the mysteries of Boolean logic and controlled vocabularies, not to mention command-driven search syntax.

Thus optical coincidence cards and other manual systems were still providing good service in places such as Technical Help to Exporters (THE), the office where I worked in the first part of the decade. THE was also the birth-place in 1981 of the *BSI ROOT Thesaurus* [35], which deserves mention as the first of Aitchison's thesauri to be managed by computer. Development of programs which could derive a standard alphabetical display entirely automatically from the faceted classification was an important breakthrough [36]. (Incidentally this is still a challenge, as described by Vanda Broughton [37] at the NKOS ECDL workshop in 2007. The 1981 software was developed for a minicomputer and there is no commercially available software today to match it.)

The step-change came in the next decade, when personal computers began to appear on the desks of ordinary mortals. And it leapt even higher when the internet brought remote computers to our fingertips. The role of the information intermediary was threatened. The value of controlled vocabularies seemed more questionable than ever, given the improbability of persuading end-users to learn how to apply them.

But the progressive roll-out of corporate intranets soon posed a cruel question: what was the point of having all those resources ostensibly at your fingertips if you could not find them? The software vendors were quick to spot the opportunity. They would provide a search/navigation facility, and what better name for it than 'taxonomy'? Software products have proliferated, and so too have websites with all manner of ways of selecting from a top list of subject areas and 'drilling down' to progressive levels of specificity.

As the taxonomy buzz-word spread around, many information professionals seized a different opportunity. They rescued their existing home-grown thesauri, subject heading schemes and classification schemes, dusted them off a little, and re-branded them 'taxonomy'. The controlled vocabulary had now become more popular than ever before! The website at www.taxonomywarehouse.com/ gives some idea of the wide range of vocabularies currently available.

For serious researchers in classification theory and practice, the opportunity was now to adapt the long-established principles of classification to the electronic medium. Faceted classification in particular seems well suited to electronic applications, and since the 1990s has been a very active focus for R&D. The challenge for evolving classification schemes has been to recognize and retain the baby of essential principles, while discarding the bathwater associated with shelf arrangement and hardcopy housekeeping. This 'bathwater' is of course still essential in the running of physical libraries, but, in the words of Steve Pollitt [38], 'The need to maintain a single relative physical position on a bookshelf is the major source of complexity in classification. Extensive latent benefits will be realized when systematic subject arrangements [...] are coupled to view-based browse and search techniques.'

Thesauri too needed a face-lift to suit the new context and user expectations. The popularity of taxonomies has led to development of a number of vocabularies which combine some of the precoordination properties of a classification scheme with thesaural features such as reciprocal inter-term relationships and scope notes. See, for example, the Integrated Public Sector Vocabulary (IPSV) [39] at www.esd.org.uk/standards/ipsv/, released by the UK Cabinet Office in 2005 for use throughout the public sector [40, 41].

## Networking and interoperability: another dimension

Not long after the stimulus provided by widespread availability of desktop computers, the evolutionary path of knowledge organization schemes took another twist to adapt to networking opportunities. Designing a vocabulary for a specific retrieval application had always been a challenge. But to make it work across multiple networked applications adds a new dimension of complexity. The networks have opened up an array of different resources, systems and applications, and users want to search them all, at one pass. Indexing vocabularies can no longer be designed in isolation, if they are to serve in the interconnected world. Interoperability between systems is not just a buzz-word; there is a real demand.

Important progress has been realized through the Dublin Core Metadata Initiative (DCMI), emerging from an OCLC workshop held in 1995 in Dublin, Ohio. The metadata element set published by DCMI [42] has provided a framework within which other, more specialized metadata schemas and application profiles have been developed. Controlled vocabularies find their application here, especially for populating the subject element of metadata descriptions. Key advances in the field are discussed at the annual DCMI conference, and full papers are available from the website at http://dublincore.org/workshops/.

Another forum for addressing interoperability concerns is provided by Networked Knowledge Organization Systems and Services (NKOS), which holds workshops approximately annually in both Europe and the USA. Links to the workshop presentations and other key resources may be found on the website at http://nkos.slis.kent.edu/. Topics attracting interest and action at recent workshops include mapping between vocabularies, social tagging, user-centred design, a typology of knowledge organization schemes, and metadata registries.

Beginning to address the interoperability needs as they affect controlled vocabularies and other forms of knowledge organization scheme, revision of ISO 2788 and ISO 5964 is under way [43]. The revised standard will eventually be known as ISO 25964, and it will be based on the recently published five-part standard BS 8723 *Structured vocabularies for information retrieval* [44–48]. As well as updating the guidelines for monolingual and multilingual thesauri, BS 8723 now covers:

- Functions of software for vocabulary management

- Characterization and comparison of the different vocabulary types, such as classification schemes, taxonomies, subject heading schemes, thesauri, name authority lists and ontologies
- Mapping between vocabularies
- Formats and protocols for data exchange

Standardization of these aspects is an important step towards enhanced interoperability for systems incorporating knowledge organization schemes. But eight years into the twenty-first century, at least one question is wide open: will developers of new applications, vocabularies and systems be content to follow the standards to realize the interoperability advantages, or will practices continue to diverge as new technologies stimulate innovative approaches to knowledge organization?

## So where is it all heading?

In following the thread of developments associated with controlled vocabularies, this paper has failed to mention a wealth of other approaches to knowledge organization that have been gaining momentum over the last one or two decades. A look through the programmes and proceedings of recent conferences of ISKO, the International Society for Knowledge Organization (www.isko.org/), soon reveals that alongside faceted classification, metadata and thesauri, members are very actively studying ontologies, folksonomies, the challenges of organizing images and multimedia resources, cross-language information retrieval, and many more areas of fruitful development. Technology developments such as clustering, automatic categorization, collaborative filtering, the Google search algorithm, are all shaping the practice of knowledge organization, if not the principles. Google in particular has revived the debate as to whether controlled vocabularies are worth the effort. Let us not fall into the trap of trying to predict which of these approaches and technologies, if any, will dominate the coming decades.

The future will certainly be influenced by the Semantic Web vision expounded by Tim Berners-Lee (founding father of the world wide web) and others in 2001 [49]. They painted a scenario in which networked computer agents are able to communicate with each other in order to undertake a chain of actions on the user's behalf, without further instruction. For example, when medical help and action is needed, the computers work together to find the nearest place where the right medicine can be obtained, organize the next appointment at the health clinic (checking it against the diaries of all the people involved) and arrange transport for the patient.

This influential paper has already sparked a wave of interest in development of tools such as ontologies and other forms of knowledge organization scheme. While many of us feel the Semantic Web is still a long way off, some applications that demonstrate the feasibility of at least parts of it are already with us. (See, for example, the SWAD-Europe (Semantic Web Advanced Development) projects at www.w3.org/2001/sw/Europe/.) Such is the respect commanded by Berners-Lee, that project funding is likely to flow freely for some time to come.

## Last words

While researching for this paper I came across the final draft of a student project I did back in 1971, a faceted classification scheme for organometallic chemistry. Among the 78 pages of painful handwriting were recorded several changes of mind, for example where notation had shifted to accommodate an extra facet, and all the subsequent notation had been adjusted and columns laboriously re-alphabetized. No doubt the subsequent typing up had been equally painful.

It reminded me, too, of the 11 man-years that went into preparation of the BSI ROOT Thesaurus, much of it spent on meticulous tabulation of hand-written entries, to be subsequently typed up, proof-read, corrected, proofed again, sent off to the data processing agency for keyboarding into the PDP8e minicomputer, the results proofed again, and so on until the final (exceedingly rapid) generation of camera-ready outputs.

Our capabilities for managing information have since then undergone a revolution. Such inefficiency is now unthinkable. But the greatest part of the credit, I feel, goes to enhanced information technology rather than fundamental new thinking in knowledge organization. Certainly, we have had to adapt to changing circumstances and apply original thinking to the challenges of networking and interoperability. But the basic techniques of grouping like with like, and labelling the groups so that they can be recognized and found again, have been around for a very long time. For term-based access, we are still very much reliant on the principles established in the 1950s and 1960s, and extended multilingually in the 1970s. The subsequent work, in my view, has mostly been about exploiting and adapting to changes in technology, the market-place and user expectations.

Gone are the preoccupations with keeping knowledge organization schemes and other tools down to a manageable size. Gone too are most of the difficulties of getting hold of the published literature. In their place we are now grappling with how to make easily navigable and searchable an increasingly diverse and complex network of systems, languages and resources.

# References

[1]   W.C. Berwick Sayers, *A Manual of Classification for Librarians and Bibliographers*, 3rd Edition (London, Andre Deutsch, 1962).

[2]   I.C. McIlwaine, UDC in the twenty-first century. In: R. Marcella and A. Maltby (eds), *The Future of Classification* (Aldershot, Gower, 2000) 93–104.

[3]   K. La Barre, Bliss and Ranganathan: synthesis, synchronicity or sour grapes? In: C. Beghtol et al. (eds), *Dynamism and Stability in Knowledge Organization: Proceedings of the Sixth ISKO Conference; July 10–13 2000, Toronto, Canada* (Ergon Verlag; Würzburg, 2000) 157–63.

[4]   Classification Research Group, The need for a faceted classification as the basis of all methods of information retrieval. Originally drafted in 1955 and published in 1957, but reprinted in: A. Gilchrist (ed.), *From Classification to 'Knowledge Organization': Dorking Revisited or 'Past is Prelude'* (International Federation for Information and Documentation, The Hague, 1997) 1–9.

[5]   B.C. Vickery, *Faceted Classification: a Guide to Construction and Use of Special Schemes* (Aslib, London, 1960).

[6]   N. Roberts, The pre-history of the information retrieval thesaurus, *Journal of Documentation* 40(4) (1984) 271–85.

[7]   D.A. Krooks and F.W. Lancaster, The evolution of guidelines for thesaurus construction, *Libri* 43(4) (1993) 326–42.

[8]   *Thesaurus of Engineering and Scientific Terms (TEST)* (Engineers Joint Council and US Department of Defense, New York, 1967).

[9]   J. Aitchison and S. Dextre Clarke, The thesaurus: a historical viewpoint, with a look to the future. *Cataloging and Classification Quarterly* 37(3/4) (2004) 5–21.

[10]  International Organization for Standardization, *ISO 2788–1974: Documentation – Guidelines for the Establishment and Development of Monolingual Thesauri*, 1st Edition (International Organization for Standardization, Geneva, 1974).

[11]  J. Viet, *Macrothesaurus for Information Processing in the Field of Economic and Social Development*, 1st Edition (OECD Development Centre, Paris, 1972).

[12] J. Aitchison, A. Gomersall and R. Ireland, *Thesaurofacet: a Thesaurus and Faceted Classification for Engineering and Related Subjects* (English Electric Company, Whetstone, 1969).

[13] J. Aitchison and A. Gilchrist, *Thesaurus Construction: a Practical Manual*, 1st Edition (Aslib, London, 1972).

[14] J. Aitchison, A. Gilchrist and D. Bawden, *Thesaurus Construction and Use: a Practical Manual*, 4th Edition (Aslib, London, 2000).

[15] *Medical Subject Headings (MeSH)* (National Library of Medicine; Bethesda, MA, annually updated). Available at: www.nlm.nih.gov/mesh/MBrowser.html

[16] W. Ashworth, A review of mechanical aids in library work. In: W. Ashworth (ed.), *Handbook of Special Librarianship and Information Work*, 3rd Edition (Aslib, London, 1967) 524–53.

[17] J.R. Sharp, Information retrieval. In: W. Ashworth (ed.), *Handbook of Special Librarianship and Information Work*, 3rd Edition (Aslib, London, 1967) 141–232.

[18] S.G. Dextre, Industrial information in Latin America, *The Information Scientist* 10(4) (1976) 149–56.

[19] H.P. Luhn, The automatic derivation of information retrieval encodements from machine-readable texts. In: A. Kent (ed.), *Information Retrieval and Machine Translation* (Interscience, New York, 1961) 1021–8.

[20] C.W. Cleverdon and J. Mills, The testing of index language devices. *Aslib Proceedings*, 15(4) (1963) 106–30.

[21] C.W. Cleverdon, J. Mills and E.M. Keen, *Factors Determining the Performance of Indexing Systems* (College of Aeronautics, Cranfield, 1966).

[22] C.W. Cleverdon, The Cranfield tests on index language devices. *Aslib Proceedings* 19(6) (1967) 173–92.

[23] E. Svenonius, Unanswered questions in the design of controlled vocabularies, *Journal of the American Society for Information Science* 37(5) (1986) 331–40.

[24] R.C. Henzler, Free or controlled vocabulary? Some statistical user-orientated evaluations of biomedical information systems. *International Classification* 5(1) (1978) 21–6.

[25] M.L. Calkins, Free text or controlled vocabulary? A case history: step-by-step analysis ... plus other aspects of search strategy, *Database* 3(2) (1980):56–67.

[26] C.P.R. Dubois, The use of thesauri in online retrieval, *Journal of Information Science* 8(2) (1984) 63–6.

[27] C.P.R. Dubois, Free text vs controlled vocabulary: a reassessment, *Online Review* 11(4) (1987) 243–53.

[28] C. Tenopir, Full text database retrieval performance, *Online Review* 2 (1985) 149–64.

[29]   R. Betts and D. Marrable, Free text vs controlled vocabulary: retrieval precision and recall over large databases. In: D.I. Raitt (ed.), *Online Information 91: Proceedings of the 15th International Online Information Meeting, Dec 10–12 December 1985* (Learned Information Europe, London/Oxford, 1991) 153–65.

[30]   J.L. Milstead, Needs for research in indexing, *Journal of the American Society for Information Science* 45(8) (1994) 577–82.

[31]   K. Markey, P. Atherton and C. Newton, An analysis of controlled vocabulary and free text search statements in online searches, *Online Review* 4(3) (1982) 225–36.

[32]   J. Rowley, The controlled versus natural languages debate revisited: a perspective on information retrieval practice and research, *Journal of Information Science* 20(2) (1994) 108–19.

[33]   V. Bush, As we may think, *Atlantic Monthly* 176(July) (1945) 101–8.

[34]   International Organization for Standardization, *ISO 5964–1985: Documentation – Guidelines for the Establishment and Development of Multilingual Thesauri* (International Organization for Standardization, Geneva, 1985).

[35]   British Standards Institution, *BSI ROOT Thesaurus*, 1st Edition (British Standards Institution, Milton Keynes, 1981).

[36]   S.G. Dextre and T.M. Clarke, A system for machine-aided thesaurus construction, *Aslib Proceedings* 33(3) (1981): 102–12.

[37]   V. Broughton, *Facet Analysis as a Fundamental Theory for Structuring Subject Organization Tools* (2007) [web page]. Available at: www.comp.glam.ac.uk/pages/research/hypermedia/nkos/nkos2007/programme.html (accessed 11 February 2008).

[38]   S.A. Pollitt, The application of Dewey Classification in a view-based searching OPAC. In: W.M. el Hadi et al. (eds), *Structures and Relations in Knowledge Organization: Proceedings of the 5th International ISKO Conference, 25–29 1998 Lille, France* (Ergon Verlag, Würzburg, 1998) 176–83.

[39]   S.G. Dextre Clarke, *IPSV Maintenance Guide* (2005) [web page]. Available at: www.esd.org.uk/documents/IPSVMaintenanceGuide.pdf (accessed 11 February 2008).

[40]   S.G. Dextre Clarke, A devolved architecture for public sector interoperability. In: A. Gilchrist and B. Mahon (eds), *Information Architecture: Designing Information Environments for Purpose* (Facet, London, 2004) 145–60.

[41]   S.G. Dextre Clarke, e-GIF, e-GMS and IPSV: what's in it for us? *Legal Information Management* 7(4) (2007) 275–6.

[42]   DCMI Usage Board, *DCMI Metadata Terms* (2006) [web page]. Available at: http://dublincore.org/documents/dcmi-terms/ (accessed 11 February 2008).

[43]    S.G. Dextre Clarke, Evolution towards ISO 25964: an international standard with guidelines for thesauri and other types of controlled vocabulary, *Information Wissenschaft & Praxis* 58(8) (2007) 441–4.

[44]    British Standards Institution, *BS 8723–1:2005: Structured Vocabularies for Information Retrieval – Guide – Definitions, Symbols and Abbreviations* (British Standards Institution, London, 2005).

[45]    British Standards Institution, *BS 8723–2:2005: Structured Vocabularies for Information Retrieval – Guide – Thesauri* (British Standards Institution, London, 2005).

[46]    British Standards Institution, *BS 8723–3:2007: Structured Vocabularies for Information Retrieval – Guide – Vocabularies Other Than Thesauri* (British Standards Institution, London, 2007).

[47]    British Standards Institution, *BS 8723–4:2007: Structured Vocabularies for Information Retrieval – Guide – Interoperability between Vocabularies* (British Standards Institution, London, 2007).

[48]    British Standards Institution, *DD 8723–5:2008: Structured Vocabularies for Information Retrieval – Guide – Exchange Formats and Protocols for Interoperability* (British Standards Institution, London, 2008).

[49]    T. Berners-Lee, J. Hendler and O. Lassila, The Semantic Web, *Scientific American* (May 2001).

# 4

# On the history of evaluation in IR

STEPHEN ROBERTSON

## Abstract

This paper is a personal take on the history of evaluation experiments in information retrieval. It describes some of the early experiments that were formative in our understanding, and goes on to discuss the current dominance of TREC (the Text REtrieval Conference) and to assess its impact.

## Introduction

The foundation of the Institute of Information Scientists in the UK in 1958 coincides closely with the beginning of the notion of experimental evaluation of information retrieval systems. Although there had been some earlier attempts, we usually mark the start of the tradition as the Cranfield experiments, which ran from 1958 to 1966. Information retrieval is commonly regarded as a core component of information science, and systematic empirical evaluation of IR systems probably represents the strongest claim that information science can make to being a science in any traditional sense. There is a nice irony here: the founder of the empirical tradition in IR, the Cranfield librarian Cyril Cleverdon, was not at all a supporter of the Institute. But more of this anon.

As for the present, and despite the concerns of the founders of the Institute, academic information science is now quite closely associated with the former library schools, many of which have adopted titles which include the word 'information'. However, a lot of current work in IR, theoretical and experimental, takes place elsewhere, mainly in computer science departments, though several other academic domains are represented. It probably comes as a considerable surprise to a current PhD student, working on (say) a machine learning optimization technique applied to search engine ranking, that he or she is in thrall to an experimental tradition founded by a librarian, working with card indexes, a half-century ago.

Thus the history that is the subject of this paper is not too readily defined in terms of institutional or academic boundaries – or national ones. Despite this, it can be seen as a remarkably coherent development of a set of principles and methods. Like all academic subjects it generates argument and disagreement and heated disputation, but there remains a relatively stable common core, which has, despite its limitations (I will argue), served us well over the last 50 years. Furthermore, while its present international status developed out of a US dominance for a large part of that period, the strength of the UK contribution has been remarkable.

In this paper, I will be surveying the history of this experimental tradition, both from the point of view of the ideas involved and also from that of some of the people and groups who contributed, and the environments in which they worked. In these latter respects, the paper will have some focus on the UK, and on groups and projects in which I have been involved myself in one way or another. I make no apology for this personal focus; the paper is as much 'history as I remember it' as formal documented history.

## A note on sources

I will be citing original material throughout this paper, but the single best source for the first half of the period covered (up to 1980) is the book called *Information Retrieval Experiment*, edited by Karen Spärck Jones [1]. The project that has dominated the last fifteen years of experimental work in the field is TREC, the Text REtrieval Conference; this too has been the subject of a recent book [2] which makes a great introduction to a huge volume of work.

## Cranfield

In the 1950s, many of the ideas (there were indeed many) about how to do information retrieval could be traced back to library classification schemes and their embodiment in card catalogues. Printed indexes, which now survive only as back-of-the-book indexes, were also common; there were also pre-computer forms of mechanization, specifically a whole range of different forms of punched cards used in different ways. But the library classification model was the dominant one. Under this model a document had to be classified/indexed by a human being, and the result of this process was a short description or representation of the document in a more-or-less formal indexing language. The particular form of the indexing language; the kind of analysis that went into constructing it in the first place, and then applying it to a document; the amount of detail you could represent in this way; the specificity of the representation and its divisibility; all of these and more were subjects of fierce argument.

## Arguments

Some of this argument revolved around anecdote. That is, researchers would try to come up with examples to understand the differences between methods, or to demonstrate why one particular system would work and others would not. Two such examples were 'Venetian blinds' (as distinct from 'blind Venetians'[1]) and 'lead coatings on copper pipes'.[2]

But the core of the argument was generally not empirical, but philosophical. Library classification schemes tend to carry with them entire philosophical world-views, concerning the nature of human knowledge, and to some extent of its representation in documents. But the nature of *language* as such was somewhat separate and peripheral – in some sense the object of a formal classification or indexing system is to avoid all the vagaries and pitfalls of natural language. Of course one has to describe and define the concepts or categories of the scheme in natural language, but the function of this description might be regarded as pedagogic – to help the librarian or user towards an understanding of what the concept or category *really* is, and to see underneath the surface of language. In constructing such a scheme, one might appeal to literary warrant, but that would not absolve one of the responsibility of understanding the concept.

In the context of these arguments, empiricism (let alone a formal scientific experiment) was a radical notion. There was resistance to a strictly functional view of such schemes, quite apart from the difficulties of first formulating the functionality and then operationalizing an experimental framework.

## The beginning of experimentation

Some ideas were being floated in the literature in the 1950s (stimulated by the Royal Society Scientific Information Conference in 1948 [3]), and one or two small experiments were reported in the UK, the USA and the Netherlands. Interest was further developed by the International Conference on Scientific Information in Washington DC in 1958 [4]. But by this time Cyril Cleverdon, Librarian at the then Cranfield College of Aeronautics, had got the bit between his teeth, and started (with funding from the US National Science Foundation) the first of two Cranfield projects, eventually published in 1962 [5]. This project tackled the philosophical divisions in the field head-on, by subjecting four indexing schemes – exemplars of opposing views of how information should be organized – to a direct experimental competition.

Each scheme was to be operated by experts in that scheme. They would construct the scheme itself, index the documents, design the search strategies and undertake the searching. Thus we might regard the necessary human expertise as part of the 'system' in a broad sense. The four schemes were: the Universal Decimal Classification (a hierarchical library classification); an Alphabetical Subject Catalogue (subject headings expressed as phrases); a Faceted Classification Scheme (allowing the construction of complex categories by combination of elements from different facets); and the Uniterm System of Co-ordinate Indexing (terms relatively freely assigned and combined).

Both the methods used and the results obtained provoked much debate and led to the formulation of a second Cranfield project. Methods will be discussed further below, but one of the results is worth noting. On the primary measure of effectiveness used, the four competing systems did not show huge differences; however, the faceted classification scheme came out worst of the four. An analysis of failures then identified an issue with the chosen card-index representation of the faceted classification (a form of so-called 'chain indexing'), and an alternative representation was tried – this boosted the scheme to best of the four. This was somewhat surprising to the proponents of the various schemes: it meant that, at least to some degree, the determinants of effectiveness might not be the major principles on which the schemes were based, but the details of implementation.

## Cranfield 2

In terms of both methodology and content, the transition from Cranfield 1 to Cranfield 2 was a great leap forward [6]. For content, the focus was still on 'indexing languages': artificial languages constructed to allow the representation of documents and requests in some partially formalized way. But rather than treating such a language as a black box defined by some overriding general principle, an attempt was made to disentangle the detailed processes of building a language into small steps and to evaluate the steps. The broad-brush conclusion, that the best thing to do was to search on combinations of words, leaving the natural language words almost untouched, was quite shocking to many people at the time, although it would be much less surprising now, given the predominance of word-based search engines.[3]

But the more significant achievement of Cranfield 2 was to define our notion of the methodology of IR experimentation. The basic ideas of collecting documents and queries were inherited from Cranfield 1, but the biggest change concerned the notion of a good answer. The method in Cranfield 1 was to use a 'source document' – that is, to start from a known document and formulate a question to which that document was a suitable answer. (More specifically, the author of the document was asked to formulate the question which prompted the work to be done in the first place.) Then the criterion for the search system was whether or not it retrieved this source document.

This method was explicitly intended to avoid judgements of relevance. Some earlier work had attempted to obtain relevance judgements by agreement among a group of judges, but found it very difficult. But the source document method was severely criticized, for three main reasons:

- The queries might be regarded as unrealistic;
- Retrieval of the source document is not a good test;
- The resulting measure evaluates recall only, not precision.[4]

The response in Cranfield 2 was to continue to use the method as a way of generating queries, but to deal with items 2 and 3 as follows. Source documents were removed from the test collection, and relevance judgements were made by judges. No attempt was made to get agreement between judges; the judgements for each query were made by a single judge.

Documents to be judged for each query were selected by a variety of methods including manual searching and the use of a form of citation-based indexing. The aim was completeness – to discover all (or nearly all) the relevant documents in the collection. (The extent to which this aim was achieved was the subject of much argument.)

## Cyril and Jason

As an aside from the main theme of this paper, it may be of interest to reflect on the characteristics of some of the disputations involved. In this regard, two people stand out.

Cyril Cleverdon I have already named; the other is Jason Farradane, one of the founders of the Institute of Information Scientists, as well as of the Information Science Department at City University. Farradane had been a technical information officer in the food industry, and before that a chemist, and his views of the field of information science were strongly influenced by this hard-science background. Both men had strongly held opinions, and both expressed themselves forcibly – and they could not stand each other. Give one of them a platform at a conference or meeting, and the other would be in the audience, just itching to jump up and explain why the speaker had got it all wrong. Farradane conducted his own rather smaller evaluation of his own rather idiosyncratic method of indexing in the middle 1960s, and believed that Cleverdon's application of scientific method to the construction of index languages and to experimental design for the test was fundamentally flawed. Their arguments were fierce and unrelenting, sometimes well beyond the boundaries of civility.[5]

This particular animosity was perhaps extreme in its mixture of the personal and the professional, but it was by no means the only argument engendered by the project. In the USA, Don Swanson [7] was almost equally trenchant in his criticisms of the methods and results of Cranfield, albeit in the form of a paper published five years later, rather than a person-to-person public confrontation. Many other authors have contributed arguments and criticisms to the debate, and Cranfield-type methods tend to generate strong reactions both for and against. A later example (now in relation to TREC) can be found in a paper by Blair and the subsequent responses [8a, 8b].

Nevertheless, the methods pioneered at Cranfield survived and prospered over the next 40 years, most directly through the agency of TREC, the Text REtrieval Conference. They did so despite their very real limitations and distortions. There are indeed many things wrong with them, but (I will argue further below) they have also yielded real and valuable results.

## Some experiments

In this section, I will describe a small selection of experiments that took place in the quarter-century or so following Cranfield 2. This is selective both in respect of the set of experiments and in respect of the details concerning each one. But both the selection and the sequence are chosen to bring out the development of some of the critical ideas in the field.

## SMART

The most significant early series of experiments in computer-based retrieval was that on the SMART[6] system from the very early 1960s [9]. The project, led by Gerard Salton, started at Harvard but was based for most of its life at Cornell University in the USA, and continued until the 1990s. Many of the ideas that are currently taken for granted in the web search engines were pioneered there; in particular, the use of purely automatic methods based on the text of the documents, the notion of a scoring function (to measure the extent to which each document matches the query), and the consequent ranking of documents or references to documents for display to the user. It is worth observing that the scoring-and-ranking idea, built into SMART from the very beginning and taken up by many other researchers, did not even begin to appear in any commercial system until the late 1980s, and really only took off with the web search engines in the middle 1990s.

The model used in the SMART system is normally described as the vector space model. It can be conceived as a vector space where the axes are defined by terms (typically words), and each document and each query is represented by a vector of weights – a point in the vector space. Document similarity, or the similarity between a document and a request, is seen as (the reverse of) a distance measure in the space. The scoring function most commonly used in SMART was not based on a Euclidean distance measure, but on cosine correlation, which itself is based on angles between vectors.

The vector components, the weights, can be simple binary values (1 = 'term present', 0 = 'term absent'), but can be more complex, based for example on statistical information. The SMART team used the term frequency in the document (TF), and then combined it with the inverse document frequency (IDF) devised by Spärck Jones (see Section 3.3). The idea of relevance feedback was also pioneered in SMART, by Rocchio [10]: using relevance judgements by the searcher to improve the ranking for the current search, or to enhance the indexing of documents for the benefit of subsequent searches.

The early SMART evaluation experiments, from the middle 1960s on, were conducted on a variety of small test collections (perhaps tens or hundreds of documents), either built in-house or re-used from other experiments. In particular, they made use of the Cranfield collection when it became available in machine-readable form (again, see Section 3.3 for further discussion of this issue). By the early 1980s, they were using and in some cases constructing somewhat larger test collections. But it is worth noting here, in this age of plentiful and cheap computing power on every desktop, that in 1973 a single computer run on the 1400-document Cranfield collection took 11.2 minutes of processor time and cost $86.22.[7]

## Medlars

The Medlars[8] Demand Search Service was one of the early operational computer-based retrieval systems – the predecessor of Medline and PubMed today, covering the medical research literature. Most of the early computer retrieval systems were devoted to the scientific and technical literature, riding on the back of the computerization of the production of abstracts journals. At the time searching on Medlars was based solely on human-assigned indexing terms, from a controlled indexing language (MeSH).[9] Queries used Boolean logic; output was an unranked set of references. Queries were typically formulated by expert searchers, on the basis of an interaction with the user, a face-to-face reference interview or correspondence by mail. Readers much younger than myself might like to note that this was well before the days of network access, let alone online operation, and the computer was located in the USA, at the National Library of Medicine (NLM) outside Washington DC. Searches were run in batches overnight, and a printout of results was posted back to the user.

The experiment, conducted by Lancaster [11], was completed in 1968. It was aimed at evaluating the index language itself and the methods and procedures used to index documents and formulate searches. Users were invited to participate at the time of initial contact with NLM; thus the queries were real ones representing real information needs, and the users made relevance judgements in relation to those needs. The study was unusual in including a very detailed failure analysis: an attempt was made to attribute each failure in search (either type: in identifying good documents or in rejecting bad ones) to one or more of a variety of system causes, for example the structure of the index language, indexing policy or practice, the language or logic of query formulation.

One particular result of the Medlars experiment is of some interest. As mentioned, the interaction between the user (medical researcher) and the intermediary (expert searcher) might take place by correspondence or by face-to-face interview – although all searches took place at NLM, intermediaries were located at significant centres around the world, and users could visit them. One experimental question was: how much does it help to have a face-to-face interview? The answer was surprising: it hinders! That is, effectiveness on the searches arising from face-to-face interviews was somewhat worse than on those arising from correspondence. The explanation put forward by the researchers was that a user who writes a letter has to think carefully about his/her information need and how to define and describe it, without being constrained by the language of the system. A user who walks into the office of an intermediary has probably not gone through this process, and the intermediary is liable to go straight into the system language without spending enough time on understanding the information need. Training of intermediaries was changed as a result of this discovery.

## Karen Spärck Jones

For about 20 years from the early 1960s, Karen Spärck Jones (at the Computer Laboratory, Cambridge, UK) conducted a series of computer-based experiments into term clustering and term weighting.

Unlike Cleverdon (or indeed most of the other experimenters working at that time), she did not build her own test collection. That made her particularly receptive to the idea of re-using collections built by other researchers; she was one of the first to perceive the possibilities and difficulties of this mode of operation. As soon as she could after the completion of Cranfield 2, she obtained that collection (now in machine-readable form), and her first series of experiments [12] was based entirely on this collection. During this period she invented the form of term weighting based on the number of documents in which the term occurs (inverse document frequency weighting, IDF) [13, 14]. The combination of IDF with within-document term frequency TF, by the SMART team, was to dominate thinking on document-ranking systems for many years, and to have a profound influence on the next generation of term-weighting and document-ranking algorithms.

However, when she subsequently repeated the experiments on further collections, while IDF proved itself, some of the clustering results she had obtained on Cranfield were not confirmed. This encouraged her to think more seriously about the design and construction of test collections. From the middle 1970s until the early 1980s, she led a significant effort to clarify and explain the basic paradigm and to improve both the methods and the materials of experimentation in information retrieval. The effort involved many other people, in the UK and elsewhere (including for example Keith van Rijsbergen [15], who has lived and worked in many countries, but spent the bulk of his working life in the UK). The effort had two main outcomes: a proposal and a book.

The second of these, the book *Information Retrieval Experiment* [1], appeared in 1981. It was a collection of papers by a dozen other authors working in the field, with two contributed by Spärck Jones herself. But she also ensured a rare level of coherence in the whole enterprise, by careful planning of the whole, by writing introductory and connecting material, and by suggestion and comment to the other authors. This book was for many years the sole coherent source on how to plan and execute an information retrieval experiment, arguably until the publication of the book on TREC in 2005 [2].

The other outcome of Spärck Jones's work in that period was a design for a new and better test collection. Each of the collections existing at that time had been designed and created for a specific experimental comparison, but typically these same collections were then re-used for many other experiments, for which they were clearly not ideal. So the proposal for the 'ideal' test collection was born. The quotation marks were deliberate, reflecting not so much what might be achievable as an aspiration. The study included some careful preparatory work on a number of important details, such as the pooling technique for obtaining relevance judgements in a relatively large collection [15, 16]. A costing was also made.

But the proposal then hit a wall. The financial support available for basic IR research in the UK in the late 1970s was deemed insufficient to fund the project. The 'ideal' test collection idea went onto a back shelf, and sat there for more than a decade, until the TREC project began in the US in the early 1990s (Section 4 below). Spärck Jones herself diversified her research into areas relating to natural language processing. However, she returned to very active involvement in experimental IR with the development of TREC.

## Keen

Michael Keen was a member of the Cranfield 2 team, who then went to the USA to join the SMART team for a period, and returned to the UK (the College of Librarianship Wales at Aberystwyth) to conduct his own experiments throughout the 1970s. While in the USA he made a significant analysis of the various measures of retrieval effectiveness that had evolved over the course of many experiments from Cranfield on [17]. The issue of the choice of measures and their analysis was then and remains now a common concern of researchers in the field – a theme which generates a significant and probably increasing number of new papers every year.

Keen then undertook an evaluation of index languages in the information science domain [18], followed by a study of the searching of printed subject indexes [19]. The first provided some further evidence (confirming the Cranfield 2 conclusion) that straight English words make for a good and effective indexing language, and that it is seriously hard to do better.

Somewhat unlike Cranfield 2 but perhaps more in tune with Cranfield 1, both of Keen's studies, particularly the second on printed subject indexes, are characterized by serious attempts to address questions relating to human searching behaviour. That is, they tended to regard the searcher as being as much part of the 'system' as any set of rules or algorithms. This required them to allow searchers to take the kind of on-the-fly, intelligent decisions that searchers typically take, rather than trying to reduce every aspect of search to the application of predefined rules. In keeping with the usual practice of the times, the model was of 'delegated search' rather than 'end-user' search – in other words, the searcher was assumed to be a professional information scientist acting on behalf of the real user or person needing the information. However, despite this delegated-search idea, these experiments look forward to the more user-oriented search studies of recent years, as much as to the more mechanistic and algorithmic approaches that tend to dominate TREC and the SIGIR[10] conferences.

## Belkin and Oddy

This user-orientation also characterizes (although in quite a different fashion) the smaller project of Robert Oddy [20], and his subsequent work with Belkin.

Oddy, doing a PhD in Newcastle, UK in the early 1970s, in the Computer Science department, was interested in designing highly interactive systems, and in the difficulties of so-called 'end-user' search (the person with the information need searching on his or her own behalf).[11] These include the difficulty of constructing a good search strategy, which in the days of Boolean search was quite a technical skill; but also the conceptual difficulty of describing an imprecisely understood need for information. Oddy designed a prototype system, Thomas,[12] which was intended to maintain some kind of model of the user's interest, inferred from the user's actions and responses, which would minimize the user's effort in reaching some information goal, and particularly avoid the search strategy issue. Although he was not able to get real users to use the system, his experiments involved a form of simulation of real-user interaction, using real queries and real relevance judgements obtained from experiments similar to the Medlars experiment described above. The primary objective, which the experiments suggested had been achieved, was to allow the user to obtain similar results to the more conventional system but with less effort.

Nick Belkin, also doing his PhD in the UK in the 1970s,[13] had come up with the ASK model, addressing exactly this idea of an imprecisely understood need [21]: that which stimulates a user to start seeking information is characterized as an Anomalous State of Knowledge. Belkin went to City University, and teamed up with Oddy for a design study [22] of an IR system based on the ASK model. This study did not include any search evaluation tests of the sort described above, but attempted instead to validate and explore certain aspects of the user model, by means in part of small-scale user experiments. Belkin has continued, initially at City and then at Rutgers University after his return in 1985 to the USA, to explore the areas of user interaction, user cognitive processes and the task context of information seeking. Some of this work has taken the form of more-or-less conventional retrieval system tests, on the Cranfield-TREC model and in particular within TREC, but the emphasis has always been on the user side, with the challenge of integrating into the experimental methodology a real understanding of user behaviour. The interaction between the user orientation and TREC is explored further below.

## Okapi

The final two projects I would like to discuss in this section came a little later. The Okapi[14] project began in the early 1980s. At that time, there was much interest in OPACs, online public access catalogues, in libraries. One could argue that this was the first sign that information retrieval might become something of interest to the man-in-the-street (or, in the traditional UK phrase, the 'man on the Clapham omnibus').[15] The web search engine was still well over a decade away, but the notion that someone walking into a library (say, a student in a college library, or even a user of a public library – not a search expert) might reasonably want to do a search on a computer-based system was clearly in the air.

Okapi started life as just such a system, intended to provide access to a library catalogue, primarily in the form of subject searches. It was developed initially at the then Polytechnic of Central London, by Stephen Walker and colleagues [23], then moved with Walker in 1989 to join my team at City University.[16] Here it was developed into a general-purpose text search engine, used both with library catalogue data and the somewhat older domain of scientific abstracts. Although it was an experimental system, its raison d'être was to provide a real, live service to users, whose behaviour could be studied, or who could be enlisted to take part in further experiments.

Okapi implemented a simple text search based on a free-language query, typed into a box – in a form that would be instantly recognizable today but was then quite unfamiliar. The search mechanisms were based on IR methods developed experimentally (but with no real users) in the 1970s, including weighting of terms and ranking of output. The interface mechanisms were relatively primitive, though some advance on the command lines of the 1970s.[17]

The service to real user groups allowed a range of different kinds of experiment [24–26] with user-based evaluation. These included extensive experiments in relevance feedback with automatic query expansion. In general, Okapi users were asked to provide relevance judgements as a matter of course; these could be used both for evaluation and for improving the current search (relevance feedback). On the other hand, it was not normally possible in such an environment to make any kind of attempt to discover all the relevant documents in the collection.

## Croft

Bruce Croft, originally from Australia, and then taking a PhD under Keith van Rijsbergen in Cambridge in the late 1970s, moved on to the USA and joined the University of Massachusetts, where he has been ever since. The group built around him at UMass, the Center for Intelligent Information Retrieval

(CIIR), has become the strongest IR research group in the USA and indeed in the world, supplanting the SMART group at Cornell in this respect.

One characteristic of CIIR's work is the prime status of experiment. A succession of experimental systems and toolkits (I3R, Inquery, Lemur, Indri...) has provided the basis for this work; but the main determining factor is the attitude to theory and experimentation. CIIR has generated a wide range of exciting ideas and models, but these ideas and models do not count for much (in the view of the group) until they have been subjected to rigorous experimentation. Furthermore, experiments are required to have good baselines – to have a chance of surviving, an idea has to be shown not only to be good, but to be better than previous ideas.

CIIR has tended not to get involved in test collection creation, but to use test collections and materials built elsewhere. A recent book on the work of CIIR [27] contains just one chapter specifically on experimental methodology, devoted to a form of exploratory data analysis. But almost every chapter reports experiments, many using TREC data. However, as we shall see below, the dominant model is now changing – many test collections are built cooperatively over a number of research groups, often involving individuals from the groups taking part as request formulators and relevance judges. In this respect, CIIR now contributes extensively as one of the collaborating groups.

## Postscript to three decades

After the apparent failure of the 'ideal' test collection project, and being closely involved in the Okapi projects, Micheline Beaulieu and I wrote a paper in 1991 [28] in which we argued that we seemed to be moving away from the Cranfield test collection paradigm, towards much more user-oriented work. This turned out to be a bad call, both for the field as a whole and for ourselves. In between the writing and the publication of this paper in 1992, TREC was announced. TREC was the 'ideal' test collection writ large, underwritten by US funds, and planned on a grand scale. While we did not abandon our commitment to live-user experiments, TREC was too good an opportunity to miss, and the Okapi team joined the TREC effort with enthusiasm.

Nevertheless, the fault-line had been there from the beginning and remains there to this day. On the one hand, we can do experiments in a laboratory, characterized by control and artifice. The control enables us to set up formal experimental comparisons and to expect scientifically reliable answers, confirmed by statistical significance tests whose primary requirement is simply enough data; but the artifice requires us to abstract from the real world, to eliminate whatever messiness it might introduce as noise into our experiments. On the other hand, we can seek external validity and attempt to observe real world events in their natural setting, which involves waiting for them to happen and minimizing any controls and any observer effects – and therefore get potentially rich but messy and noisy results, probably both unreliable and hard to interpret.

This is not a strict dichotomy, but is very much an opposition. The technology has a strong influence – sometimes technical developments make real-world observation easier, but sometimes they require us to invent new forms of control or put phenomena beyond our reach. In the days of library buildings and physically located catalogues, we could and did stand beside the catalogue or at the entrance to the library and ask users questions (rich data but potential for observer interference). Nowadays we can log all their activities on a previously unimaginable scale (much more data, no observer interference) but it is seriously hard to ask a user *why* they did something which we observed.

In the end, any experimental design is a compromise, a matter of balancing those aspects which the experimenter feels should be realistic with those controls which are felt to be necessary for a good result. Furthermore, the field advances not by deciding on a single best compromise, but through different researchers taking different decisions, and the resulting dialectic.

## TREC

The initial organizer of TREC, and main architect of its success, is Donna Harman; for the last few years it has been run by Ellen Voorhees [2]. Among the many people who contributed to both its design and its success was Karen Spärck Jones, main author of the 'ideal' test collection proposal a decade and a half earlier.

At the time of writing, TREC is in its 16th year. It is an annual competition/collaboration/bake-off/get-together between research groups interested in different aspects of information retrieval. Every year, a set of tasks is defined, broadly information retrieval/search tasks. They may be defined by any or all of the following: the nature of the material to be searched, the type of user, the type of search request, the task context in which the user is operating, the timescale of the information need, the form(s) of interaction allowed, etc. Specific tasks typically persist over several TRECs, but may eventually be replaced by others. At the beginning there were just two tasks, to which all participants contributed; now there are separate tracks each with its own handful of tasks, and participants typically choose one or a small number of tracks.

The entire process is masterminded by the US National Institute of Standards and Technology (NIST), but tracks are largely organized by the participant research groups. The usual process goes something like this. Track co-ordinators and participants agree their tasks and their raw data; this last might consist of:

1. a collection of documents, obtained from some external source;
2. a collection of requests or topics, which may also be obtained externally or may be created internally; and
3. a set of relevance judgements.

The creation of the topics and/or the relevance assessments may be done by people employed by NIST for this purpose; the main group of assessors is a set of retired news analysts, formerly employed by one of the security agencies.

The documents and requests are distributed to participants, and each participant indexes the documents and runs the requests through some experimental search system. Some set of results is submitted to NIST, and results for each request from all participants are then pooled in some way for relevance assessment. Everyone gets together for a conference in November each year, and discovers (normally only on arrival) how well they have done in the competition.

This broad-brush sketch is intended only to provide an overview; individual tracks and tasks often deviate from this model. A few of the tasks are described further below; but interested readers are referred to the book cited earlier [2] or to the annual reports at [29].

## Ad-hoc retrieval

The user model invoked here is what has now become the most obvious one for search: a user has an information need, sits down in front of a system and conducts a search against an existing collection of documents, over a limited time period. This is known in TREC jargon as an 'ad-hoc' search – an earlier more-or-less equivalent term was 'retrospective searching'. The system produces a ranked list of items, which the user consults in rank order. Users may judge documents good or bad, but in principle there may be any number of good documents in the collection. (The one significant change in this model from the Cranfield view is that there is now an assumption that each system will rank its results list.) It is often asserted that there is also an assumption that requests are topical or subject-based (documents *about* X); indeed the TREC jargon, which is to call requests 'topics', encourages that view.[18] However, although most of the requests used in TREC (all of those in early TRECs) are indeed topical, there is no necessary requirement of the model that this should be so, or that they should be *purely* topical. In some sense the nature of the requests is determined by the relevance judgements; if the judgements depend on other criteria than pure topicality, then that is the nature of the task.

However, it is fundamental to the model that the judge or assessor should indeed be able to make a judgement on each document, actually a binary one for most of the TREC ad-hoc tasks, and should be able to make the judgement irrespective of the order of presentation of the documents. This last precludes, for example, embedding a criterion of novelty in the usual ad-hoc task relevance judgements (although one track did investigate novelty by making judgements of novelty separated from the relevance judgements).

### Methodology

There are many methodological issues here, but a major one concerns the set of documents to be judged for relevance. The ideal since Cranfield has been completeness – discovering all (or in practice most) of the documents in the collection that might be judged relevant. The practice of employing people to create the topics in the first place and then to make judgements allows a significant amount of effort to go into this phase, but certainly does not allow a complete scan of a reasonable size collection by each judge. Therefore relevance judgements have to be selective. One method used extensively in TREC is the pooling method – given the outputs of a range of different systems, judging a pool of the top 100 ranked items from each system is likely to give a reasonable variety of relevant documents. Furthermore, there is some evidence that under some conditions this is likely to result in the discovery of most of the relevant documents in the collection.

What are the required conditions? Well, the evidence suggests that we need to start with a good range of different kinds of systems – preferably, in particular, including some manual systems involving human-designed search strategies and (preferably again) some degree of interaction in the search. Second, we need reasonably deep pools (preferably 100+ from each system, not 10). Third, the collections themselves cannot be too big.

In all these respects, the pooling method is currently under suspicion. Given the increasing range of tasks at TREC, the number and variety of participants in each task has declined. Although some tracks involve an explicit manual or interactive task, such tasks are hard for participants to undertake, and many of the TREC tracks do not attempt such a task. Finally, the scale of the document collections used for TREC has increased hugely since the beginning. One target for the last few years has been to reach or at least approach web scale. TREC is not there yet, but has been taking large steps in that direction.

A further issue is that in some of the tracks (and also in many of the more recent TREC-like initiatives) either or both of the request formulations and relevance judgements are made by the track participants rather than by judges employed by NIST. This is essentially volunteer effort, and effectively precludes the judging of thousands of documents per query.

Thus some effort in the last few years has been devoted to alternatives to the pooling method. Various methods based on sampling are currently being tried. A major motivation for the completeness target has always been the re-use of test collections by other researchers after relevance judgements have been obtained. A challenge for the sampling approaches is to maintain re-usability.

## Ranking algorithms

At the heart of a search engine in the modern sense is a scoring-and-ranking algorithm. This may be used for various tasks, but most directly for ad-hoc retrieval, and therefore these algorithms became a major focus for the TREC ad-hoc task.

At the start of TREC, the best-known and most well-established ranking algorithms were those associated with SMART and the vector-space model – essentially cosine correlation, either with simple TF*IDF term weighting or with one of a small number of variants developed as part of SMART. There were several other algorithms in existence, including the Robertson/Karen Spärck Jones relevance weight (RSJ [30]: IDF, no TF, but with a relevance feedback component) and some other approaches implemented in Inquery (based on an inference model of retrieval [31]). But most researchers would treat one of the SMART variants as baseline: that which they would like to improve on.

The early years of TREC proved revolutionary in this respect. Using a further development of an old probabilistic model, we in the Okapi team developed a much extended version of RSJ weighting, now commonly known as (Okapi) BM25: this makes effective use of TF and also document length [32]. Its success at TREC helped stimulate a whole host of other developments in ranking. A new form of model, known as Language Modelling [33], appeared in the late 1990s, and has also been influential. There is absolutely no doubt that today's ranking algorithms are *far* better than those of 1990.

Nowadays, BM25 has something of the status that the vector space model had in 1992. That is, many researchers use BM25 as baseline: that which they try to beat. It is also the case that BM25 has made it into several commercial search systems. However, modern commercial ranking algorithms tend to be much more complex, leveraging different kinds of information. They do not treat documents as undifferentiated blobs of text (which is what both the vector space model and BM25 do), but extract different kinds of evidence which need to be combined in an optimal way for good ranking. Typically in such an environment, an algorithm like BM25 will provide part of the evidence, but will be combined with other clues for the final ranking.

## Feedback

A second strand of experiments that was present from the beginning of TREC is those associated with feedback, specifically with per-request feedback based on relevance judgements. Relevance feedback (RF) is the process of getting the system to learn some characteristics of relevant documents, over and above what can be inferred directly from the request itself. The idea has been around since Rocchio's work on the SMART system in the 1960s [10], and as indicated above, was also implemented in the Okapi system.

It is not so easy to design a good evaluation of an RF system. The SMART researchers devised various methods simulating an initial search, user examination of a few top documents, followed by a new search. A tricky issue concerns the treatment, while evaluating the new search, of the documents already 'seen' by the user. Okapi evaluation with real users concluded that given a simple interface,

1.  after having made some relevance judgements (as required anyway by the system), some users would make use of an RF facility;[19]
2.  some of these users would then mark as relevant items that they would have been unlikely to find in the original search.

Such data provides circumstantial evidence that RF can be beneficial, but does not provide a good basis for comparative evaluation of different methods.

The first few rounds of TREC had a task called 'routing'; the model was as follows. We assume we have an existing collection of documents, and for each request we already have (that is, the system has access to) relevance judgements, more-or-less complete, on this existing collection. Now we want to search a new collection – we need to formulate a query based on the original request and the relevance judgements from the old collection. This particular formulation of RF task is relatively clean from an experimental point of view but very unrealistic.

Subsequently, a task called 'adaptive filtering' was developed.[20] Here the model is that documents arrive in the system in a stream; for each request, a decision has to be taken on each incoming document, concerning whether the requester should be notified about it or not. If yes, the requester is then assumed to provide a relevance judgement on it; s/he is also assumed to have provided two or three examples of relevant documents on initially formulating the request. This design, while still artificial in many ways, is clearly more defensible than the routing model.

In many of these experiments, the RF notion has proved extremely powerful. In general, documents judged relevant (or not) by the user or requester provide extremely rich information about the (hidden) user information need, above and beyond what is provided by the stated request. In fact the idea has extended into theories and models; the notion that documents may be judged for relevance to the need becomes not just a mechanism for evaluating systems, but a basic concept in design.[21]

*Machine learning*

Feedback-related tasks, or similar ones like text categorization based on human-assigned examples, have also been instrumental in introducing a new community into IR. The machine learning (ML) community thrives on learning from examples, and although much of the early work on routing was based on home-grown methods from the IR world (e.g.

Rocchio, Okapi), it became increasingly common to see methods and ideas brought in from the ML community. Nowadays, such ideas and methods are pervasive in IR, not just in the RF context. In particular, modern ad-hoc scoring-and-ranking algorithms often depend on ML methods for optimization. This is no longer a question of learning about a particular user's underlying information need, but about learning at some level of abstraction, about what characteristics or features of request and document combined are good predictors of a user relevance judgement.

## Tackling the web

When TREC was announced at the tail end of 1991 the world wide web scarcely existed, though the problems of information discovery on the internet were already being recognized. The initial technical challenge at TREC-1 was to index and search a text collection of the order of 2 Gb in size[22] – and this was indeed a seriously hard task for some of the participating groups. But beside today's web search engines (which claim to index 20 billion *pages* and upwards), 2 Gb pales into insignificance. Nor is size the only characteristic of the web which differentiates it from other collections of documents for search purposes. Its heterogeneity, its extremely variable quality, the presence of web spam are all major features. In addition, there are features which (as we have discovered over the past decade) are positively useful for search purposes, the most obvious one being the linkage between pages.

TREC has tried to tackle some of the issues of web search – both the technical problems of dealing with the sheer size of data and the search effectiveness issues which are the main theme of this paper (and which may also be related to size). A succession of tracks has pushed up the size of experimental collections, starting with the Very Large Collection, through the Web Track, and to the Terabyte Track. This last was based on a crawl of the .gov domain in the USA, and resulted in a collection which was actually somewhat less than half a terabyte, but nevertheless much larger than previous TREC collections. At the same time, the issue of query types has been tackled. It is now understood that web search engines receive a variety of types of query. The commonly cited classification is informational/ navigational/transactional; however, at TREC the following types have been used, in addition to traditional topical queries: 'topic distillation' (find a good overview page to browse from); 'home page' (find a home page for e.g. a person, company, product); 'named page' (find a specific page such as a form for a particular purpose).

The amount and variety of evidence that can be used to help web search engines rank effectively, beyond the text of the page, is surprisingly wide. Google has made famous PageRank, which is a query-independent measure of how good a page is, based on linkage; but all web search engines make extensive use of other kinds of evidence. Anchor text (taking snippets of text from a referring page to describe the referred-to page) is probably the strongest single piece of evidence to help home page queries. Usage data, based for example on click-through logs, also appears to be of major importance. All of this poses challenges to the TREC environment – it might be seriously hard for a public project like TREC to get hold of the necessary data to do experiments. At the time of writing, TREC has clearly demonstrated the benefits of anchor text, but has yet to tackle click-through, or web spam (there has, however, been a track devoted to spam email detection).

## Interactive experiments at TREC

Typically, a TREC task involves each group trying out a small number of variants of its own system, with a view to addressing a research question or questions of particular interest to that group. In addition, there is the cross-group comparison, which makes up the competitive element of TREC.

Probably for most participants and observers, the competitive element dominates: the scope for serious internal experimentation to be covered by a set of submissions for a TREC task is somewhat limited, and is probably better done offline, on some existing set of TREC test material.

However, using human searchers in interactive searching experiments within the TREC framework introduces serious problems into the competitive aspects of TREC. The primary issue is that human searchers vary vastly.

In statistical terms, a typical TREC set of results has two main sources of statistical variability, between systems and between requests, and also an interaction effect between the two. The variability between requests is well-known to be large (actually larger than the variability between systems); this in itself is problematic, though it can be dealt with by having enough requests. But if we now include human searchers in the equation, they introduce their own variability, and also probably two more interaction effects, any or all of which may be large. Even if it were feasible to control such variability by numbers, it is very likely that different groups would have access to different types of searcher, so it would be very hard to impose controls sufficient to allow cross-group comparisons.

This lesson was learnt, somewhat painfully, over three or four successive years of the TREC interactive track. In part, therefore, the emphasis has been on developing methodologies which allow a group to set up a relatively controlled internal experiment, and hope to get statistically valid and reliable results on its own research questions. In particular, this means a design which allows the teasing out of the various main and interaction statistical effects mentioned above. Also required was a rich set of additional data-gathering tools, including detailed records or logs of the search processes followed by the searchers, both automatic logs and methods such as think-aloud recordings.

The development of these methods and tools has been impressive, but it is probably true that we have only scratched the surface of what we might learn from them.

Of the research groups most active in the TREC interactive track, we have come across two already. Nick Belkin's group at Rutgers took part in the track in all nine years that it ran, and the Okapi group (from various institutional homes in the UK) in the first seven. Two other groups, one from the US and one from Australia, also took part most years.

## Final remarks on TREC

The extraordinary success of TREC, over a decade and a half, has transformed both the state of the art of information retrieval in general and that of IR experimentation in particular. Even if TREC were to stop today, it would have had the following effects.

It has stimulated a series of substantial advances in information retrieval techniques, particularly for example in ranking algorithms.

This stimulation has fed back into the theories and models that underlie the techniques. The most significant advances are those that required the re-thinking of old theories or the development of new ones.

One mechanism for this stimulation has been the element of explicit, open competition in TREC itself. Although it has been engineered to avoid claims of 'winning', and retains a very strong collaborative atmosphere, relative success at TREC has nevertheless carried considerable kudos, and has also encouraged the rapid spread of good ideas.

Another mechanism has been the development and provision of test material, of a quality, quantity and variety quite unlike anything that went before. The proportion of research papers in the field that make some use of TREC-derived data is huge.

In addition to test material, TREC has also greatly encouraged the development of good methods of experimentation. The standard of rigour of experimental methodology has been vastly improved.

TREC has stimulated a number of imitations. I do not use the word in a pejorative sense; on the contrary, these projects (NTCIR, CLEF, INEX etc.) are themselves producing important results as TREC has done.

These achievements are huge and extraordinary, and deserve to be shouted from the rooftops. Without in any way belittling them, we need also to be aware of the negative aspects of TREC. I will mention three.

The first concerns its competitive nature. This has in itself been immensely stimulating, in exactly the ways described above; but it also engenders a focus on results (based on effectiveness measures like recall and precision) which sometimes gets in the way of other things. It is very unusual now to see the kind of detailed failure analysis that characterized the early Medlars experiment. Similarly, theories or models tend to be the subject of experimental investigation *only* in terms of the effectiveness of the resulting system. Seen as an application of the usual scientific method, of challenging theories by trying to derive falsifiable consequences, which may then be tested experimentally, this is extremely limited.

The second aspect concerns TREC's laboratory nature. It is a laboratory experiment, and the materials and methods it has generated are materials and methods for laboratory experiments. Any laboratory experiment is an abstraction, based on a set of choices: choices to represent certain aspects of the real world (directly or indirectly) and to ignore others. Choices are made deliberately for the end in view – to isolate certain variables in order to be able to understand them. But choices are also made perforce – because certain aspects of the real world are highly resistant to abstraction. This factor introduces inevitable biases in what is studied: some groups of variables are more amenable than others to abstraction into a laboratory setting. From this point of view, the most important grouping of variables in the IR field is of those that directly concern users and those that do not. On the whole, user variables are resistant to abstraction.

The standard way to deal with this issue in laboratory experiments, inherited from Cranfield, is to reduce the user variables to requests and relevance judgements. This is, we have seen, an extraordinarily powerful abstraction; but it does not allow us to answer all the research questions we might reasonably ask. Parts of TREC, particularly the interactive tracks, have attempted and to some extent succeeded in pushing outside this limitation, but the bias remains. It is very much easier for (say) a PhD student in the field to work on mathematical models and ranking algorithms, using the TREC material in the usual way and never questioning the validity of relevance judgements, than to venture into the jungle of real users with real anomalous states of knowledge.

Other aspects of the real world make their way into TREC, but with more or less difficulty. While TREC was originally designed to allow experiments to scale up to collections of realistic size, at the same time real-world collections have themselves got bigger and more complex. In respect of the web in particular, as indicated above, TREC has so far addressed only a few of the issues.

The third limitation I would like to address relates to the second, but is distinct. In the process of abstracting from the real world, we define artificial and restricted goals for our systems. The primary system goal addressed in TREC and in most such experiments is the retrieval of items of information. From the point of view of a user engaged in a larger task, or from the point of view of an organization or institution or community trying to improve communication among its members, the retrieval of items of information must at best be a sub-goal. Our understanding of the validity of this as a sub-goal, and how it relates to the achievement of wider goals, is limited, and deserves more analysis – theoretical, observational, and experimental.

Experimentation in IR is a large domain. TREC occupies a big part of it, but by no means all.

## Some current concerns

The various TREC 'imitations' use TREC-like methods to conduct further experiments and to generate new test materials.[23] In part this involves applying essentially the same methods as developed and used for TREC, but to different materials. For example, CLEF (the Cross-Language Evaluation Forum, based in Europe) covers retrieval in multiple mainly European languages, mixed-language collections, and queries and documents in different languages. NTCIR (NII Test Collection for IR Systems, based in Japan) has included material in Japanese, English, Chinese and Korean, and also has some patent data and scientific abstracts. However, some of the tasks force the development of new methods. For example, INEX (Initiative for Evaluation of XML, based in Europe) addresses the question of retrieval from collections of structured documents, where the appropriate unit of retrieval might, depending on the request, be a section or subsection of an original document. Since the traditional Cranfield/TREC method involves treating documents as indivisible units, both for retrieval and for relevance judgement, the INEX tasks require significantly different methods.

Moving a little away from search tasks, DUC (the Document Understanding Conference, USA-based) addresses various questions around summarizing documents (single documents or sets), which requires very different kinds of evaluation. Within TREC itself, there has been for some time a Question-Answering track: the aim is to generate a specific answer to a question, to be extracted or inferred from a collection of documents, rather than to retrieve (references to) documents which might contain such an answer. In such ways the experimental approach is being extended to a wider range of information-related functions and tasks.

As discussed above, there are interesting new concerns even within the Cranfield/TREC paradigm, for example the discovery of relevant documents in the collection. This is even more critical for many of the TREC imitations, which are often trying to accomplish TREC-like results with much less in the way of resources. In some cases (including some TREC tracks), either or both of request generation and relevance judgements are done by the participating research groups (that is, by the researchers themselves) rather than by assessors employed for the purpose. Thus there is very considerable interest in methods which promise to reduce the amount of effort needed to obtain a useful set of results.

A recurring theme in current work is the issue of measures. There are many things that cause researchers to worry about measures, including for example the case of retrieving parts of structured documents, or the use of graded rather than binary relevance judgements, or methods such as sampling for choosing which documents to judge. In this last case, one of the concerns is with measures that are robust under incomplete judgements. More broadly, methods of analysis of results, including for example statistical significance analysis, are the subject of much current work.

## Finally

At an earlier stage in the history of IR experimentation, one might have been tempted to conclude that the basic methodological work was already done – that we might settle down into a common, agreed way of doing experiments. This is far from the case. Although some of the ideas have remained remarkably stable, the field of IR experimentation is as exciting now, and is changing as fast, as it was at the time of my own initial immersion, in the days of Cyril Cleverdon and Jason Farradane.

## Acknowledgements

I am grateful to the following for extremely useful comments on drafts of this paper: Alan Gilchrist, Donna Harman, Ellen Voorhees, Chris Buckley, Bob Oddy, and an anonymous referee. The historical inaccuracies and misinterpretations, however, are all mine.

## Notes

1  The 39th Doge of Venice at the turn of the 13th century, Enrico Dandolo, was blind.

2  One is somewhat reminded of Noam Chomsky's famous example, dating from the same period, of a sentence that is grammatically correct but apparently meaningless: 'colourless green ideas sleep furiously'.

3  We may note again that even this word-based searching experiment at Cranfield 2 was done without the aid of computers in any form.

4  Recall: proportion of the relevant documents in the collection that are retrieved (ability of the system to find the relevant documents). Precision: proportion of the retrieved documents that are relevant (ability of the system to weed out non-relevant documents). In the present state of the art, we have a large menagerie of measures in common use; most of them derive directly from, or are inspired in some way by, these primitive notions of recall and precision, albeit adapted to measure ranked output rather than set retrieval (ability of the system to rank relevant documents highly).

5  Personal anecdote: as a master's student of Farradane's in 1967–8, and publishing my first paper, based on my master's dissertation on evaluation measures, in 1969, I incurred by association some of Cleverdon's wrath. It was some years before my relations with Cleverdon recovered from that poor start.

6  It is hard to find the origin of some of the names of systems discussed here. A dictionary of information science defines SMART as System for the Mechanical

Analysis and Retrieval of Text. However, in one of the very early reports from Cornell by one of the researchers there, it was said to mean 'Salton's Magic Automatic Retriever of Texts' (almost exactly this form also appears in Wikipedia). I can find no reference by Salton himself to any expansion.

7   Professors were charged for computer time for their research projects, and had to include such expenses in grant applications. On the above figure, 20 runs might easily cost more than a professor's salary for a month. I am indebted to Donna Harman for this datum.

8   The Medical Literature Analysis and Retrieval Service.

9   Medical Subject Headings.

10  SIGIR is the ACM Special Interest Group on Information Retrieval.

11  Technological note: Oddy was working in an environment which gave him access to visual display units, as opposed to the printing terminals that I was using at the same time. However, the interaction mechanisms were strictly keyboard input/command line/scrolling character/line display – nothing remotely like windows or mice yet.

12  Thomas is not an acronym. One source of inspiration for it was Thomas the Tank Engine, a character in a children's book (my thanks to Bob Oddy for this information, which has not been published before). Not to be confused with a later system called THOMAS from CIIR, based on Inquery, for the Library of Congress.

13  At the same time and place as I did mine, under the supervision of Bertie Brookes at University College London.

14  'If this has to be an acronym it stands for "Online keyword access to public information"' [23].

15  The full phrase, due to the journalist Walter Bagehot in the nineteenth century, is 'the bald-headed man at the back of the Clapham omnibus'. The Clapham in question is a suburb of south London; since my home is in south London, I do use London buses, and I am bald-headed, he might mean me!

16  Where I had moved in the late 1970s.

17  One version of the Okapi interface was based on a vt100 terminal protocol. This had a screen of 24 lines of 80 characters. Each character position in the grid was addressable, and the available characters included a limited number of graphics characters which could be used to construct very limited visual display devices, such as rectangular boxes. Menus could be displayed, and menu items chosen by hitting a single numeric or alphabetic key.

18  A typical TREC 'topic' has a short title (which might be used directly as a query), and additional information about the supposed information need under the headings 'description' and 'narrative'. The narrative contains explicit rules for judging the relevance of documents. An example title and description are: Hydroponics –

Document will discuss the science of growing plants in water or some substance other than soil.

19    Although the usage of the RF facility declined as we moved into the window display era and interfaces became more complex.

20    Old hands will recognize in the idea of filtering an earlier form of search system known as 'current awareness' or 'selective dissemination of information'. The latter phrase was usually abbreviated to SDI – long before Ronald Reagan purloined the acronym for his star wars project.

21    The first theory to incorporate relevance explicitly was a probabilistic indexing model due to Maron and Kuhns in the US in 1960 [34], around the time that the relevance idea was being operationalized for experimentation but more or less independently. Subsequently Rocchio's method [10] and, in the UK, the Robertson/Spärck Jones model [30] tied the two together more firmly.

22    Actually two collections of approximately 1 Gb each.

23    Websites for various initiatives: CLEF, http://clef.iei.pi.cnr.it/; NTCIR, http://research.nii.ac.jp/ntcir/; INEX, http://inex.is.informatik.uni-duisburg.de/; DUC, http://duc.nist.gov/; TREC QA, http://trec.nist.gov/data/qamain.html (all accessed 6 September 2007).

# References

[1]    K. Spärck Jones (ed.), *Information Retrieval Experiment* (Butterworths, London, 1981).

[2]    E.M. Voorhees and D.K. Harman (eds), *TREC: Experiments and Evaluation in Information Retrieval* (MIT Press, Cambridge, MA, 2005).

[3]    *The Royal Society Scientific Information Conference, 21 June–2 July 1948: Report and Papers Submitted* (Royal Society, London, 1948).

[4]    *Proceedings of the International Conference on Scientific Information, Washington, DC* (National Academy of Sciences, Washington, DC, 1958).

[5]    C.W. Cleverdon, *Report on the Testing and Analysis of an Investigation into the Comparative Efficiency of Indexing Systems* (College of Aeronautics, Cranfield, 1962). [Aslib Cranfield Research Project]

[6]    C.W. Cleverdon, J. Mills and E.M. Keen, *Factors Determining the Performance of Indexing Systems* (2 vols) (College of Aeronautics, Cranfield, 1966). [Aslib Cranfield Research Project]

[7]    D.R. Swanson, Some unexplained aspects of the Cranfield tests of index language performance, *Library Quarterly* 41(3) (1971) 223–8.

[8a]   D.C. Blair, Some thoughts on the reported results of TREC, *Information Processing and Management* 38(3) (2002) 445–51, 2002.

[8b]   Letters to the editor, *Information Processing and Management*, 39(1) (2003) 153–9.

[9]    G. Salton (ed.), *The SMART Retrieval System: Experiments in Automatic Document Processing* (Prentice-Hall, Englewood Cliffs, NJ, 1971).

[10]   J.J. Rocchio, Relevance feedback in information retrieval. In: G. Salton (ed.), *The SMART Retrieval System: Experiments in Automatic Document Processing* (Prentice-Hall, Englewood Cliffs, NJ, 1971) 313–23.

[11]   F.W. Lancaster, MEDLARS: report on the evaluation of its operating efficiency, *American Documentation* 20(2) (1969) 119–48.

[12]   K. Spärck Jones, *Automatic Keyword Classification for Information Retrieval* (Butterworths, London, 1971).

[13]   K. Spärck Jones, A statistical interpretation of term specificity and its application in retrieval, *Journal of Documentation*, 28(1) (1972) 11–21.

[14]   S.E. Robertson, Understanding Inverse Document Frequency: on theoretical arguments for IDF, *Journal of Documentation*, 60(5) (2004) 503–520. Available at http://www.soi.city.ac.uk/~ser/idf.html (accessed 17 August 2007).

[15]   K. Spärck Jones and C.J. van Rijsbergen, *Report on the Need for and Provision of an 'Ideal' Information Retrieval Test Collection* (Computing Laboratory, University of Cambridge, Cambridge, 1975).

[16]   K. Spärck Jones and R.G. Bates, *Report on a Design Study for the 'Ideal' Information Retrieval Test Collection* (Computing Laboratory, University of Cambridge, Cambridge, 1977).

[17]   E.M. Keen, Evaluation parameters. In: G. Salton (ed.), *The SMART Retrieval System: Experiments in Automatic Document Processing* (Prentice-Hall, Englewood Cliffs, NJ, 1971) 74–111.

[18]   E.M. Keen, The Aberystwyth index languages test, *Journal of Documentation* 29(1) (1973) 1–35.

[19]   E.M. Keen, *Evaluation of Printed Subject Indexes by Laboratory Investigation: Final report to the British Library Research and Development Department, BLR&D Report 5454* (BLR&DD, London, 1978).

[20]   R.N. Oddy, Information retrieval through man-machine dialogue, *Journal of Documentation* 33(1) (1977) 1–14.

[21]   N.J. Belkin, Anomalous states of knowledge as a basis for information retrieval, *Canadian Journal of Information Science*, 5(May) (1980) 133–43.

[22]   N.J. Belkin, R.N. Oddy and H.M. Brooks, ASK for information retrieval. Part I: background and theory; part II: results of a design study, *Journal of Documentation*, 38(2) (1982) 61–71 and 38(3) 145–64.

[23]    N. Mitev, G. Venner and S. Walker, *Designing an Online Public Access Catalogue: Okapi, a Catalogue on a Local Area Network* (The British Library, London, 1985). [Library and Information Research Report no. 39]

[24]    S. Walker, The Okapi online catalogue research projects. In: C. Hildreth (ed.), *The Online Catalogue: Developments and Directions* (Library Association, London, 1989) 84–106.

[25]    S.E. Robertson, Overview of the Okapi projects, *Journal of Documentation* 53(1) (1997) 3–7. [Introduction to special issue of *Journal of Documentation*]

[26]    M. Hancock-Beaulieu, Experiments on interfaces to support query expansion, *Journal of Documentation* 53(1) (1997) 8–19.

[27]    W.B. Croft (ed.), *Advances in Information Retrieval: Recent Research from the Center for Intelligent Information Retrieval* (Kluwer, Boston, MA, 2000).

[28]    S.E. Robertson and M. Hancock-Beaulieu, On the evaluation of IR systems, *Information Processing and Management*, 28(4) (1992) 457–66.

[29]    NIST (National Institute of Standards and Technology), *Text REtrieval Conference*. Available at: http: //trec.nist.gov/ (accessed 13 August 2007).

[30]    S.E. Robertson and K. Spärck Jones, Relevance weighting of search terms, *Journal of the American Society for Information Science* 27 (1976) 129–46. Available at: http://www.soi.city.ac.uk/~ser/papers/RSJ76.pdf (accessed 17 August 2007).

[31]    H.R. Turtle and W.B. Croft, Evaluation of an inference-network based retrieval model, *ACM Transactions on Information Systems*, 9(3) (1991) 187–222.

[32]    K. Spärck Jones, S. Walker and S.E. Robertson, A probabilistic model of information retrieval: development and comparative experiments. *Information Processing and Management*, 36 (2000) 779–808 (Part 1) and 809–40 (Part 2). Available at: http://www.soi.city.ac.uk/~ser/blockbuster.html (accessed 17 August 2007).

[33]    W.B. Croft and J. Lafferty (eds), *Language Modelling for Information Retrieval* (Kluwer, Dordrecht/Boston/London, 2003).

[34]    M.E. Maron and J.L. Kuhns, On relevance, probabilistic indexing and information retrieval, *Journal of the ACM* 7(3) (1960) 216–44.

# 5

# The information user: past, present and future

TOM WILSON

## Abstract

The emergence of research on various aspects of 'information behaviour' is explored and its growth as a subject of academic research is documented. The origin of the field as a potential aid to the development of library and information services is noted, as is the transition from this status to that of a subject for research at PhD level and beyond. The development of the field has thus led to a division between the needs of academia for theoretically grounded work, and the needs of the field of practice for guidance for service development. There is, today, a disconnection between research and practice, to a significant extent: early research was undertaken by practitioners but today academic research dominates the scene. Suggestions are made as to how this disconnection can be repaired.

## Introduction

The 'user' has been of interest in librarianship and information science for much longer than either has existed as a focus for research. Virtually every development in the field has been concerned with making it easier for the user to access documents or information. Thus, the first 'union catalogue' in England was devised to make it easier for the scholar monks to locate wanted manuscripts in monastery libraries:

> In the late thirteenth century a union catalog was constructed, which
> included a unified list of holdings of English monastery libraries, '*Registrum*
> *librorum Angliae*'... [1: p. 126].

Charles Ami Cutter's 'shelf marks' [2] were designed to make easier the location of a specific book on the shelf, 'open access' [see, e.g., 3] was devised to make it easier for the library visitor to get the book he or she wanted without undue delay, Kaiser's 'systematic indexing' [4] was devised to enable the rapid location of wanted pieces of information, and so on throughout the history of libraries and information centres.

It took some time, however, before the 'user' as a living, breathing person became the focus of attention in information research. Initially, the focus was on the system used, how it was used and by whom. Thus, the first library surveys were designed to discover what *categories* of persons used libraries, not what those persons did when they were in a library nor what life or work issues were behind their library use. Similarly, early readership studies were designed to discover the social class (and, hence, spending power) of newspaper readers [see 5 for background] to enable advertisers to focus their efforts: what the *individual* reader read, how they read and why they read was not a subject of interest at the time.

## Early research on information use

When the Royal Society Scientific Information Conference was held in 1948, the information user was the focus of some attention, but, again, the attention was directed towards the systems used; most of the reports and papers related to the documentation of science and to technical methods (from microfilm to punched cards) of handling the documents. The outstanding exception to the general run of papers was that by Professor J.D. Bernal on *Preliminary analysis of pilot questionnaire on the use of scientific literature* [6]. Bernal's aim was

> to find out directly from working scientists, what they read, why they read it and what use they made of the information [6: p. 589].

The method employed was interesting, since the 'questionnaire' actually consisted of three forms: form A consisted of cards, small enough to fit into a pocket, upon which the scientist was asked to record what journals they read, where the reading was done and what amount of time they spent doing it. Form B concerned the specific papers read, and sought information on the source of the reference to the paper, how the paper was obtained and the use to which it was put. Form C was a questionnaire with 16, mostly open, questions about the individual scientist's reading habits, use of abstracts, language abilities and so forth. A case could be argued that this was, in fact, the first 'user study' in the field and I do not know of any study since that has attempted to use a similar method of data collection. From the example of a completed questionnaire given in the paper, the time involved must have been considerable. One of the conclusions resonates interestingly with the present:

> The demand for more reprints and for central distribution of reprints, which might be combined with microfilm reproduction of papers difficult to obtain, has also been repeatedly made [6: p. 602].

The descendants of these scientists are still trying (successfully, in some areas) to implant the notion of disciplinary and institutional repositories of papers.

The repeat conference, 10 years later, held in Washington DC under the auspices of the National Academy of Sciences, had more papers relating to information use but, still, much related to the user's distribution of time and resources over different kinds of documents: scientific journals, books, patents, abstracting and indexing services, and so on. Hogg and Smith [7] used methods somewhat similar to those of Bernal in 1948 to explore the way journals and abstracting services were used by scientists in the United Kingdom Atomic Energy Authority, while Herner and Herner [8] sought to derive information requirements from the records of reference enquiries, also in the field of atomic energy. Both studies were directed towards the discovery of guidelines for the development of information services or retrieval systems and, indeed, this was the overall focus of papers in this section of the conference.

Unsurprisingly, given that research into these matters was in its infancy in the Schools of Librarianship in the USA, and almost non-existent in those in the UK, practitioners represented the majority of those presenting papers at the Conference and there was only one academic from a School of Librarianship – Hazel Mews of the Department of Librarianship, University of the Witwatersrand. There were, however, many academics from other disciplines and a small number of participants (not presenting papers) from library schools in the USA and Canada.

It is evident, from examining this research, however, that the study of 'information needs' was not, after all, particularly useful for its intended purpose. What were libraries supposed to divine from the discovery that scientists subscribed to two or three journals, regularly scanned other journals in their field in the library, perused a relevant abstracting journal to discover what was not immediately available in the library, and often requested offprints from researchers around the world?

At this early stage of investigation (that is, up to the early 1970s), there was little in the way of genuine academic or scholarly interest in the subject: when we look at the authors of the papers in the two scientific information conferences, for example, we discover that most of them were practitioners in library and information work, with the occasional scientist discovering an interest in this aspect of scholarly communication. As late as 1971, when the INFROSS (Information Requirements of the Social Sciences) study was published [9], none of the three main researchers (Line, Brittain, and Cramer) was a library school staff member, and the research was based in the Library of Bath University. Up to this point I believe that there were only two persons with PhDs in librarianship or information science in the UK: as a research field, the subject was in its infancy.

However, information user research in this early period was also carried out by the Aslib Research Group. Members of the group, such as Margaret Slater and John Martyn, undertook a number of projects from the mid-1960s onwards; for example, Martyn's investigation into literature searching by scientists [10] and Slater's study of social scientists [11]. In the same era, we have the emergence of the *Annual Review of Information Science and Technology* and the beginning of its series of chapters on information needs, with Menzel's 'Information needs and uses in science and technology' [12] and Paisley's 'Information needs and uses' [13]. Somewhat later, in the 1970s, the Centre for Research on User Studies was established in the then Postgraduate School of Librarianship and Information Science (now the Department of Information Studies) at the University of Sheffield. The Centre carried out a wide variety of investigations [e.g., 14–16] before lack of funding led to its closure in 1989.

In the early years, the research paradigm was positivist: the aim, in common with much of social science at the time, was to make the research 'objective', in the same way that scientific research was assumed to be objective. The principal research methods employed were questionnaire-based surveys and interviews and, in large part, there was little or no attention to theoretical conceptualisation: the focus was on the discovery and description of aspects of library and document usage. The situation began to change in the late 1970s and early 1980s, through the example of the INISS Project [17] and Wilson's advocacy in 'On user studies and information needs' [18].

It is true, of course, that there were papers and reports with an implicit theoretical basis: for example, the early studies of library users were implicitly or explicitly concerned with the occupations and class origins on library users. The Hild Regional Branch Library of Chicago undertook a survey of the occupations of its users, showing that the largest group consisted of 'housewives' [19], while a study of Montclair Public Library in New Jersey focused on the holders of library cards by persons in groups such as the 'College Woman's Club', those listed in *Who's Who in America*, 1934, and 'Other key people, including teachers and ministers' [20].

## The growth period

Overall, however, specific theories in relation to the information user did not appear until the 1980s. By this time, information use and users had become a curriculum topic in the schools of librarianship in the UK, particularly those that had become part of the newly emergent polytechnics (subsequently to be designated universities). Accompanying their new status within degree-offering institutions, the schools found a need to develop undergraduate and Masters' degrees and, accordingly, new subjects for a full curriculum. In addition to the curriculum development, there came the need for teachers to engage in research; many had done so before the emergence of the polytechnics, but all were required to after that development.

In the USA, at about the same time, pressure to engage in research, to raise the status of the parent institution, also began to be felt, and there was a gradual interest in the number of PhD students overall, and in the information-seeking behaviour field in particular.

The development of PhD studies in library and information science also emerged in the UK at this time: to begin with, probably the largest number of doctorates was awarded to the academic staff of the polytechnic schools, who were seeking to upgrade their qualifications to fit themselves for the newly emergent research culture in which they worked. Soon, however, they were replaced by newly or recently graduated students who moved on to the PhD either directly from a Master's programme or shortly thereafter.

Since these developments in the 1980s, the sub-discipline of information behaviour has developed apace, with more and more PhD students choosing this area of research. The growth, in general, can be shown by reference to the increase in papers indexed by the Web of Science with the terms *information seeking, information behavio(u)r,* or *information seeking behavio(u)r* anywhere in the

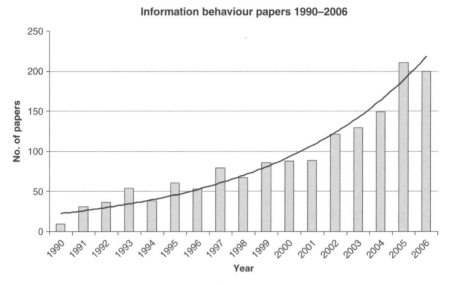

**Information behaviour papers 1990–2006**

**Figure 1** Growth in information behaviour papers 1990–2006. It is also apparent from the source data that the subject has never been the province solely of the information science community. For example, the nine papers produced in 1990 were published in eight journals, as shown in Table 1.

**Table 1** Distribution of papers, 1990

| | |
|---|---|
| Research in Nursing & Health | 2 |
| Bulletin of the Medical Library Association | 1 |
| Health Education Quarterly | 1 |
| Journal of Documentation | 1 |
| Journalism Quarterly | 1 |
| Medical Care | 1 |
| Proceedings of the ASIS Annual Meeting | 1 |
| Technovation | 1 |

record – there were nine such papers in 1990 and 200 in 2006 (see Figure 1). As may be seen from the trend line on the figure, the growth has been close to exponential.

It is worth commenting here that, even in the early days of the sub-discipline, only two papers were published in what might be considered 'core' information science journals, while five were published in health related journals, one in journalism and one in the field of technical innovation.

By 2006, the 200 papers listed by Web of Science were published in 94 journals. Fifty percent of the papers were published in 13 journals, some of

**Table 2** The 13 journals covering 50% of the listed papers in 2006

| | | |
|---|---|---|
| Journal of the American Society for Information Science and Technology | 22 | 11.00% |
| Information Research – an International Electronic Journal | 18 | 9.00% |
| Information Processing & Management | 11 | 5.50% |
| Journal of Health Communication | 8 | 4.00% |
| Journal of Academic Librarianship | 7 | 3.50% |
| Journal of Documentation | 6 | 3.00% |
| Journal of Librarianship and Information Science | 5 | 2.50% |
| Library & Information Science Research | 5 | 2.50% |
| Patient Education and Counseling | 5 | 2.50% |
| Journal of the Medical Library Association | 4 | 2.00% |
| Electronic Library | 3 | 1.50% |
| Health Services Research | 3 | 1.50% |
| Human Communication Research | 3 | 1.50% |
| | 100 | 50.00% |

which are core journals in the information science field and, consequently, accept papers in this area as a matter of editorial policy. Others are in journals from a diverse range of fields where the motivation to accept papers on this subject is more difficult to determine, as shown in Table 2.

The growth of the field within information science is clearly discernible here: 77 of the papers were published in core information science journals, 20 in a small number of health-related journals, and three in the communication studies journal *Human Communication Research*. The remaining journals in which papers were published covered a wide variety of fields: other health related (21 journals), psychology (16), information systems (14), other information science journals (10), communication studies (6), management topics (6), artificial intelligence (2), education (2), general social sciences (2) and linguistics (1). Clearly, although information science and health-related journals are dominant, interest in the subject has spread into a wide variety of disciplines, to the extent that a researcher in the field would have considerable difficulty in covering all of the material of interest.

When we compare the early work in this area with that of the period since 1980, three things are evident: first, in the early years the focus was on the information needs of scientists and, to a smaller degree, engineers; secondly, the methods employed were predominantly quantitative, mainly questionnaires with some records analysis and interviews; and, thirdly, there was little or no attempt to evoke or develop theoretical perspectives – the intention of the research was entirely pragmatic.

Today, the situation is quite changed. If, for example, we take the papers presented at the ISIC Conference in 2006, we find that out of 34 papers published, only five could be said to be concerned with the world of work of any kind (railway workers, the military, engineers, office workers and business) compared with seven papers with an educational context; that qualitative methods dominate the field; and that 11 of the 34 papers were directly concerned with theoretical issues. Furthermore, most of the remaining papers had a theoretical orientation and discussed that orientation. Apart from the papers concerned with the world of work, however, few papers discussed the relevance of the research to library or information services. A further difference between 1958 and 2006 is that virtually all of the presenters in the Information Seeking in Context (ISIC) conference were PhD students, academic staff members of schools and departments of library and information science, or full-time researchers in academic or research institutions.

It is evident, then, that we have seen a move, over the past 60 years, from a concern by practitioners to discover guidelines for the improvement of practice to research within an academic discipline. Although that discipline is connected, through the training of librarians and other information specialists, to a world of practice, there is the danger of a disconnection between the two.

This disconnection is understandable on two grounds: first, members of academe must observe the norms of the academy in terms of the kind of research they carry out and the journals in which they publish; they are judged on the extent to which they satisfy these norms. The world of practice may be a source of researchable problems but, as the discipline develops an identity within the world of academe, the researchable problems become more and more theoretically grounded. Secondly, the role of the PhD student in academic research, in this particular discipline, which has the character of a social science, is that of the solitary scholar, pursuing a research problem independently of others (although guided by a supervisor or doctoral committee). A researcher may enter a field of practice and, indeed, may form excellent personal and professional relationships with the practitioners there, but, however participatory may be the character of the research, the researcher will ultimately withdraw. In the best of all possible worlds, the researcher will provide feedback on his or her research to the practitioners and discuss how the research may help them in their work, but this does not always happen and sometimes it is not even expected. Figure 2 illustrates the disconnection at its most severe.

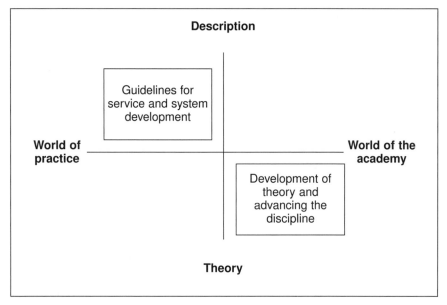

**Figure 2** Practice and the academy

It may be, of course, that education and training programmes in the UK, at the Master's level, are producing, through research training and the completion of a dissertation, practitioners who are comfortable with in-house research and have little need for collaboration with academe. If so, there is little evidence to this effect in the form of publications in the key journals of the field.

## The future?

One of the consequences of a disconnection between practice and academe is the danger that the division may become so complete that both sets of players simply ignore what is happening in the other 'world'. The consequence of this for education for the information professions would be grave, and some may believe that the position has already been reached that professional education and research are irrelevant to practice.

The question arises, therefore, of what the future holds for 'user research' and, as with all questions about the future, the answer is uncertain. However, it is clear from Table 2 above, and the related comments, that there are sub-fields within the sub-discipline, with health-related and 'everyday life' studies being prominent. There is also the field of 'information searching', which has not been dealt with here, but which has emerged as separate from information retrieval research – there is a link, through work on interactive information retrieval systems, but much of the research deals with approaches to search using Web search engines, using similar conceptual frameworks to those used in information seeking. This sub-field has been subject to similar levels of growth to that experienced by information seeking research, and with the increasing digitization of the outputs of research and scholarship, its significance is likely to grow.

In spite of the growth in research in the field, it is evident from the data presented that some areas have had meagre interest devoted to them. For example, information seeking in the public library is almost barren of research; a simple search on the Web of Science revealed only 25 papers from the entire file that combined *information seeking* and *public library*. Can we expect growth in this area, or is the future of the public library system in so much doubt that there will be no growth?

The decline of interest in the information seeking behaviour of scientists and engineers has already been noted and the reasons are difficult to determine. It may be that researchers in the information seeking field come themselves mainly from the humanities and social sciences and so fear that they have insufficient understanding of science and technology and prefer to work in familiar fields. This situation is not likely to change, since there is little sign of any influx of science-education researchers into the field. It may be that practitioners in the scientific and technical information area will, once again, emerge to fill the gap in studies, but that, again, seems unlikely, given the work pressures that everyone is under.

One area of practice that is open to social-science-oriented research is non-health-related organizations in the public sector. There has been only a limited amount of work in this area and, given the spread of intranets and the internet into such organizations, the time would seem to be ripe for research studies. This may be the most likely area of growth for future studies.

To a degree, the rise of doctoral studies in the field has tended to distort studies towards 'captive audiences': students in the same universities as the researchers, and school children. It is not clear how much such investigations have done to improve information services to these groups, although the work of Kuhlthau [21] in taking her work into educational practice through focused workshops stands out in this respect. Recently, in Sweden, Limberg [22] has followed suit.

This still leaves us with the problem of the connection (or disconnection) between research and practice and, in the author's opinion, the best way to bridge the gap is to adopt 'action research' as a methodological approach. This was advocated some years ago [23], but there appears to have been little take-up of the idea, and it is difficult to understand why, other than that the academic drivers have become more and more important to researchers as Research Assessment Exercises and other modes of 'performance assessment' have come to dominate educational life. As in so many other areas, the urge for 'efficiency' appears to drive out effectiveness.

As for theory: Fisher, Erdelez and McKechnie [24] show how diverse the field is from this point of view and Case's [25] presentation of models, paradigms and theories is a well-structured introduction to the range of such conceptual frameworks. Although there is a proliferation of papers on various aspects of theory, it seems that four models or approaches dominate: these are Wilson's models of 1981 and 1996 [26, 27], Kuhlthau's 'information search process' [28] (which is based on Kelly's 'personal construct theory') and Dervin's [29] 'sense-making'. One or another of these approaches is referred to or cited by practically everyone working in the field and, at least at present, there does not appear to be a majority in favour of any one contender, although Wilson has proposed that 'activity theory' might serve as a unifying framework [30, 31].

Whatever the future holds for any of these issues, it seems likely that the need to understand how people search for and use information is likely to continue and, as technologies change and information services continue to develop, the understanding gained may become more and more important for the effective design of systems and services.

## References

[1]   S. Shoham, *Library Classification and Browsing: the Conjunction of Readers and Documents* (Sussex Academic Press, Brighton, UK, 2000).

[2]   C.A. Cutter, *Rules for a Dictionary Catalog (4th edn)* (Government Printing Office, Washington, DC, 1904).

[3]   A. Black, *The Public Library in Britain, 1914–2000* (British Library, London, UK, 2000).

[4]   J. Kaiser, *Systematic Indexing* (Pitman, London, UK, 1911).

[5]   J.P. Wood, Leaders in marketing: George H. Gallup, *Journal of Marketing* 26(4) (1962) 78–80.

[6]   J.D. Bernal, Preliminary analysis of pilot questionnaire on the use of scientific literature. In: *The Royal Society 1948 Scientific Information Conference: Report and Papers Submitted* (Royal Society, London, 1948) 589–637.

[7]   I.H. Hogg and J.R. Smith, Information and literature use in a research and development organization. In: *Proceedings of the 1958 International Conference on Scientific Information* (National Academy of Sciences – National Research Council, Washington, DC, 1959) 131–162.

[8]   S. Herner and M. Herner, Determining requirements for atomic energy information from reference questions. In: *Proceedings of the 1958 International Conference on Scientific Information* (National Academy of Sciences – National Research Council, Washington, DC, 1959) 181–188.

[9]   M.B. Line, The information uses and needs of social scientists: an overview of INFROSS, *Aslib Proceedings* 23(8) (1971) 412–434.

[10]  J. Martyn, *Report of an Investigation on Literature Searching by Research Scientists* (Aslib Research Department, London, UK, 1964).

[11]  M. Slater, Social scientists' information needs in the 1980s, *Journal of Documentation* 44(3) (1988) 226–237.

[12]  H. Menzel, Information needs and uses in science and technology, *Annual Review of Information Science and Technology* 1 (1966) 41–69.

[13]  W.J. Paisley, Information needs and uses, *Annual Review of Information Science and Technology* 3 (1968) 1–30.

[14]  C. Corkill and M. Mann, *Information Needs in the Humanities: Two Postal Surveys* (Postgraduate School of Librarianship and Information Science, CRUS, University of Sheffield, Sheffield, UK, 1978).

[15]  C. Harris and C. Harrop, *Metals Information Needs in Industry: a Pilot Study in South Yorkshire* (Postgraduate School of Librarianship and Information Science, CRUS, University of Sheffield, Sheffield, UK, 1984).

[16]  N. Roberts and B. Clifford, *Regional Variations in the Demand and Supply of Business Information: a Study of Manufacturing Firms* (Postgraduate School of Librarianship and Information Science, CRUS, University of Sheffield, Sheffield, UK, 1986).

[17]  D.R. Streatfield and T.D. Wilson, Information services in English local authority social services departments: implications of Project INISS, *Behavioural and Social Sciences Librarian* 1 (1980) 189–199.

[18]  T.D. Wilson, On user studies and information needs, *Journal of Documentation* 37(1) (1981) 3–15.

[19]  Hild occupational survey, *A.L.A. Bulletin* 32 (1938) 525. Cited by: E.W. McDiarmid, *The Library Survey: Problems and Methods* (American Library Association, Chicago, IL, 1940).

[20]     M.C. Quigley and W.E. Marcus, *Portrait of a Library* (Appleton-Century, New York, NY, 1936). Cited by: E.W. McDiarmid, *The Library Survey: Problems and Methods* (American Library Association, Chicago, IL, 1940).

[21]     C.C. Kuhlthau, *Seeking Meaning: a Process Approach to Library and Information Services (2nd edn)* (Libraries Unlimited, Westport, CT, 2004).

[22]     L. Limberg, Experiencing information seeking and learning: a study of the interaction between two phenomena, *Information Research* 5(1) (1999). Available at: http://InformationR.net/ir/5–1/paper68.html (accessed 10 December, 2007).

[23]     T.D. Wilson, *Recent trends in user studies: action research and qualitative methods (1980)*, (Projekt Methodeninstrumentarium zur Benutzerforschung in Information und Dokumentation, MIB P1 11/80, Freie Universität, Institut für Publizistik und Dokumentationswissenschaft, Berlin, Germany, 1980). Available at: http://InformationR.net/ir/paper76.html (accessed 10 December, 2007).

[24]     K.E. Fisher, S. Erdelez and L.E.F. McKechnie (eds), *Theories of Information Behavior* (Information Today, Medford, NJ, 2005).

[25]     D.O. Case, *Looking for Information: a Survey of Research and Information Seeking, Needs and Behavior (2nd edn)* (Academic Press, Amsterdam, The Netherlands, 2007).

[26]     T.D. Wilson, On user studies and information needs, *Journal of Documentation* 37(1) (1981) 3–15.

[27]     T.D. Wilson and C. Walsh, *Information Behaviour: an Inter-Disciplinary Perspective* (British Library Board, London, UK, 1996). Available at: http://informationr.net/tdw/publ/infbehav/index.html (accessed 10 December, 2007).

[28]     C.C. Kuhlthau, *Seeking Meaning: a Process Approach to Library and Information Services (2nd edn)* (Libraries Unlimited, Westport, CT, 2004).

[29]     B. Dervin, L. Foreman-Wernet and E. Lauterbach (eds), *Sense-making Methodology Reader: Selected Writings of Brenda Dervin* (Hampton Press, Creskill, NJ, 2003).

[30]     T.D. Wilson, A re-examination of information seeking behaviour in the context of activity theory, *Information Research* 11(4) (2006). Available at: http://InformationR.net/ir/11–4/paper260.html (accessed 10 December, 2007).

[31]     T.D. Wilson, Activity theory and information seeking behavior, *Annual Review of Information Science and Technology* 42 (2008) 119–161.

# 6

# The sociological turn in information science

BLAISE CRONIN

## Abstract

This paper explores the history of 'the social' in information science. It traces the influence of social scientific thinking on the development of the field's intellectual base. The continuing appropriation of both theoretical and methodological insights from domains such as social studies of science, science and technology studies, and socio-technical systems is discussed.

## Introduction: an inter-discipline?

I first published in the *Journal of Information Science* (*JIS*) in 1980 [1]. My gossamer paper – that was how I described it to the then editor – most certainly did not set the world alight, nor did it languish in the capacious dustbin of the uncited, though, truth be told, it probably deserved such a fate. 'Some reflections on citation habits in psychology' was a (very) brief communication containing three references, one of which was to Jack Meadows' estimable book, *Communication in Science* [2]. The two other cited works were articles in *American Psychologist* and *Social Studies of Science*. It seems appropriate, this being the Ruby anniversary that never was, to take as my starting point that first foray into print with the official organ of the late lamented Institute of Information Scientists (IIS); doubly so, given that it was, in retrospect at least, an early indicator of my long-standing interest in the intersection of information science and social scientific thinking and practice.

For almost three decades I have been reading and drawing upon the literature of the social and behavioral sciences, specifically sociology of science, science and technology studies (STS) and, more recently, the somewhat amorphous domain of social informatics. By way of illustration, many of the references in both my earliest and most recent books, *The Citation*

*Process* [3] and *The Hand of Science* [4], are to monographs and articles sourced from these and cognate fields. It strikes me as inconceivable that the issues which define the sub-fields of information science in which I primarily work – scholarly communication, citation analysis, scientometrics – could have evolved and matured to the extent they have without appropriating insights, both theoretical and methodological, from the social sciences, not least of which is sociology. That early paper in *JIS* is but one of many over the years in which I have tried, more or less systematically, to connect the literature of information science with the larger social scientific literature. To be sure, one aspiring boundary spanner does not a sociological spring make, but this anniversary does at least provide a convenient pretext to ask: 'Has there been a sociological turn in information science?'

In raising the question, or indeed presuming the answer as the title of this paper does, I am not suggesting that our interest in matters sociological is either powerfully dominant or exclusionary of other disciplines that could shape the conduct of enquiry in information science. Far from it: in fact, information science both imports from and exports to a wide range of intellectual trading partners; and, it would appear, is doing so with increasing intensity, as a recent large-scale, diachronic study suggests [5]. That should hardly come as a surprise, given that Irene Farkas-Conn concluded her chronicle of the field in North America [6, p. 210] as follows:

> The history of the American Society for Information Science follows the move from documentation to information science, an era of profound changes in the world, the development of information becoming a new body of knowledge, emerging from *several disciplines*. (Emphasis added.)

Information science, being as it is both relatively youthful and modest of size, routinely interacts with and draws liberally upon other subject fields for intellectual enrichment; it engages enthusiastically in, to use Julian Warner's terminology, 'exoteric and esoteric communication' [7] in an effort to achieve theoretical maturity. That need not be problematic or viewed as a negative, since, as Gernot Wersig noted some years ago, 'inter-conceptual work' [8, p. 214] is arguably a defining feature of any 'new/postmodern science' [8, p. 209].

The chunky concepts which make up our field's intellectual core (e.g. knowledge, information, communication, representation) are neither owned by information science nor likely to be assembled into an entirely credible canon without the judicious addition of perspectives and approaches taken from established disciplines such as computer science, linguistics, philosophy, psychology and sociology, as well as from newer fields such as cognitive science and human–computer interaction.

## A short history of the social in information science

Of course, I am far from being the only one, or even one of the first, to see the relevance of 'the social' to information science; or for that matter to its disciplinary ancestors: documentation and librarianship. Here are a few brief illustrations of early awareness within the field.

Chapter 2 of Pierce Butler's *An Introduction to Library Science* [9], first published in 1933, was entitled *The sociological problem*. In an essay reviewing the historical importance of Butler's short book (astonishingly, 20,000 copies were sold in paperback) I both acknowledged the influence of the University of Chicago's fabled school of sociology on his thinking and also suggested that we should see Butler's 'inchoate thoughts on societal knowledge, knowledge epistemology and social agency as a harbinger of social epistemology' [10, p. 185]. The term 'social epistemology' – now also the title of a journal edited, until recently, by the sociologist Steve Fuller – was coined and introduced into the literature of the field by Margaret Egan and Jesse Shera in the early 1950s [11], revisited recently by Jonathan Furner in *Library Trends* [12] and, more recently still, reviewed by Don Fallis in the pages of the *Annual Review of Information Science and Technology (ARIST)* [13].

In the 1970s, Norman Roberts outlined a cogent case for utilizing the social scientific approach in information science [14], a case subsequently elaborated by his University of Sheffield colleague, Tom Wilson, who, in his paper 'The sociological aspects of information science', asserts confidently and correctly that 'studies in this area range from all-embracing theories in the sociology of knowledge to small-scale studies of collaboration in the writing of scholarly papers' [15]. In the 1990s, Rob Kling emerged as a forceful advocate for social informatics, which he defined as 'the interdisciplinary study of the design, uses and consequences of information technologies that takes into account their interaction with institutional and cultural contexts' [16]. He made considerable use of symbolic interactionism as a means of understanding 'the social structure of the computing world' [17]. The socio-cultural dimensions of knowledge and the socially embedded nature of information and communication technologies (ICTs) are, and to some extent always have been, integral to the theory base of information science, an assertion that is easily confirmed by inspection of the published literature.

More generally, and over the course of several decades, information science has drawn upon the ample if scattered scholarly literature devoted to the so-called information society. Although the starting points and interpretative frameworks favored by different scholars and schools of thought in what is sometimes referred to as information society studies may vary, the common intent has been to turn the spotlight on the social dimensions and ramifications of informatization. It is not uncommon to see the work of sociologists such as Daniel Bell, Manuel Castells and Frank Webster cited in the pages of *JIS* and other leading information science journals, e.g. [18–20]. Large-scale social theorizing has enabled the field to better understand the complex interplay of technical factors and social forces that together drive developments in ICTs and also to avoid the pitfalls of parochialism and reductionism.

As so often, one is tempted to say that there is nothing new under the sun. The importance of socio-technical design was recognized more than half a century ago by the Tavistock Institute in London and the core precepts of Tavistock thinking were carried over into the realm of information systems design by the late Enid Mumford, whose pioneering work has continued to influence thinking in the fields of information systems, information science and social informatics [21]. Suffice it to say, 'the social' has long been part of our field, either implicitly or explicitly.

Talk of inter-concepts and interconnectivity is not mere words; the inter-dependence of disciplines can be demonstrated bibliometrically. Citation matrices and co-citation maps – techniques, it is worth noting in passing, that have been developed, refined and successfully exported by information science over the years – allow one to visualize the ideational interpenetration of fields; to see the intellectual trade routes that exist between discrete scholarly communities, e.g. [22–25].

## The linguistic turn

Disciplinary interdependence is also suggested discursively. Only the Rip van Winkles of the academy cannot have noticed the increasing frequency with which disciplines, from geography to information science, are said to have exhibited a 'turn' of one kind or another. A few examples should clarify what

I mean and also underscore the growing porosity of traditional disciplinary boundaries.

The original turn can probably be claimed by philosophy. The movement known as analytical philosophy – and here I am necessarily over-simplifying – broke with tradition by viewing philosophical problems as problems fundamentally and inherently to do with language. Meaning was constituted by language and thus the proper focus of philosophers should be ordinary language and everyday speech acts. The linguistic turn was inspired partly by Ludwig Wittgenstein's later work [26] (by way of an aside, he is much quoted in some sections of the literature of information science) and promoted by Oxford philosophers such as J.L. Austin [27] and Gilbert Ryle [28]. This *bouleversement* was not greeted warmly by grandees such as Bertrand Russell [29].

The linguistic turn, dismissed memorably by Ernest Gellner as 'Conspicuous Triviality' [30, p. 273] and indirectly by Samuel Beckett with the pithy 'Being is not syntactical' [31, p. 129], morphed into heavily French-flavoured structuralism. In university literature departments this resulted in an intensified focus on texts, intertextuality, reader response and, ultimately, the much-ballyhooed 'death of the author' [32]. Theory worship and ideological absolutism in turn triggered the toxic culture wars and the eventual dismantling of the ancien regime in its transatlantic ivory towers.

This particular sequence of events has been chronicled in elegiac fashion by Alvin Kernan, and here I quote from his book [33, p. 192], *In Plato's Cave*:

> The authors of the great works of literature were stripped of their literary property and reduced to the status of 'scriptors' who did not create their works but merely exploited the stock of ideas common to their languages and cultures.

Post-structuralism, new historicism, feminism, post-colonialism and the rest came to rule the academic roost. Once again the grandees harrumphed, but for every Harold Bloom doughtily defending aesthetic criticism and the Western canon (e.g. [34]) there was a congeries of theory fetishists promoting the latest 'ism'.

What happened in the humanities may not seem at first blush to be of great import for the world of classical Anglo-American information science, but critical theory – which I shall use as a portmanteau for all the 'isms' – has diffused in recent years from departments of literature and cultural studies to many other areas, including information studies. Though significantly social scientific in character, our field has a strong humanities tradition and not surprisingly the new thinking rapidly found adherents within those ranks. Even the intellectually conservative *Library Quarterly*, published by the prestigious University of Chicago Press, opened its pages to papers on postmodernity and post-positivist research methods in library and information science, e.g. [35]. I certainly do not mean to imply by any of the foregoing that postmodern theorizing and interpretative methods are incapable of sharpening our understanding of informational phenomena and discourses; well deployed they can promote much-needed analytic rigor and clarity of thought. Indeed, I commissioned a chapter for *ARIST* on post-structuralism, the first of its kind to appear in the venerable review since its inception almost four decades earlier [36], though I suspect its content and tenor remain anathema to the field's unreconstructed Popperians.

### 'To every season, turn, turn, turn' – The Byrds
Critical theory à la mode

Since the linguistic turn in its various manifestations, we have witnessed the advent of the cognitive turn (further over-simplification), a paradigmatic shift from a focus on linguistic acts to individual thought processes; from observable utterances to unobservable cognitions. The so-called cognitive turn was followed – though not in any strict linear sense – by the 'cultural turn', the 'practice turn' and the 'pragmatic turn', to name but three. Not all disciplines embrace each and every turn with comparable enthusiasm or at the same pace; tolerances and timelines seem to vary. One might be forgiven for assuming that a relatively minor (and, one might have thought, uncomplicated) academic field such as theatre studies would have been oblivious if not immune to both the linguistic and cognitive turns, but the evidence suggests otherwise, e.g. [37].

Sometimes the effects are dispiriting. Roger Kimball has exposed the pernicious influence of willfully obscurantist postmodern criticism on art historical scholarship in his spirited book, *The Rape of the Masters* [38]. Few corners of the academy have not succumbed to the lure of theory, sometimes for 'behavioral and scholarly reasons' [39, p. 420], sometimes for just one or the other. For a number of academia's less fashionable areas – and one is reminded here of George Stigler's [40, p. 171] description of information economics as 'a slum dwelling in the town of economics' –

theory is the engine of gentrification. Certainly, the importance of theory in the eyes of the academy's ruling elite has never been greater. Doctoral students and untenured faculty know all too well that theory fluency is a *conditio sine qua non* of career advancement. Nevertheless, there are occasional signs of jadedness; Tom Erickson's couplet, cited in Nardi [41, pp. 269–70], springs to mind:

> Theory weary, theory leery,
> Why can't I be theory cheery?'

Theory (and theory renewal) is important not only in the social sciences but also in the humanities, where, in the words of Louis Menand, the 'antifoundationalists were followed by the feminists and the postcolonialists and the multiculturalists' [42, p. 11]. The colorful parade to which he refers has, of course, included many other sects and splinter groups, all fiercely protective of their particular dogmas and distinctive dialects. The 'isms' may wax and wane, the disciplinary doxas may come and go, but for now the Age of Theory flourishes as never before in the academy – *pace* Terry Eagleton [43] and all those who would argue that we live in a post-theoretical world. Just as history did not end (see Fukuyama [44]), theory has not exhausted itself.

Information studies (a more expansive territory than information science) has proved to be an enthusiastic, if not always the most discriminating, adopter of vogue theoretical approaches, notably continental philosophy. The names of, for example, Baudrillard, Derrida, Foucault and Lacan, along with those of Hegel and Heidegger, are invoked as regularly as they are in the literatures of ostensibly unrelated fields. What Kingsley Amis [45, p. 377] called 'gimcrack theorizing' is at once the great elevator and great leveller.

The compendious *Theories of Information Behavior* [46], though cleverly conceived and well received, illustrates my general point. This multi-author compilation (in the interests of full disclosure, I should note that I supplied a pre-publication blurb) comes close to being *Information Theory for Dummies*. But there are many other options, many other publications in the now theory-rich literature of the field; for instance, Talja, Tuominen, and Savolainen [47] have produced a very thoughtful overview of some of the more fashionable 'isms' (collectivism, constructivism and constructionism) in information science. Their table (p. 82) depicting the main features, influences and representatives of these three Cs should be of considerable help to those unfamiliar with the 'isms' in question, confused as to the underlying differences, or simply curious to know where they are to be found in the literature of the field and with which authors they are typically associated. These are but two random examples of the growing body of work devoted to critical theory in information science and related areas.

## Other turns

Howard Rosenbaum has spoken of the 'user turn' in information studies, a conceptual refocusing of the field dating from the 1980s that few would contest, even though this particular phrase seems to lack traction [48, p. 429). Today, the qualifier 'user-centered' (or 'user-centric') has become a cliché. Gregory Downey [49, p. 685) for his part has expressed surprise that information studies has been slow to engage with what in the social sciences and humanities has been referred to as the 'spatial turn', which, for him, would entail the use of 'both familiar interpretative methods, such as ethnographic interviewing and theory-building and analytical concepts such as 'place', 'space', and 'scale'. Slow or not, parts of the information science community have in fact engaged with issues such as spatiality, hybrid space, physical presence and the social shaping of space, e.g. [50, 51]. More particularly, City University's long-established Department of Information Science has in recent years become an important locus for research and teaching in geographical information science (e.g. [52]). There is even a renaissance of sorts in the area of documentation studies, as evidenced by the series of conferences organized by the Document Academy and the appearance of a self-consciously entitled monograph, *A Document (Re)turn* [53].

## The physical paradigm and the cognitive turn

Taking the celebrated Cranfield experiments [54] of the 1960s as a starting point, David Ellis has shown how the 'physical paradigm' in information retrieval (IR) – with its emphasis on laboratory-based research into best match searching and weighted relevance feedback, an emphasis that was carried forward in the early 1990s with the launch of the highly successful Text REtrieval Conference (TREC) series [55] – firmly established itself in information science. Information retrieval is a core component of almost anyone's definition of information science, yet as Stephen Robertson – a self-confessed theorist – concedes, the IR field 'is not a very theoretical one' and lacks 'a capital-T Theory' [56, pp. 1, 8].

The dominance of traditional IR was challenged by the emerging 'cognitive paradigm' [57, p. 180], which sought to develop an understanding of the user's mental models and knowledge states with a view to constructing more effective retrieval systems, stressing agency, contexts and tasks as much as recall-precision ratios and other quantifiable performance measures. The jousting between the lab retrievalists and the cognitive camp had begun [58], though some optimistic souls maintain that 'user-oriented research has started to have an increased impact on the systems-oriented IR research and vice versa' [59, p. 956].

Among those most closely associated with the cognitive viewpoint were (and are) Nick Belkin, who coined the oft-quoted phrase 'anomalous states of knowledge' [60], and Peter Ingwersen who has argued in his aptly entitled book, *The Turn*, for a tighter coupling of research in IR and information seeking (IS); and also for greater attention to be paid to contextual understanding and situational awareness in systems development [61]. Although the Cranfield-TREC tradition (often associated with names such as Bookstein, Croft, Spärck Jones, Robertson and Willett) remains strong, the cognitive viewpoint has established itself within the information retrieval and seeking (IR&S) communities. It is not, however, without its detractors (e.g. [62]).

My potted account of IR is not inconsistent with the results of Howard White and Kate McCain's [63, p. 342] meticulous co-citation analysis of information science for the period 1972–95. Although experimental IR remains important, the authors conclude that 'the cognitive side of information science, which some retrievalists tend to ignore in favor of algorithms, has emerged during the 1980s and 1990s as a major enterprise'. The right-hand sides of Figures 2, 3 and 4 in their paper show the clustering of various sub-tribes of information retrievalists (experimental, practical, theoretical) over time. I have to say that their objective representation of the field matches my subjective sense.

## The social side of information science

The cognitive viewpoint's emphasis on the individual's knowledge state can cause us to lose sight of the epistemological significance of social relations and social structures. As I have noted elsewhere ([50, p. 1]:

The texts we write and the texts we cite bear the marks of the epistemic cultures, socio-cognitive networks and physical places to which we belong at the different stages of our professional lives.

Cognition is not an exclusively individual phenomenon nor is it readily amenable to scrutiny either inside or outside the lab; rather, it is multi-componential and interactive in character. We are, after all, social animals. Edwin Hutchins's book, *Cognition in the Wild* [64], is a good introduction to notions such as distributed and collective cognition and in that regard a welcome, in some respects commonsensical, antidote to the more extreme formulations of (cognitive) constructivism. There is, too, growing appreciation of the economic significance of distributed cognition; the revolutionary potential of 'open distributed innovation' [65, p. 238] is widely acknowledged in the business and innovation literatures.

Let me now illustrate the limitations of the cognitivist approach with reference to bibliometrics. Classical bibliometric/informetric studies (think of Bradford, Lotka, Zipf et al.) have described and analyzed a family of mathematical and statistical generalizations relating to the production, distribution and use of documents, words, etc. One might be forgiven for thinking that a Bradford distribution was a purely mathematical matter, untouched by 'the social' (on this subject, see Brookes [66]). That, though, would be to ignore the fact that individual authors select specific references, which are then aggregated and transformed into frequency distributions. It is reasonable to assume that these choices may have been influenced, to some measure, by extra-scientific factors such as collegial ties, collaborations, social networks or document availability issues. To what extent, then, to use Derek de Solla Price's memorable words, are these cited authors 'known to each other as warm bodies rather than labels on literature' [67, p. 4]? To what extent does the social intrude on the cognitive?

The fact that pre-existent social ties can shape authors' citation practices has given rise to the related notions of 'socio-bibliometric mapping' [68, p. 81] and 'socio-scientometrics' [50, p. 1]. As Alesia Zuccala has shown, invisible colleges have a social as well as a cognitive structure [69], a point that has received relatively little attention, historically, from bibliometricians and co-citationists. The potential for synergies between bibliometrics and the fast-growing field of social network analysis is clear, further evidence, I would argue, of the importance of social theory and related modelling techniques to the traditional concerns of quantitatively-inclined information science research. This kind of social constructivism highlights the interplay between knowledge structures and the wider environment, typically expressed as a continuous process of co-constitution. Knowledge is created in the world, socially constructed to use an over-used phrase; it is not something that is only created and contained sub-cranially.

In the fields of sociology of science and STS, social constructivism in various guises and strengths proved to be very popular during the 1980s, and some of the associated acronyms, such as SCOT (Social Construction of Technology) and ANT (Actor-network Theory), continue to be widely used within those literatures and also within the research literatures of social informatics and information science. Indeed, many of these domains' intellectual vanguard (e.g. Bijker, Bloor, Collins, Knorr-Cetina, Latour, Law, MacKenzie, Pinch, Woolgar) are cited routinely in the leading information science journals; regrettably, there is little citation in the reverse direction: information science listens, but is either not heard or heard and largely ignored by the aforementioned prime movers.

## From structural-functionalism to social constructivism

Social constructivists tend to take issue with grand narratives and the Great Man approach to history; they challenge the unquestioned authority of science and the automatic privileging of its truth claims. Instead, they focus on the contingent and socially negotiated nature of knowledge: relativism trumps absolutism; universalism cedes to localism. It need hardly be said that information scientists wedded to the scientific method have had little time for micro-sociology of the relativistic kind. Yet, it is not – or at least need not – be an either–or choice.

Perhaps the clearest and most thoughtful review of the topical connections between STS and information science is Nancy van House's compendious *ARIST* chapter [70] on the potential for symbiosis between the two fields. She makes the point that STS focuses on 'practice and the materiality of knowledge work' which provides 'an alternative to the mentalist approaches' prevalent in much of information science [70, p. 71]. This allusion to the 'practice turn', which I mentioned in passing above, is by no means an isolated example within the recent information science literature. Bernd Frohmann, for example, has written a fine book, *Deflating Information: From Science Studies to Documentation*, in which he argues for a 'shift of focus from cognitive to labour processes' in order to reveal scientific work as 'the construction of localized assemblages of things, persons, devices, and social relations' [71, p. 100] – a melange of the tangible and intangible, in other words.

Carole Palmer and Melissa Cragin's recent *ARIST* chapter is good on the practice turn in the social sciences generally and in information science in particular [72]. Coincidentally, the same volume of ARIST includes a useful chapter on activity theory and its potential relevance to information science by Tom Wilson [73] who quotes Bonnie Nardi [74, p. 7]:

> Activity theorists argue that consciousness is not a set of discrete disembodied cognitive acts [...] rather, consciousness is located in everyday practice: you are what you do.

Knowledge, *tout court*, emerges from practice; it is grounded in the material world. This is a very different take on events from that favored by proponents of the cognitivist approach.

Returning to the three co-citation maps of information science's top 100 authors produced by White and McCain [63, Figs. 2, 3, 4], one can see that quite a few of the most influential names in the field are 'outsiders', that is to say scholars whose primary disciplinary home is (or was) somewhere other than information science/information studies. Prominent outsiders for the 24-year period in question included Derek de Solla Price (history of science), Thomas Kuhn (history and philosophy of science), and Michael Moravcsik (theoretical physics), whose main contributions were made in literatures other than information science, but some of whose ideas nonetheless had a formative influence on the nascent field of information science. On the left-hand side of the White/McCain maps there is a small cluster of notable social scientists that includes Thomas Allen (management and organizational psychology), William Garvey (psychology), and the polymathic Herbert Simon (political science, psychology, cognitive science, economics). In their different yet complementary ways, all of these individuals helped fashion the intellectual foundations that have allowed information science to move well beyond the physical paradigm; they also stimulated early interest in the socio-psychological and behavioral aspects of information creation, transfer and use. An exemplary case in point was William Garvey and Belver Griffith's influential study of formal and informal modes of communication in psychology [75].

Also appearing on the left-hand side of the three White/McCain figures is a group of distinguished sociologists: Diana Crane, Daryl Chubin,

Jonathan Cole, Stephen Cole, Robert Merton and Harriet Zuckerman. The Cole brothers and Zuckerman were once students of Merton at Columbia University and together this quartet made notable contributions to the (pre-constructivist) sociology of science. One thinks in particular of their writings on the reward system in science, the bases of individual and institutional prestige in academia, the stratification of scholarly journals, and the structural and normative dimensions of scholarly production and communication.

And where do I feature on the White/McCain maps? Not with any of the aforementioned retrievalists, nor with the mathematical bibliometricians, such as Leo Egghe, but alongside the sociologists of science, which if nothing else provides empirical validation of my opening autobiographical remarks. The structural-functionalist accounts of science crafted by Merton and his followers have fallen out of popularity in recent years; social constructivists are typically averse to large abstractions and skeptical of, for instance, claims that the behavior of scientists, including their writing and citation practices, is normatively governed. Merton and his fellow institutional (and neo-institutional) theorists view science as a largely self-regulating social system, whose structures and collectively sanctioned norms shape, impel and constrain social actors. Such sweeping analyses are very different from the richly descriptive case studies, with their close-ups of 'the materialities of experimentation' (e.g. Rheinberger [76, p. 309]) which are beloved of social constructivists. Yet, all things considered, I remain sympathetic to Merton's [77, p. 276] view that there exists 'a distinctive pattern of institutional control of a wide range of motives which characterizes the behavior of scientists' and I am happy to live with the 'noble fiction' – Plato's idea of the useful lie – since the alternative to accepting that there are commonly held imperatives which guide the actions of scientists and scholars is rampant relativism and, ultimately, epistemological anarchy.

One of the behaviors being alluded to above by Merton is citation. Do we assume that citation practices are essentially whimsical in character because individual citers' motivations differ; that citations cannot be aggregated because the contexts and conditions under which individual authors select and cite the works of others are particularistic (see Moed, [78, p. 213–14] on this issue)? Or, do we line up behind Howard White [79, p. 90]?:

> Those who want to 'psychologize' citing as a way of undermining trust in the counts seem to over-rely on individual experience in a way typical of humanists, who tend to see universals in anecdotal particulars.

I think I know where I stand.

## Conclusion

Robert Merton, as it happens, was one of the sociologists identified by Howard Rosenbaum and Inna Kouper in their preliminary analysis of major sociological influences on information science [80]. They conducted a content analysis of all chapters in volumes 36–40 of *ARIST* – whose founding editor, by the way, was a social/behavioral scientist: Carlos Cuadra held a PhD in clinical/experimental psychology from the University of California at Berkeley – to determine which sociologists, both classical and contemporary, and also which sociological theories, had been imported into information science within the recent past. Among the most frequently cited names were Pierre Bourdieu (social and cultural capital), Manuel Castells (networked society), Harold Garfinkel (ethnomethodology), Anthony Giddens (structuration), Bruno Latour (Actor-Network theory) and Robert Merton (Matthew effect). These names and others of that ilk are not only to be found in *ARIST* – and not only for the five years covered by Rosenbaum and Kouper's survey – but also appear regularly in the pages of *JIS, JASIST* and other core information science journals. In some cases, the theories, methods and terminology associated with these eminences, a few of which I have listed parenthetically above, have become standard elements of our field's scholarly apparatus and professional discourse.

Impressionistically, and speaking as someone who is reasonably familiar with the information science canon, I would say that our field has long been mindful of, and indeed receptive to, sociological thinking. That being the case, it is probably misleading to speak of a 'sociological turn' as such. It is not clear that there was in fact a particular historical moment at which the field became somehow sociologically enlightened, or shifted gears paradigmatically as a result of concentrated exposure to insights from mainstream sociology, though some might cite the establishment in 1980 of the *Journal of Social Science Information Studies* (edited by Tom Wilson and Norman Roberts) as a significant milestone. In any case, perhaps I should have used 'social' instead of 'sociological' in the title of this paper and/or appended a question mark.

## Acknowledgments

I am grateful to both Howard Rosenbaum and Inna Kouper for sharing their preliminary findings and to HR for reading the draft manuscript. The comments of an anonymous referee are also appreciated.

## References

[1]    B. Cronin, Some reflections on citation habits in psychology, *Journal of Information Science* 2(6) (1980) 309–11.

[2]    A.J. Meadows, *Communication in Science* (Butterworths, Seven Oaks, 1974).

[3]    B. Cronin, *The Citation Process: the Role and Significance of Citations in Scientific Communication* (Taylor Graham, London, 1984).

[4]    B. Cronin, *The Hand of Science: Academic Writing and Its Rewards* (Scarecrow Press, Lanham, MD, 2005).

[5]    B. Cronin and L.I. Meho, The Shifting Balance of Intellectual Trade in Information Studies, *Journal of the American Society for Information Science and Technology* 59(4) 551–64.

[6]    I.S. Farkas-Conn, *From Documentation to Information Science: the Beginnings and Early Development of the American Documentation Institute – American Society for Information Science* (Greenwood Press, Westport, CO, 1990).

[7]    J. Warner, W(h)ither information science?/! *Library Quarterly*, 71(2) (2001) 243–55.

[8]    G. Wersig, Information science and theory: a weaver bird's perspective. In: P. Vakkari and B. Cronin (eds), *Conceptions of Library and Information Science: Historical, Empirical and Theoretical Perspectives* (Taylor Graham, London, 1992) 201–17.

[9]    P. Butler, *An Introduction to Library Science* (University of Chicago Press, Chicago, 1933).

[10]   B. Cronin, Pierce Butler's *An Introduction to Library Science*: a tract for our times? *Journal of Librarianship and Information Science* 36(4) (2004) 183–8.

[11]   M. Egan and J. Shera, Foundations of a theory of bibliography, *Library Quarterly* 22(2) (1952) 125–37.

[12]   J. Furner, 'A brilliant mind': Margaret Egan and social epistemology, *Library Trends* 52(4) (2004) 792–809.

[13]   D. Fallis, Social epistemology and information science, *Annual Review of Information Science and Technology* 40 (2006) 475–519.

[14]   N. Roberts, Social considerations towards a definition of information science, *Journal of Documentation* 32(4) (1976) 249–57.

[15]   T.D. Wilson, Sociological aspects of information science, *International Forum on Information and Documentation* 6(2) (1981) 13–18. Available at: http://informationr.net/tdw/publ/papers/socasp81.html (accessed 11 August 2007).

[16]   R. Kling, What is social informatics and why does it matter? *D-Lib Magazine* 5(1) (1999). Available at: www.dlib.org:80/dlib/january99/kling/01kling.html (accessed 11 August 2007).

[17]   A. Robbin and R. Day, *On Rob Kling: the Theoretical, the Methodological, and the Critical* (2006). Available at: https://scholarworks.iu.edu/dspace/bitstream/2022/183/1/Robbin-Day.pdf (accessed 11 August 2007).

[18]   D. Bell, *The Coming of Post-Industrial Society: a Venture in Social Forecasting* (Basic Books, New York, 1999).

[19]   M. Castells, *The Rise of the Network Society* 2nd edn (Blackwell, Oxford, 2000).

[20]   F. Webster, *Theories of the Information Society* 2nd edn (Routledge, London, 2002).

[21]   E. Mumford, *Systems Design: Ethical Tools for Ethical Change* (Macmillan, London, 1996).

[22]   C.L. Borgman and R.E. Rice, The convergence of information science and communication: a bibliometric analysis, *Journal of the American Society for Information Science* 43(6) (1992) 397–411.

[23]   P.G.W. Keen, MIS research: reference disciplines and a cumulative tradition. In: E.R. McLean (ed.), *First International Conference on Information Systems* (AIS, Philadelphia, 1980) 9–18.

[24]   A. Lockett and A. Williams, The balance of trade between disciplines: do we effectively manage knowledge? *Journal of Management Inquiry* 14(2) (2005) 139–50.

[25]   S. Miyamoto, N. Midorikawa and K. Nakayama, A view on studies on bibliometrics and related studies in Japan. In: C.L. Borgman (ed.), *Scholarly Communication and Bibliometrics* (Sage, Newbury Park, CA, 1990) 73–83.

[26]   L. Wittgenstein, *Philosophical Investigations* [translated by G.E.M. Anscombe] (Prentice Hall, London, 1999).

[27]   J.L. Austin, *How to Do Things with Words* (Harvard University Press, Cambridge, MA, 1975).

[28]   G. Ryle, *The Concept of Mind* (Hutchinson, London, 1949).

[29]   B. Russell, *Mysticism and Logic* (Routledge, London, 1949).

[30]   E. Gellner, *Words and Things* (Pelican, London, 1968).

[31]   J. Knowlson and E. Knowlson (eds), *Beckett Remembering, Remembering Beckett: a Centenary Celebration* (Arcade, New York, 2006).

[32]   R. Barthes, The death of the author, *Aspen* 5/6 (1967). Available at: www.ubu.com/aspen/aspen5and6/threeEssays.html#barthes (accessed 11 August 2007).

[33]   A. Kernan, *In Plato's Cave* (Yale University Press, New Haven, 1999).

[34]   H. Bloom, *The Western Canon: the Books and School of the Ages* (Harcourt Brace, New York, 1994).

[35]   G.P. Radford, Positivism, Foucault, and the fantasia of the library: conceptions of knowledge and the modern library experience, *Library Quarterly* 62(4) (1992) 408–24.

[36]   R.E. Day, Poststructuralism and information studies, *Annual Review of Information Science and Technology* 39 (2005) 575–609.

[37]   B. McConachie, Doing things with image schemas: the cognitive turn in theater studies and the problem of experience for historians, *Theatre Journal* 53(4) (2001) 569–94.

[38]   R. Kimball, *The Rape of the Masters: How Political Correctness Sabotages Art* (Encounter, New York, 2004).

[39]   I. Cornelius, Theorizing information for information science, *Annual Review of Information Science and Technology* 36 (2002) 393–425.

[40]   G. Stigler, The economics of information, *Journal of Political Economy* 69(3) (1961) 213–25.

[41]   B.A. Nardi, Coda and Response to Christine Halverson, *Computer Supported Cooperative Work* 11 (2002) 269–75.

[42]   L. Menand, Dangers within and without, *Profession* 8 (2005) 10–17.

[43]   T. Eagleton, *After Theory* (Basic Books, New York, 2005).

[44]   F. Fukuyama, The end of history? *National Interest* 16(Summer) (1989) 3–18.

[45]   Z. Leader, *The Life of Kingsley Amis* (Pantheon Books, New York, 2006).

[46]   K.E. Fisher, S. Erdelez and E.F. McKechnie (eds), *Theories of Information Behavior* (Information Today, Medford, NJ, 2005).

[47]   S. Talja, K. Tuominen, and R. Savolainen, 'Isms' in information science: constructivism, collectivism and constructionism, *Journal of Documentation* 61(1) (2005) 79–101.

[48]   H. Rosenbaum, The death of the user. In: *Proceedings of the 66th Annual Meeting of the American Society for Information Science* (Information Today, Medford, NJ, 2003). Presentation available at: www.slis.indiana.edu/hrosenba/www/Pres/asist_03/index.htm (accessed 11th August 2007).

[49]   G. Downey, Human geography and information studies, *Annual Review of Information Science and Technology* 41 (2007) 683–727.

[50]  B. Cronin, Warm bodies, cold facts: the embodiment and emplacement of knowledge claims. In: P. Ingwersen and B. Larsen (eds), *Proceedings of the 10th International Conference on Scientometrics and Informetrics* (Karolinska University Press, Stockholm, 2005) 1–12.

[51]  P. Turner and E. Davenport (eds), *Spaces, Spatiality and Technology* (Springer, Dordrecht, 2005).

[52]  J. Raper, J. Dykes, J. Wood, D. Mountain, A. Krause and D. Rhind, A framework for evaluating geographical information, *Journal of Information Science* 28(1) (2002) 39–50.

[53]  R. Skare, N.W. Lund and A. Vårheim (eds), *A Document (Re)Turn: Contributions from a Research Field in Transition* (Peter Lang, Frankfurt, 2007).

[54]  C.W. Cleverdon, J. Mills and E.M. Keen, *Factors Determining the Performance of Indexing Systems* (Aslib Cranfield Research Project, College of Aeronautics, Cranfield, 1966) [Volume 1: Design; Volume 2: Results].

[55]  D.K. Harman and E.M. Voorhees, TREC: an overview, *Annual Review of Information Science and Technology* 40 (2006) 113–55.

[56]  S. Robertson, Salton Award lecture: on theoretical argument in information retrieval, *ACM SIGIR Forum* 34(1) (2000) 1–10.

[57]  D. Ellis, Paradigms and proto-paradigms in information retrieval research. In: P. Vakkari and B. Cronin (eds), *Conceptions of Library and Information Science: Historical, Empirical and Theoretical Perspectives* (Taylor Graham, London, 1992) 165–86.

[58]  K. Järvelin, An analysis of two approaches to information retrieval: from frameworks to study designs. *Journal of the American Society for Information Science and Technology* 58(7) (2007) 971–86.

[59]  F. Åstrom, Changes in LIS research front: time-sliced cocitation analysis of LIS journal articles, *Journal of the American Society for Information Science and Technology* 58(7) (2007) 947–57.

[60]  N. Belkin, Anomalous states of knowledge as a basis for information retrieval, *Canadian Journal of Information Science* 5(May) (1980), 133–43.

[61]  P. Ingwersen and K. Järvelin, *The Turn: Integration of Information Seeking and Retrieval in Context* (Springer, Dordrecht, 2005).

[62]  B. Hjorland, *Information Seeking and Subject Representation: an Activity-Theoretical Approach to Information Science* (Greenwood Press, Westport, CT, 1997).

[63]  H.D. White and K.W.McCain, Visualizing a discipline: an author co-citation analysis of information science, 1972–95, *Journal of the American Society for Information Science* 49(4) 327–55.

[64]  E. Hutchins, *Cognition in the Wild* (MIT Press, Cambridge, Massachusetts, 1995).

[65]   E. von Hippel, Democratizing innovation: the evolving phenomenon of user
       innovation. In: B. Kahin and D. Foray (eds), *Advancing Knowledge and the Knowledge
       Economy* (MIT Press, Cambridge, MA, 2006) 237–55.

[66]   B.C. Brookes, Bradford's law and the bibliography of science, *Nature* 224 (1969)
       953–6.

[67]   D.J. de Solla Price, Citation measures of hard science, soft science, technology,
       and nonscience. In: C.E. Nelson and D.K. Pollock (eds), *Communication Among
       Scientists and Engineers* (Heath Lexington, Massachusetts, 1970) 3–22.

[68]   P. Mählck and O. Persson, Socio-bibliometric mapping of intra-departmental
       networks, *Scientometrics* 49(1) (2000) 81–91.

[69]   A. Zuccala, Modeling the invisible college, *Journal of the American Society for
       Information Science and Technology* 57(2) (2006) 152–68.

[70]   N. van House, Science and technology studies and information studies, *Annual
       Review of Information Science and Technology* 38 (2004) 3–86.

[71]   Frohmann, B., *Deflating Information: from Science Studies to Documentation* (Toronto
       University Press, Toronto, 2004).

[72]   C.L. Palmer and M.H. Cragin, Scholarship and disciplinary practices, *Annual
       Review of Information Science and Technology*, 43 (2008) (165–212).

[73]   T.D. Wilson, Activity theory and information seeking, *Annual Review of Information
       Science and Technology* 43 (2008) (in press).

[74]   B. Nardi, Activity theory and human-computer interaction. In: B. Nardi (ed.),
       *Context and Consciousness: Activity theory and Human-Computer Interaction* (MIT Press,
       Cambridge, MA, 1996) 8–16.

[75]   W.D. Garvey and B.C. Griffith, Communication and information processing
       within scientific disciplines: empirical findings for psychology, *Information Storage
       and Retrieval* 8(3) (1972) 123–36.

[76]   H.-J. Rheinberger, 'Discourses of circumstance': a note on the author in science.
       In: M. Biagioli and P. Gallison (eds), *Scientific Authorship: Credit and Intellectual
       Property in Science* (Routledge, New York, 2003) 309–23.

[77]   R.K. Merton, The normative structure of science. In: R.K. Merton, *The Sociology
       of Science: Theoretical and Empirical Investigations* (University of Chicago Press,
       Chicago, 1973) 267–278. [Edited and with an introduction by N.W. Storer]

[78]   H.F. Moed, *Citation Analysis in Research Evaluation* (Springer, Dordrecht, 2005).

[79]   H.D. White, Author co-citation analysis: overview and defense. In: C.L. Borgman
       (ed.), *Scholarly Communication and Bibliometrics* (Sage, Newbury Park, CA, 1990)
       84–106.

[80]   H. Rosenbaum and I. Kouper, *Borrowing from Sociology: a Study of the Importation of
       Theory into Information Science* (forthcoming).

# 7

# From chemical documentation to chemoinformatics:
# 50 years of chemical information science

PETER WILLETT

## Abstract

This paper summarizes the historical development of the discipline that is now called 'chemoinformatics'. It shows how this has evolved, principally as a result of technological developments in chemistry and biology during the past decade, from long-established techniques for the modelling and searching of chemical molecules. A total of 30 papers, the earliest dating back to 1957, are briefly summarized to highlight some of the key publications and to show the development of the discipline.

## Introduction

Chemistry is, and has been for many years, one of the most information-rich academic disciplines. The very first journal devoted to chemistry was *Chemisches Journal*, which was published 1778–84 and then, under the name of *Chemische Annalen*, till 1803 [1]. The growth in the chemical literature during the nineteenth century led to a recognition of the need for comprehensive abstracting and indexing services for the chemical sciences. The principal such service is Chemical Abstracts Service (CAS), which was established in 1907 and which acts as the central repository for the world's published chemical (and, increasingly, life-sciences) information. The size of this repository is impressive: at the end of its first year of operations, the CAS database contained *ca* 12,000 abstracts; by the end of 2006, this had grown to *ca* 25 million abstracts with *ca* 1 million being added each year. Most chemical publications will refer to one or more chemical substances. The structures of these substances form a vitally important part of the chemical literature, and one that distinguishes chemistry from many other disciplines. The CAS

Registry System was started in 1965 to provide access to substance information, initially registering just small organic and inorganic molecules but now also registering biological sequences [2]. At the end of 1965 there were ca 222,000 substances in the System; by the end of 2006 this had grown to *ca* 89 million substances, of which *ca* one-third were small molecules and the remainder biological sequences, with *ca* 1.5 million being added each year. There are also many additional molecular structures in public databases such as the Beilstein Database [3], and corporate files, in particular those of the major pharmaceutical, agrochemical and biotechnology companies.

The presence of chemical structures requires very different computational techniques from those used for processing conventional textual information. These specialized techniques – now referred to by the name of 'chemoinformatics' as discussed further below – have developed steadily over the 50 years that have passed since the founding of the Institute of Information Scientists in 1958. This paper provides an historical overview of the development of these techniques by highlighting some of the key papers that have been published over the years. The focus is on the representation and searching of small molecules; the reader is referred elsewhere for the processing of textual chemical information (e.g. [4–6]) and of biological sequence information (e.g. [7, 8]). Readers interested in the history of chemoinformatics are referred to Williams and Bowden's *Chronology of Chemical Information Science* [1], Metanomski's history of the Division of Chemical Information (formerly the Chemical Literature Group and then the Division of Chemical Literature) of the American Chemical Society [9], and Chen's recent historical review [10].

## Historical development of the field

The importance of chemical information was recognized in 1961 by the establishment of what has since become the core journal for the field, the *Journal of Chemical Documentation* (as it was then named) published by the American Chemical Society. The focus on the documentation of the literature is evidenced by the journal's title, and an inspection of early tables-of-content demonstrates the importance of the published literature and of manual, rather than computerized, information processing. Very soon, however, papers began to appear in the journal that focussed on the computer handling of structural information so that, for example, the first issue of Volume 2 contained articles describing the use of fragmentation-code and linear-notation systems based on punched card systems.

The 1960s and 1970s were a time of intensive research, with techniques being introduced that are, with appropriate development, still playing an important role in present-day systems. Examples include: the introduction of efficient algorithms for (sub)structure searching of databases of chemical molecules and for the indexing of databases of chemical reactions; the application of expert-systems technology to chemical problems; and the use of statistical correlation methods for the prediction of molecular properties (called QSAR for quantitative structure–activity relationships). The early 1970s saw the publication of the first two books devoted to the computer handling of chemical structure information. The first of these was that by Lynch et al., providing not just a snapshot of the current state-of-the-art but also summarizing much of his early research at the University of Sheffield into methods for searching molecules and reactions [11]. The second was the proceedings of a NATO Advanced Study Institute held in Noordwijkerhout in Holland and attended by all the key researchers of the time [12], with the published proceedings including contributions from what have proved to be the three longest-lived academic research groups in the field: the DARC group in Paris under Dubois; the group in Sheffield initially under Adamson and Lynch and more recently under Gillet and Willett; and the group under Gasteiger, initially in Munich and more recently at Erlangen–Nuremberg. Then, in 1975, there was published what became the standard text for the next decade, Ash and Hyde's *Chemical Information Systems* [13], with further books from the same lead-author and publisher appearing in 1985 [14] and then in 1991 [15]. The year 1975 also saw the first change of name of the core journal, with its new title – the *Journal of Chemical Information and Computer Sciences* – emphasizing the centrality of computerized techniques in the handling of chemical information.

The 1980s and early 1990s were – in part at least – developmental in nature, with much of the work building on techniques that had been introduced in the two previous decades. For example, similarity and generic searching methods were developed to complement structure and substructure searching, and the much enhanced computer technology of the time enabled the widespread implementation of operational systems, both public and in-house, for searching chemical databases. Perhaps the major enhancement was the move from two-dimensional (2D, i.e. the conventional chemical structure diagram) to three-dimensional (3D, i.e. full atomic coordinate information) representations of molecular structure. This move was spurred by the appearance of structure-generation programs that permitted the conversion of 2D structure databases to 3D form, the latter necessitating the extension of existing systems for 2D searching and structure–property correlation to encompass the increased dimensionality of the structure representation. Developments in this period are exemplified by the third issue of Volume 25 of the *Journal of Chemical Information and Computer Sciences*, which celebrated the silver anniversary of the founding of the journal, and the sixth issue of Volume 3 of *Tetrahedron Computer Methodology*, which contained the papers from the first major symposium on 3D structure handling to be held by the American Chemical Society. Noordwijkerhout has been mentioned already as the location of the 1973 NATO Advanced Study Institute: 1987 saw it being the venue for the first of what has proved to be a three-yearly International Conference on Chemical Structures [16]. This rapidly established itself as the principal conference in the field, with the next in the series to be held in June 2008. The other major international conference dedicated to chemoinformatics has been held in Sheffield, co-sponsored by the Chemical Structure Association Trust and the Molecular Graphics and Modelling Society, every three years since 1998, in the year preceding the Noordwijkerhout meeting.

The commercial importance of many chemicals has meant that industry – in particular the pharmaceutical industry – has long played a vitally important role in the development of chemical structure handling. The pharmaceutical industry is based on the synthesis of novel molecules that exhibit useful biological activities. Both the synthesis of molecules and the subsequent testing of these molecules for bioactivity underwent dramatic changes in the 1990s: taken together, the developments in these two areas resulted in significant increases in the volumes of data associated with pharmaceutical research programmes. Specifically, combinatorial chemistry provided the ability to synthesize not just one, but hundreds or even thousands of structurally related compounds at a time; and high-throughput screening provided the ability to test very small samples of these large numbers of molecules at a time. There was thus an explosion in the volumes of structural and biological data that needed to be assimilated and rationalized, and this resulted in the emergence of what has come to be called chemoinformatics to deal with these requirements [17]. To quote Brown (who first used the term):

The use of information technology and management has become a critical part of the drug discovery process. Chemoinformatics is the mixing of those information resources to transform data into information and information into knowledge for the intended purpose of making better decisions faster in the area of drug lead identification and optimization. [18]

This definition ties chemoinformatics very firmly to pharmaceutical research; whilst many of the techniques have their roots in that industry, they are of much broader applicability, as noted by Paris and quoted by Warr:

Chem(o)informatics is a generic term that encompasses the design, creation, organization, storage, management, retrieval, analysis, dissemination, visualization and use of chemical information. [19]

Note the use of 'chem(o)informatics' above, since there has been some discussion as to whether the term should be 'cheminformatics' or 'chemoinformatics' [17]: we shall use the latter form here. Finally, a particularly succinct definition is given by Gasteiger:

Chemoinformatics is the application of informatics methods to solve chemical problems. [20]

Chemoinformatics is not really new: instead, it is the integration of two previously separate aspects of chemical structure-handling. The group of researchers considered thus far had developed techniques to store, search and process the molecules in databases of chemical structures, so as to identify useful (in some sense) sets of compounds; a second, almost totally distinct group of researchers had for many years developed techniques to model and to correlate the structures of those molecules with biological properties, so as to enable the prediction of bioactivity in previously untested molecules [21–23]. At the risk of simplification, the former techniques were designed to handle the large numbers of molecules (hundreds of thousands or even millions) that would exist in a database; the latter techniques were designed to handle the few tens (or the few hundreds at most) of molecules for which the appropriate biological training data was available. Chemoinformatics is thus, at heart, a very specialized type of data mining, involving the analysis of chemical and biological information to support the discovery of new bioactive molecules [18, 20].

The recent emergence of chemoinformatics has been marked by the publication of several new books, and by a further change in the title of the core journal, which has been called the *Journal of Chemical Information and Modeling* since 2005. The new title makes clear the linkage between chemical information (the archival and repository functions of chemical information systems) and the modelling and prediction of biological activity (the QSAR functions of molecular modelling systems) noted above. The emergence is also evidenced by the appearance of specialist educational programmes in chemoinformatics. Skolnik suggested that four elements are needed to characterize a discipline: a body of active researchers; a forum for the interaction of these researchers; a journal for the presentation of leading-edge papers in the discipline; and roots in the educational structure [24]. The first three of these had been present for many years, but it was not till the start of this century that the fourth was achieved with the appearance of several masters-level programmes in chemoinformatics in higher-education institutions in Europe and in the USA: the need for these is discussed by Schofield et al. [25] while Wild and Wiggins provide a detailed review of current provision [26].

## Selection of key papers

This section reviews some of the most important papers in the development of chemoinformatic techniques. In each case, we briefly summarize the key paper, mention a few significant subsequent publications and give a recent review article (if available) to summarize the current status. More detailed accounts of all the topics considered here are provided in the textbooks by Leach and Gillet [27] and by Gasteiger and Engels [28], and in the extremely comprehensive *Handbook of Chemoinformatics* edited by Gasteiger [29]. As with any selection of key papers, the choice is inevitably biased by my own research interests and those of my colleagues, especially as I have spent my working life in an institution that has hosted for some four decades one of the most active research groups in the field [30, 31]: as Alexander Pope noted

> To observations which ourselves we make, we grow more partial for
> th'observer's sake.

Table 1 lists the papers that have been chosen for discussion, many of which will be very familiar to workers in the field. Others are less well known. In

**Table 1** Key papers in the development of chemoinformatics

1. Ray and Kirsch (1957) Substructure searching of connection tables [32]
2. Hansch et al. (1962) Correlation of bioactivity with physicochemical properties [46]
3. Vleduts (1963) Indexing of reactions and generation of synthetic pathways [33]
4. Free and Wilson (1964) Correlation of bioactivity with substituent contributions [43]
5. Morgan (1965) Canonicalisation of connection tables [47]
6. Sussenguth (1965) Set reduction technique for substructure searching [48]
7. Hyde et al. (1967) Conversion of WLNs to connection tables [49]
8. Corey and Wipke (1969) Interactive computer-aided synthesis design [50]
9. Crowe et al. (1970) Selection of dictionary-based screens [51]
10. Topliss and Costello (1972) Sample-feature ratios in QSAR [52]
11. Adamson and Bush (1973) Calculation of inter-molecular structural similarity [37]
12. Cramer et al. (1974) Correlation of bioactivity with substructural fragments [53]
13. Blair et al. (1974) Non-interactive computer-aided synthesis design [54]
14. Feldman and Hodes (1975) Selection of superimposed-coding screens [55]
15. Ullmann (1976) Efficient algorithm for substructure searching [56]
16. Gund (1977) Possibility of 3D substructure searching [57]
17. Lynch and Willett (1978) Indexing of chemical reactions [58]
18. Marshall et al. (1979) Active analogue approach for pharmacophore mapping [59]
19. Lynch et al. (1981) Representation and searching of Markush structures [34]
20. Kuntz et al. (1982) Protein–ligand docking [44]
21. Crandell and Smith (1983) Graph matching approach for pharmacophore mapping [35]
22. Jakes and Willett (1986) Selection of distance screens for 3D substructure searching [60]
23. Cramer et al. (1988) CoMFA method for 3D QSAR [42]
24. Danziger and Dean (1989) De novo molecular design [61]
25. Gasteiger et al. (1990) Generation of 3D atomic coordinates [62]
26. Johnson and Maggiora (1990) Similar property principle [63]
27. Martin et al. (1995) Computer selection of diverse molecules [64]
28. Brown and Martin (1996) Comparison of methods for compound selection [65]
29. Patterson et al. (1996) Neighbourhood behaviour [66]
30. Lipinski et al. (1997) Physicochemical properties of drug-like molecules [45]

some cases, this is because they are by now very old, such as the seminal – and I use the word advisedly – contributions by Ray and Kirsch [32] and by Vleduts [33] to the searching of molecules and of reactions, respectively. In other cases, the original work was over-shadowed by subsequent publications: for example, the 1981 paper by Lynch *et al.* [34] was merely the first in a sequence of over 20 publications on the representation and searching of generic structures; and the 1983 graph-matching paper by Crandell and Smith [35] resulted a decade later in the first successful commercial system for pharmacophore mapping [36] (see below). In still other cases, the importance of the work was simply not fully recognized at the time; e.g. the paper by Adamson and Bush [37] on comparing fragment bit-strings to compute molecular similarity preceded the first descriptions of similarity searching systems by over a decade [38, 39]. Indeed, it was this 1973 paper that was one of the principal drivers for work in Sheffield on fingerprint-based searching and clustering that commenced in the 1980s [40] and that continues to the present day [41]. Even with such less well-recognized papers included, the 30 selected papers in Table 1 had attracted a total of 7363 citations in the Web of Science by May 2007, with four of those in the drug discovery area [42–45] each receiving over 500 citations in the literature.

The focus here is on the computational techniques underlying operational systems, but there are at least two further ways in which we could chart the development of chemoinformatics. The first approach would be by reference to the major operational systems (which are, of course, based on the techniques considered here). Examples of such milestones include the appearance of: the batch [67] and then online [68, 69] implementations of the CAS Registry System; the NIH-EPA Structure and Nomenclature Search System (the first fully interactive structure and data retrieval system) [70]; ORAC [71] and REACCS [72] (the first in-house systems for storing and searching chemical reactions); and the Cambridge Structural Database [73] and the Protein Data Bank [74] (the two principal sources of experimental 3D coordinate data for organic molecules). The second approach would be by reference to the activities of those individuals responsible for the most important research findings. There is, however, a ready source of such information, this being the winners of the Herman Skolnik Award of the Division of Chemical Information of the American Chemical Society. The Division established this award in 1976 to recognize outstanding contributions to, and achievements in the theory and practice of, chemical information science. It is named in honour of the first recipient, Herman Skolnik (the editor of the *Journal of Chemical Documentation* and then the *Journal of Chemical Information and Computer Sciences* from 1961 to 1982), and the awardees (listed at http://acsinf.org/dbx/awards/skolnik.asp, together with links to supporting information) comprise many of the pioneers in the field.

We have identified five broad categories of technique to structure the discussion below, these being techniques for: searching databases of 2D molecules; searching databases of patents, reactions and 3D molecules; quantitative structure–activity relationships and molecular modelling;

knowledge-based systems; and diversity analysis and drug-likeness. It must be emphasized that these categories are rather arbitrary; for example, one could have separate sections for processing information about molecules and reactions, with the latter encompassing material about reaction databases and synthesis planning that are currently discussed in two separate sections (Sections 5 and 7, respectively). The reader should also note that the categories chosen here overlap to some considerable extent; e.g. pharmacophore mapping is discussed in Section 6, despite one of its main applications being for 3D database searching as discussed in Section 5.

## Searching databases of 2D molecules

Database search is one of the principal facilities in any information system, and much of the early research in chemoinformatics targeted the development of efficient access mechanisms for databases of 2D structures. The key paper here, and the earliest to be discussed in this review, is that by Ray and Kirsch [32]. These authors were the first to describe an automated procedure for *substructure searching*, i.e. the identification of those molecules in a file that contain a user-defined query substructure. The paper described the use of a 'connection table', a labelled graph representation in which the nodes and edges of a graph encode the atoms and bonds of a 2D chemical structure diagram, to describe each of a file of 200 steroid molecules, and then the use of a subgraph isomorphism algorithm based on an exhaustive, depth-first tree-search to analyse each molecule's connection table for the presence of a query substructure.

The connection table format was chosen for the CAS Registry System, which started operations in 1965 following several years of intensive research and development [75]. An important criterion in the development of the System was the need to provide a unique machine-readable identifier for each distinct molecule. The creation of a unique, or 'canonical', graph requires that the nodes of the graph are numbered, and for a graph containing $N$ nodes there are up to $N!$ possible sets of numberings. Drawing on ideas first presented by Gluck [76], Morgan [47] described an algorithm to impose a unique ordering on the nodes in a graph, and hence to generate a canonical connection table that could provide a unique molecular identifier for computer processing (in much the same way as systematic nomenclature uniquely describes a molecule in a printed subject index). With subsequent enhancements [77, 78], the Morgan algorithm continues to lie at the heart of the CAS Registry System (and also of many other chemoinformatics systems) right up to the present day.

The issue of the *Journal of Chemical Documentation* that contained Morgan's paper on graph canonicalization also contained the paper by Sussenguth describing his 'set reduction' algorithm. Ray and Kirsch's substructure search algorithm was certainly effective but was also extremely inefficient, requiring a huge amount of backtracking. Sussenguth [48] realized that much of the backtracking could be eliminated, and hence the number of atom-to-atom comparisons minimized, by partitioning a graph into sets of nodes that possessed common characteristics, e.g. nodes of type nitrogen linked to not more than two other nodes. Nodes from the graph describing the query substructure then need to be considered for matching only against those nodes from a database structure that possess the same characteristics. It is interesting to note that this work was carried out in collaboration with Gerard Salton, as part of his pioneering work on statistical methods for retrieval that laid the foundation for present-day information retrieval systems [79]. The idea of linking query nodes to database nodes is fundamental to all substructure searching algorithms, including the refinement procedure that lies at the heart of the subgraph isomorphism algorithm due to Ullmann [56]. Although not designed specifically for the processing of chemical graphs, subsequent studies showed that it was particularly well suited to these sorts of graphs [80, 81], and the Ullmann algorithm now forms the basis for most current substructure searching systems, both 2D and 3D.

However, even the use of set reduction was not sufficient to enable subgraph searching of chemical databases with acceptable response times, and it was only with the introduction of fragment-based screening methods that substructure searching became feasible on a large scale. The idea of screening is a simple one: to filter out that great fraction of the molecules in the search file that do not contain all of the substructural fragments that are contained in the query substructure (in much the same way as keywords are used to filter searches of text databases). This idea was first suggested by Ray and Kirsch, who experimented with a simple molecular-formula screen but who realized that more sophisticated approaches might be required for large-scale operations [32]. This is now normally done using a fragment 'bit-string', in which the presence or absence of small substructural fragments in a molecule is encoded in a binary vector. Two main approaches have been developed for selecting the fragments that are used for screening: *dictionary-based* approaches in which there is a pre-defined list of fragments with normally one fragment allocated to each position in the bit-string; and *fingerprint-based* approaches, where hashing algorithms are used to allocate multiple fragments to each bit-position.

Effective dictionary-based screening requires that the fragments encoded in the bit-string have been selected so as to maximize the degree of filtering. In particular, the best use will be made of the available bits if the selected fragments are statistically independent of each other and if they occur with intermediate frequencies of occurrence [82]: if the fragments occur very frequently in the database that is to be searched then their presence in a query will eliminate only a small fraction of the database; if the fragments occur very infrequently in the database that is to be searched then they are most unlikely to be specified in a query. The use of frequency criteria was first studied by Lynch et al. in a series of papers, commencing with a study by Crowe et al. [51] of the frequencies of occurrence of bond-centred fragments. Subsequent papers in this series considered atom- and ring-centred fragments, culminating in a prototype system [83] that strongly influenced the subsequent design of dictionary-based screening systems such as that used for the CAS Registry System [67, 68]. The screening methods developed by Feldman and Hodes at the National Institutes of Health do not make use of a dictionary of carefully selected fragments; instead, fragments are grown in an algorithmic fashion, one atom at a time, until they meet a frequency criterion, with a superimposed coding procedure being used to allocate multiple bits to each fragment and multiple fragments to each bit-position [55]. The fragments here are hence closely tuned to the specific database that is to be screened, and the methods have strongly influenced the design of subsequent fingerprint-based screening systems.

Substructure searching requires the availability of a substructural query, this in turn requiring detailed insights into the structural requirements for biological activity. A common alternative situation is when the only information available is the existence of a known active molecule, such as a literature compound or a competitor's product. Use can then be made of the *Similar Property Principle*, which states that molecules that have similar structures will have similar properties. It is not clear where this was first stated explicitly; many people (including the present author) have cited the 1990 book by Johnson and Maggiora [63] as the source but the principle had certainly been articulated prior to the book's publication in 1990. For example, writing in 1980, Wilkins and Randic [84] noted that it is

> generally accepted that molecules of similar structural form may be expected
> to show similar biological or pharmacophoric patterns [...]

and such considerations clearly underlie the 1973 paper by Adamson and Bush that is discussed further below. It is, however, appropriate to include the Johnson and Maggiora book [63] as one of the key contributions since it was the first publication to highlight the role played by similarity in a whole range of chemoinformatics applications, including database searching, property prediction, and computer-aided synthesis design inter alia. While there are many minor exceptions to the principle, there is now a considerable body of experimental evidence for its general correctness [40, 85–87]: the principle provides a rational basis for a wide range of applications in chemoinformatics, including not just similarity searching and molecular diversity analysis (both of which are discussed later in this paper) but also database clustering and property prediction inter alia.

In a similarity search, a known active molecule, often referred to as a 'reference' or 'target' structure, is compared with all of the molecules in a database; molecules that are structurally similar to the reference structure are more likely to be active than are molecules that have been selected at random from a database. A similarity search hence provides a simple way of identifying further compounds for testing, and is thus one example of the more general concept of 'virtual screening', i.e. the use of computational, rather than biological, methods to identify bioactive molecules [88–90]. At the heart of any similarity searching system is the measure that is used to quantify the degree of structural resemblance between the target structure and each of the structures in the database that is to be searched. There are many such measures but by far the most common are those obtained by comparing the fragment bit-strings that are used for 2D substructure searching, so that two molecules are judged as being similar if they have a large number of bits, and hence substructural fragments, in common. This approach was first described by Adamson and Bush for property prediction purposes [37]; over a decade was to pass, however, before bit-string similarities started to be used on a large scale for database searching, as exemplified by the first operational similarity searching systems at Lederle Laboratories [38] and Pfizer UK [39]. Similarity searching has now established itself as one of the most important tools for virtual screening, with widespread and continuing interest in the development of new similarity measures and search algorithms [91–93].

Thus far, we have considered only connection table records of 2D molecules. There is, however, an alternative type of representation that was very popular in the early days, at least in part since it had significantly lower processing costs at a time when computers were orders of magnitude slower than is the case today. This representation was the 'line notation', which encodes the topology of a molecule in an implicit form in an alphanumeric string, rather than explicitly as in a connection table. The Wiswesser Line Notation (WLN) system enjoyed widespread use for both in-house and public chemical information systems during the 1960s and early 1970s [13]. In 1967, Hyde et al. showed that it was possible to convert between WLN and a connection table [49], thus opening the way to providing full substructure searching capabilities on WLN-based systems, something that had previously been difficult to achieve with a high degree of effectiveness [94]. Although we have chosen normally to ignore systems papers, the paper by Hyde et al. is included here not just because of the relationship between linear notations and connection tables, but also because it (and two subsequent papers by this group [95, 96]) described CROSSBOW, probably the first fully integrated in-house chemoinformatics system that allowed for compound registration, substructure searching and, importantly, structure display. This work set a standard that has driven the development of in-house systems ever since. WLN is now of historical interest only, but two other line notations – the SMILES [97] and IUPAC International Chemical Identifier (InChI) (details available at www.iupac.org/inchi/) notations – are widely used today as convenient input and storage representations.

## Searching databases of reactions, patents and 3D molecules

Chemistry is as much about reactions as it is about molecules, but the development of databases of chemical reactions lagged behind the development of databases of chemical molecules for many years. The principal problem was the need to characterize not just the sets of reactant and product molecules, but also the 'reaction sites' (or 'reaction centres'), i.e. those parts of the reacting molecules where the substructural transformation takes place and which are the focus of many reaction queries. The key role of the reaction site in developing reaction database systems was first highlighted by Vleduts in an important 1963 paper [33]. This paper made three contributions: it suggested that the sites could be detected by comparing the connection tables of the reactant and product molecules to identify the structural commonalities and differences; it described a simple classification scheme based on bonds broken or formed that could be used to organize and to search a database of chemical reactions; and it considered the use of computers to suggest synthetic pathways (as discussed further in Section 7 below). Starting in 1967 [98], Lynch and collaborators studied a range of comparison methods for the mapping of reactant and product atoms, but some 10 years passed before an effective and efficient procedure for reaction-site detection was identified, based on a maximum common subgraph (MCS) isomorphism algorithm [58]. Lynch and Willett's original procedure used an approximate MCS algorithm that was based on an adaptation of the Morgan algorithm, but the operational systems that soon emerged (such as CASREACT [99] and REACCS [100]) used exact graph-matching procedures for reaction-site detection that, with appropriate development, are used to the present day [101].

Specialized techniques are also required for the handling of the structural information that occurs in chemical patents. In many cases, a patent will describe specific chemical molecules, but it may also describe 'generic', or 'Markush', structures, which encode many, or even an infinite number of, different specific molecules in a single representation. The individual specific molecules normally result from variations in the nature, position and frequency of substituents on a central ring system, or scaffold, with further complexities arising from, for example, a variable substituent itself being capable of variation. These complexities drove a long-term research programme by Lynch's group to develop the connection-table, screening and atom-by-atom components of conventional substructure searching systems so that they could be used to represent and to search Markush structures. The basic strategy is outlined by Lynch et al. [34], this being the first of over 20 papers that are summarized and reviewed by Lynch and Holliday [102]. These studies resulted in a body of algorithms and data structures that provided much of the theoretical and practical basis for the current sophisticated systems for structure-based access to generic chemical structures [103]. Many of the techniques that were developed on this project have found further application in the representation and searching of 'combinatorial libraries', large (and sometimes extremely large) sets of structurally related molecules that can be generated using the techniques of combinatorial synthesis [104] as discussed further in Section 8.

Thus far, we have considered only 2D molecular representations. However, the 3D structure of a molecule is of crucial importance in determining its properties, and it is thus hardly surprising that interest turned to the provision of facilities for 3D searching, often referred to as 'pharmacophore' searching where a pharmacophore is the geometric pattern of features in a drug that interacts with a biological receptor [105]. Pharmacophore searching was first described by Gund. His 1977 paper (there is an earlier, difficult-to-obtain report in the proceedings of a 1973 conference [106]) showed that the graph matching techniques that were by then well established for 2D substructure searching could be applied to 3D substructure searching using graphs in which the edges denoted inter-atomic distances, rather than bonds as in a conventional connection table [57]. However, there was little interest in this remarkable achievement for over a decade, because two problems had to be addressed before searching systems could be developed.

The first problem was the lack of data. The principal source of experimental atomic coordinate data for small molecules is the Cambridge Structural Database (CSD) produced by the Cambridge Crystallographic Data Centre [73,107], which started in 1964 and which now contains the 3D structures for *ca* 400,000 molecules. Although the database is a vital resource for drug research, it contains only a very small fraction of the molecules that might be of interest to a pharmaceutical company. Accurate 3D structures for many molecules can be obtained using computational techniques such as quantum mechanics, molecular dynamics and molecular modelling, but these are too time-consuming for large numbers of molecules. There was hence much interest in 1987 when two programs for 'structure generation' were reported. These could rapidly convert a 2D structure into a reasonably accurate 3D structure, thus opening up the possibility of converting chemical databases to 3D form. These two programs were CONCORD, developed by Pearlman and co-workers [108], and CORINA, developed by Gasteiger and co-workers [109]: despite many subsequent programs for structure generation [110], these two remain the principal sources of computed 3D structures to the present day. The two listed papers are both hard to get – one is in an informal newsletter and the other in a German conference proceedings – so the paper chosen for inclusion here is that by Gasteiger et al. in the 1990 issue of *Tetrahedron Computer Methodology* mentioned previously [62].

The second problem was that while Gund had demonstrated that 3D substructure searching was possible, the matching algorithm was far too slow for large-scale processing. We have noted that operational systems for 2D substructure searching only became feasible with algorithmic developments such as the use of set reduction and bit-string screening. In a series of papers, Willett and co-workers developed the basic algorithmic techniques necessary for efficient 3D substructure searching. In the first of these, they reported the development of a screening system in which the bit-strings encoded the distances between pairs of heavy atoms in a molecule as a distance range, these ranges being chosen using frequency-based methods analogous to those developed previously for selecting screens for 2D substructure searching [60]. Subsequent papers compared subgraph isomorphism algorithms that could be used for 3D substructure searching, and reported the first operational 3D searching system developed in collaboration with Pfizer UK; they then extended their techniques to take account of the fact that most molecules are not rigid but can, instead, exhibit some degree of flexibility owing to the existence of one or more rotatable bonds in a molecule. The work of the Sheffield group is summarized by Willett [111] and 3D substructure searching, both rigid and flexible, is now a standard facility for in-house chemoinformatics systems [105, 112].

There is a further type of 3D database search that is now one of the key components of systems for virtual screening: 'protein–ligand docking' or, more simply, docking. Docking assumes that a 3D structure has been obtained, typically by X-ray crystallography, of the biological receptor, such as the active site of an enzyme, that is involved in a biological pathway of interest. The 'lock-and-key' theory of drug action assumes that a drug fits into a biological receptor in much the same way as a key fits a lock; thus, if the shape of the lock is known, one can identify potential drugs by scanning a 3D database to find those molecules that have shapes that are complementary to the shape of the receptor. The original description of docking, by Kuntz et al. [44], considered the fitting of just a single molecule into a protein active site, with the molecule and the binding site being described by sets of spheres that were checked for a steric match. However, it was soon realized that if this fitting operation was repeated for all of the molecules in a database then docking could provide a highly sophisticated approach to virtual screening, with a database being ranked in order of decreasing goodness of fit with the active site (and hence in decreasing likelihood of activity). Developments in the basic technique involved matching not just geometric but also chemical characteristics of a molecule and a protein; however, the recent surge in interest in docking has come about as the result of systems that take account of the inherent flexibility of many small molecules, with docking systems such as GOLD [113] and FlexX [114] being used on a very large scale in industrial lead-discovery programmes. Rester [115] and Leach et al. [116] summarize the current state of the art, the latter in the preface to a special issue of *Journal of Medicinal Chemistry* that focusses on studies of protein–ligand docking.

## Quantitative structure–activity relationships and molecular modelling

Chemoinformatics is principally concerned with the lead-discovery and lead-optimization stages of drug discovery: finding one or more exemplars of a class of compounds that exhibits the bioactivity of interest; and then identifying those members of that class that possess the best combination of potency, synthetic feasibility, pharmacokinetic properties (e.g. solubility and metabolic stability) and minimal side-effects. Early studies of computational methods in drug discovery focussed on the second of these two stages, whilst modern work also contributes to the lead-discovery stage, most obviously by means of virtual screening as described previously.

The classical approach to quantitative structure–activity relationships (QSAR) is Hansch analysis. In a series of papers in the early 1960s, Hansch and his co-workers showed that it was possible to use multiple linear regression (MLR) to derive statistically significant correlations between the biological activities of sets of structural analogues and experimental or computed physicochemical parameters that describe the molecules' steric, electrostatic and hydrophobic properties; once the correlation has been obtained, the resulting equation can be used to predict the bioactivity of previously untested molecules. The first such paper was published in 1962 [46], with this being followed by several others that, taken together, provided an approach to lead optimization that has played a crucial role in the development of QSAR and that continues to be used to the present day [117, 118]. Many different physicochemical parameters have been used in Hansch analysis, but by the far the most common is the octanol–water partition coefficient, which has spurred the development of many different programs for the calculation of this important descriptor [119]. Just two years after Hansch's seminal paper, Free and Wilson published a further technique for lead optimization that was again based on MLR but that used structural, rather than physicochemical, variables in the analysis [43]. The basic idea is that the presence of a specific substituent at a specific position on a ring scaffold makes a constant and additive contribution to the overall activity of those molecules that contain it. These contributions are obtained using MLR, and then used to suggest new analogues for synthesis and testing.

The use of MLR to predict biological activities was rapidly adopted as a key tool for lead optimization. There is, however, a problem – common to many statistical and machine-learning methods – that is related to the 'sample-feature ratio', i.e. the ratio of the number of variables to the number of observations. Specifically, it is possible to derive seemingly strong correlations even if no meaningful correlation exists in practice when the value of this ratio is less than some threshold value, typically 5–10 being quoted in the literature. The importance of these statistical considerations was first demonstrated by Topliss and Costello [52] (see also [120]), who showed that seemingly good QSAR correlations could be obtained using random variables if sufficient of them were included in the predictive equation; indeed the crucial factor is the number of variables considered for inclusion (a number that is often greater than the number included in the final equation) [121, 122]. Such statistical considerations need to be taken into account whenever a new predictive tool becomes available, as evidenced by studies of the applications of neural networks to the prediction of biological activity [123]. Sample-feature ratios continue to be of importance given the very large numbers of descriptors that can now be generated for a molecule [124, 125], although techniques such as cross-validation and data scrambling can help to confirm the significance of potential structure–activity correlations [126, 127]. Other problems associated with the use of MLR for QSAR are discussed by Wold and Dunn [128].

A limitation of Free-Wilson analysis is the large number of analogues that need to be synthesized and tested if multiple substituent positions are allowed on the central scaffold, and this has restricted the use of the approach as originally described. However, the applicability of the method is significantly enhanced if the location-specific criterion is relaxed, and the biological activity is expressed merely in terms of the presence of a substituent (or, more generally, substructural fragment) rather than its location. Thus Adamson and co-workers correlated several biological and physical properties with the occurrences of fragments generated from connection tables or WLN using MLR (see e.g. [129, 130]), an approach that foreshadows the commercial HQSAR package [131]. However, the most important development of Free-Wilson analysis is probably 'substructural analysis', as first described by Cramer et al. in 1974 [53]. This used qualitative, i.e. active/inactive, biological data, and also allowed the analysis of large, structurally diverse datasets, thus enabling the analysis of the screening data that forms one of the principal components of lead-discovery programmes. Substructural analysis involves calculating a weight for each fragment (often denoted by a particular bit-location in a fingerprint) that is used to characterize the molecules in the training data, this weight being a function of the numbers of active and inactive molecules that contain this fragment [132]. A score is then obtained for a molecule of unknown activity by summing the weights for its constituent fragments. The resulting score represents the molecule's probability of activity, and untested molecules can hence be prioritized for screening in order of decreasing probability of activity; the anti-cancer screening programme that was carried out during the 1980s by the National Cancer Institute [133] is an important example of such an approach. Substructural analysis is important not just in its own right but also as the first example of machine learning being used on a large scale in chemoinformatics since, although not realized at the time [134], substructural analysis is an example of a naive Bayesian classifier, a machine-learning technique that is now widely used for the analysis of biological screening data [135].

The QSAR methods discussed thus far take no explicit account of the 3D structures of molecules, despite the fact that molecular size and shape are key factors in determining the interactions between a potential drug molecule and its biological receptor. The methods of computational chemistry – quantum mechanics, molecular dynamics and molecular modelling – provide effective tools for analysing the conformations that molecules can adopt in 3D space but, as noted previously, these can be very demanding of computational resources. Marshall et al. were the first to describe a conformational searching procedure that was sufficiently rapid in operation to investigate the shapes of sets of molecules such as those that might be encountered in a QSAR analysis [59]. With programs such as this, and then structure-generation procedures such as CONCORD and CORINA, it was not long before QSAR methods started to appear that sought to correlate bioactivity with the 3D structures of molecules. Two papers were published in 1988 describing the hypothetical active site lattice (HASL) approach of Doweyko [136] and the Comparative Molecular Field Analysis (CoMFA) approach of Cramer et al. [42]. The latter has been far more widely used, not least because it rapidly became available as a successful commercial product. A molecule in a CoMFA analysis is placed at the centre of a regular 3D grid, and the steric and electrostatic interaction energies between the molecule and a standard probe then computed at each point in the grid. The resulting sets of interaction energies for each molecule are then correlated with those molecules' bioactivities using not MLR but an alternative multivariate technique, partial least squares (PLS). PLS describes the variations in the bioactivity by means of latent variables that are linear combinations of the original variables, i.e. the grid-point interaction energies. The use of latent variables, rather than the original variables, makes analysis of the resulting correlation equations rather more difficult than in the case of MLR, but this is compensated for by the fact that PLS can handle datasets with very large numbers of variables, i.e. with sample-feature ratios that would preclude the use of MLR. This it does by means of a multiple-sampling technique known as cross-validation that ensures the statistical significance of the resulting predictive equations. There are several factors that need to be taken into account when carrying out a CoMFA analysis [137] but these have not prevented it becoming the method of choice for present-day QSAR [138].

Many of the techniques that are used in molecular modelling are too time-consuming for use in chemoinformatics applications, although this is starting to change [139]. There is, however, one such technique that has proved of considerable value, and that is the application of methods for conformational searching, i.e. a detailed exploration of the conformations that a molecule can adopt in 3D space, to the identification of 'pharmacophoric patterns', where a pharmacophoric pattern, or pharmacophore, is the geometric arrangement of features that is responsible for some particular type of bioactivity. A pharmacophoric pattern can be used both to rationalize the activities of molecules and to act as the query for a 3D substructure search to find new molecules that contain the pattern and that are hence also possible actives. The active analogue approach of Marshall et al. [59] was the first automated procedure for pharmacophore mapping. Given a set of molecules with a common biological activity, the low-energy conformational space of each of the molecules is explored to find a conformation (or conformations) that allows the chosen features (typically hydrogen-bond donors or acceptors, or the centres of aromatic rings) to appear in the same geometric arrangement in all of the molecules. The effectiveness of the approach was demonstrated by the identification of the pharmacophore common to a set of diverse angiotensin–converting enzyme (ACE) inhibitors [140], and its efficiency was later increased by means of an improved conformational searching algorithm [141].

The active analogue approach is widely used but does require the specification of the matching features prior to the conformational search, implying some knowledge of the protein–ligand interactions that are involved in the observed bioactivity. This limitation was first overcome in a study by Crandell and Smith [35], who described the use of an MCS algorithm to find 3D patterns common to sets of molecules. The work was carried out as an aid to structure elucidation (see below) but is also clearly applicable to the problem of pharmacophore mapping. The Crandell–Smith algorithm involves a breadth-first search and becomes very slow if multiple molecules are required. However, a detailed study of a range of algorithms for 3D MCS detection [142] demonstrated the general efficiency of the clique-detection algorithm of Bron and Kerbosch [143] for this application. An operational implementation of the Bron–Kerbosch algorithm by Martin et al. [36] resulted in DISCO, the first widely used program for pharmacophore mapping and a direct influence on the many such programs that are now available [105, 144].

## Knowledge-based systems

It may be argued that the term 'knowledge-based' is rather non-specific since any computer system must have at least some knowledge of the types of data that are to be processed and the results that are required. However, it is a term that has come to be applied to a class of systems that encode human expertise – either explicit or implicit – in machine-readable form to facilitate the solution of some problem, normally one that cannot be tackled efficiently by a conventional, deterministic computer program. Such systems, often referred to as 'expert systems', 'intelligent knowledge-based systems' or 'fifth-generation computer systems' were much to the fore during the 1980s and early 1990s; they are rather less prominent now, with many of the basic techniques that were developed then having been assimilated into more conventional types of computer system. Interestingly, much of the early work on expert systems was carried out in the field of structural chemistry, with three applications being of particular importance: computer-aided structure elucidation (CASE); computer-aided synthesis design (CASD); and 'de novo' design.

Structure elucidation is the task of identifying an unknown molecule given knowledge of its properties, which can be of any type although spectral properties have been the principal focus of work in CASE. There are two ways in which a computer can be used to assist the analyst when faced with an unknown molecule. The first, and simpler, approach is to carry out a database search, matching the spectrum of the unknown molecule with those available in an existing database; a complete or partial match can then suggest the identity or the principal substructural components of the unknown molecule [145, 146]. The second, expert-systems, approach derives from some of the very earliest work in the area of expert systems. This was the DENDRAL project at Stanford University for the analysis of mass spectra [147], which derived from work by Lederberg [148]. Given the mass spectrum and the molecular formula of the unknown molecule, the program would exhaustively generate all possible molecules satisfying these constraints. The spectrum of each generated molecule would be computed, and then compared with the source data, this process identifying further constraints that could be included in subsequent iterations of the generation cycle. The process continues until the unknown has been identified or until it is not possible to identify any further constraints. Although massively influential in the development of expert systems in general, DENDRAL was never as successful in practice as some of its proponents claimed [146]. However, the techniques that were developed for generating structures have proved to be of widespread applicability, and systems based on a range of types of spectral data (including not just mass spectra but also nuclear magnetic resonance and infra-red spectroscopy) are widely used [149], as are systems for searching databases of spectra [150–152].

Another application of expert systems to structural chemistry is the area of computer-aided synthesis design (CASD), as reviewed recently by Ott [153]. CASD was first suggested as a possible area of research in Vleduts' 1963 paper on automatic reaction indexing that has been mentioned in Section 5 above [33]. Given stored information about the most common reactions and the conditions under which they could be applied successfully, Vleduts suggested that a computer could be used to generate a sequence of reactions that would result in the generation of a user-specified synthetic target in acceptable yield. Descriptions of synthesis in the chemical literature move from the starting materials to the final products, even though a synthetic chemist will normally design the synthesis by starting with the final product and then working backwards until known starting materials are reached. This 'retrosynthetic' approach was the basis for the first published description of a CASD system: Corey and Wipke's OCSS (for Organic Chemical Simulation of Syntheses) program [50]. The retrosynthetic approach attracted much attention in the

1970s and 1980s, with programs such as LHASA [154] and SECS [155] undergoing extensive development, much of it in collaboration with industry who saw such programs as a complement to the work of their synthetic chemists [156]. However, it came to be realized that very large amounts of synthetic knowledge needed to be captured from the chemists and then encoded in machine-readable form before the programs could be expected to perform at a reasonable level of effectiveness [157]. Ugi and Gillespie [158] were the first to advocate an alternative approach in which the computer would take a set of starting materials and then generate synthetic pathways by the making and breaking of bonds. The program CICLOPS operated in a fully automated mode that was not constrained by the existing chemical knowledge, and that could thus generate all syntheses that were mathematically feasible [54], whereas retrosynthetic programs involve considerable interaction with the chemist running the program. Gasteiger and colleagues suggested that the effectiveness of CICLOPS and similar programs could be enhanced by the inclusion of chemical knowledge, in the shape of computed physical properties such as heats of formation and reaction enthalpies, that could be used to assess the feasibility of the suggested molecules [159]. The resulting EROS program has undergone extensive development over the years [160] and there is an associated program, called WODCA, for reaction prediction that uses both forward and backward planning [161]. An important component of any CASD program is a module to predict the synthetic feasibility of the molecules under consideration, and such procedures are now being used more generally in drug discovery programmes [162].

The final example of knowledge-based systems to be described here are the 'de novo' design programs, which produce novel molecules that possess specific properties, typically the ability to fit within the binding site of a biological target such as an enzyme. They can hence be regarded as complementary to the docking programs discussed in Section 5: docking identifies known molecules that are able to fit into the binding site, whereas de novo design generates unknown molecules with this ability. The approach was first described by Danziger and Dean [61], whose HSITE program identified those regions in a receptor that could form strong hydrogen-bonding interactions with a ligand, thus specifying geometric constraints that must be satisfied by potential ligands. A new molecule is then designed by placing appropriate molecular fragments – typically individual atoms or substructures chosen from a dictionary – into the binding site at locations that satisfy these constraints, and then by linking these fragments together to form a connected entity. Other programs soon followed; examples that continue to be widely used include LUDI [163], which includes one of the most widely used functions for estimating the energy of binding for a suggested molecule, and SPROUT [164], which includes both hydrogen-bonding and hydrophobic interactions in its scoring function. Most work on de novo design has focussed on molecules that will fit a binding site, but any type of constraint can be used, for example ranges of values for chemical and physical properties [165]. Schneider and Fechner review the current state of the art, and include several examples of the use of de novo programs in the design of bioactive molecules, while emphasizing that the principal role of such programs is to suggest novel structural types for further consideration rather than to provide fully fledged lead molecules [166].

## Diversity analysis and library design

The last area of research to be discussed here is also the most recent, being driven by the developments in combinatorial chemistry and high-throughput screening that took place in the early 1990s. These technological improvements meant that it was now possible to synthesize and to test vastly more molecules than had previously been the case. However, real-world experiments were still expensive and there was hence much interest in computational methods to ensure that those molecules that were put forward for testing could provide the maximum amount of information to support lead discovery in a cost-effective manner. This requirement led initially to work on maximizing the structural *diversity* (i.e. the level of dissimilarity) of the molecules that are submitted for biological testing, whilst minimizing the numbers of molecules that are tested. The Similar Property Principle discussed in Section 4 implies that structurally similar molecules are likely to exhibit the same bioactivity, and hence the synthesis of large numbers of structurally related molecules is unlikely to result in a commensurate amount of useful structure–activity data. Patterson et al. [66] postulated the related, but distinct, concept of 'Neighbourhood Behaviour', which states that structurally dissimilar molecules may give different biological responses. The maximum amount of structure–activity information that can be extracted from testing some fixed number of molecules (as determined by the testing capacity that is available) will thus be obtained by selecting a set of molecules that are as diverse as possible.

Structural diversity had long been recognized as an important factor in the selection of compounds for testing [167], but it was the vast libraries of compounds that became available as a consequence of combinatorial chemistry that focussed interest on computer techniques for diversity analysis. Two problems were of initial interest: selecting a set of molecules from those already available, either from a corporate database or from commercial suppliers; or selecting a set of molecules that could be obtained from an appropriately designed combinatorial synthesis. The basic problem of selecting the most-diverse subset of a set of available (or possible) molecules is a very simple one; however, it is also one that is computationally infeasible, as there are an astronomical number of subsets that can be chosen from a dataset of non-trivial size. A wide range of techniques was hence suggested for selecting diverse sets of molecules, whilst not being able to guarantee the identification of the optimally diverse subset. Examples of these techniques are described in detail in two books [168, 169] and a recent review [170], with Martin et al. providing an interesting overview of the early history of molecular diversity analysis [171]. We exemplify this work by two of the earliest, and most heavily cited, studies, those by Martin et al. [64] and by Brown and Martin [65].

Combinatorial synthesis operates by reacting together sets of reactant molecules in parallel to yield a set of products called a combinatorial library, e.g. sets of acids and sets of amines to yield a combinatorial library of amides. Martin et al. [64] described the use of similarity measures based on fingerprints and on computed properties to select diverse sets of reactants, with the expectation that this would yield a diverse set of products in the resulting combinatorial library. This approach was rapidly taken up, and there is now an extensive literature on the use of reactant-based selection to ensure diverse combinatorial libraries. Later work focussed on the diversity of the final library rather than of the input reactants, and demonstrated that such product-based approaches could yield more diverse libraries, albeit at the cost of increased computational complexity [172]. The paper by Brown and Martin [65] compared different types of clustering method and structural descriptor in terms of their ability to predict a range of types of property, and hence of their suitability for compound selection. The study is notable not only in terms of the very detailed comparisons that were carried out (and also in a second, related paper [173]) but also because it concluded that simple, 2D descriptors were at least as effective as more sophisticated 3D descriptors for database-scale operations such as compound selection. The latter, surprising result has been confirmed in several subsequent studies of compound selection, although it is probably the case that an appropriate level of 3D representation has yet to be identified, rather than that

3D representations are inherently less suitable for database-scale operations. It is also the case that much 3D information is implicit in the 2D structure of a molecule, especially if there are few rotatable bonds.

Initial studies of methods for diversity analysis focussed on the identification of sets of molecules that were structurally diverse, but it was soon realized that other factors also needed to be taken into account when selecting molecules for biological testing. For example, Gillet and co-workers have described the use of multiobjective optimization to ensure the design of libraries that are not only structurally diverse but that contain molecules whose physicochemical properties resemble those of known drugs [174]. There is widespread interest in such 'drug-likeness' (or 'drugability') studies, driven in large part by the 'Rule of Five' first suggested by Lipinski et al. [45]. Methods of combinatorial synthesis had been rapidly adopted by the pharmaceutical industry; however, whilst these had resulted in very large numbers of molecules, they had not resulted in significantly larger numbers of bioactive molecules than could be obtained using conventional synthetic methods. Lipinski et al. analysed over 2000 molecules that had entered phase II clinical trials (i.e. the phase in drug discovery where a potential drug is given to a small number of patients for initial studies of efficacy and side-effects) and observed that many of these obeyed simple physicochemical constraints that were simple multiples of five, e.g. the molecular weight should be less than 500 and the molecule should contain not more than five hydrogen-bond donor features. Molecules not satisfying these physicochemical constraints were likely to exhibit poor absorption or permeation, thus providing an obvious filtering mechanism for the selection of molecules and for the design of new combinatorial libraries. Subsequent studies have involved more detailed analyses of the physicochemical requirements for activity [175], the differences in properties between leads (i.e. molecules that are considered appropriate for detailed study in a drug-discovery programme) and drugs (i.e. molecules that get to the stage of being administered to patients) [176, 177], the use of machine-learning tools to differentiate between databases of drugs and (assumed) non-drugs [178–180], and the development of analogous techniques for the design of agrochemicals [181].

## Conclusions

In this paper, we have sought to highlight some of the major contributions to the historical development of chemoinformatics, although considerations of length inevitably mean that many other important papers have had to be omitted or merely mentioned in passing. However, it is hoped that this personal selection – however biased – is sufficient to make clear the intellectual debts that we owe to the early pioneers, many of whose techniques are still in widespread use many years after they were first published.

Chemoinformatics is, of course, continuing to develop, with three areas of particular importance for the next few years. The first, already mentioned, area is the use of machine-learning methods for virtual screening. Machine learning and data mining are subjects of intense research in computer science, with the resulting methodologies starting to be applied in very many application areas, including chemoinformatics. Thus techniques such as decision trees, kernel discrimination, and support vector machines have been rapidly adopted for chemoinformatics applications and this trend will undoubtedly continue as new techniques become available [182]. The second area is ADMET prediction (standing for absorption, distribution, metabolism, excretion and toxicity). Work in QSAR over many years has resulted in reasonably effective methods for the prediction of biological activity; the aim now is to extend these methods to enable the prediction of these more complex types of pharmacokinetic and biological properties. The work mentioned previously on drug-likeness can be regarded as a first step in this direction, with measures of drug-likeness representing an implicit codification of the pharmacokinetic properties required for a molecule to be not just bioactive but also potentially a drug; ADMET prediction studies try to model these properties explicitly [183]. The third area arises from the observation that QSAR uses computationally simple, but surprisingly effective, techniques to model the requirements for bioactivity. As noted previously, the emergence of chemoinformatics has been driven in large part by the scaling-up of these techniques, which had traditionally been aimed at just a few tens of molecules, to the very large datasets that characterize modern pharmaceutical research. Given the successes that have been achieved thus far, it seems not unreasonable to expect that further increases in effectiveness could be achieved by application of the sophisticated techniques of computational chemistry. These have traditionally been aimed at the detailed analysis of small numbers of molecules, but improvements in computer hardware and software mean that the methods are starting to be applied on a significantly larger scale than heretofore, as exemplified by the work of Beck et al. [139], and this trend can only increase further. In brief, we can expect the next 50 years to be at least as productive as the 50 years that have passed since the founding of the Institute of Information Scientists.

## Acknowledgements

I thank Val Gillet and Wendy Warr for their comments on this paper.

## References

[1]   R.V. Williams and M.E. Bowden, *Chronology of Chemical Information Science*. Available at: www.libsci.sc.edu/bob/chemnet/chchron.htm (accessed 12 November 2007).

[2]   D.W. Weisgerber, Chemical Abstracts Service Chemical Registry System: history, scope and impacts, *Journal of the American Society for Information Science* 48(4) (1997) 349–60.

[3]   S.R. Heller (ed.), *The Beilstein Online Database – Implementation, Content, and Retrieval* (American Chemical Society, Washington, DC, 1990).

[4]   R.T. Bottle and J.F.B. Rowland (eds), *Information Sources in Chemistry* (4th Edition) (Bowker-Saur, London, 1993).

[5]   R.E. Maizel, *How to Find Chemical Information* (3rd Edition) (Wiley, New York, 1998).

[6]   W.A. Warr and C. Suhr, *Chemical Information Management* (VCH, Weinheim, 1992).

[7]   C.A. Orengo, J.M. Thornton and D.Y. Jones (eds), *Bioinformatics* (Bios Scientific Publishers, Abingdon, 2002).

[8]   A.M. Lesk, *An Introduction to Bioinformatics* (2nd Edition) (Oxford University Press, Oxford, 2005).

[9]   W.V. Metanomski, *50 Years of Chemical Information in the American Chemical Society 1943–1993* (American Chemical Society, Washington, DC, 1993).

[10]  W.L. Chen, Chemoinformatics: past, present and future, *Journal of Chemical Information and Modeling* 46(6) (2006) 2230–55.

[11]  M.F. Lynch, J.M. Harrison, W.G. Town and J.E. Ash, *Computer Handling of Chemical Structure Information* (Macdonald, London, 1971).

[12]  W.T. Wipke, S. Heller, R. Feldmann and E. Hyde (eds), *Computer Representation and Manipulation of Chemical Information* (John Wiley, New York, 1974).

[13]  J.E. Ash and E. Hyde (eds), *Chemical Information Systems* (Ellis Horwood, Chichester, 1975).

[14]  J.E. Ash, P.A. Chubb, S.E. Ward, S.M. Welford and P. Willett (eds), *Communication, Storage and Retrieval of Chemical Information* (Ellis Horwood, Chichester, 1985).

[15] J.E. Ash, W.A. Warr and P. Willett (eds), *Chemical Structure Systems* (Ellis Horwood, Chichester, 1991).

[16] W.E. Warr (ed.), *Chemical Structures: The International Language of Chemistry* (Springer, Berlin, 1988).

[17] P. Willett, A bibliometric analysis of chemoinformatics, *Aslib Proceedings*, 60(2008), 4–17.

[18] F.K. Brown, Chemoinformatics: what is it and how does it impact drug discovery? *Annual Reports in Medicinal Chemistry* 33 (1998) 375–84.

[19] W.A. Warr, Balancing the needs of the recruiters and the aims of the educators (1999). Paper presented at the 218th American Chemical Society National Meeting, New Orleans, August 22–26, 1999. Available in part at: www.warr.com/warrzone2000.html (accessed 13 November 2007).

[20] J. Gasteiger, The central role of chemoinformatics, *Chemometrics and Intelligent Laboratory Systems* 82(1/2) (2006) 200–209.

[21] H. Kubinyi, QSAR and 3D QSAR in drug design: Part 1, *Drug Discovery Today* 2(11) (1997) 457–67.

[22] H. Kubinyi, QSAR and 3D QSAR in drug design: Part 2, *Drug Discovery Today* 2(12) (1997) 538–46.

[23] H. Kubinyi, From narcosis to hyperspace: the history of QSAR, *Quantitative Structure–Activity Relationships* 21(4) (2002) 348–56.

[24] H. Skolnik, The journal for chemical information and computer scientists: a 25-year perspective, *Journal of Chemical Information and Computer Sciences* 25(3) (1985) 137–40.

[25] H. Schofield, G. Wiggins and P. Willett, Recent developments in chemoinformatics education, *Drug Discovery Today* 6 (18) (2001) 931–4.

[26] D.J. Wild and G.D. Wiggins, Challenges for chemoinformatics education in drug discovery, *Drug Discovery Today* 11(9/10) (2006) 436–39.

[27] A.R. Leach and V.J. Gillet, *An Introduction to Chemoinformatics* (Kluwer, Dordrecht, 2003).

[28] J. Gasteiger and T. Engel (eds), *Chemoinformatics: A Textbook* (Wiley-VCH, Weinheim, 2003).

[29] J. Gasteiger (ed.), *Handbook of Chemoinformatics* (Wiley-VCH, Weinheim, 2003).

[30] M.F. Lynch and P. Willett, Information retrieval research in the Department of Information Studies, University of Sheffield: 1965–1985, *Journal of Information Science,* 13(4) (1987) 221–34.

[31] N. Bishop, V.J. Gillet, J.D. Holliday and P. Willett, Chemoinformatics research at the University of Sheffield: a history and citation analysis, *Journal of Information Science* 29(4) (2003) 249–67.

[32]  L.C. Ray and R.A. Kirsch, Finding chemical records by digital computers, *Science* 126(3278) (1957) 814–19.

[33]  G.E. Vleduts, Concerning one system of classification and codification of organic reactions, *Information Storage and Retrieval* 1(2/3) (1963) 117–46.

[34]  M.F. Lynch, J.M. Barnard and S.M. Welford, Computer storage and retrieval of generic chemical structures in patents, part 1: introduction and general strategy, *Journal of Chemical Information and Computer Sciences* 21(3) (1981) 148–50.

[35]  C.W. Crandell and D.H. Smith, Computer-assisted examination of compounds for common three-dimensional substructures, *Journal of Chemical Information and Computer Sciences* 23(4) (1983) 186–97.

[36]  Y.C. Martin, M.G. Bures, E.A. Danaher, J. Delazzer, I. Lico and P.A. Pavlik, A fast new approach to pharmacophore mapping and its application to dopaminergic and benzodiazepine agonists, *Journal of Computer-Aided Molecular Design* 7(1) (1993) 83–102.

[37]  G.W. Adamson and J.A. Bush, A method for the automatic classification of chemical structures, *Information Storage and Retrieval* 9(10) (1973) 561–8.

[38]  R.E. Carhart, D.H. Smith and R. Venkataraghavan, Atom pairs as molecular-features in structure activity studies – definition and applications, *Journal of Chemical Information and Computer Sciences* 25(2) (1985) 64–73.

[39]  P. Willett, V. Winterman and D. Bawden, Implementation of nearest-neighbour searching in an online chemical structure search system, *Journal of Chemical Information and Computer Sciences* 26(1) (1986) 36–41.

[40]  P. Willett, *Similarity and Clustering in Chemical Information Systems* (Research Studies Press, Letchworth, 1987).

[41]  P. Willett, Similarity-based virtual screening using 2D fingerprints, *Drug Discovery Today* 11(23/24) (2006) 1046–53.

[42]  R.D. Cramer, D.E. Patterson and J.D. Bunce, Comparative Molecular-Field Analysis (CoMFA), 1: effect of shape on binding of steroids to carrier proteins, *Journal of the American Chemical Society* 110(18) (1988) 5959–67.

[43]  S.M. Free and J.W. Wilson, A mathematical contribution to structure-activity studies, *Journal of Medicinal Chemistry* 7(4) (1964) 395–99.

[44]  I.D. Kuntz, J.M. Blaney, S.J. Oatley, R. Langridge and T.E. Ferrin, A geometric approach to macromolecule–ligand interactions, *Journal of Molecular Biology* 161(2) (1982) 269–88.

[45]  C.A. Lipinski, F. Lombardo, B.W. Dominy and P.J. Feeney, Experimental and computational approaches to estimate solubility and permeability in drug discovery and development settings, *Advanced Drug Delivery Reviews* 23(1) (1997) 3–25.

[46]    C. Hansch, P.P. Maloney, T. Fujita and R.M. Muir, Correlation of biological
        activity of phenoxyacetic acids with Hammett substituent constants and partition
        coefficients, *Nature* 194(4824) (1962) 178–80.

[47]    H. Morgan, The generation of a unique machine description for chemical
        structures – a technique developed at Chemical Abstracts Service, *Journal of
        Chemical Documentation* 5(2) (1965) 107–13.

[48]    E.H. Sussenguth, A graph-theoretic algorithm for matching chemical structures,
        *Journal of Chemical Documentation* 5(1) (1965) 36–43.

[49]    E. Hyde, F.W. Matthews, L.H. Thomson and W.J. Wiswesser, Conversion of
        Wiswesser notation to a connectivity matrix for organic compounds, *Journal of
        Chemical Documentation* 7(4) (1967) 200–204.

[50]    E.J. Corey and W.T. Wipke, Computer-assisted design of complex organic
        syntheses, *Science* 166(3902) (1969) 178–92.

[51]    J.E. Crowe, M.F. Lynch and W.G. Town, Analysis of structural characteristics of
        chemical compounds in a large computer-based file, I: non-cyclic fragments,
        *Journal of the Chemical Society (C)* (1970) 990–96.

[52]    J.G. Topliss and R.J. Costello, Chance correlations in structure-activity studies
        using multiple regression analysis, *Journal of Medicinal Chemistry* 15(2) (1972)
        1066–8.

[53]    R.D. Cramer, G. Redl and C.E. Berkoff, Substructural analysis: a novel approach
        to the problem of drug design, *Journal of Medicinal Chemistry* 17(5) (1974) 533–5.

[54]    J. Blair, J. Gasteiger, C. Gillespie, P.D. Gillespie and I. Ugi, Representation of the
        constitutional and stereochemical features of chemical systems in the computer-
        assisted design of syntheses, *Tetrahedron* 30(13) (1974) 1845–59.

[55]    A. Feldman and L. Hodes, An efficient design for chemical structure searching, I:
        the screens, *Journal of Chemical Information and Computer Sciences* 15(3) (1975)
        147–52.

[56]    J.R. Ullmann, An algorithm for subgraph isomorphism, *Journal of the ACM* 23(1)
        (1976) 31–42.

[57]    P. Gund, Three-dimensional pharmacophoric pattern searching, *Progress in
        Molecular and Subcellular Biology* 5 (1977) 117–43.

[58]    M.F. Lynch and P. Willett, The automatic detection of chemical reaction sites,
        *Journal of Chemical Information and Computer Sciences* 18(3) (1978) 154–9.

[59]    G.R. Marshall, C.D. Barry, H.E. Bosshard, R.A. Dammkoehler and D.A. Dunn,
        The conformational parameter in drug design: the active analogue approach in
        computer-assisted drug design. In: E.C. Olson and R.E. Christoffersen (eds),
        *Computer-Assisted Drug Design Vol. 112* (American Chemical Society, Washington
        DC, 1979).

[60]   S.E. Jakes and P. Willett, Pharmacophoric pattern-matching in files of 3-D chemical structures – selection of interatomic distance screens, *Journal of Molecular Graphics* 4(1) (1986) 12–20.

[61]   D.J. Danziger and P.M. Dean, Automated site-directed drug design: a general algorithm for knowledge acquisition about hydrogen-bonding regions at protein surfaces, *Proceedings of the Royal Society of London B* 236(1283) (1989) 101–13.

[62]   J. Gasteiger, C. Rudolph and J. Sadowski, Automatic generation of 3D atomic coordinates for organic molecules, *Tetrahedron Computer Methodology* 3 (1990) 537–47.

[63]   M.A. Johnson and G.M. Maggiora (eds), *Concepts and Applications of Molecular Similarity* (John Wiley, New York, 1990).

[64]   E.J. Martin, J.M. Blaney, M.A. Siani, D.C. Spellmeyer, A.K. Wong and W.H. Moos, Measuring diversity: experimental design of combinatorial libraries for drug discovery, *Journal of Medicinal Chemistry* 38(9) (1995) 1431–6.

[65]   R.D. Brown and Y.C. Martin, Use of structure-activity data to compare structure-based clustering methods and descriptors for use in compound selection, *Journal of Chemical Information and Computer Sciences* 36(3) (1996) 572–84.

[66]   D.E. Patterson, R.D. Cramer, A.M. Ferguson, R.D. Clark and L.E. Weinberger, Neighbourhood behaviour: a useful concept for validation of 'molecular diversity' descriptors, *Journal of Medicinal Chemistry* 39(16) (1996) 3049–59.

[67]   W. Graf, H.K. Kaindl, H. Kniess, B. Schmidt and R. Warszawski, Substructure retrieval by means of the BASIC Fragment Search Dictionary based on the Chemical Abstracts Service Chemical Registry III System, *Journal of Chemical Information and Computer Sciences* 19(1) (1979) 51–5.

[68]   P.G. Dittmar, N.A. Farmer, W. Fisanick, R.C. Haines and J. Mockus, The CAS ONLINE search system, I: general system design and selection, generation and use of search screens, *Journal of Chemical Information and Computer Sciences* 23(3) (1983) 93–102.

[69]   R. Attias, DARC substructure search system: a new approach to chemical information, *Journal of Chemical Information and Computer Sciences* 23(3) (1983) 102–8.

[70]   S.R. Heller, G.W.A. Milne and R.J. Feldmann, A computer-based chemical information system, *Science* 195(4275) (1977) 253–9.

[71]   A.P. Johnson, Computer aids to synthesis planning, *Chemistry in Britain* 21(1) (1985) 59–67.

[72]   W.T. Wipke, Exploring reactions with REACCS. In: Abstracts of the Papers of the American Chemical Society 188th Meeting (August 1984, Philadelphia) 43-CINF, (ACS, Washington, DC, 1984).

[73]   F.H. Allen, S. Bellard, M.D. Brice, B.A. Cartwright, A. Doubleday, H. Higgs, T. Hummelink, B.G. Hummelink-Peters, O. Kennard, W.D.S. Motherwell, J.R. Rogers and D.G. Watson, The Cambridge Crystallographic Data Centre: computer-based search, retrieval, analysis and display of information, *Acta Crystallographica B* 35 (1979) 2331–9.

[74]   F.C. Bernstein, T.F. Koetzle, G.J.B. Williams, E.F. Meyer, M.D. Brice, J.R. Rodgers, O. Kennard, T. Shimanouchi and M. Tasumi, The Protein Data Bank: a computer-based archival file for macromolecular structures, *Journal of Molecular Biology* 112 (1977) 535–42.

[75]   D.P. Leiter, H.L. Morgan and R.E. Stobaugh, Installation and operation of a registry for chemical compounds, *Journal of Chemical Documentation* 5(4) (1965) 238–42.

[76]   D.J. Gluck, A chemical structure storage and search system developed at DuPont, *Journal of Chemical Documentation* 5(1) (1965) 43–51.

[77]   W. Wipke and T. Dyott, Stereochemically unique naming algorithm, *Journal of the American Chemical Society* 96(15) (1974) 4825–34.

[78]   R. Freeland, S. Funk, L. O'Korn and G. Wilson, The Chemical Abstracts Service Chemical Registry System, II: augmented connectivity molecular formula, *Journal of Chemical Information and Computer Sciences* 19(2) (1979) 94–8.

[79]   G. Salton and E.H. Sussenguth, Some flexible information retrieval systems using structure matching procedures, *AFIPS Conference Proceedings, Spring Joint Computer Conference* 25 (1964) 587–97.

[80]   A.T. Brint and P. Willett, Pharmacophoric pattern matching in files of 3-D chemical structures: comparison of geometric searching algorithms, *Journal of Molecular Graphics* 5(1) (1987) 49–56.

[81]   G.M. Downs, M.F. Lynch, P. Willett, G.A. Manson and G.A. Wilson, Transputer implementations of chemical substructure searching algorithms, *Tetrahedron Computer Methodology* 1(3) (1988) 207–17.

[82]   L. Hodes, Selection of descriptors according to discrimination and redundancy – application to chemical-structure searching, *Journal of Chemical Information and Computer Sciences* 16(2) (1976) 88–93.

[83]   G.W. Adamson, J. Cowell, M.F. Lynch, A.H.W. McLure, W.G. Town and A.M. Yapp, Strategic considerations in the design of screening systems for substructure searches of chemical structure files, *Journal of Chemical Documentation* 13(3) (1973) 153–7.

[84]   C.L. Wilkins and M. Randic, A graph theoretical approach to structure–property and structure–activity correlation, *Theoretica Chimica Acta* 58(1) (1980) 45–68.

[85] Y.C. Martin, J.L. Kofron and L.M. Traphagen, Do structurally similar molecules have similar biological activities?, *Journal of Medicinal Chemistry* 45(19) (2002) 4350–58.

[86] R.P. Sheridan, B.P. Feuston, V.N. Maiorov and S.K. Kearsley, Similarity to molecules in the training set is a good discriminator for prediction accuracy in QSAR, *Journal of Chemical Information and Computer Sciences* 44(6) (2004) 1912–28.

[87] J. Bostrom, A. Hogner and S. Schmitt, Do structurally similar ligands bind in a similar fashion?, *Journal of Medicinal Chemistry* 49(23) (2006) 6716–25.

[88] H.-J. Böhm and G. Schneider (eds), *Virtual Screening for Bioactive Molecules* (Wiley-VCH, Weinheim, 2000).

[89] G. Klebe (ed.), *Virtual Screening: an Alternative or Complement to High Throughput Screening* (Kluwer, Dordrecht, 2000).

[90] J. Alvarez and B. Shoichet (eds), *Virtual Screening in Drug Discovery* (CRC Press, Boca Raton, 2005).

[91] P. Willett, J.M. Barnard and G.M. Downs, Chemical similarity searching, *Journal of Chemical Information and Computer Sciences* 38(6) (1998) 983–96.

[92] R.P. Sheridan and S.K. Kearsley, Why do we need so many chemical similarity search methods? *Drug Discovery Today* 7(17) (2002) 903–11.

[93] A. Bender and R.C. Glen, Molecular similarity: a key technique in molecular informatics, *Organic and Biomolecular Chemistry* 2(22) (2004) 3204–18.

[94] J.E. Crowe, P. Leggate, B.N. Rossiter and J.F.B. Rowland, The searching of Wiswesser line notations by means of a character-matching serial search, *Journal of Chemical Documentation* 13(2) (1973) 85–92.

[95] L.H. Thomson, E. Hyde and F.W. Matthews, Organic search and display using a connectivity matrix derived from Wiswesser notation, *Journal of Chemical Documentation* 7(4) (1967) 204–9.

[96] E. Hyde and L.H. Thomson, Structure display, *Journal of Chemical Documentation* 8(3) (1968) 138–46.

[97] D. Weininger, SMILES, a chemical language and information system, 1: introduction to methodology and encoding rules, *Journal of Chemical Information and Computer Sciences* 28(1) (1988) 31–6.

[98] J.E. Armitage and M.F. Lynch, Automatic detection of structural similarities among chemical compounds, *Journal of the Chemical Society (C)* (1967) 521–8.

[99] P.E. Blower and R.C. Dana, Creation of a chemical reaction database from the primary literature. In: P. Willett (ed.), *Modern Approaches to Chemical Reaction Searching*, (Gower, Aldershot, 1986).

[100] T.E. Moock, J.G. Nourse, D. Grier and W.D. Hounshell, The implementation of atom-atom mapping and related features in the Reaction Access System

(REACCS). In: W.A. Warr (ed.), *Chemical Structures: The International Language of Chemistry*, (Springer, Berlin, 1988).

[101] L. Chen, J.G. Nourse, B.D. Christie, B.A. Leland and D.L. Grier, Over 20 years of reaction access systems from MDL: a novel reaction substructure search algorithm, *Journal of Chemical Information and Computer Sciences* 42(5) (2002) 1296–1310.

[102] M.F. Lynch and J.D. Holliday, The Sheffield Generic Structures project: a retrospective review, *Journal of Chemical Information and Computer Sciences* 36(5) (1996) 930–36.

[103] A.H. Berks, Current state of the art of Markush topological search systems, *World Patent Information* 23(1) (2001) 5–13.

[104] G.M. Downs and J.M. Barnard, Techniques for generating descriptive fingerprints in combinatorial libraries, *Journal of Chemical Information and Computer Sciences* 37(1) (1997) 59–61.

[105] O. Güner (ed.), *Pharmacophore Perception, Development and Use in Drug Design* (International University Line, La Jolla, CA, 2000).

[106] P. Gund, W.T. Wipke and R. Langridge, Computer searching of a molecular structure file for pharmacophoric patterns. In: *International Conference on Computers in Chemical Research and Education* Vol. 3 (Elsevier, Amsterdam, 1974).

[107] F.H. Allen, The Cambridge Structural Database: a quarter of a million crystal structures and rising, *Acta Crystallographica Section B-Structural Science* 58(3 1) (2002) 380–88.

[108] R.S. Pearlman, Rapid generation of high quality approximate 3D molecular structures, *Chemical Design Automation News* 2 (1987) 1–7.

[109] C. Hiller and J. Gasteiger, Ein automatisierter Molekülbaukasten. In: J. Gasteiger (ed.), *Software-Entwicklung in der Chemie 1*, (Springer, Berlin, 1987).

[110] D.V.S. Green, Automated three-dimensional structure generation. In: Y.C. Martin and P. Willett (eds), *Designing Bioactive Molecules: Three-Dimensional Techniques and Applications*, (American Chemical Society, Washington DC, 1998).

[111] P. Willett, Searching for pharmacophoric patterns in databases of three-dimensional chemical structures, *Journal of Molecular Recognition* 8(5) (1995) 290–303.

[112] Y.C. Martin and P. Willett (eds), *Designing Bioactive Molecules: Three-Dimensional Techniques and Applications* (American Chemical Society, Washington, 1998).

[113] G. Jones, P. Willett and R.C. Glen, A genetic algorithm for flexible molecular overlay and pharmacophore elucidation, *Journal of Computer-Aided Molecular Design* 9(6) (1995) 532–49.

[114]  M. Rarey, B. Kramer, T. Lengauer and G. Klebe, A fast flexible docking method using an incremental construction algorithm, *Journal of Molecular Biology* 261(3) (1996) 470–89.

[115]  U. Rester, Dock around the clock – current status of small molecule docking and scoring, *QSAR & Combinatorial Science* 25(7) (2006) 605–15.

[116]  A.R. Leach, B.K. Shoichet and C.E. Peishoff, Prediction of protein–ligand interactions, docking and scoring: successes and gaps, *Journal of Medicinal Chemistry* 49(20) (2006) 5851–5.

[117]  Y.C. Martin, *Quantitative Drug Design: A Critical Introduction* (Marcel Dekker, New York, 1978).

[118]  C. Hansch and A. Leo, *Exploring QSAR: Fundamentals and Applications in Chemistry and Biology* (American Chemical Society, Washington, DC, 1995).

[119]  R. Mannhold and H. van de Waterbeemd, Substructure and whole molecule approaches for calculating log P, *Journal of Computer-Aided Molecular Design* 15(4) (2001) 337–54.

[120]  J.G. Topliss and R.P. Edwards, Chance factors in studies of quantitative structure–activity relationships, *Journal of Medicinal Chemistry* 22(10) (1979) 1238–44.

[121]  D.J. Livingstone and D.W. Salt, Judging the significance of multiple linear regression models, *Journal of Medicinal Chemistry* 48(3) (2005) 661–3.

[122]  D.W. Salt, S. Ajmani, R. Crichton and D.J. Livingstone, An improved approximation to the estimation of the critical F values in best subset regression, *Journal of Chemical Information and Modeling* 47(1) (2007) 143–9.

[123]  D.T. Manallack, D.D. Ellis and D.J. Livingstone, Analysis of linear and nonlinear QSAR data using neural networks, *Journal of Medicinal Chemistry* 37(22) (1994) 3758–67.

[124]  D.J. Livingstone, The characterisation of chemical structures using molecular properties, *Journal of Chemical Information and Computer Sciences* 40(2) (2000) 195–209.

[125]  R. Todeschini and V. Consonni, *Handbook of Molecular Descriptors* (Wiley-VCH, Weinheim, 2002).

[126]  A. Golbraikh and A. Tropsha, Beware of $q^2$!, *Journal of Molecular Graphics and Modelling* 20(4) (2002) 269–76.

[127]  D.M. Hawkins, The problem of overfitting, *Journal of Chemical Information and Computer Sciences* 44(1) (2004) 1–12.

[128]  S. Wold and W.J. Dunn, Multivariate quantitative structure–activity relationships (QSAR): conditions for their applicability, *Journal of Chemical Information and Computer Sciences* 23(1) (1983) 6–13.

[129] G.W. Adamson and J.A. Bush, A method for relating the structure and properties of chemical compounds, *Nature* 248 (1974) 406–7.

[130] G.W. Adamson and D. Bawden, A method of structure–activity correlation using Wiswesser Line Notation, *Journal of Chemical Information and Computer Sciences* 15(4) (1975) 215–20.

[131] W. Tong, D.R. Lowis, R. Perkins, Y. Chen, W.J. Welsh, D.W. Goddette, T.W. Heritage and D.M. Sheehan, Evaluation of quantitative structure–activity relationship methods for large-scale prediction of chemicals binding to the estrogen receptor, *Journal of Chemical Information and Computer Sciences* 38(4) (1998) 669–77.

[132] A. Ormerod, P. Willett and D. Bawden, Comparison of fragment weighting schemes for substructural analysis, *Quantitative Structure–Activity Relationships* 8(2) (1989) 115–29.

[133] L. Hodes, G.F. Hazard, R.I. Geran and S. Richman, A statistical-heuristic method for automated selection of drugs for screening, *Journal of Medicinal Chemistry* 20(4) (1977) 469–75.

[134] J. Hert, P. Willett, D.J. Wilton, P. Acklin, K. Azzaoui, E. Jacoby and A. Schuffenhauer, New methods for ligand-based virtual screening: use of data-fusion and machine-learning techniques to enhance the effectiveness of similarity searching, *Journal of Chemical Information and Computer Sciences* 46(2) (2006) 462–70.

[135] X. Xia, E.G. Maliski, P. Gallant and D. Rogers, Classification of kinase inhibitors using a Bayesian model, *Journal of Medicinal Chemistry* 47(18) (2004) 4463–70.

[136] A.M. Doweyko, The hypothetical active site lattice: an approach to modelling active sites from data on inhibitor molecules, *Journal of Medicinal Chemistry* 31(7) (1988) 1396–1406.

[137] H. Kubinyi, G. Folkers and Y.C. Martin (eds), *3D QSAR in Drug Design* (Kluwer/ESCOM, Leiden, 1998).

[138] R.D. Cramer and B. Wendt, Pushing the boundaries of 3D-QSAR, *Journal of Computer-Aided Molecular Design* 21(1/3) (2007) 23–32.

[139] B. Beck, A. Horn, J.E. Carpenter and T. Clark, Enhanced 3D-databases: a fully electrostatic database of AM1-optimized structures, *Journal of Chemical Information and Computer Sciences* 38(6) (1998) 1214–17.

[140] D. Mayer, C.B. Naylor, I. Motoc and G.R. Marshall, A unique geometry of the active site of angiotensin-converting enzyme consistent with structure–activity studies, *Journal of Computer-Aided Molecular Design* 1(1) (1987) 3–16.

[141] R.A. Dammkoehler, S.F. Karasek, E.F.B. Shands and G.R. Marshall, Constrained search of conformational hyperspace, *Journal of Computer-Aided Molecular Design* 3(1) (1989) 3–21.

[142]  A.T. Brint and P. Willett, Algorithms for the identification of three-dimensional maximal common substructures, *Journal of Chemical Information and Computer Sciences* 27(4) (1987) 152–8.

[143]  C. Bron and J. Kerbosch, Algorithm 457: finding all cliques of an undirected graph, *Communications of the ACM* 16(9) (1973) 575–7.

[144]  Y.C. Martin, Pharmacophore mapping. In: Y.C. Martin and P. Willett (eds), *Designing Bioactive Molecules: Three-Dimensional Techniques and Applications* (American Chemical Society, Washington, 1998).

[145]  N.A.B. Gray, *Computer Assisted Structure Elucidation* (John Wiley, New York, 1986).

[146]  N.A.B. Gray, Computer-aided structure elucidation. In: J.E. Ash et al. (eds), *Chemical Structure Systems*, (Ellis Horwood, Chichester, 1991).

[147]  R.K. Lindsay, B.G. Buchanan, E.A. Feigenbaum and J. Lederberg, *Applications of Artificial Intelligence for Organic Chemistry: the DENDRAL Project* (McGraw-Hill, New York, 1980).

[148]  J. Lederberg, Topological mapping of organic molecules, *Proceedings of the National Academy of Sciences, USA* 53(1) (1965) 134–9.

[149]  M.E. Munk, Computer-based structure determination: then and now, *Journal of Chemical Information and Computer Sciences* 38(6) (1998) 997–1009.

[150]  W. Bremser, HOSE: a novel substructure code, *Analytica Chimica Acta* 103 (1978) 355–65.

[151]  B.A. Jezl and D.L. Dalrymple, Computer program for the retrieval and assignment of chemical environments and shifts to facilitate interpretation of carbon-13 nuclear magnetic resonance spectra, *Analytical Chemistry* 47(2) (1975) 203–7.

[152]  W.A. Warr, Spectral databases, *Chemometrics and Intelligent Laboratory Systems* 10(3) (1991) 279–92.

[153]  M.A. Ott, Cheminformatics and organic chemistry: computer-assisted synthetic analysis. In: J.H. Noordik (ed.), *Cheminformatics Developments: History, Reviews and Current Research* (IOS Press, Amsterdam, 2004).

[154]  E.J. Corey, W.T. Wipke, R.D. Cramer and W.J. Howe, Computer-assisted synthetic analysis: facile man-machine communication of chemical structure by interactive computer graphics, *Journal of the American Chemical Society* 94(2) (1972) 421–31.

[155]  W.T. Wipke, G.I. Ouchi and S. Krishnan, Simulation and evaluation of chemical synthesis – SECS: an application of artificial intelligence techniques, *Artificial Intelligence* 11(1/2) (1978) 173–93.

[156]  W.T. Wipke and W.J. Howe (eds), *Computer Assisted Organic Synthesis* (American Chemical Society, Washington, 1977).

[157] F. Loftus, Computer-aided synthesis design; In: J.E. Ash et al. (eds), *Chemical Structure Systems* (Ellis Horwood, Chichester, 1991).

[158] I. Ugi and P.D. Gillespie, Matter preserving synthetic pathways and semi-empirical computer assisted planning of syntheses, *Angewandte Chemie International Edition* 10(12) (1971) 915–19.

[159] J. Gasteiger and C. Jochum, EROS: a computer program for generating sequences of reactions, *Topics in Current Chemistry* 74 (1978) 93–126.

[160] W.D. Ihlenfeldt and J. Gasteiger, Computer-assisted planning of organic syntheses: the second generation of programs, *Angewandte Chemie International Edition* 34(23/24) (1995) 2613–33.

[161] J. Gasteiger, W.D. Ihlenfeldt, P. Rose and R. Wanke, Computer-assisted prediction and synthesis design, *Analytica Chimica Acta* 235(1) (1990) 65–75.

[162] J.C. Baber and M. Feher, Predicting synthetic accessibility: application in drug discovery and development, *Mini Reviews in Medicinal Chemistry* 4(6) (2004) 681–92.

[163] H.-J. Böhm, The computer program LUDI: a new simple method for the de novo design of enzyme inhibitors, *Journal of Computer-Aided Molecular Design* 6(1) (1992) 61–78.

[164] V.J. Gillet, A.P. Johnson, P. Mata and S. Sike, Automated structure design in 3D, *Tetrahedron Computer Methodology* 3(6C) (1990) 681–96.

[165] R.C. Glen and A.W.R. Payne, A genetic algorithm for the automated generation of molecules with constraints, *Journal of Computer-Aided Molecular Design* 9(2) (1995) 181–202.

[166] G. Schneider and U. Fechner, Computer-based *de novo* design of drug-like molecules, *Nature Reviews Drug Discovery* 4(8) (2005) 649–63.

[167] P. Willett, V. Winterman and D. Bawden, Implementation of non-hierarchic cluster analysis methods in chemical information systems: selection of compounds for biological testing and clustering of substructure search output, *Journal of Chemical Information and Computer Sciences* 26(3) (1986) 109–18.

[168] P.M. Dean and R.A. Lewis (eds), *Molecular Diversity in Drug Design* (Kluwer, Amsterdam, 1999).

[169] A.K. Ghose and V.N. Viswanadhan (eds), *Combinatorial Library Design and Evaluation: Principles, Software Tools and Applications in Drug Discovery* (Marcel Dekker, New York, 2001).

[170] A.-D. Gorse, Diversity in medicinal chemistry space, *Current Topics in Medicinal Chemistry* 6(1) (2006) 3–18.

[171] Y.C. Martin, P. Willett, M. Lajiness, M. Johnson, G.M. Maggiora, E. Martin, M.G. Bures, J. Gasteiger, R.D. Cramer, R.S. Pearlman and J.S. Mason, Diverse

viewpoints on computational aspects of molecular diversity, *Journal of Combinatorial Chemistry* 3(3) (2001) 231–50.

[172] V.J. Gillet, P. Willett and J. Bradshaw, The effectiveness of reactant pools for generating structurally-diverse combinatorial libraries, *Journal of Chemical Information and Computer Sciences* 37(4) (1997) 731–40.

[173] R.D. Brown and Y.C. Martin, The information content of 2D and 3D structural descriptors relevant to ligand-receptor binding, *Journal of Chemical Information and Computer Sciences* 37(1) (1997) 1–9.

[174] V.J. Gillet, W. Khatib, P. Willett, P.J. Fleming and D.V.S. Green, Combinatorial library design using a multiobjective genetic algorithm, *Journal of Chemical Information and Computer Sciences* 42(2) (2002) 375–85.

[175] T.I. Oprea, Property distribution of drug-related chemical databases, *Journal of Computer-Aided Molecular Design* 14(3) (2000) 251–64.

[176] M.M. Hann, A.R. Leach and G. Harper, Molecular complexity and its impact on the probability of finding leads for drug discovery, *Journal of Chemical Information and Computer Sciences* 41(3) (2001) 856–64.

[177] T.I. Oprea, A.M. Davis, S.J. Teague and P.D. Leeson, Is there a difference between leads and drugs? A historical perspective, *Journal of Chemical Information and Computer Sciences* 41(5) (2001) 1308–15.

[178] Ajay, W.P. Walters and M.A. Murcko, Can we learn to distinguish between 'drug-like' and 'nondrug-like' molecules?, *Journal of Medicinal Chemistry* 41(18) (1998) 3314–24.

[179] J. Sadowski and H. Kubinyi, A scoring scheme for discriminating between drugs and nondrugs, *Journal of Medicinal Chemistry* 41(18) (1998) 3325–29.

[180] V.J. Gillet, P. Willett and J. Bradshaw, Identification of biological activity profiles using substructural analysis and genetic algorithms, *Journal of Chemical Information and Computer Sciences* 38(2) (1998) 165–79.

[181] E.D. Clarke and J.S. Delaney, Physical and molecular properties of agrochemicals: an analysis of screen inputs, hits, leads, and products, *Chimia* 57(11) (2003) 731–4.

[182] B.B. Goldman and W.P. Walters, Machine learning in computational chemistry, *Annual Reports in Computational Chemistry* 2 (2006) 127–40.

[183] D.E. Clark, Computational prediction of ADMET properties: recent developments and future changes, *Annual Reports in Computational Chemistry* 1 (2005) 133–51.

# 8

# Health informatics: current issues and challenges

PETER A. BATH

## Abstract

Health informatics concerns the use of information and information and communication technologies within healthcare. Health informatics and information science need to take account of the unique aspects of health and medicine. The development of information systems and electronic records within health needs to consider the information needs and behaviour of all users. The sensitivity of personal health data raises ethical concerns for developing electronic records. E-health initiatives must actively involve users in the design, development, implementation and evaluation, and information science can contribute to understanding the needs and behaviour of user groups. Health informatics could make an important contribution to the ageing society and to reducing the digital divide and health divides within society. There is a need for an appropriate evidence base within health informatics to support future developments, and to ensure health informatics reaches its potential to improve the health and well-being of patients and the public.

## Introduction

Health care is a complex and information-intensive process in which data concerning the health and medical conditions of individual patients are stored and used for clinical care and management. Additionally, data are aggregated for secondary purposes, such as the management of local health services, the monitoring and surveillance of diseases, and for planning the delivery of health services at regional, national and international levels. Within health care organizations, services and systems, large volumes of data are collected, stored, analysed, transferred, and accessed on a daily basis. In addition to data on individual patients, up-to-date information on how to prevent, diagnose, treat and manage diseases from research is being published and is required by healthcare professionals to provide effective and safe care for patients and the public. Health informatics is a relatively new field that has emerged in the last 20 years and has assumed a growing importance as a discipline. From a Donabedian perspective [1],[1] health informatics can be regarded as being concerned with the structures and processes, as well as the outcomes involved in the use of information and information and communications technologies (ICTs) within health. The term 'e-health' has been coined to describe the application of these technologies in health and medicine.

The aim of this paper is to review health informatics and to consider how information science can contribute to this field. The review commences by considering how health informatics, and the closely related areas of medical informatics and health information management, are defined. It discusses current developments in health informatics and particularly what it is about health and medicine that requires special consideration from an informatics perspective, as well as the contribution that informatics makes to health and medicine. It considers the implications of developments in health informatics and e-health for patients and healthcare professionals, and discusses the challenges faced within health informatics, as well as the opportunities health informatics has to offer in the twenty-first century.

## Defining health informatics and related areas

Despite numerous attempts to define informatics [3], medical informatics, health informatics and health information management, no widely accepted definitions exist for these areas [4, 5]. Related to these three areas are other specific fields, such as nursing informatics [6], dental informatics and primary care informatics [7], which consider informatics applications related to specific professions or health sectors. These can be considered sub-groups of health and/or medical informatics and whilst they are not considered in this review, they make an important contribution in health and medicine. The relationship between health and medical informatics, as well as with health information management, is less clear. Research and developments in information and the use of ICTs in health and medicine may fall into one of these areas or may overlap across two, or all three, areas. This relationship is represented in Figure 1.

Figure 1 illustrates the point that health informatics, medical informatics and health information management can be considered as three separate, but related, fields with overlap among them. Here they are first considered separately, before the overlaps between, and among, them are discussed. While there is no widely accepted definition of health informatics, in its broadest sense, it concerns how ICTs are used in the health sector. The overall aim of health informatics is to develop and improve the organization and management of information and thereby improve the overall quality of care for patients [8], and to this group should be added their families and carers, and the general public. Implicit in this aim is the need to consider health informatics developments from the perspectives of these groups, at an individual, group and societal level. In addition, the impact of ICT applications on health and information professionals and on the interaction between healthcare professionals and patients [9] requires consideration within health informatics.

Although medical informatics has no formal definition either, it can also be considered to include the use of information technology (IT), and to a lesser extent, ICT, to improve the care of patients. However, medical informatics is concerned with the use of information and computing technologies for specific

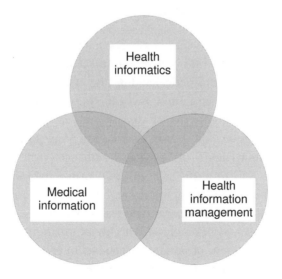

**Figure 1** Diagrammatic representation of the relationship between health informatics, medical informatics and health information management.

clinical applications in particular settings, for example storing medical images (e.g. [10]), decision support tools for patient management, architectures for electronic medical records (e.g. [11]), and data mining techniques for diagnosing clinical conditions (e.g. [12]) or predicting clinical outcomes (e.g. [13]). Research and developments within medical informatics focus more on the technical issues and pay less attention to the human and societal implications of these developments. The use of the term 'medical' in this name also implies a specific clinical focus and the involvement of clinicians/doctors, whereas the word 'health' in the other areas implies greater generality and the involvement of other health professions. This may have contributed to the rise of health informatics and health information management. Health information management is a relatively smaller area, and is more restricted conceptually, being concerned with how information is organized and managed within health, for example by patients or health professionals; or within a hospital, an organization, a service; or nationally (e.g. the level of health literacy within populations [14]; surveillance systems for public health).

The overlaps between, and among, medical and health informatics and health information management are represented by the intersections of the sets in Figure 1; they are extensive but, again, not readily defined. Specific medical informatics applications within a particular clinical setting may have implications for other aspects of a health service or organization or may consider the needs of patient, or other user groups. For example, Ma et al., in describing the Violet Technology (which prioritizes relevant information for diabetes patients), both specified the technical details and also considered how the information needs and preferences can be individualized for patients [15]. Medical informatics applications may also affect information management within an organization, e.g. understanding the effect of electronic medical records on how doctors manage and use health information [16]. Developing methods of identifying patterns of disease and deprivation is a medical informatics challenge (e.g. [17]), but also has important implications for the management of information within public health.

Developments and advances in health informatics may also improve the organization and management of information for healthcare and information professionals, health service managers and planners, as well as patients and the public, and so overlap conceptually with health information management. For example, the development of portals for patients to provide access to health information on the web has implications for the way in which people access and manage health information [18]. Information management strategies may be used to reduce problems associated with use of information systems within the health environment [4, 5], for example, to decrease dependency on paper-based systems and thereby reduce redundancy of information.

The intersection among all three areas may include those developments that have a specific medical application, but which have to be considered within the wider health context and have implications for information management. For example the development of electronic records may consider different electronic records architectures (medical informatics), their impact on the doctor–patient relationship (health informatics) and how data might be extracted for management purposes (health information management).

A citation search of the terms 'health informatics', 'medical informatics' and 'health information management' in article titles and topics in the Web of Knowledge demonstrates the relatively recent development of these fields. The results of this search are illustrated in Figure 2. The terms 'health informatics' and 'health information management' first appeared in the

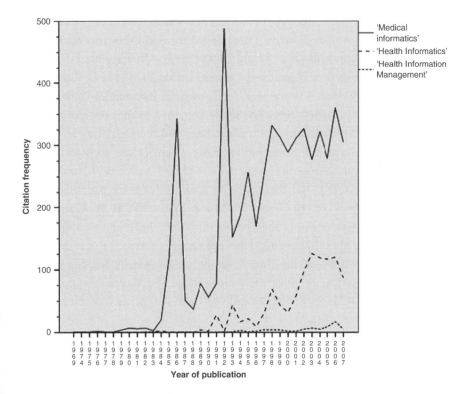

**Figure 2**  Line graph to show the frequency of articles including the terms 'health informatics', 'medical informatics' and 'health information management'. Source: Web of knowledge, 2008.

research literature in 1969 and the term 'medical informatics' first appeared in 1974. However, as shown in Figure 2, the term medical informatics rose to prominence in the mid-1980s, whereas it was not until the 1990s that 'health informatics' started to appear more frequently in the research literature, and even then it had not reached the levels of the term 'medical informatics'. The term 'health information management' started to appear more often at the start of the twenty-first century and it remains to be seen whether this term becomes more widely adopted.

Whilst it is helpful to highlight specific aspects of health and medical informatics and health information management, it must be emphasized that the distinctions and areas of overlap are not clear. This is evidenced in medical/health informatics/health information management and medical literatures, which all cover these areas: for example, the *Journal of the American Medical Informatics Association* (JAMIA) and the *International Journal of Medical Informatics* include papers that relate closely to health informatics, and the *Health Informatics Journal* publishes papers that overlap with medical informatics and health information management. This journal also publishes papers from the International Symposium for Health Information Management Research (ISHIMR), organized each year by the University of Sheffield in collaboration with other information science and health/medical informatics centres. The difficulty in the distinction between the three areas is further compounded by the limited professionalization within the field and the lack of a clear career structure. Some national organizations exist, such as the well established American Medical Informatics Association (AMIA) and Health Informatics New Zealand (HINZ), and these provide a forum for informaticians within the health services to discuss issues and share their work. Such organizations include the other areas within their remit, but while this inclusive approach is very positive, it makes the distinctions between these areas less clear. Having a sharp distinction between the three areas is not necessarily helpful, anyway, given that the purpose of all of these areas should be to improve the use of information and ICTs for the health and well-being of patients, their carers and families.

For the purposes of this review and more generally, I will use the following working definition of health informatics: health informatics is the use of information and ICTs to improve the quality of care and health and well-being of patients, their families and carers, and the general public. From a Donabedian viewpoint [1], this includes the *structures* (i.e. the information and the technologies, e.g. decision support tools, web-sites containing health information), the *processes* by which these technologies are developed, implemented and evaluated, and the *outcomes* of using information and ICTs within health (e.g. the impact on patient well-being and quality of life, user satisfaction). While this definition does not include health care professionals and managers, these are important in the overall process. Above all, the emphasis in health informatics should be on the ultimate benefit to patients and the public. This review concentrates on health informatics, i.e. the area within the bold circle in Figure 1, and pays less direct attention to pure medical informatics and/or health information management issues and developments.

## Information systems and electronic records

A major focus of activity in health informatics (and medical informatics/health information management) has been the development of information systems for medical and health care. During the last 10–20 years the focus has moved away from departmental or ward-based systems to institutional/hospital-based systems and on, to operate at a regional, national or global level [4, 5]. The earlier development of individualized systems that fulfilled specific functions for their unit resulted in legacy systems that successfully met the objectives of that unit but were unable to exchange or transfer data to other parts of the service or organization due to incompatibility [19]. The increasing realization that this exchange of information is important, if not vital, for continuity of care and multidisciplinary care of patients has been a major driver for the development of organization- or service-wide systems. However, this transition has not been without problems and there are notable examples of huge financial investments in IT systems in health care that have been wasted. Systems developers have been faced with the choice of either developing systems to integrate existing legacy systems, or of developing completely new systems that meet the needs of all parts of an organization. Integrating existing systems has proved problematic and developing new systems has to overcome obstacles to incorporating previous data from a variety of systems. This has been compounded by mixtures of paper-based systems and electronic systems [4, 5] resulting in continuing problems of data redundancy and duplication of data collection and information storage. Further problems occur when integrating systems developed for, or in, different geographical locations, or that use different operating systems.

A further change in recent years in the development of information and communication systems has been the move to patient-centred systems away from systems that collect data for management purposes. The problem with systems developed for collecting management data is that clinical staff perceive little benefit for patient care, and are reluctant to add data and to use systems for which they feel there is little purpose. The UK White Paper, *Information for Health* [19], presented an information management and technology (IM&T) strategy for the National Health Service and two key principles underlying this strategy were that systems should be person-based and that management data should be collected from these operational systems. Although the implementation of the IT strategy was beset with problems and difficulties [20], and the strategy has since been replaced by the National Programme for IT (NPfIT), the movement towards a national patient-based system has continued.

The issues in developing electronic records for patient care help to illustrate the complexity of health information and issues faced within health informatics. The volume and range of information collected within a single episode of health care for an individual patient can be large. The required information can include textual, numeric, high resolution image and complex signal data [4,5] collected by different health professionals, including doctors, nurses, radiologists, pathologists and physiotherapists. These data record the personal details and medical history, symptoms and clinical measurements, diagnosis and prognosis, and treatment of the patient. An additional level of complexity is that health professionals are used to recording their observations as free text and using annotated diagrams; incorporating such data into an electronic format is not straightforward [21]. These data may be collected and may be required in different locations, e.g. in an Emergency Department, on a hospital ward, within a radiology department, or in the home; and appropriate devices need to be available for entering and accessing these data. These requirements must be considered in developing electronic records. The parallel development of new technologies, for example personal computers and laptops, increased computer disk storage, mobile telephony, wireless networks, PDAs, satellite television, has facilitated the development of electronic records and helped overcome some of the challenges outlined here. The technology requirements themselves are not the limiting factor in the development of electronic records; rather it is the human, managerial and organizational issues that are key to the successful integration of electronic records into health care. A lack of consideration of these types of issues has been a significant factor in the failure of past systems.

The movement towards integrated and patient-centred electronic records and information systems will have a major impact on the way that healthcare professionals and service managers utilize information and information systems within health and will transform the way health care is delivered. Whilst data may be collected within a single patient episode, they need to be combined with information collected at previous stages in the patient's life, and this has led to the development of lifelong electronic health records [20]. Berner and Moss [22] described the very real possibility that all the necessary clinical data and information will become available to healthcare professionals for treating individual patients whenever and wherever they are needed. However, a critical factor in the future success of electronic records and information systems is ensuring that the health professionals and patients are involved in the research, design and evaluation of these developments. Health informatics, and more broadly, information science can play an important role in consideration of the information needs of these groups and how they seek, obtain and use information for health care.

## Information needs and use within health care

As indicated in the previous section, an important area for consideration in the overlap between health informatics and health information management is information needs and information behaviour in the context of health. Whilst user-based studies of information needs and behaviour might once have been considered pure health information management, or information science, the development of the web and of Web 2.0 technologies has stimulated interest in understanding how ICTs might be used to benefit patients and the general public, as well as health professionals, by providing support and help, education and information [8].

Research in information science and the development of different models of information behaviour (e.g. by Dervin, Wilson, Ellis, Kuhltau and Savolainen among others, reviewed in [23]) have developed a better understanding of people's information seeking in a variety of contexts. Research in the health, medical and social sciences includes a large number of studies, which have identified information needs of patients, family members and carers for numerous conditions, as well as for the general public, in order to develop interventions, e.g. patient information leaflets, and web-sites to improve information provision for particular groups.

An important conclusion from this body of research is that information needs are not necessarily the same within a particular group, and that one size does not fit all: the information needs of individuals must be considered when designing information interventions and providing information. For example, the acquisition of information is not always beneficial and there are circumstances in which individuals may avoid information [24–26]. This is particularly true in health and medicine when information needs and behaviour can change during the patient pathway. For example, at the time of diagnosis, when patients are coming to terms with a diagnosis, they may want little or no information about their condition [27], but this may change once they have adapted to their situation, when they may need information on treatment options, prognosis, etc.

Although a large volume of research has been undertaken on information behaviours in general and on information needs for particular patient groups or conditions, there has been relatively little research that has explored the applicability of established information behaviour models in the context of health care. For example, Williams et al. used Dervin's sense-making framework to examine information behaviour among women visiting their family doctor [28], and Beverley et al. examined Wilson's model of information seeking in relation to people with a visual impairment [29]. The numbers of these studies are limited and there is a need to examine how well these and other models of information behaviour can be applied to groups of patients, their families and carers and the general public [26]. There is also a need to increase awareness of models of information behaviour within health and health care. While these models are very well known within information science, they are relatively unknown among health care professionals and health researchers: increasing awareness of these models may help to develop better information-related interventions.

In addition, a growing body of research has reported the information needs of healthcare professionals, for example, doctors (e.g. [30, 31]), general practitioners and family doctors [32, 33], and nurses (e.g. [34–36]). As in knowledge management there is an understanding that there is both implicit and explicit knowledge within organizations, and recently there has been an interest in implicit and explicit information needs within the medical profession [31]. Explicit information needs are the needs for information that are recognized by a healthcare professional, e.g. treatments available for a diagnosed condition; whereas implicit information needs are those of which the healthcare professional is not aware, e.g. the symptoms of diseases which the clinician does not realize that the patient is suffering from. As a consequence, while healthcare professionals may seek information about explicit information needs, they cannot do this for implicit information needs, and the latter needs will only be met through serendipity, or when it is too late, perhaps following a post-mortem. One possible solution to overcome this problem has been to explore how implicit information needs can be made explicit [31].

Braun et al.'s literature survey and interview study [31] identified physicians' information needs, before abstracting the information needs to produce natural language representations of these needs and make them context independent. The resulting information needs templates were instantiated with clinical data from electronic medical records, in order to relate information needs directly to patients. While this approach resulted in too high a level of information need, and therefore possible information overload across a group of physicians and patients, Braun et al. proposed ways of reducing this volume to manageable levels by the use of additional knowledge, e.g. relating to the temporal aspects of the patient/condition or using domain knowledge. Clearly, using generalized models of information need has the potential to identify implicit information needs, and similarly models of information need and information behaviour developed in information science could help contribute to the understanding of implicit, as well as explicit, information needs.

The possibility of ever more clinical data and information becoming available to healthcare professionals and of patients having greater access to their own health information is likely to lead to the need for ways in which to deal with this information [22]. For example, although clinicians require specific information about individual patients, as well as general information on the interventions etc. available to treat the particular condition [30], there is a danger of having too much information and not being able to use it efficiently [22]. While the summarizing of information, the filtering of information and the tailoring of it to the needs of individual healthcare professionals takes place routinely throughout the process of clinical care, e.g. during change-over in shifts on wards, or in hospital ward rounds, there is a need to develop more robust tools that will serve this function as more information becomes available electronically [22].

Similarly, patients, their families and carers, and the general public need access to accurate, up-to-date and reliable information [37] on specific health topics. With the advent of the web and the resulting availability of large amounts of information of variable quality at a global level, ways to filter and evaluate this information are required [22, 38]. In addition to information being made available by health care providers, e.g. the NHS Direct online web-site in the UK, other organizations such as charities, non-governmental, not-for-profit and commercial organizations provide information for patients and the public via the web. However, given the differing functions and motivations of these types of organizations, there is a need for evaluating and checking the quality of web-based information. Although a large number of tools have been developed to evaluate the quality of information available on the web [39, 40], many of these are generic tools and evaluate technical issues, such as when the site was last updated or the accuracy of information. These tools do not consider the information needs of specific groups, and the number of tools that are designed for specific conditions (e.g. diabetes [41]; Alzheimer's Disease [42, 43]; multiple sclerosis [44]), taking into account the needs of individuals, is limited.

In addition to patients' being able to access information 24 hours a day and seven days a week [8], ICTs, and the web in particular, can benefit patients by improving access to health care, e.g. in the UK through NHS Direct online and NHS Choices; and using Web 2.0 technologies, such as blogs and wikis that enable patients and the public to interact directly with healthcare and information professionals. Three main groups using the internet for accessing health information (Cain, 2000, cited in [8]) are people who are:

- well but who are seeking health-related information;
- chronically ill, and their informal carers; or
- newly diagnosed and seeking information about their condition.

Perceived benefits of using ICTS include improvements in well-being and quality of life, reduced distress, and increased role or function within the family [8]. ICTs are being utilized to develop communication and information sharing among patients with similar conditions and this may provide benefits additional to, or even in preference to, support received from healthcare professionals [8]. Not only can patients' retrieving information from the web and sharing information with other patients relieve pressures on, and reduce expectations of, healthcare staff but it also supports the notion of the 'expert patient' and this can increase patient empowerment and strengthen patient autonomy, improving satisfaction with care. Information science models could help to understand better how people are using the internet to access and share health-related information [26, 44] and to understand how different behaviour may influence the information that is obtained [45].

There is a danger, however, that ICTs can be used to replace verbal and face-to-face communication, adversely affecting the relationship between the healthcare professional and the patient. In addition, ICTs have the potential to increase expectations of healthcare professionals, and Åkesson et al. commented on the need to balance the demands of consumers with the capacity of health care organizations to provide information and services [8]. However, patients' being able to manage their own conditions can give a greater sense of coherence, that is, an ability to cope and manage in their life, which has a mediating effect on the stressful events surrounding their condition [8]. Using ICTs might increase a patient's capacity to live in their own home and improve their quality of life through better interaction with friends, family and healthcare professionals, although these benefits require further research evaluation [8]. A further danger is, however, that developments in health informatics will be focussed on professional groups to the extent that the needs of patients, their families and carers, and the general public are either overlooked or ignored. While the latter groups may still benefit, there is the potential for their care and well-being to be adversely affected. Further, we need to understand how developments in e-health are changing health behaviour [46, 47] and the interaction between a healthcare professional and a patient, i.e. the doctor–patient relationship. The psychosocial aspects of decision-making need to be taken into consideration in designing, developing, implementing and evaluating informatics solutions within health care [7].

## Data mining

Data mining, also called knowledge discovery in databases, is a term used to describe the process of analysing large amounts of data to identify patterns within data or relationships among variables contained within the database. Particular features of data within health and medicine lend themselves to data mining approaches, although there are unique aspects of health and medicine that must also be considered. Because, typically, data in clinical medicine and the health sector relate to individuals, and aspects of their health and well-being, this is a safety-critical context, in which analyses conducted, and decisions made, can affect the lives of people, in contrast to other application areas of data mining, such as applications in business and commerce [48]. This means that there must be a critical understanding of the process of data analysis and interpretation of the findings by those involved in the process of health care. Furthermore, it is important for those who develop methods of analysing data that even though there is a statistical relationship among a group of variables, the clinical importance may be quite limited [49]. Although large clinical data warehouses may contain vast amounts of information that can be exploited using a range of data mining methods, many clinical applications of data mining have been based on relatively small data sets, collected in specific clinical situations, and the results from these may not be generalizable to other areas. Additionally, clinical databases may be particularly prone to large amounts of missing data, and although methods have been developed to deal with this problem, or variables or cases containing missing data can be removed prior to analysis, the fact that data may be missing for a specific value and case may be a key feature in developing a predictive model.

In health and medicine, clinical data warehouses, epidemiological studies and genomic databases are good examples of large datasets and may therefore be particularly suited to data mining [48]. As noted by previous authors [48, 49], the success of using data mining methods within specific domains such as health and medicine is dependent, in no small part, on the involvement of domain experts, in the interpretation of results and application of clinical knowledge derived from the process of data mining.

## Ethical issues

The collection, storage and retrieval of personal data on the health and medical conditions of individual patients is an important area of ethical concern within health informatics, and more widely in health and medicine [50]. In addition to ethical issues surrounding the way these data are processed, the replacement of the traditional paper-based medical records with electronic records, and the movement to computer-based, and ultimately paperless systems in health care organizations raises important ethical issues for those concerned in the care of patients and emphasizes the need for respecting human rights, security and privacy of data within health [46, 51]. The development of the 'Spine', a national database containing the personal health data and summaries of patient records, as part of the UK National Programme for IT (NPfIT) will make available online patient-identifiable health data on 50 million people in the UK. While this has considerable potential benefits for healthcare professionals and patients to access data, it also raises concerns about the security of the data and the threats to patient privacy and confidentiality [52]. As Kluge noted [53], there are more fundamental questions about whether the driving force behind e-health technology should be the technology itself, service providers and/or governments, or the interests of patients and the public.

Patient health data and individual medical records are regarded as private, because they may contain sensitive personal details, for example about the illnesses or medical conditions for which a patient is treated. While there are issues regarding the privacy of personal data and information in other domains, such as the financial sector, the education sector, and within the legal system, there is particular concern within the health sector, because of the inherent sensitivity of health. Even for relatively minor, and non-life-threatening, medical problems, e.g. acne among teenagers, or an older person experiencing a fall, people are naturally sensitive about these conditions, and information regarding these is considered private. There is even greater sensitivity about more serious medical conditions, often for financial or employment reasons (e.g. experiencing a heart attack or visual impairment); or due to fear or shame (e.g. lung cancer, sexually transmitted diseases); or because of possible stigmatization within society (e.g. mental health problems, being HIV positive). Whilst issues connected with privacy and confidentiality have been important since the development of medicine as a profession, the principle of confidentiality extending back to the Hippocratic oath [54], developments within health informatics have raised new concerns about how health data and information are managed and controlled [53, 55]. Healthcare professionals, patients and the public are rightly sensitive about the ways in which health data are stored and transferred from one location to another [56].

The development of ICTs and electronic records systems, and e-health initiatives in particular, raise concerns regarding data security, patient privacy and confidentiality because they are making data potentially accessible and available on an unprecedented scale [53]. Although paper-based medical records had limitations regarding security, e.g. their physical nature meant that they could be lost, or left lying on a hospital trolley for passers-by to view, generally they could be stored securely and access could be controlled. Storing medical data on computers, coupled with the ability to connect computers via networks and the web, and the use of wireless systems raise concerns about how safe these data are, whether data can be transferred securely, and how access to sensitive information might be controlled. The increased availability of individual patient information raises ethical questions about who should be allowed access to this information, and whether particular types of information should be made available to different types of healthcare professionals on a need to know basis, e.g. details about HIV status, history of mental health problems, genetic diseases within the family [22]. These, in turn, raise technical questions about how access to electronic data can be controlled [55].

The potential for providing patients and the general public with access to their medical records via the web has emerged more recently, and raises further ethical questions, as well as issues regarding ownership and censorship of data. There is a need to avoid what is increasingly regarded as the traditional paternalistic approach of the medical profession [57], in which the doctor knows best, and to give patients and the public greater autonomy and control over the information that is stored about them. It was only with the passing of the *Access to Medical Reports Act* (1988) and the *Access to Health Records Act* (1990) in the UK, that patients and the public were granted the legal right to have access to their own medical records. Prior to this, doctors were under no legal obligation to allow patients to view their own records. While, to some extent, a doctor could control access, and restrict a patient's access if s/he felt it was detrimental to their well-being [54], e.g. for patients with mental health conditions, making patient records available online 24 hours a day potentially removes this control and has led to the development of protocols for developing electronic clinician sealed envelopes, which contain information that the patient is not able to view [52].

In addition to ethical and technical issues arising through the advent of electronic records, Kluge identified the need to ensure that health information professionals who develop and implement e-health initiatives have appropriate ethical qualifications [53]. In the last few years formal qualifications in information governance have been developed to meet this need. Training health informatics professionals in information governance and ethical issues will not only increase understanding of the importance but will empower them to influence decision-making in e-health initiatives [53].

Kluge highlighted the need for international standards for ensuring that health information professionals have appropriate ethical qualifications [53], and educational programmes are now available in information governance for health, for example at the University of Bath in the UK. There is a difference between healthcare professionals and information professionals in terms of their roles in undertaking health care and facilitating this care respectively [53]. This difference has implications for the access they have to information systems and data, the former to data on individuals and the latter the development and implementation of information systems and e-health interventions that affect these data. Kluge pointed out that while there are these differences, the ethical issues that relate to access to these data and the systems themselves cannot be separated and there is a need for appropriate qualifications for both health professionals and information professionals regarding the ethical use of information [53]. The very nature of e-health, i.e. electronic communication of health data or information, means that it transcends national boundaries, so that internationally accepted standards are required. This is complicated by the fact that ethical standards and values vis-a-vis patients' data and their rights may be very different in different countries; for example, the patients' rights to see their own data may be quite different in Western countries compared with developing countries.

## Challenges in health informatics

A major challenge within health informatics is the financial investment required to develop, implement and maintain e-health initiatives, and Anderson identified a lack of financial support and high initial costs as barriers to adopting ICT in health care [56]. While health informaticians and information professionals may perceive the future benefits of investments in ICTs, health professionals and managers may be sceptical about such developments, particularly when they are satisfied with current methods of working and wish to maintain the status quo, and may perceive such initiatives as diverting financial resources away from under-resourced clinical care. The diversion of funds ear-marked for local developments under the UK White Paper, *Information for Health* [19], was cited by Protti as a major reason for the limited progress with implementing the strategy [20]. Individual and shared feelings about the perceived value of IT systems may lead to a more general resistance to using these systems.

Resistance to the development of ICT systems by health professionals and managers can create further problems once systems are implemented and the limited use of health informatics applications has meant that their potential has not always been realized. For example, decision support systems may be ignored or over-ridden, and there may be instances when evidence-based information has limited applicability for an individual patient. Clinicians are making life-affecting decisions or are acting in life-threatening situations, and if they do not understand enough about the reasoning behind computer-based decision support systems, they will not trust them, nor will they utilize them effectively [22]. This emphasizes the need not only to involve clinicians and healthcare professionals in the development of systems and in the interpretation of results, but also to provide sufficient explanation and information at the point of care for healthcare professionals to trust the systems [22]. As noted above, identifying the types of information that clinicians need, and the ways they access and utilize information are important in ensuring that developments not only meet the needs of the users, but that they are also perceived to be of value, so that health professionals and other users will want to maximize their potential. Addressing the concerns of healthcare professionals, patients and the public regarding the security of data and the threats to patient privacy and confidentiality will also be important in developing online access to patient records [52]. Ensuring greater security measures are incorporated into the design of systems [56] will help improve confidence in systems, though the possibility of third parties gaining access to sensitive patient-identifiable data remains a risk.

Quality within health informatics initiatives is a further issue that can affect successful development and implementation. The quality, both actual and perceived, of data entered into systems and then utilized for health care is critical not only for ensuring systems are utilized but more importantly, for the safety and well-being of patients. If data are not entered, or not entered correctly, the accumulation of missing or poor quality data will dissuade others from utilizing the system and will create further mistrust and scepticism about future developments. The imperative for data that are complete and correct will increase as lifelong electronic records are developed [22], for records developed prospectively as individuals are born, and also for those developed retrospectively using data accumulated over an existing person's lifetime to date.

As discussed above, the earlier development of small-scale information systems within individual departments or hospitals led to systems being incompatible and problems in exchanging or transferring data when larger-scale systems were subsequently developed. One way to overcome this problem is to build greater interoperability and the use of established electronic record architectures into the design of new systems. Allied to this is the lack of standards for data within health which creates further difficulties for transferring and sharing data across systems [56]. Attempts to overcome these problems include the development of standards for managing information: including Digital Imaging and Communications in Medicine (DICOM), Health Level Seven (HL7), and terminologies and coding systems (e.g., the International Classification of Diseases (ICD), Read coding, and Snomed) to standardize the ways in which medical conditions and diseases are represented in computer-based systems and to try to codify the natural language used by medical staff in describing patient symptoms. The ICD was developed to provide a standard means of classifying medical diagnoses for epidemiology and health service purpose: originally, it included only causes of death, but more recent versions have included causes of morbidity and it is now in its tenth version [58].

## Opportunities for health informatics
### Supporting an ageing society

Throughout the developing world the numbers and proportion of older people are increasing, and are likely to continue to rise until at least 2050. Within health informatics there is the opportunity to utilize ICTs and e-health initiatives to benefit older people and ageing populations [4, 5], particularly in those countries in which the ratio of people of working age to those of pensionable age is, or is becoming, low. The increasing population of older people and the associated increase in the prevalence of chronic diseases in society has lead to increased demand for health care services, and the need for services that can support individuals in their own homes [59]. The parallel developments in ICTs are providing opportunities to meet these additional needs through tele-health services, web-based information resources and interactive digital television [60]. Additional driving forces behind the development of tele-health are patient empowerment and the need for shared care among people with acute and chronic conditions [59].

The focus on developing telemedicine services, which provide remote consultations and diagnosis for patients with acute clinical conditions at a distance, such as for people living in rural areas far from specialist centres, has changed to developing tele-health services, in which chronic conditions can be managed at home through remote data collection and transfer of data through ICTs. This allows a more holistic approach, encompassing health promotion and disease prevention [59].

Health-enabling technologies, such as sensor and sensor-based technologies that can collect data on an ongoing basis and transmit the data using ICTs, are relatively new. They are of particular value within an ageing society to help older people and other groups to live longer in their homes, rather than being admitted to residential/nursing home care [4, 5]. As well as obvious benefits for the patients in terms of improving health and quality of life, there are potential economic benefits to reducing admissions to these types of care. ICTs also have an important role to play in the detection and prevention of diseases during the stages before clinical manifestation of a disease, as well as in the management of chronic illnesses. ICTs can be used to collect and transfer a variety of data from patients on an ongoing basis (for example physical and clinical measurements, biochemical markers, respiratory measurements) and combining these data can provide additional value [59]. Applications of health-enabling technologies include the remote detection of falls in older people, reminders for taking medications, or helping to orient people with early-onset dementia [4, 5, 59]. As ICTs and these health-enabling and monitoring technologies develop, the opportunity for health informatics to contribute to the ageing society will increase throughout the twenty-first century.

## Spanning the digital divide

Providing access to information on the internet may improve health care for individuals and for groups but may not meet the needs of all groups, and may lead to some groups being neglected and ignored. This has the potential to increase both the digital divide and the health divide for particular groups, such as homeless people, older people, people with specific disabilities (e.g. visual or cognitive impairment) and people in developing countries. This may be because either technology or resources are not available to a group or they do not have the ability to utilize the ICTs or information, so that they are effectively excluded. However, as Åkesson et al. reported in their review of consumers' use of ICTs [8], specific groups (e.g. older people, people with early-onset dementia, children, people with lower levels of education) did not report difficulties in using the technologies, and it may be that assumptions about their ability to utilize the ICTs are a greater barrier than having access or the ability to use the ICTs/information.

Healy stressed the importance of giving support to developing countries to overcome the digital divide at a global level [46]. Kapiriri and Bondy reported the need to ensure that health professionals in developing countries have access to the internet, particularly in rural and less affluent areas, in order to provide access to necessary information resources and reduce current inequalities in access to information and health resources [61].

The American Medical Informatics Association has focussed on how informatics might be applied to specific groups with particular needs. Chang et al. highlighted the difference between vulnerable groups, i.e. those that are particularly at risk from particular health problems, and under-served groups, that is, those that receive fewer health care resources than they need for either actual or potential health care problems [62]. While there is some overlap between the groups, they are different and it is possible for individuals to be in one group but not the other, e.g. older people with low blood pressure may be at increased risk of falls, but there may be support services available that reduce the risk. However, individuals in groups that are both vulnerable and under-served, e.g. older people from minority ethnic backgrounds living in deprived areas, can be particularly at risk of adverse health outcomes, and Chang et al. discussed how the digital divide that has emerged within society meant that people in both of these groups were even worse off compared to those in only one group [62]. A challenge, therefore, for health informatics is to explore ways in which the digital divide can be reduced, if not removed altogether, for the benefit of people in vulnerable and under-served groups. Barriers to vulnerable and under-served groups being able to access appropriate health information technology include community factors, such as e-health applications not being focussed on the needs of specific groups, mistrust of health organizations and technology, low levels of computer and health literacy, the lack of financial incentives for developing health information and informatics resources and lack of training in health education and health literacy among informatics professionals [62].

## The need for an evidence base in health informatics

As has been discussed earlier in this review, further research is necessary to evaluate the experiences of consumers in using ICTs and to investigate the impact of ICTs on consumer satisfaction with health care [8] and to understand the factors that affect information seeking behaviour among healthcare professionals, including those in developing countries [61]. In addition to evaluating information systems within health, there is the need to develop an appropriate evidence base by evaluating information systems in health (Rigby, 2001, cited in [63]), e.g. tele-health systems [59], so that future development and implementation of information technology and information systems in health is based on the best available evidence.

A problem with the evidence base, in health and medicine as in other fields, is the negative publication bias brought about by a failure to report unsuccessful interventions in the medical and health literature, and in medical and health informatics [64]. A consequence of this is that further money and resources may be invested in information systems that are prone to failure, because previous problems have not been reported. Heeks reported the need for a better understanding of definitions of success and failure in information systems in health, due to the subjective nature of these concepts. The subjectivity inherent in defining partial failure and success is particularly problematic, and positivist approaches to research and evaluation of systems adopt an objective viewpoint, at the expense of more subjective aspects. More rigorous and independent evaluations of information systems are required, as 'both the conceptualization and the evidence base for HIS [health information systems] success and failure are weak' [64, p.127]. A problem with the literature is that individual studies are either too specific, in which case generalizations to other situation are not possible, or too general and studies assume that the findings apply to all systems. Heeks proposed a design–reality gap model for more effectively evaluating the success or failure of information systems within healthcare, i.e. the gap between the situation, or reality, as it is now and the intended design of the health information system [64]. This model might be useful in not only evaluating the success or failure of systems that have been implemented, but in predicting the future success or failure of a new information system through risk assessment. Heeks acknowledged the possible influence of other driving forces, e.g. political motivation that might overcome the problem of a large design–reality gap and contribute to the success of an information system.

Although recent work has reported improvements in the quality of evaluation studies and in increased use of multi-centre trials and increased use of randomized-controlled trials (RCTs) [63], Ball supported the notion that evaluations should look beyond RCTs and consider other forms of research evidence when evaluating e-health interventions [51]. De Lusignan, in his review of the emergence of primary care informatics as a discipline [7], emphasized the need to value the importance of tacit knowledge, as well as explicit knowledge, in primary care and made the important point that an evidence-based approach to medicine ignored the importance of tacit knowledge.

Berg, Aarts and van der Lei [65] and Aarts and Gorman [66] emphasized the importance of socio-technical approaches to design, implementation and evaluation of information systems within health, indicating that a variety of research methodologies are important in contributing to our understanding of how information systems and technologies interact with the social practice in an organization and that the interaction between humans and systems has to be studied in context. Three questions are emerging: to what extent 'technological failures are due to technological system issues'; to what extent problems are encountered when implementing health informatics systems or solutions due to 'lack of awareness and understanding of the sociocultural environment in which such applications are implemented'; and to what extent changes in one or other of 'people, technologies, and processes of care' cause problems in the other aspects or the interaction between them (systems view) [66, p. S1].

## Conclusion

This review has considered current issues and developments in health informatics and has discussed the distinctions and overlaps between medical informatics and health information management. It has highlighted some important challenges and key issues that are faced within health informatics, as well as the opportunity to make a difference to how it can make a positive contribution to the health and well-being of patients and the public. Throughout the review a number of themes have emerged which may determine the success of health informatics in the coming years and decades, and which highlight the potential contribution that information science can contribute.

A central theme emerging is that health and medicine is a unique and highly important field, and requires particular consideration in comparison to other areas, for example, education, finance and commerce. If one accepts this argument [53], it follows that health informatics requires particular consideration as an emerging discipline within information science. There are several reasons for this. First, personal health data are private and people are very sensitive about the ways in which information on health is stored and processed. Second, the process of health care is complex, and the amount of health information that is collected in an episode of care, and ultimately throughout a person's life is potentially huge, and this information is complex. Third, a large number of people may be involved in the care of a person, and this will be different for each patient, dependent on the condition and circumstances of the individual: these may include generalist and specialist doctors, nurses, therapists, informal carers, family members, as well as the person themselves. The implication of all this is that developments in health informatics require particular care and attention: information science can make a valuable contribution to health informatics, but needs to consider issues above and beyond other areas within the discipline.

A second, but related, theme underlying this review is that the success of health informatics applications and e-health initiatives depends on the active involvement of users in the design, development, implementation and evaluation of e-health initiatives. Given the large number and variety of people involved in health care, this is no small undertaking, but it is nonetheless important. Identifying the health information needs and information behaviour of health professionals and other health workers, patient and carer groups, as well as the general public, is an important first step in the process, and research in information science and in the health and social sciences has made considerable progress towards identifying health information needs. However, further research is required to explore how people search for health information, what the intervening variables are and the barriers to their acquiring information, and how ICTs may help to overcome these barriers. Models of information behaviour developed in information science may help to provide a better understanding of these issues but the applicability of these models in health requires investigation. Models of information use and methodologies for evaluating information systems developed in information science may also help to develop and test e-health initiatives and understand how ICTs can improve the use of information within health. This leads to the third, and final, theme emerging from this review, i.e. the need for independent, and therefore objective, evaluation and research of developments in health informatics [51]. This particular theme follows on from the second theme, and as has been discussed earlier, incorporates the views of users in all phases of health informatics developments. While research and evaluation in health informatics need to be objective and independent, they should not be constrained by particular paradigms such as positivism, but should be appropriate for the particular situation in question. This will help to ensure that the full impact of ICT on the health and well-being of patients, their families and carers and the general public is effective.

In conclusion, Berner and Moss described the impending golden decade of heath informatics [22]: the three themes identified here are key to the development and maturation of health informatics and ensuring that it reaches its full potential. Health informatics is a specialized field and can benefit from multidisciplinary contributions from information science, health and medicine and the social sciences. Health informatics must address the specific issues that are unique to medicine and health. Understanding the needs of all users in the care process through research and evaluation of health informatics developments and e-health initiatives are important for the ultimate well-being and safety of patients.

## Acknowledgements

I would like to thank Professor Peter Willett (Department of Information Studies, University of Sheffield) and the two anonymous reviewers for their constructive and helpful comments on earlier drafts of this paper. I would also like to thank the editor of this special issue of the *Journal of Information Science*, Alan Gilchrist, for his helpful suggestions and support in preparing the paper.

## Note

1   Avedis Donabedian is widely regarded as one of the leading figures of quality assurance in public health in the twentieth century. His seminal paper entitled 'Evaluating the quality of medical care' [1] introduced the idea of evaluating quality of care and services in terms of the structures (e.g. number of beds in a hospital), processes (e.g. number of operations conducted over a period of time) and outcomes (e.g. the survival rate of patients). This article is one of the most cited articles in public health and is a Current Contents citation classic [2].

## References

[1]   A. Donabedian, Evaluating the quality of medical care, *Milbank Memorial Fund Quarterly* 44 (3 Supplement) (1966) 166–206.

[2]   R. Suñol, Avedis Donabedian, *International Journal for Quality in Health Care* 12(6) (2000) 451–4.

[3]   J.H. van Bemmel and M.A. Musen (eds), *Handbook of Medical Informatics* (Springer-Verlag, Heidelberg, 1997).

[4]   R. Haux, Health information systems: past, present, future, *International Journal of Medical Informatics* 75(3/4) (2006) 268–81.

[5]   R. Haux, Individualization, globalization and health: about sustainable information technologies and the aim of medical informatics, *International Journal of Medical Informatics* 75(12) (2006) 795–808.

[6]   N. Staggers and C.R. Thompson, The evolution of definitions for nursing informatics: a critical analysis and revised definition, *Journal of the American Medical Informatics Association* 9(3) (2002) 255–61.

[7]    S. de Lusignan, What Is primary care informatics? *Journal of the American Medical Informatics Association* 10(4) (2003) 304–9.

[8]    K.M. Åkesson, B.-I. Saveman and G. Nilsson, Health care consumers' experiences of information communication technology: a summary of literature, *International Journal of Medical Informatics* 76(9) (2007) 633–645.

[9]    J. Hsu, J. Huang, V. Fung, N. Robertson, H. Jimison and R. Frankel, Health information technology and physician-patient interactions: impact of computers on communication during outpatient primary care visits, *Journal of the American Medical Informatics Association* 12(4) (2005) 474–80.

[10]   Y.-Y. Chen, Medical image compression using DCT-based subband decomposition and modified SPIHT data organization, *International Journal of Medical Informatics* 76(10) (2007) 717–25.

[11]   W.W. Simons, K.D. Mandl and I.S. Kohane, The PING personally controlled electronic medical record system: technical architecture, *Journal of the American Medical Informatics Association* 12(1) (2005) 47–54.

[12]   P.S. Heckerling, G.J. Canaris, S.D. Flach, R.S. Wigton, T.G. Tape and B.S. Gerber, Predictors of urinary tract infection based on artificial neural networks and genetic algorithms, *International Journal of Medical Informatics* 76(4) (2007) 289–96.

[13]   R. Ahmad and P.A. Bath, Identification of risk factors for 15-year mortality among community-dwelling older people using Cox regression and a genetic algorithm, *Journal of Gerontology (medical science)* 60A(8) (2005) 1052–8.

[14]   A.T. McCray, Promoting health literacy, *Journal of the American Medical Informatics Association* 12(2) (2005) 152–63.

[15]   C. Ma, J. Warren, P. Phillips and J. Stanek, Empowering patients with essential information and communication support in the context of diabetes, *International Journal of Medical Informatics* 75(8) (2006) 577–96.

[16]   H. Lærum, T.H. Karlsen and A. Faxvaag, Effects of scanning and eliminating paper-based medical records on hospital physicians' clinical work practice, *Journal of the American Medical Informatics Association* 10(6) (2003) 588–95.

[17]   P.A. Bath, C. Craigs, R. Maheswaran, J. Raymond and P. Willett, Use of graph theory to identify patterns of deprivation, high morbidity and mortality in public health data sets, *Journal of the American Medical Informatics Association* 12(6) (2005) 630–41.

[18]   A. Moen and P. Flatley Brennan, Health@home: the work of health information management in the household (HIMH): implications for consumer health informatics (CHI) innovations, *Journal of the American Medical Informatics Association* 12(6) (2005) 648–56.

[19]   F. Burns, *Information for health: an information Strategy for the Modern NHS 1998–2005. A National Strategy for Local Implementation* (NHS Executive, Leeds, 1998).

[20]   D.J. Protti, *Implementing Information for Health: Even More Challenging Than Expected?* (Department of Health, London, 2001). Available at: http://hinf.uvic.ca/archives/Protti.pdf (accessed 21 February 2008).

[21]   W. Hersh, *Information Retrieval: a Health and Biomedical Perspective*, 2nd Edition (Springer, New York, 2003).

[22]   E.S. Berner and J. Moss, Informatics challenges for the impending patient information explosion, *Journal of the American Medical Informatics Association* 12(6) (2005) 614–17.

[23]   A. Spink and C. Cole, Human information behavior: integrating diverse approaches and information use, *Journal of the American Society for Information Science and Technology* 57(1) (2006) 25–35.

[24]   B. Dervin, Libraries reaching out with health information to vulnerable populations: guidance from research on information seeking and use, *Journal of the Medical Library Association* 93(4) (2005) S74-S80.

[25]   D.O. Case, J.E. Andrews, J.D. Johnson and S.L. Allard, Avoiding versus seeking: the relationship of information seeking to avoidance, blunting, coping dissonance and related concepts, *Journal of the Medical Library Association* 93(3) (2005) 353–62.

[26]   J.A. Harland and P.A. Bath, Understanding the information behaviours of carers of people with dementia: a critical review of models from information science, *Aging and Mental Health* 12(4) (2008), 467–77.

[27]   C. Rees and P.A. Bath The information needs and source preferences of women with breast cancer and their family members: a review of the literature published between 1988 and 1998, *Journal of Advanced Nursing* 31(4) (2000) 833–41.

[28]   P. Williams, D. Nicholas and P. Huntington, Non-use of health information kiosks examined in an information needs context. *Health Information and Libraries Journal* 20(2) (2003) 95–103.

[29]   C. Beverley, P.A. Bath and R. Barber Can two established information models explain the information behaviour of visually impaired people seeking health and social care information? *Journal of Documentation* 63(1) (2007) 9–32.

[30]   R. Smith What clinical information do doctors need? *British Medical Journal* 313(7064) (1996) 1062–8.

[31]   L.M.M. Braun, F. Wiesman, H.J. van den Herik, A. Hasman and E. Korsten, Towards patient-related information needs. *International Journal of Medical Informatics* 76(2/3) (2007) 246–51.

[32]  P.N. Gorman, Information needs of physicians, *Journal of the American Society for Information Science*, 46(10) (1995) 729–36.

[33]  J.W. Ely, J.A. Osheroff, M.H. Ebell, G.R. Bergus, B.T. Levy, M.L. Chambliss et al., Analysis of questions asked by family doctors regarding patient care, *British Medical Journal* 319(7206) (1999) 358–61.

[34]  C. Urquhart and S. Crane, Nurses' information-seeking skills and perceptions of information sources: assessment using vignettes, *Journal of Information Science* 20(4) (1994) 237–46.

[35]  M. Wakeham, Nurses, their information needs and use of libraries: the views of some librarians, *Health Libraries Review* 10(2) (1993) 85–94.

[36]  D. Bawden and K. Robinson, Information behaviour in nursing specialities: a case study of midwifery, *Journal of Information Science* 23(6) (1997) 407–21.

[37]  A. Coulter, Evidence based patient information, *British Medical Journal* 317(7153) (1998) 225–6.

[38]  E.V. Bernstam, D.M. Shelton, M. Walji and F. Meric-Bernstam, Instruments to assess the quality of health information on the World Wide Web: what can our patients actually use? *International Journal of Medical Informatics* 74(1) (2005) 13–19.

[39]  A.R. Jadad and A. Gagliardi, Rating health information on the internet: navigating to knowledge or to Babel? *Journal of the American Medical Association* 279(8) (1998) 611–14.

[40]  A. Gagliardi and A.R. Jadad, Examination of instruments used to rate quality of health information on the internet: chronicle of a voyage with an unclear destination, *British Medical Journal* 324(7337) (2002) 569–73.

[41]  J.J. Seidman, D. Steinwachs and H.R. Rubin, Design and testing of a tool for evaluating the quality of diabetes consumer information web sites, *Journal of Medical Internet Research* 5(4) (2003) e30. Available at: www.jmir.org/2003/4/e30/ (accessed 8 April 2008).

[42]  H. Bouchier and P.A. Bath, Evaluation of websites that provide information on Alzheimer's disease, *Health Informatics Journal* 9(1) (2003) 17–32.

[43]  P.A. Bath and H. Bouchier, Development and application of a tool designed to evaluate websites providing information on Alzheimer's disease, *Journal of Information Science* 29(4) (2003) 279–97.

[44]  J.A. Harland and P.A. Bath, Assessing the quality of web-sites providing information on multiple sclerosis: evaluating and comparing web-sites, *Health Informatics Journal* 13(3) (2007) 207–21.

[45]  G. Eysenbach and C. Köhler, How do consumers search for and appraise health information on the world wide web? Qualitative study using focus groups,

usability tests, and in-depth interviews, *British Medical Journal* 324(7337) (2002) 573–7.

[46]   J.C. Healy, Editorial of the special health and the internet for all, *International Journal of Medical Informatics* 75(1) (2006) 5–7.

[47]   S. Ross and C.-T. Lin, The effects of promoting patient access to medical records: a review, *Journal of the American Medical Informatics Association* 10(2) (2003) 129–38.

[48]   R. Bellazzi and B. Zupan, Predictive data mining in clinical medicine: current issues and guidelines, *International Journal of Medical Informatics* 77(2) (2008) 81–97.

[49]   P.A. Bath, Data mining in health and medical information, *Annual Review of Information Science and Technology* 38 (2004) 331–69.

[50]   E.-H.W. Kluge, *A Handbook of Ethics for Health Informatics Professionals* (The British Computer Society, Swindon, 2003).

[51]   M.J. Ball, Hospital information systems: perspectives on problems and prospects, 1979 and 2002, *International Journal of Medical Informatics* 69(2/3) (2003) 83–9.

[52]   M.Y. Becker, Information governance in NHS's NPfIT: a case for policy specification, *International Journal of Medical Informatics* 76(5/6) (2007) 432–7.

[53]   E.-H.W. Kluge, Secure e-health: managing risks to patient health data, *International Journal of Medical Informatics* 76(5/6) (2007) 402–6.

[54]   British Medical Association, *Medical Ethics Today: Its Practice and Philosophy* [Chapter 2: Confidentiality and Medical Records] (BMJ, London, 1993).

[55]   R. Anderson, NHS-wide networking and patient confidentiality, *British Medical Journal* 311(1) (1995) 5–6.

[56]   J.G. Anderson, Social, ethical and legal barriers to e-health, *International Journal of Medical Informatics* 76(5) (2007) 480–83.

[57]   M. Dixon-Woods, Writing wrongs? An analysis of published discourses about the use of patient information leaflets, *Social Science and Medicine* 52(9) (2001) 1417–32.

[58]   World Health Organization, *International Classification of Diseases (ICD)* (2008). Available at: www.who.int/classifications/icd/en/ (accessed 21 February 2008).

[59]   S. Koch, Home telehealth: current state and future trends. *International Journal of Medical Informatics* 75(8) (2006) 565–76.

[60]   D. Nicholas, P. Huntington and H. Jamali, with P. Williams, *Digital Health Information for the Consumer: Evidence and Policy Implications* (Ashgate, Aldershot, 2007).

[61]   L. Kapiriri and S.J. Bondy, Health practitioners' and health planners' information needs and seeking behavior for decision making in Uganda, *International Journal of Medical Informatics* 75(10) (2006) 714–21.

[62]   B.L. Chang, S. Bakken, M.P.H. Brown, T.K. Houston, G.L. Kreps, R. Kukafka, C. Safran and P.Z. Stavri, Bridging the digital divide: reaching vulnerable populations, *Journal of the American Medical Informatics Association* 11(6) (2004) 448–57.

[63]   N.F. de Keizer and E. Ammenwerth, The quality of evidence in health informatics: how did the quality of healthcare IT evaluation publications develop from 1982 to 2005? *International Journal of Medical Informatics* 77(1) (2008) 41–9.

[64]   R. Heeks, Health information systems: failure, success and improvisation, *International Journal of Medical Informatics* 75(2) (2006) 125–37.

[65]   M. Berg, J. Aarts and J. van der Lei, ICT in health care: sociotechnical approaches, *Methods of Information in Medicine* 42(4) (2003) 297–301.

[66]   J. Aarts and P. Gorman, IT in health care: sociotechnical approaches 'to err is system', *International Journal of Medical Informatics* 76S (2007) S1–S3.

# 9

# Social informatics and sociotechnical research – a view from the UK

ELISABETH DAVENPORT

## Abstract

This paper explores the connections between two historical lines of research: social informatics in the United States, and sociotechnical studies in the United Kingdom. The author discusses samples of work from three long established UK research sites, at Manchester, Edinburgh and the London School of Economics, to give the reader a sense of sociotechnical work at different historical periods. Though the US and UK traditions share a common interest in the production of technology, and work with complementary concepts and methods, formal links between the two have not been strong for much of the historical period under review. However, there are signs of fusion in the work of a current generation of researchers on both sides of the Atlantic.

## Introduction

Social Informatics is concerned with computerization, or the

> transformation in human activity that follows the implementation, use and adoption of computers in different types of organization [1].

Historically, separate disciplines have explored this phenomenon from perspectives that focus on different stages of technological development: Human Computer Interaction has handled interface design and ergonomics; Information Systems has addressed analysis, design and implementation; LIS (Library and Information Science) has addressed information retrieval and use; Business and Management have addressed adoption and impact; Operations Research has modelled processes. Social

Informatics (SI), in contrast, is transdisciplinary, tracing antecedents and consequences across these different phases of development, and treating technology as an evolving assemblage of interests, activities and artefacts that is shaped over time in local conditions.

## The US tradition

In the United States, an explicit SI line of thinking was first articulated in the early 1970s by an eclectic group of analysts working at the University of California, Irvine, exploring information systems in local government across the US. Perplexed by the mismatch between accounts from engineering, managerial and operating staff of the impact of ICTs on organization, Kling and Scacchi [2] produced an explanatory frame, the 'web of computing', in a seminal paper that was in effect a manifesto for a new line of inquiry. Organizational computing must be understood as a web, woven from front line issues and concerns, from organizational contests and interest groups (the production lattice), from infrastructural constraints, and from larger societal visions about humans and machines, the future of work, and so on. The web of computing could be explored systematically to produce a corpus of work that was conducive to more realistic expectations of computing. In a further paper [3], Kling scoped out the approaches that would characterize the new field – mixed and multidisciplinary methods, multiple perspectives that cross institutional boundaries and different levels of organization, local observation across time, explanation rather than prescription, and an interest in the negotiated orders that stabilize technology – in terms that were deeply subversive of the IS systems methodologies of the time.

According to Kling and his colleagues [4], the problems that SI researchers find interesting do not tend to be formal engineering puzzles (the domain of Computer Science). They focus instead on technologies as social products that emerge, sometimes in surprising forms, from complex interactions, and the starting point of an inquiry may be conflicting views about a product, or unexpected failure or success. What is seen as a successful project, for example, by senior management, may not be seen that way from other points of view, and a Social Informatics analyst attempts to unravel the complex of moves, alliances, resources, and rhetoric that constitute a technological formation over time, to produce an account ('technological realism') that may well differ from the utopian or romantic account offered by developers, gurus, CEOs and other instigators of ICT development. Kling has been described as 'arguably the foremost proponent of social informatics during his lifetime' [5: p.575] and hailed as the man who 'brought computing and sociology together' [6]. While such claims may hold in a North American context (those who wish to know more about this are referred to the chapter by Sawyer and Eschenfelder in the 2002 *Annual Review of Information Science and Technology* [7], and the recent article by Sawyer and Tapia [8]), the current article considers a different tradition: the fusion of sociology and computing in ICT research in the UK that predates the establishment of SI in the United States. In the 1970s, Rudy Hirschheim, then a young and aspiring North American graduate with an interest in sociotechnical analysis was told to go to England, where 'the experts are' [9: p. 362]. The text that follows shows that the historical traditions of SI research in the US have much in common with those of sociotechnical research in the UK, although there is little evidence of formal links between them, a point that is discussed briefly in the concluding section.

## The UK tradition

Though there are a number of centres in the UK where sociotechnical research is undertaken (for example at the Oxford Internet Institute, Brunel University, Lancaster University, the University of York, the Judge Institute at Cambridge and the Said Business School at Oxford), a comprehensive review is not possible here. The article focuses instead on three significant sites, or 'truth spots', Gieryn's [10] term for sites with a long track record of sustained and substantial research that makes them reference points. It seems fitting in this *JIS* anniversary issue to focus on institutions where the span of activity is roughly commensurate with the 50 year period since the IIS was founded. On this basis, Manchester, Edinburgh and the London School of Economics have been selected – each has a long tradition of sociotechnical research, characterized by the concerns described above. The sections that follow present examples of work at each site, to give the reader a sense of the scope, methods and concepts that have characterized research there at different points in time. The sample is highly selective, and the account impressionistic.

## The socio-technical approach at Manchester

The first 'truth spot' is Manchester, and this section focuses on a corpus of work initiated by Enid Mumford (and influenced by her association with the

Tavistock Institute) that places social context and human consequences at the heart of systems design. Mumford's first major project was one of a series of investigations into office automation across Europe, initiated in 1957 by an 'international committee for social research in industry' to establish

> a body of sociological knowledge concerning the effects of new techniques on the formal and informal structures of firms and on different occupational groups within these firms [11: p.1].

The UK investigations were sponsored by the Department of Scientific and Industrial Research, and started in 1957, though the research was not undertaken until 1960, as the research team had difficulty in finding sites – in 1958 there were about 100 computers in industry in the UK. The final study involved nine companies, in the manufacturing, pharmaceutical, banking and retail sectors. This was the era of first generation computing in the UK – a world of bureaucratic organizations migrating from manual to electronic data processing where *de novo* programming and process design could be contoured to local practice. Confident that the social consequences of technology could be assessed in advance using standard social science techniques – surveys and on-site interviews with stakeholders – Mumford and her colleagues focused on persuading managers across all of the functions implicated in their case studies that

> any change policy is most likely to be successful if it is logically derived from an analysis of the variables [12].

Attitudinal and demographic data should be gathered by trained specialists – industrial sociologists and psychologists who can complement the facilitation work of personnel managers as business becomes more computer intensive. The full findings of the study were presented in *The computer and the clerk*, which makes a strong case for work-centred design:

> Managers, computer manufacturers and consultants often appear content to do a partial analysis of the effects of electronic data processing … virtually no attention may be given to the sociological problems of seeing how, for example, a firm's management structure may change once managerial functions are automated, and how this may in turn affect the balance of power within the firm or to find out in advance the likely reaction of the different groups whose work will be affected by the new systems [11: p. 17].

Socio-technical analysis is a way to 'cushion the shock' of new technology – Mumford and Banks declare that

> Technical change is like a bomb explosion – if no precautions are taken, there may be widespread panic and confusion [11: p. 16].

By 1979, Mumford and her colleagues had consolidated the findings from this and subsequent projects into a methodology they called 'ETHICS' ('Effective Technical and Human Implementation of Computer Systems'). The starting point is work design, rather than systems, and the method

> recognises the interaction of technologies and people and produces work systems which are both technically efficient and have social characteristics which lead to high satisfaction [13: p. 6].

A work system that is designed to achieve objectives solely in technical terms is 'likely to have unpredictable human consequences' [13: p. 9]. ETHICS is uncompromisingly humanistic in its approach, scoring quality of working life in terms of 'fit' between personal aspirations and organizational goals – if managers do not work with employees to align these aspirations, idiosyncratic practices around computing technology may compromise efficiency. Mumford's concern with lifeworlds is prescient – they are a major conceptual resource in contemporary interaction design.

One of the most ambitious applications of ETHICS involved an expert systems implementation (XSEL) in the sales group of a global computing manufacturer (DEC) in the 1980s. Organizational computing had entered a new phase: this was now a world of global corporate infrastructures where complex artefacts were assembled from components designed and manufactured at several different sites. (An example is the expert systems shell that was a focal artefact in the XSEL project). In such a context, the scope and reach of humanistic work-centred design need to be greatly extended. Mumford addresses the issues in a masterful review of current and future expert systems research and offers a comprehensive vision of integrated design:

> Such an examination needs to cover the philosophy and values of the designers and their sponsors, the way in which the design task has been defined, the nature of the decisions taken, including technological decisions,

the skills, knowledge and interests of the project group who have responsibility for design and the processes which they use to move from problem identification to system implementation [14: p. 146].

She warns against single variable research and advocates the adoption of methods that address the 'total situation':

multidisciplinary rather than from the perspective of a single discipline; focusing on ... the technology and its social and organizational context, rather than examining the impact of one or two variables and qualitative as well as quantitative so that is can take account of values as well as behaviour [14: p. 148].

She concludes that

All those involved – designers, experts, users and society – should gain from this technological breakthrough; the objective must be to have no losers [14: p. 151].

An interesting feature of this chapter is Mumford's interest in observations that are 'concurrent with events', and in 'the processes of choice', signature themes in the work of the Edinburgh group that is the focus of the next section:

The objective or subjective choices which a project group makes at each stage of the design process are what causes the organization to change. A different set of choices or different weightings for individual variables will result in different organizational consequences [14: p. 146].

The message that systematic exploration of social consequences can mitigate adverse effects is more urgent in an era of distributed production and use:

It is the responsibility of the researcher to draw the attention of managers and politicians to consequences and to identify the nature of stimuli that cause them. It is also the responsibility of the researcher to draw the attention of managers and politicians to consequences which are having adverse effects for particular groups in society. The researcher can provide powerful evidence even if others take the decisions [14: p. 149].

The suggestion that expert systems might have adverse effects was bold, given the utopian optimism of UK policy-makers and researchers, and the heavy national and international investment in large-scale research programmes like Alvey in the UK and ESPRIT in Europe.

In focusing on design methodology and evidence-based intervention, Mumford took a path followed by a number of UK sociotechnical researchers, who saw commoditized methodologies as a vehicle to transport research into industry. Wood-Harper and Avison, for example, developed the Multiview method [15] as a synthesis of the ideas of Mumford and Kling (in a response to Kling's charge that there was no transdisciplinary method available for organizational research). Without strong commercial or industrial sponsors, however, such a labour-intensive and time-consuming approach was unlikely to work in the 1980s and 1990s in the UK in an environment hostile both to sociological academic research, and to socially rich accounts of implementation [15–17].

A memorial issue of the *Information Systems Journal* [18] published in 2006 shortly after Mumford's death provides ample evidence of her influence, both conceptual and methodological, on a generation of sociotechnical researchers. In a posthumous piece in the same issue, she reflects on the 'story of socio-technical design'. Her tone is sybilline and sombre. ETHICS as a design method has not been widely adopted, and where it has been, the results have been uneven (XSEL, for example, could achieve only regional reach). The current political and social climate is presented as dystopian – a world where vested interests and monopolies shape the workplace, and where global capitalism has produced complex and chaotic effects. A focus on human values and individual rights are all that Mumford can salvage:

> The most important thing that socio-technical design can contribute is its value system. This tells us that although technology and organizational structures may change, the rights and needs of the employee must be given as high a priority as those of the non-human parts of the system [19: p. 338].

She concludes that we badly need 'a more specific concept than the concept of humanism' [19: p. 340]. The next section presents a line of social informatics work whose conceptual base is indeed 'more specific'.

## The social shaping of technology approach at Edinburgh

The second 'truth spot' is Edinburgh. Socially oriented studies of science, technology and innovation were supported at Edinburgh University from the mid 1960s, when David Edge (a physicist) was appointed as founding director of the Science Studies Unit in 1966 [20]. The Unit was multidisciplinary from the start, combining physics expertise with sociology, philosophy and history. Science studies researchers at Edinburgh aimed to provide an unbiased sociological account (recognizing that this is only one of many possible accounts) of the conditions that give rise to scientific insights, and to treat such insights symmetrically regardless of their truth or falsity. They would apply these criteria to their own work [21]. By 1984, this line of work had been extended to include the study of technology. The methodological case for parity of treatment between science and technology is made in the 1984 paper [22] by Pinch and Bijker, 'The social construction of facts and artefacts'. This is a manifesto for a strongly relativist research programme, the Social Construction of Technology (SCOT), to explore technology, complementing the research agenda proposed for science by Bloor and his colleagues.

The principles underlying the Science Studies research agenda remain controversial, notably the stance that for scientificity to be revealed, all knowledge claims (whether they prove to be scientific or not) must initially be treated as equal. SCOT has also provoked controversy. In 1991, for example, Winner [23] exposed the 'poverty' of the research programme, indifferent to moral values and human consequences. He suggested that technological determinism (the 'straw-man' of SCOT proponents) has simply been replaced by social determinism. A close reading of Pinch and Bijker's paper belies such claims. Their accounts of technological development are imbued with moral and aesthetic detail: the 'invention' of the safety bicycle, for example, is presented not as the product of a moment, but of a 20-year trajectory where the eventual artefact was shaped at every stage by the judgments (on the decency of women among other things) and interests of groups who cared about the device. This social process involved selection and rejection (sometimes based on empirical warrant, sometimes not) of each of the component parts – frames, gear mechanisms, handlebars, wheels, tyres and so on: the story is one of participative process, a circuit of advances and retreats. Bijker and Pinch talk of 'getting inside the technology', or 'inside the content'. Like social informatics, SCOT is sensitive to multiple points of view, consequences and the boundaries of inquiry, concerns captured in the core SCOT concepts of 'interpretive flexibility', 'closure', and 'relevant social groups'.

In the 1980s and 1990s, socially oriented research into innovation and technology was strongly supported by UK and EC funding agencies, notably the Economic and Social Research Council (ESRC) whose 10-year PICT (Programme for Information and Communication Technologies) supported investigations at sectoral and societal levels. The genesis and progress of the PICT programme are reviewed in Mansell and Steinmuller [24] and Dutton [25]. PICT can be seen as 'big science' sociotechnical research. It provided resources for trans-sectoral longitudinal research, and, thus, supported extensively scoped social explanations of technology trajectories. Edinburgh was one of six major sites of research, with wide-ranging investigations of the manufacturing sector (focusing on robotics), the financial sector, and, in the 1990s, the emerging field of multimedia technologies – an arena that blurred the boundaries of work and non-work and challenged existing accounts of ICTs and innovation. A set of principles was derived from observations across these different domain studies, corralled under the rubric of 'social shaping of technology', a framing that emphasizes the cumulative nature of development (a 'technology trajectory' shaped by 'technological choices') and the mutual agency (or reflexivity) of shaping and technology. The Institute for the Study of Science, Technology and Innovation (ISSTI) at Edinburgh continues to explore emerging technologies – most recently genomics. The focus here is ICT research – the major output of the Research Centre in the Social Sciences (the precursor, founded in 1984, of ISSTI) in the 1980s and 1990s. This strand of the work continues with current projects on standardization, health informatics, e-science and e-social science.

In 1996, Williams and Edge (at that time current and past directors of RCSS respectively) scoped out the domain [26] describing it as a 'broad church', encompassing a variety of scholars with differing concerns and intellectual traditions, including, for example, 'industrial sociology, evolutionary economics, economic history, sociology of science'. The authors meticulously review the contributions that these, and other cognate research traditions (SCOT, Actor Network Theory for example), have made to sociotechnical thinking, and suggest that sociotechnical research into ICTs has revealed a number of recurring issues and problems, though they may be resolved differently in different periods and contexts. A repertoire of SST concepts and terms has emerged from empirical work over the years that provides analysts with a means to 'get inside' complex technology. In a subsequent review of this framework, Russell and Williams [27] acknowledge that it has been criticized as an externally imposed description of local conditions that can provide little general insight, but they defend it as a means of providing valid insights into contingent and emergent ITC development. The framework opens up the notions of design and development: the language used is processual, presenting development as an open and indeterminate activity. Fleck and Howell, for example, describe this in terms of a 'technology complex', or 'knowledge and activities related to artefacts' [28: p. 525]. The text that follows presents three core SST concepts, with brief discussions of their implications.

The first is a term introduced by Fleck in his PICT-funded studies of robotics on the shop floor [29]. Empirical work at a number of sites showed that innovation continues through implementation, consumption and use – a process that he labelled 'innofusion'. This is a process of protracted learning that involves an array of actors, all with different commitments to a project in terms of each one's past experience and expertise. Such actors may be outside the focal organization – producers of competing products for example – and artefacts typically emerge 'through a complex process of action and interaction between heterogeneous players' – what Fleck calls 'learning by trying' [30], or (in many cases) 'learning by struggling'. This has a number of implications. If technology development is always an occasion for organizational learning, then current performance measures can only be partial as they focus on downstream effects like cost efficiencies or improved performance, and upstream benefits are invisible. In addition, if 'the potential uses and utility of a project cannot be fully understood at the outset' [31: p. 252], then the visions that are presented in project proposals and policy-making documents cannot be considered as prescriptive, and must be analysed as more complex discourse types [27: p.60]. It may be noted that 'vision' has been under-explored in accounts of ICT project work, and it is only recently that a few analysts have turned their attention to this topic [32–34].

The second core concept, 'configuration', develops further the notion of open design and implementation by considering technology in cases where an array of heterogeneous components is arranged locally into some kind of working order. Where sites of use are remote from sites of production, suppliers must 'prefigure' products, which will then be configured locally – and consumers show remarkable inventiveness in adapting technologies [31]. A configuration is 'a complex array of standardized and customized automation elements' [35] – knowledge of how to configure these may be distributed among a number of intermediary suppliers. Configuration is common in integration projects, a form of implementation that is typical of organizational ICT development. To 'get inside' configurational technology, analysts need to shift their focus:

> It is … not helpful to look for the social implications of a technology at the level of specific artefacts (e.g. particular components, or even the integrated artefact given the potential range of configurations available for the same function) but rather at how they are inserted into broader systems of technology and social practice [35: p. 311].

This requires analysts to examine supplier tactics, and to explore the tensions and negotiations that allow commodified products to sit with local innovations. To understand this process in detail, Williams [31, 35] suggests that we need to understand standardization – firstly the process by which technologies become stabilized (and de-stabilized), and secondly, the ways in which the generic potential of new technologies (the 'supplier' focus) is to be matched with current and emerging user and societal requirements that tend to undermine the trend to stabilization. Producers attempt to align co-producers and enrol future users through alliance building, which will allow them to share costs and risks, and 'reduce uncertainties by foreclosing options in advance'. Williams observes that

> Future technologies/markets are being pre-constructed in a virtual space constituted by the collective activities of players around standards for the interconnection between products [35: p. 311],

as major actors seek to align expectations around their particular offerings.

Alignment requires actors to mobilize around an artefact, and build sustainable alliances – the process of multi-actor and multi-level 'social learning', the third core concept that is explored here [31]. If the earlier projects in the RCSS programme explored 'domestication' in the context of organizations [31: p. 251], later projects broadened the scope:

> social learning is not restricted to the learning economy of supplier-user interaction around the design and appropriation of artefacts, but also

encompasses the activity of public policy-makers, as well as promoters and other players in civil society in setting the 'rules of the game' [31: p. 251].

Mobilization and alliance building often happen around demonstrator projects (think of the big EC IST programmes) that provide convincing evidence of technological futures. According to Williams

> governments (and supra-governmental bodies such as the European Union and the G7 group of countries) are trying to match or outdo each other in setting up different kinds of experiments ... This tie between government and industry elites is geared towards a consensus about the need for greater ICT investments in order to achieve competitiveness and social advance ... associated with particular rhetorics about what ICTs will deliver [31: p. 252].

Large trials and pilots (in more or less natural settings) are a way to learn how to develop, as much as a way to learn about what products and services will look like – experimental projects may not need to proceed to roll-out/widespread use to be deemed worthwhile, as a key social learning ability is the capacity to

> unbundle different elements; to build upon relationships established to retain and transfer relevant knowledges and creatively apply them in different settings [31: p. 255].

Particular industrial experiences rapidly become disseminated and discussed across the field and thus come to form part of the strategic repertoire for further technological and commercial strategies.

A major implication of such macro-level social learning is a shift in policy configuration. In an environment where informal sectoral knowledge drives macro-level alliance building, government's role becomes more complex as it moves from commissioning evidence-based sociological research (the scenario for Mumford's early work) to direct participation in experiential policy-making, sometimes 'acting in its own right as a powerful intermediary in development', or more usually 'providing resources for other intermediaries ... bringing groups together, and supporting demonstrator and awareness programs' [31: p. 258]. Official evaluation of such large-scale collaborations in both the UK and Europe has focused on operational and functional performance, and more comprehensive accounting mechanisms are not yet in place to assess the Return on Investment for alliance-building [36, 37]. Both public and private sector agencies seek to protect their sunk investments in this area as they do for R & D – and accountability becomes problematic.

The 20-year trajectory of research that is described in this section is important for a number of reasons. By defining and elaborating a number of core concepts (three are discussed here) for the exploration of dynamic and complex infrastructures, researchers at Edinburgh were able to explicate the ICT research and policy problems that emerged from a developing global infrastructure. ICT development is revealed as an open process, imbued with politics and learning opportunities, whose stability is not guaranteed. Critical engagement with this process is a major part of the work of the group that is the focus of the next section.

## The Critical Informatics approach at the LSE

The third site is the London School of Economics (LSE), whose association with a sociotechnical tradition can be traced to the appointment of Frank Land in 1967, bringing practical experience of the groundbreaking implementation of an office automation system at J.S. Lyons, 'LEO' [38]. LEO was a thoroughly sociotechnical project, involving work processes that would later be described as 'participative design' and 'social learning'. LSE's long track record in organizational computing research is not, however, reviewed here (readers interested in a more comprehensive account of organizational ICT analysis at LSE can consult the edited monographs by Currie and Galliers [39] and Avgerou, Ciborra and Land [40]). In this section a specific line of work, critical IS, is explored. Many of the concepts and methods developed and explored by critical IS researchers at LSE overlap (consciously and unconsciously) with the sociotechnical and social shaping approaches discussed in earlier sections; the group has, however, contextualized these in a wider European theoretical tradition (Heidegger, Foucault, Latour, etc.). The work of the LSE group is empirical and locally grounded: in some case studies, concepts are probed; in others they are elaborated on; and, in others again, new ways are presented of framing 'knowledge and activities' around computational artefacts. At the end of the 1990s, Claudio Ciborra joined the group, a *genius loci* who constantly challenged the 'Gestell' of established methods and concepts in his search for detailed and authentic explanations of the organizational phenomena that constitute technology. His death, in 2005, was marked by a memorial issue of the *European Journal of Information Systems* – the contributions are unusually rich and affective and the obituaries work as a form of collective bricolage [41] and as a form of stock taking for critical IS.

Ciborra's prior work is summarized in his 2002 monograph, *The labyrinths of information* [42]. Here he distils what he has learned from years of empirical work. To critique standard approaches, Ciborra often adopted and adapted available terms and concepts. In Heidegger, for example, he found the concepts of caretaking (we attend to things that matter to us) and disclosure: we need to drop the old methodologies in order to

> better be able to see the new dimensions the technology is going to disclose – technology reveals what was hidden [43].

From Unger, he took the notion of 'formative context' to explain that we can never fully anticipate the effects of new technology, as the world presents itself to us in terms of past experience. From Weick, he appropriated the notion of bricolage ('leveraging the world' by using what is to hand), coupling and contrasting the term with the notion of improvization, the transgressive energy that breaks the given order, or 'jumps Gestalt'. Such concepts were operationalized in a lexicon, of 'caring', hospitality' and 'cultivation', for analysing organizational computing that challenges the validity of mainstream accounts and received ideas.

The group's probing and elaboration of received concepts and methods is evident in a 1999 case study by Whitley [44] of systems implementation in Prêt à Manger, a fresh food takeaway retail chain with a strong participative ethos. The systems design approach observed by the researchers was less participatory than the team expected, and they wished to find out why. In a highly reflexive account, Whitley and his colleagues explore both participative and autocratic decisions about design across the project. The first attempt at analysis shoehorns their observations into a linear model of stakeholder alignment that uses the terminology of Actor Network Theory – intéressement, engagement and so on; but they are rebuked for this by both the Prêt à Manger actors, and by Latour, the author of the approach [45]. A second attempt at analysis explores the relationship between participative and autocratic decision-making by looking at the antecedents and outcomes associated with each style, and shows how the hybrid approach revealed aspects of entrepreneurial working that were previously hidden – Heidegger's notion of disclosive space is invoked here. In a different study, a similar method is used in an exploration of the notion of 'regulation' in a case study of peer to peer networking [46]. A number of received ideas ('free cyberspace' and 'code as regulation', for example) are tested against observations of a localized working group – and a more nuanced account is provided of regulation that suggests that the regulatory effects of code differ according to users' experience and technical competence: 'black boxes' perform a service for novices, but not for more experienced users.

Whitley explicitly embraces Ciborra's vocabulary in co-authored account [47] of a project - Digital Business Ecology (DBE) funded by the European Commission [45] where the tension between the 'promissory' machine (a notion discussed in the previous section) and a convincing material prototype is explored. This is, of course, the world of the large scale pilot projects or experiments in social learning described by the Edinburgh group. The paper presents the dynamic between the development of an abstract schematic organization (the PERT chart, the software) and demonstration of a material artefact, and the authors chart failures to deliver at milestones, and the emergence of an alien product from the network. Whitley and his colleagues frame the story in terms of two complementary experiences of organizing, 'fluid' and 'fire', Ciborra's dense and concise metaphors for routine work and improvization. Anyone who has worked on such projects will recognize the authenticity of the narrative – the sudden bursts of improvization as deadlines are missed, the triage of deliverables as the project progresses and the tinkering with elements of the project that are revealed as lesser priorities. Standard project management protocols cannot contain complexity – but the effects of complexity can be mastered by experienced actors.

A concern with the effects (and thus the quality) of policy-making (anticipated or experienced) is at the core of social informatics at the LSE and elsewhere. In 2004, Ciborra [48] turned his attention to UK policy on grid technologies, observing that they

> are bound to produce a techno-socio-economic assemblage that has the potential of becoming a pervasive technology for managing individuals' life projects in ways that have not been possible [48: p. 469].

Scrutinizing the role of government (national, international and global) in promoting and securing such platforms is a major focus of LSE critical research, and a number of projects, on e-health, and on e-government for example, are under way. One of these, the 'Identity Project', seeks to provide evidence-based input into UK policy-making on Identity Cards. This is one of a number of 'mega-projects' [49], or 'mega-programmes' [50] that have been initiated in the UK in the past ten years, many of which have failed to deliver to specification, on time or on budget, for identifiable reasons [51]. In these projects, the problems identified in the earlier DBE study (virtual artefact versus material artefact, promises versus demonstrable effects) are amplified – as UK e-government projects attempt integration (of data, of operating systems, and of labour across multiply outsourced contractors) on a previously unattempted scale. Over the past three years, LSE researchers have critically assessed the claims made for such programmes, gathering evidence from analogous initiatives elsewhere, and addressing the 'misplaced expectations' and 'overly optimistic' promises of politicians [50], by offering evidence at various stages of public inquiry and scrutiny. The group's attempts to 'improve the terms of debate and public discourse' have required integrity and tenacity at every level of the institution [52].

The archive of the project consists of the technical reports that have been presented as evidence, press coverage, and academic publications that reflect on the project as a critical IS initiative. Costs, the overt focus of a 2005 public controversy about the project, are only one component of this complex technological assemblage; by offering alternative models [53] for costs and other components, and experiencing the processes by which these possibilities were acknowledged or rejected, the LSE group is working 'inside the technology' as participants and observers. But the archive also documents a process of social learning, by conserving evidence of the interactions that have placed this particular group of academic actors in an authentically critical relationship with government and industry. A corollary of this experience is the group's suggestion [54] that we need a shift in academic values to legitimize engagement with society as an activity that earns points in terms of career trajectories.

## Conclusion

Sociotechnical research is sometimes presented as an overly localized, non-analytic line of work. Kallinikos, for example, characterizes much of critical IS as suffering from 'ethnographic positivism':

small sets of observations, plus selected documentation used as reality ... the macro-sociological indifference means that some technological characteristics that embody a wider historical and institutional context are ignored [55].

Cronin [56] makes similar observations. This article has shown that though such ethnographic work may be part of a line of inquiry, many UK sociotechnical researchers undertake a larger task, that of tracing links between local observations and a wider set of social phenomena, addressing micro-, meso- and macro-level developments. They share with SI researchers in the United States a fundamental interest in the production of technology, and the complex processes that are involved.

Formal bibliographic links between the two traditions discussed here are surprisingly few. Kling, for example, mentions the work of Mumford and Pettigrew in his early work; Williams [31] and Sauer and Willcocks [50] invoke concepts developed by Kling. A recent analysis of Kling's citation habits [57] reveals that his citation identity (the sources cited) is very US-centric. Yet a current generation of researchers in both the UK and the US can see clear affinities between SI and sociotechnical research [1, 8], and it may be noted that a number of Social Informatics research groups (explicitly labelled as such) have emerged in the UK – at Napier University in Edinburgh, at York and at Brighton for example. These researchers work with an eclectic repertoire of concepts and methods that draws on both traditions. For a number of us, SI/sociotech is one of the more interesting games in town.

## Acknowledgment

I would like to thank Trevor Wood-Harper for help with sources on Enid Mumford, and Blaise Cronin for discussion and feedback on earlier drafts of the paper.

## References

[1]   K. Horton, E. Davenport and T.W. Wood-Harper, Exploring sociotechnical interaction with Rob Kling: five 'big' ideas, *Information, Technology and People* 18(1) (2005) 50–67.

[2]   R. Kling and W. Scacchi, The web of computing, Computing technology and social organization, *Advances in Computers* 21 (1982) 3–90.

[3] R. Kling, Defining the boundaries of computing across complex organizations. In: R. Boland and R. Hirschheim (eds), *Critical Issues in Information Systems* (John Wiley, New York, 1987) 307–362.

[4] R. Kling, What is social informatics and why does it matter? *DLIB Magazine* 5(1) (1999). Available at: http://www.dlib.org/dlib/january99/kling/01kling.html (accessed 6 January 2008). Reprinted in *The Information Society* 23 (2007) 205–220.

[5] R. Day, Kling and the 'critical': social informatics and critical informatics, *Journal of the American Society for Information Science and Technology* 58(4) (2007) 575–582.

[6] B. Wellman and R. Hiltz, Sociological Rob: how Rob Kling brought computing and sociology together, *The Information Society* 20 (2004) 91–95.

[7] S. Sawyer and K. Eschenfelder, Social informatics: perspectives, examples and trends. In B. Cronin (ed.), *Annual Review of Science and Technology* 36, (Information Today, Medford, NJ, 2002) 427–425.

[8] S. Sawyer and A. Tapia, From findings to theories: institutionalising social informatics, *The Information Society* 23 (2007) 263–275.

[9] R. Hirschheim, in: D. Avison, N. Bjørn-Andersen, E. Coakes, G.B. Davis, M.J. Earl, A. Elbanna, G. Fitzgerald, R.D. Galliers, R. Hirschheim, J. Iivari, H.K. Klein, F. Land, M. de Marco, A.M. Pettigrew, J. Porra, B. C. Stahl, C. Sørensen, B. Wood and T. Wood-Harper, Enid Mumford: a tribute, *Information Systems Journal* 16(4) (2006) 343–382.

[10] T. Gieryn, City as truth spot, *Social Studies of Science* 36(1) (2006) 5–38.

[11] E. Mumford and O. Banks, *The Computer and the Clerk* (Routledge and Kegan Paul, London, 1967).

[12] E. Mumford, *Living with a Computer* (Institute of Personnel Management, London, 1964).

[13] E. Mumford and M. Weir, *Computer Systems in Work Design – the ETHICS Method* (Associated Business Press, London, 1979).

[14] E. Mumford, Managerial expert systems and organizational change: some critical research issues. In R.J. Boland and R.A. Hirschheim (Eds), *Critical Issues in Information Systems Research* (John Wiley, New York, 1987) 135–155.

[15] D.E. Avison and A.T. Wood Harper, Multiview – an exploration in information systems development, *Australian Computer Journal* 18(4) (1986) 174–179.

[16] R. Singh, B. Wood and T. Wood-Harper, Socio-technical design of the 21st century. In: T. McMaster, D. Wastell, E. Ferneley and J.I. DeGross (eds), *Organizational Dynamics of Technology-based Innovation: Diversifying the Research Agenda* (International Federation for Information Processing, Vol. 235, Springer, Berlin, 2007) 503–406.

[17]   T.D. Wilson, *Professor Tom Wilson – a (mainly) professional biography*. Available at: http://informationr.net/tdw/biog.html (accessed 19 December 2007).

[18]   D. Avison, N. Bjørn-Andersen, E. Coakes, G.B. Davis, M.J. Earl, A. Elbanna, G. Fitzgerald, R.D. Galliers, R. Hirschheim, J. Iivari, H.K. Klein, F. Land, M. de Marco, A.M. Pettigrew, J. Porra, B. C. Stahl, C. Sørensen, B. Wood and T. Wood-Harper, Enid Mumford: a tribute, *Information Systems Journal* 16 (2006) 343–382.

[19]   E. Mumford, The story of socio-technical design: reflection on its successes, failures, and potential, *Information Systems Journal* 16(4) (2006) 317–342.

[20]   D. Mackenzie, B. Barnes, S. Jasanoff and M. Lynch, Life's work, love's work. Four tributes to David Edge (1932–2003), *EASST Review* 22(1/2) (2003).

[21]   D. Bloor, *Knowledge and Social Imagery* (Routledge, London, 1976).

[22]   T. Pinch and W. Bijker, The social construction of facts and artefacts: or how the sociology of science and the sociology of technology might benefit each other, *Social Studies of Science* 14(3) (1984) 399–441.

[23]   L. Winner, Upon opening the black box and finding it empty: social constructivism and the philosophy of technology, *Science Technology & Human Values* 18(3) (1993) 362–378.

[24]   R. Mansell and E. Steinmuller, *Mobilizing the Information Society, Strategies for Growth and Opportunity* (Oxford University Press, Oxford, UK, 2000).

[25]   W. Dutton, The web of technology and people: challenges for economic and social research, *Prometheus* 17(1) (1999) 5–20.

[26]   R. Williams and D. Edge, The social shaping of technology, *Research Policy* 25 (1996) 865–899.

[27]   S. Russell and R. Williams, Social shaping of technology: frameworks, findings and implications for policy with Glossary of social shaping concepts. In K. Sorensen and R. Williams (eds), *Shaping Technology, Guiding Policy* (Edward Elgar, Cheltenham, UK, 2002) 37–131.

[28]   J. Fleck and J. Howells, Technology, the technology complex and the paradox of technological determinism, *Technology Analysis and Strategic Management* 13(4) (2001) 523–532.

[29]   J. Fleck, *Innofusion or Diffusation? The Nature of Technological Development in Robotics* (Edinburgh PICT Working Paper No. 7, Edinburgh University, Edinburgh, UK, 1988).

[30]   J. Fleck, Learning by trying: the implementation of configurational technology, *Research Policy* 23 (1994) 637–652.

[31]   R. Williams, Public choices and social learning; the new multimedia technologies in Europe, *The Information Society* 16 (2000) 251–262.

[32]   N. Pollock, *The promise organisation and the market for ICT* (Presented at the University of Edinburgh, Edinburgh, UK, 14 December 2007).

[33]   N. Thrift, *Knowing Capitalism* (Sage, London, 2005).

[34]   K. Vann and G. Bowker, Interest in production: on the configuration of technology-bearing labours for epistemic IT. In C. Hine (ed.), *New Infrastructures for Knowledge Production: Understanding E-Science* (Information Science Publishing, London, 2006) 71–79.

[35]   R. Williams, The social shaping of information and communications technologies. In: H.Kubicek, W. Dutton and R. Williams (eds), *The Social Shaping of Information Superhighways: European and American Roads to the Information Society* (St Martin's Press, New York, 1997) 299–338.

[36]   B. Kahin and D. Foray (eds), *Advancing Knowledge in the Knowledge Economy* (MIT Press, Cambridge, MA, 2006).

[37]   E. Davenport, Minding the Galison gap, *The Information Society* (in press).

[38]   F. Land, A historical analysis of implementing IS at J. Lyons. In: W. Currie and R. Galliers (eds), *Rethinking Management Information Systems* (Oxford University Press, Oxford, UK, 1999) 310–325.

[39]   W. Currie and R. Galliers (eds), *Rethinking Management Information Systems* (Oxford University Press, Oxford, UK, 1999).

[40]   C. Avgerou, C. Ciborra and F. Land, *The Social Study of IT* (Oxford University Press, Oxford, UK, 2004).

[41]   B. Stahl, The obituary as bricolage: the Mann Gulch disaster and the problem of heroic rationality, *European Journal of Information Systems* 14 (2005) 487–491.

[42]   C. Ciborra, *The Labyrinths of Information: Challenging the Wisdom of Systems* (Oxford University Press, Oxford, UK, 2002).

[43]   S. Zuboff, Ciborra disclosed: aletheia in the life and scholarship of Claudio Ciborra, *European Journal of Information Systems* 14 (2005) 470–473.

[44]   E. Whitley, Understanding participation in entrepreneurial organizations: some hermeneutic readings, *Journal of Information Technology* 14 (1999) 193–202.

[45]   B. Latour, On using ANT for studying information systems: a (somewhat) Socratic dialogue. In: C. Avgerou, C. Ciborra and F. Land (eds), *The Social Study of Information and Communication Technology* (Oxford University Press, Oxford, UK, 2004) 61–76.

[46]   A. Micakova and E. Whitley, Configuring peer-to-peer software: an empirical study of how users react to the regulatory features of software, *European Journal of Information Systems* 13 (2006) 95–102.

[47]   E. Whitley and M. Darking, Object lessons and invisible technologies, *Journal of Information Technology* 21 (2006) 176–184.

[48] C. Ciborra, *Digital Technologies and the Duality of Risk* (CARR, the London School of Economics, London, UK, 2004).

[49] B. Flyvberg, N. Bruzelius and W. Rothengatter, *Megaprojects and Risk: an Anatomy of Ambition* (Cambridge University Press, Cambridge, UK, 2003).

[50] C. Sauer and L. Willcocks, Unreasonable expectations – NHS IT, Greek choruses and the games institutions play around mega-programmes, *Journal of Information Technology* 22 (2007) 195–201.

[51] P. Dunleavy, H. Margetta, S. Bastow and J. Tinkler, *Digital Era Governance: IT Corporations, the State and E-Government* (Oxford University Press, Oxford, UK, 2006).

[52] E. Whitley, I.R. Hosein, I. Angell and S. Davies, Reflections on the academic policy analysis process and the UK identity cards scheme, *The Information Society* 23 (2007) 51–58.

[53] E. Whitley and I. Hosein, *Departmental Influences on Policy Design: how the UK is Confusing Identity Fraud with Other Policy Agendas* (Department of Management, Information Systems Group, Working Paper Series 160, London School of Economics and Political Science, London, UK, 2007).

[54] E. Whitley and I. Hosein, *Policy Engagement as Rigorous and Relevant Information Systems Research: the Case of the LSE Identity Project* (Department of Management, Information Systems Group, Working Paper Series 159, London School of Economics and Political Science, London, UK, 2007).

[55] J. Kallinikos, Farewell to constructivism: technology and context-embedded action. In: C. Avgerou, C. Ciborra and F. Land (eds), *The Social Study of Information and Communication Technology* (Oxford University Press, Oxford, UK, 2004) 140–161.

[56] B. Cronin, *Journal of Information Science* 34(4) (2008) in press.

[57] B. Cronin and D. Shaw, Peers and spheres of influence: situating Rob Kling, *The Information Society* 23 (2007) 221–234.

# 10

# The evolution of visual information retrieval

PETER ENSER

## Abstract

This paper seeks to provide a brief overview of those developments which have taken the theory and practice of image and video retrieval into the digital age. Drawing on a voluminous literature, the context in which visual information retrieval takes place is followed by a consideration of the conceptual and practical challenges posed by the representation and recovery of visual material on the basis of its semantic content. An historical account of research endeavours in content-based retrieval, directed towards the automation of these operations in digital image scenarios, provides the main thrust of the paper. Finally, a look forwards locates visual information retrieval research within the wider context of content-based multimedia retrieval.

## The context of visual information retrieval

The retrieval of images or image sequences that are relevant to a query is a long-established activity which has evolved quite remarkably during the last 50 years, from the special preserve of a relatively few professional practitioners to the forefront of research in computer vision and a leading edge domestic application of information technology. This extension of traditional information retrieval activity includes both still and moving images, the former usually characterized in the literature as 'image retrieval', the latter as 'video retrieval', and the two in combination, sometimes, as 'visual information retrieval' [1,2].

The literature of visual information retrieval has grown at a stupendous rate. To quote Jörgensen, in her landmark text within the field:

Adjectives such as 'vast' are often applied to the various literatures … related to image processing, but even this designation is an understatement [3: p. 199].

More remarkable still is the fact that almost all of that growth has taken place since the early 1990s, and reflects those technological advances which brought the digital image to the attention of the computer scientist. Greatly increased availability of images via the internet, then via mobile platforms, and most recently as an aspect of the social networking phenomenon, has been said to place us

on the hinge of an important historical swing back towards to what may be called the primacy of the image [3: p. ix].

Jörgensen's observation reflects the huge upsurge in image and video retrieval activity by the general public, which finds expression in such diverse activities as searching for visual materials using search engines such as Google Images (http://images.google.co.uk/) or a social networking facility such as YouTube (http://uk.youtube.com/), the browsing of online television broadcast archives, and the recovery of images from increasingly voluminous personal stores of digital photographs.

Visual images exist in a wide variety of forms, but it is those whose features can be captured and/or viewed by unenhanced human vision, encountered typically as photographs or artwork, which have predominated in the literature of image retrieval. The curatorial or commercial imperative to collect other types of still image, including those the features of which must be captured and/or viewed by means of equipment which expands the range of human vision, such as microscopes, telescopes and electronic imaging devices, has been less pronounced. In part this is because some classes of image, notably in the medical, architectural and engineering domains, tend to occur as adjuncts to parent records, and it is these parent records which are usually the object of retrieval, rather than the images themselves. However, researchers in medicine – and in defence and criminology – came to an early realization that images within those domains must be treated as important information objects in their own right, rather than mere appendices to other database information, leading to the formation of specialized collections for research and training purposes [3: p. 139].

The technology to support the display of sequences of images in rapid succession in order to create the illusion of moving imagery has only given rise to collections of film and video material in more recent times. Because of their scale and growth rate, however, such collections have also figured significantly in the literature of visual information retrieval, and the locating of that activity within the wider context of multimedia retrieval.

In the pre-digital era, requests of varying degrees of urgency would be addressed to image repositories in the form of telephone calls, written specifications and sometimes by the presence of the client in person. Where necessary, the repository's picture researchers would act as mediators, seeking to introduce greater precision into the natural language requests, perhaps translating them into the terminology of a controlled vocabulary associated with the repository's classification scheme, and helping the client towards an explicit articulation of the mental image for which the client was seeking some physical realization [4]. In other words, this mediation process exactly paralleled that of the reference librarian in a traditional library, except that it was conducted among hanging files or archival boxes stuffed with monochrome prints and colour transparencies, backed up by a store of negatives, in a scenario engagingly captured, albeit with some dramatic license, in Stephen Poliakoff's television play *Shooting the Past* [5].

The success with which material appropriate to a client's request could be extracted from such stores reflected the picture researcher's knowledge of the collection, and of the classification and indexing practices adopted by the repository; it also reflected the researcher's judgement, based on visual inspection of any candidate images.

Film and video libraries presented a different appearance, their shelves laden with tins containing reels of film, the chemical properties of which called for special knowledge and a controlled environment [6]. Prior to viewing, determination of the potential relevance of complete films was assisted by the short synopses which sometimes augmented their catalogue records. The retrieval of image sequences, as opposed to whole films, was more challenging. Protracted viewing of material in order to make selections might be assisted by time-coded listings of each shot within a film, but the compilation of such tools was itself a highly labour-intensive operation, the undertaking of which reflected a clear commercial imperative.

In general, although a number of cataloguing standards have been developed for image and film material, and are comprehensively described by the Technical Advisory Service for Images (TASI) [7], visual asset management has lacked the adherence to universal standards of cataloguing and classification which characterized traditional library practice with text-based material. In large measure this reflected the problems posed in attempting to capture in indexing language the semantic content of images. These problems have been a recurring theme in the literature of image and video retrieval, and an understanding of their nature is central to an appreciation of the evolution of visual information retrieval.

## Image indexing

Greisdorf and O'Connor [8] and Jörgensen [3: pp. 7–68), in particular, have drawn on the literature of cognitive psychology to assist our understanding of how humans interact with images. They describe an initial physiological response to the visual primitives of colour, texture and the spatial distribution of blobs and regions within an image. This perception of the syntactic content of the image is rapidly overtaken by cognitive reasoning about the semantic content in the form of objects, activities and scenes. This is followed by high-level, inductive interpretation of the wider semantic context in which the image is located, which brings into play the viewer's subjective belief system. Analysis of user responses to images, whilst revealing 'wildly differing assessments' of particular images, found that

> user assertions about interactions with pictures … form a richer descriptive palette than ordinary indexing [9].

The principles and practice of image indexing by means of which semantic content can be represented have been the subject of comprehensive reviews [3,10,11], together with a variety of other contributions, notably [12–27]. This literature provided the backcloth to the increasingly elaborate conceptual frameworks which came to be built as a means of informing the image indexing process.

The simplest such frameworks recognized three levels, which corresponded with visual primitives (colour, texture, shapes), logical or 'derived' features (objects, activities, events) and inductive interpretation (abstract features) [8,26]. A more developed model, which has figured quite prominently in the literature, rests on the formal analysis of Renaissance art images by the art historian Panofsky [28], who recognized primary subject matter ('pre-iconography') which required no interpretative skill; secondary subject matter ('iconography'), which did call for an interpretation to be placed on the image; and tertiary subject matter, denoted 'iconology', embracing the intrinsic meaning of the image, and demanding of the viewer high-level semantic inferencing.

Shatford [14] was instrumental in generalizing Panofsky's analysis, simplifying the first two modes in terms of 'generic' and 'specific', and amplifying these by distinguishing between what a picture is 'of' and what it is 'about'. The notion of 'generic', 'specific' and 'abstract' semantic content has since figured prominently in the literature, the more developed formulations containing multiple levels, comprising both syntactic or pre-conceptual visual content, to which are added semantic layers of interpretive attributes which invoke the viewer's inferential reasoning about the local object and global scenic content of the image [29,30].

Most recently, the basic level theory expounded by Rosch et al. [31], together with extensions to a facet analysis of the subject attributes of an image [16], have been combined in a more developed form of conceptual model which gives explicit recognition to the combination of semantic content and context in image material [22]. Hare et al. [32] have shown how the keywords allocated by expert indexers to a museum's image collection can be mapped to this rich conceptual model.

Whatever the level of sophistication attained by conceptual models, the manual indexing of images has remained a matter of trying to represent visually encoded semantic content in a verbal surrogate. The problematic nature of this translation process found expression in Markey's observation that individual differences in image perception give rise to 'extraordinary idiosyncrasy' in the assignment of image terms [12], and Hogan et al.'s observation that

> If an image carries a great deal of information for the user which is dependent on contextual and situational factors, the assumption that meaning rests in a pre-defined set of subject terms is of limited utility to control access to the contents of an image base [33].

Besser [34] had already noted that

> Historically, text-based intellectual access systems have been woefully inadequate for describing the multitude of access points from which the user might try to recall the image

and Svenonius [17] went on to state that

> it is useless to attempt to point to unspeakable reality with an index term

because subject indexing presupposes that what is depicted can be named, whereas there are messages addressed to our visual and aural perceptions, the content of which cannot be named.

Arguably, the semantic indexing of film and video poses even greater challenges. The task has to address different levels of semantic structure, from the frame, through shot and scene to the film or video stream as a complete entity, together with other semantically coherent sequences in the form of clips, episodes and news stories [2: pp. 10, 35, 36]. In the absence of exhaustive shot lists the minimalist nature of synopses in standard sources of reference makes them particularly blunt instruments for leveraging the full semantic content of these forms of information object.

The phenomenon of social tagging has brought a new dimension to the representation of the semantic content of visual materials. Exemplified in such products as Flickr (http://www.flickr.com/) and YouTube(http://uk.youtube.com/), the ability to contribute personal tags to image and video metadata challenges the supremacy of professionally sourced, authoritative subject representation, whilst introducing opportunities for beneficial enhancement of both exhaustivity and specificity in subject indexing.

## Analysis of user needs

In an attempt to gain insight into effective indexing practice, a rich vein of enquiry was opened up in the 1980s, directed at the analysis of users' needs for images and image sequences. The oft-quoted observation

> The delight and frustration of pictorial resources is that a picture can mean different things to different people [14],

amplified by a recognition that a picture can mean different things to the same person at different times or under different circumstances, provided the platform for these endeavours. Observations such as Falconer's [37], that the subjects most often sought by a particular archive's clients fell into a 'no-man's land of categories' which could not be adequately or precisely classified by any existing system, and Besser's [34], that the retrieval utility of an image is inherently unpredictable, led naturally to the conclusion that the appropriate level of indexing exhaustivity is indeterminate, and that subject indexing is of low utility [19]. Only in those scenarios where the clients are well-defined and their needs well-understood could the negative impact of this unpredictability be lessened.

Jörgensen [3: p. 127] reviewed a number of these user studies, the most widely cited of which analysed some 2700 requests addressed by a variety of client types to the Hulton Deutsch collection – a major, general-purpose picture archive (now part of Getty Images) [4,38]. A preliminary analysis of these requests revealed a very wide variation in subject foci and terminological specificity, and also that the majority of the requests were for specific objects or events, frequently 'refined' by spatial, temporal or other combinations of facets. A number of other studies subsequently confirmed the relatively high incidence of requests for specific, named features [27,39–42], whilst other studies reported quite different user behaviour in which emphasis was placed on more generic or affective visual features [43–48].

The behavioural patterns exhibited in these studies ranged across a number of application areas, including art history [39,42], journalism [18,27], and medicine [43]. In combination, all these user studies contributed to a perception that the further removed the image retrieval scenario is from the scenario of a specialist archival collection, with expert mediation and an experienced user, the lower is the significance of carefully constructed metadata, and the greater is the significance of browsing facilities. Coupled with the latter came a developing appreciation of the significance of relevance feedback, with users able to interact freely with displayed output, using their innate capacity to perceive at a glance the potential interest of an image [49–51]. Fidel [23] captured the essence of this argument in an important paper which described a continuum of image searching tasks, at the extremities of which were an 'object pole' and a 'data pole'. The former referred to the situation where interest lay in retrieving a specific image identified, for example, by title, whereas the latter denoted the need to retrieve the data or information portrayed by the image. Any particular image might satisfy a number of different requests located at various points along this continuum, but recognition of the two poles carried significant implications for the design and evaluation of image retrieval systems. Towards the 'object pole' relevance becomes more difficult to determine, which lends added emphasis to browsing facilities; conversely, relevance feedback increases in importance towards the 'data pole'. It was towards this latter pole that the image retrieval research community increasingly turned their attention.

Whereas earlier user studies involved the collection of image requests recorded manually by image archive staff, and often reflecting some degree of expert mediation by them, the increasing incidence of Web-based, end-user searching of image collections has generated unmediated requests culled automatically from transaction logs. Studies of these have been able to analyse very much larger numbers of requests, as in the case of the analysis by Goodrum and Spink [52] of the transaction logs of over 33,000 image requests submitted to the Excite search engine (http://search.excite.com).

Web-enabled access to digitized image collections, whether through general search engines such as Google (http://images.google.co.uk) and Yahoo! (http://images.search.yahoo.com), specialized image search engines such as Picsearch (http://www.picsearch.com) or collection-specific search engines, brought about a revolution in image retrieval. The factors involved in the design and implementation of web image search engines were discussed by Kherfi et al. [53], who identified a need for more advanced tools to enhance retrieval performance. The user's search behaviour has also been the subject of study: Smeulders et al. [54] proposed a useful categorization which recognized 'target search', 'category search' and 'search by association' (corresponding to the 'text-based', 'subject-based' and 'browsing' labels used in an earlier study [39]). The first of these aims at a specific image, identified by title or other unique identifier, and conforms with Fidel's [23] notion of the 'object pole'. In a 'category search' the client requests images which feature some particular semantic content at the local or global level. In a 'search by association' the client may approach an image collection with no particular semantic content requirement in mind, and is content to browse in order to retrieve images by serendipity.

The evidence available thus far about Web-based searching of image collections points to the increased significance of the 'search by association' relative to the 'category search', which has been the traditional focus of effort in the professional practice of image retrieval [48,52,55]. In reality, little intelligence has been gathered on user interaction with the vast array of visual resources made available, either freely by search engines or in password-protected repositories, in the Web environment. Roddy's [56: p. 48] observation in 1991 that one of the great failures of image access was its inability to provide reliable information on a typical search session was thought by Jörgensen [3: p. 129) to remain true over a decade later, and it seems to the present author that the situation has not changed greatly in the interim.

In comparison with studies of users' needs for still image content, search requests and behaviour in the context of film and video material has received comparatively little attention. Studies involving archival film collections have been reported [35,57,58], but a fully comprehensive study of user interaction with moving images is still awaited.

## Towards content-based image retrieval

The first milestones along the development path which led to content-based image retrieval (CBIR) were encountered in the late 1970s in the form of databases constructed specifically for picture storage and retrieval [51,54]. Tony Cawkell's [59] detailed analysis of the design factors involved in their construction provides a good insight into the state-of-the-art as it had evolved by the early 1990s. The earliest attempts at image database construction were characterized by the difficulties encountered in attempting integration of image data and relational database structures [60–67]. By the beginning of the 1990s, however, Besser [34] was able to report on the benefit of clients being able to browse screen displays of thumbnail images without recourse to library personnel and without physical handling of the images themselves, in products such as Imagequery, characterized as the marriage of a standard text-oriented online library catalogue with a powerful image browsing mechanism [33].

Substantial development of image databases followed, usefully surveyed in [68], with digitized images co-located with their metadata, albeit with widely varying levels of adherence to a number of different image metadata standards. Notwithstanding the advances made since the early 1990s in digital visual asset management systems, the traditional paradigm of image retrieval remained that of textual string matching between the client's verbal search request statement and the subject annotations embedded within the image collection metadata. By this time, however, the image retrieval research community had perceived the need to:

> relinquish the idea of the utility of using words to index non-verbal
> understanding … We are looking for alternative ways of image retrieval, ways
> that are less dependent on familiarity with existing taxonomies and their
> assigned authorities [33].

There was a complementary wish to reduce dependency on the collection knowledge locked into the heads of the curators of image collections. A compelling case for this was made by the Challenger space shuttle explosion in 1986, in the aftermath of which there was an urgent requirement to retrieve from NASA's huge visual archive all possibly relevant images depicting the Challenger launch sequence and the failed booster rocket. The manual retrieval system, 'highly dependent on the corporate memories of a few dedicated individuals', could not meet this requirement [69]. Such perceptions highlighted the significance of a workshop organized by the National Science Foundation in 1992 to identify major research areas in visual information management systems, with emphasis on interactive image understanding in such applications as medical images and satellite images [54]. Shortly afterwards, the Mosaic Internet browser was released and the manifest difficulties associated with manual indexing of visual images placed in sharp relief the need for indexing tools appropriate for Web-enabled access to digital archives. Thus was fuelled some 15 years of intense research activity directed towards the CBIR paradigm.

The term 'content-based image retrieval' derives from the fact that the CBIR paradigm operates on the explicit content of the digitized image, which is its pixel domain. There are those within the professional image practitioner community who, like Hyvönen et al. [70], have expressed some scepticism about the 'content-based' label, arguing that the content of an image lies in the semantic inferences to which it leads the viewer, and which may be explicitly represented in textual metadata.

In the early stages of CBIR the focus was on syntactic operations conducted on the pixel domain of the digitized image, in order to generate visual feature vectors as surrogates of the image. The elements of these vectors were generated automatically from analysis of the quantifiable attributes, such as colour, texture and geometry, present within the pixel domain. Initially, the feature vectors took the form of global descriptors using relatively simple formulations such as colour histograms [71,72]. The query was similarly surrogated as a picture-by-example, usually a digitized image, although early forms of sketch retrieval system were also reported [73]. Similarity analysis was conducted between the query and the image collection, typically using histogram intersection techniques, leading to the retrieval of candidate images in decreasing order of similarity with the query.

Nurtured by an increasingly engaged research community, feature vectors rapidly grew in sophistication. Colour correlograms captured information about spatial layout of colour that could not be described using colour histograms; combinations of neighbouring pixels ('texels') underpinned textural analysis of images; pixel intensity transformations such as wavelet analysis proved effective at edge detection, as a means of determining an object's shape; and other advanced techniques were developed, capable of segmenting the image into multiple regions, or detecting features from salient regions within an image. Early reviews of these automatic indexing techniques were published by Idris & Panchanathan [74] and Eakins & Graham [36], together with an accessible review of techniques for colour, texture and shape by Forsyth [75] within a special issue of *Library Trends*, edited by Sandore [76], devoted to progress in visual information access and retrieval. Del Bimbo's monograph [2] provided an authorititive technical treatment, and was succeeded by other comprehensive reviews [3: pp. 149–154, 54, 77, 78].

The 1990s saw the launch of a number of experimental CBIR systems, one of the earliest of which, and certainly the best-known, was QBIC (Query By Image Content) [79]. Other systems, including Blobworld, Excalibur, MARS, Photobook and VisualSeek followed; comprehensively surveyed in [53,80], a comparative evaluation was also undertaken [81]. The Benchathlon network (http://www.benchathlon.net/) was established with the aim of developing benchmarking facilities in support of the experimental CBIR environment.

The CBIR paradigm and the experimental systems which it spawned had been responsible for a marked upsurge in the rate of publication about image indexing and retrieval after 1990 [82], and it was with some reluctance that the image retrieval research community responded to the view that an image retrieval paradigm which operates on the low-level, syntactic properties of an image had limited practical value [83]. The information science community, in contrast, had reached that view somewhat earlier, informed by experiments with specific illustration tasks which used similarity perceptions in a real work context [27] and by tests on CBIR features which revealed that users did not find these low-level features either intuitive to search or relevant to their queries [84]. Fidel's [23] concern, that much research effort and financial resources were being invested in improving CBIR without an awareness of the situations in which such retrieval might be useful, was echoed in the view that

> the emphasis in the computer science literature has been largely on what is computationally possible, and not on discovering whether essential generic

visual primitives can in fact facilitate image retrieval in 'real-world' applications [3: p. 197].

Indeed, none of the commercial CBIR systems launched in the first half of the 1990s achieved significant market penetration, and all have since ceased to be actively promoted [85].

Typical of the dangers of forsaking semantic integrity in the retrieval of images were observations that a colour-based CBIR algorithm will match busy city scenes containing beige brick backgrounds with scenes of desert sand [86], and a shape-based one might return images of the Statue of Liberty in response to queries seeking images of starfish – the so-called 'rhyming image' phenomenon [80]. Nevertheless, such algorithms were shown to have real value in situations where it is difficult for the perceptual saliency of some visual features to be captured in text, such as the perceptual elements of a texture, the outline of a form and the visual effects in a video sequence [2: p. 4]. In a comprehensive survey of the principles and practice of CBIR towards the end of the 1990s examples were provided of specialized applications – in medicine, fine art and textile design, for example – where the verbalization challenge was so great that CBIR provided the only effective solution [26].

## Towards semantic image retrieval

For more traditional image retrieval applications, however, 'semantic image retrieval' and the 'semantic gap' began to penetrate the literature from the mid 1990s onwards, with Gudivada and Raghavan [87], in a special issue of *IEEE Computer* devoted to CBIR systems, and Aigrain et al. [88], in a state-of-the-art review of CBIR one year later, introducing a publishing surge which drew the observation:

> while content-based image retrieval papers published prior to 1990 are rare, almost certainly obsolete, and of little direct impact today, the number of papers published since 1997 is just breathtaking [54].

The semantic gap is that rift in the image retrieval landscape between the information that can be extracted automatically from a digitized image and the interpretation that humans might place upon the image [54]. Early endeavours to bridge the semantic gap saw effort directed at the automatic identification of objects and scenes, undertaken either as a statistical classification procedure or as a knowledge-based recognition task [77]. The latter approach necessitated the construction of a model for each type of object of interest, which acted as the comparator in searches of each image in the collection, looking for regions similar to the models. The earliest approaches envisaged digitized reference images which depicted the object in a variety of light conditions, and at different angles, sizes and perspectives. Limited success has been achieved in automatic scene classification and object recognition, although one example of the latter – naked people – has been usefully applied to the automatic detection of pornographic images [89]. In general, however, the domain knowledge/effort involved in building the models is very considerable, leading to some scepticism that the problems of updating and extending complex model-based approaches to cover more than a 'toy subset of object classes' will prove insuperable unless some form of adaptive learning is employed [77].

By the late 1990s, it had become clear that the semantic gap could not be bridged by operations on the pixel domain alone, and that CBIR should be treated as a complement to, rather than a replacement for, text-based image retrieval [51]. Henceforth, the integration of the two paradigms became a significant focus of attention, especially in those application areas, such as investigative medicine, which generate enormous quantities of continuous-process visual data [90]. Automatic annotation of images came to the fore as a means of trying to achieve that integration.

In an overview of automatic annotation techniques, Hare et al. [91] note two basic approaches; one seeking to discover links between regions and words by statistical inference [92], and the other using a supervised learning technique which echoes document vector analysis in text-based information retrieval [93]. In this second case a training set of annotated images is used, each image surrogated as a textual term vector, the elements of which represent the allocation of keywords drawn from the indexing vocabulary. To this is appended a 'visual term' vector, with elements drawn from the image's quantized visual primitives. The 'dimensionality curse' [83] of the matrix formed from these stacked textual-and-visual term vectors called for a data reduction technique, which was found in latent semantic indexing (LSI), a procedure borrowed from the traditional theoretical model of text retrieval [94]. Vectors of visual terms from a test set of un-annotated images are compared with the visual term constituents of the training set, and where a sufficiently high level of similarity is encountered between a pair of images, one drawn from the training set, the other from the test set, the annotation associated with the former is propagated to the latter in the form of automatically assigned object/scene/activity labels.

Typically, experimentation in automatic annotation has been conducted using training sets of images derived from small, ground-truth image databases, where both the exhaustivity and specificity of the indexing has been low [22]. When compared with the rich semantic indexing typical of professionally managed image collections, these limited-vocabulary experimental scenarios appear unrealistic, and the precision of their results has tended to be erratic.

The limited perception of objects and scenes permitted by these highly constrained vocabularies combines with another disadvantage of automatic annotation techniques, which is their dependency on search engines which can only be trained to recognize features actually visible in the image. A peculiarity of visual images, however, is their ability to convey messages independently of visually perceived reality. Some of the facets which contribute to the rich conceptual model of image semantic content described earlier in this paper have no visual presence; they represent 'extrinsic semantics'. This has been shown, for example, in analyses of image perception, where the majority of the terms viewers used to describe the contents of a set of images were not visibly present in the images [8], and in user studies within the practitioner environment where requests very frequently incorporated non-visible facets [22]. Experimentation has failed, thus far, to provide any reliable evidence that automatic annotation can span the very considerable conceptual distance between object/scene/activity labelling and the high-level reasoning which situates those objects, scenes or activites appropriately within the user's sociocognitive space.

Partly in recognition of this, the CBIR research community has demonstrated a rapidly developing interest in semantic web technologies in general, and ontologies in particular. Schreiber et al. [95], working in the medical domain, were among the earliest proponents of ontologies for image annotation and retrieval, and interest has extended to experimentation in the generation of semantic inferencing rules, formulated by medical domain experts, that link low-level visual features to domain concepts [96,97]. Other applications have been reported in the cultural heritage sector [98–100].

As a result of the adoption of ontologically supported experimental image retrieval processes, tools which are well-established within the professional image management environment, such as the *Union List of Artist Names (ULAN), Thesaurus of Geographic Names (TGN), Art and Architecture Thesaurus*

*(AAT), ICONCLASS* and *WordNet* are beginning to penetrate the research environment, where they are treated as quasi-ontologies [98]. They make a welcome appearance – one which would not have been foreseen a few years ago – at the research frontiers of image retrieval.

Nevertheless, the challenge of semantic image retrieval remains daunting. Ontology construction – albeit assisted by the adoption of standard knowledge organization and representation tools – is technically demanding, and ontologies tend to be domain-specific. One approach to enhancing functionality within ontology-supported semantic image retrieval systems has been lexical expansion through the harnessing of multiple vocabularies [99,101]. Such approaches had their origin in query expansion using thesaural relations in text retrieval. Hollink [102: pp.90–94] has shown how diminishing returns set in under different combinations and degrees of propagation of such relations: there may be no counterpart in the visual image to the semantic relationships which link terms at the lexical level, leading to the danger of automatically adding wholly inappropriate terms to an image's subject metadata.

It seems clear that the widest reaches of the semantic gap cannot be spanned using current techniques. At the present time, most attempts at bridging the semantic gap have faltered at the very broad separation between object labelling and the high-level reasoning which situates those objects appropriately within the viewer's sociocognitive space. In effect, the semantic gap is a two-part fracture, and the focus of attention has been on the first part alone [91].

## Content-based video retrieval

Although the still image was the early focus of attention among the CBIR research community, once digitization and transmission of the moving image became a viable proposition the realization was reached that a spatio-temporal distribution of blobs was an easier target for syntactic analysis of the pixel domain than the spatial distribution offered by the still image:

> Video comes as a sequence, so what moves together most likely forms an entity in real life, so segmentation of video is intrinsically simpler than a still image [103].

Automatic segmentation of a video stream into shots using shot boundary detection techniques was an early focus of attention, a detailed technical treatment of which was provided in [2: pp. 203–264]. Each automatically detected shot makes available a set of frames, from among which keyframes are selected on some consistent basis to act as surrogates of the shot. Other useful operations on video sequences followed from the developing robustness of automatic shot boundary detection. A chronological ordering of keyframes enabled 'storyboards' to be formulated, which acted as surrogates for the entire film or video sequence [86]. Where a set of keyframes representative of every shot would generate too much data for efficient analysis, and clips, scenes and episodes formed significant semantic units, video segmentation into shot aggregates was developed [2: pp. 224–229].

For the searcher, cataloguer, programme compiler and editor, storyboarding techniques offered considerable savings in time, especially in those cases where the fast detection of highlights is valued, as in sports and news broadcasts. A further advantage for the searcher was the high probability that shots within a storyboard which were adjacent to a shot which had been deemed relevant to a query would have a close temporal relationship with that shot, and would be likely also to be relevant.

Rapid strides were made in the development of techniques for visual feature extraction, indexing, searching, browsing and summarization in video, with comprehensive reviews by Naphade and Smith [104] and Smeaton [105] making significant contributions to the literature. Initially, these techniques operated only on the visual content of video; more recently, research effort has been directed towards the full audiovisual content of this visual resource. Capabilities in automatic speech recognition (ASR) have advanced to the stage where the audio channel can be harnessed as a means of generating textual annotations to the complementary video channel. The best recognizers, trained for broadcast news, currently have a word error rate of about 15% on studio recorded anchor speech; naturally, performance degrades as constraints on identified speaker and comprehensiveness of vocabulary are relaxed [106].

The Informedia digital video library project, begun in 1994, is the most widely reported example of this approach [107]. Operating on news stories from television broadcasts, this landmark project seeks to make such material searchable by means of ASR-enabled transcripts, and the integration of speech recognition, natural language processing, image analysis and information retrieval [108]. Automatically generated metadata and indexes to multiple terabytes of video are continuously available online to local users. A very similar system, called Físchlár-News, automatically analyses the nightly Irish broadcast television news [109]. Both systems enable the user to inspect keyframes, play the associated video, and conduct other browsing and retrieval operations. Analytic functions also include speech/music discrimination, programme start/end identification, TV advertisement detection, and automatic detection of anchorperson shots. The outputs of these analyses are fed into a trained statistical classifier which segments the broadcast into discrete news stories which are then available as units of retrieval.

The Informedia project, in particular, has generated a wealth of experimental results which point to speech transcripts providing the single most important clue for successful video retrieval [86]. More advanced techniques reflecting research in computer vision have not, as yet, proved robust enough to be usable, and Hauptmann's recent advice to the research community is

> give up on general, deep understanding of video – that problem is just too hard for now [106].

Instead, he has argued that a few thousand high-level semantic concepts that have reasonably reliable detection accuracy can be combined to yield high-accuracy automatic video retrieval. Retrieval experiments, using sets of rich intermediate semantic descriptors derived from a standard lexicon and taxonomy, have provided support for such an approach [110].

The research effort in content-based video retrieval has been characterized, and stimulated, by the emphasis placed on the evaluation of techniques through the medium of the annual TRECVID benchmarking event. This video track offshoot of the Text REtrieval Conference began in 2001, and provides participating organizations with a large video test collection, embracing corpora which range from documentaries to advertising films and broadcast news [111–113]. A further stimulant has been the development of the MPEG-4 and MPEG-7 multimedia representation standards. MPEG-4 was designed to provide technological elements which enabled the production, distribution and content access paradigms of interactive multimedia, mobile multimedia, interactive graphics and enhanced digital television to be integrated [114]. Its provision of shape-based encoding of natural scene video has excited the interest of the image processing research community [105], but MPEG-4 offers limited capability for the interpretation of semantic content. MPEG-7 was born of a realization of that limitation, and has the ability to describe both low-level features and high-level semantics, together with structural aspects of any multimedia document or file. Modalities may include still pictures, graphics, 3D models, audio, speech, video, and composition information about how these elements are combined in a multimedia presentation [114]. The Físchlár-News system, to which reference was made earlier, automatically analyses and structures the broadcast into an MPEG-7 annotation [109].

## Conclusion

In this paper, an attempt has been made to draw, necessarily in a highly selective fashion, on the literature of image and video retrieval in order to outline the development of theory and practice in this absorbing variant of information retrieval. Within the last twenty years, reflecting the rapid burgeoning of interest among the computer vision research community, that body of literature has grown prodigiously, and its character has been described elsewhere as relentlessly abstruse [11]. The effect has been to create a communication gap between the researcher and professional practitioner communities in image retrieval, a separation which was first surveyed by Cawkell [49] in the form of two minimally linked citation-interconnected clusters derived from an analysis of pre-1991 publications. That separation has widened considerably in the intervening years.

With the intention of providing a forum where members of both research and practitioner communities could become better informed about each other's endeavours and environments, a conference was hosted by the Institute of Image Data Research (IIDR), at the University of Northumbria at Newcastle-upon-Tyne, UK in 1998. This proved to be the precursor to the annual *Challenge of Image and Video Retrieval International Conference (CIVR)* series (http://www.civr.org), now an official ACM conference and generally recognized as a key event in the visual information retrieval research community's calendar, but one which retains the specific brief of bringing that community together with the practitioner community

> to illuminate critical issues and energize both communities for the continuing exploration of novel directions for image and video retrieval [115].

Heralded in 2000 by the inclusion of the term 'video' in the title of what had previously been the *Challenge of Image Retrieval* conference, a shift may be detected in the focus of CIVR, and in the literature of visual information retrieval more generally, towards the end of the period reviewed in this paper, however. Fuelled by the seemingly greater capabilities of CBIR with video than with still images, and by a dawning appreciation of the exceptional difficulty in spanning the wider reaches of the semantic gap, beyond which lie the high-level semantic spaces inhabited by the majority of image practitioners and users, visual information retrieval is being subsumed within multimedia retrieval. Other fora – such as the ACM SIGMM Workshop on Multimedia Information Retrieval (http://www.liacs.nl/~mir), the IEEE International Conference on Multimedia and Expo (ICME) and the International Cultural Heritage Informatics Meeting (ICHIM) – vie with CIVR in a content-based information retrieval environment admirably surveyed by Lew et al [116]. From this paper's brief survey of recent activity in the landscape of visual information retrieval activity, the capture, representation and retrieval of semantic content in the visual medium has presented the practitioner and researcher alike with some difficult terrain. The way ahead, then, amid the broader landscape of content-based multimedia information retrieval, promises to be an exhilarating climb.

## Acknowledgements

I am grateful to the referees for their helpful comments.

## References

[1] A. Gupta and R.C. Jain, Visual information retrieval, *Communications of the ACM* 40(5) (1997) 71–79.

[2] A. Del Bimbo, *Visual Information Retrieval* (Morgan Kaufmann, San Francisco, 1999).

[3] C. Jörgensen, *Image Retrieval: Theory and Research* (The Scarecrow Press, Lanham, MD, 2003).

[4] P.G.B. Enser and C.G. McGregor, *Analysis of Visual Information Retrieval Queries, Report on Project G16412 to the British Library Research & Development Department* (British Library R&D Report 6104, British Library, London, 1992).

[5] S. Poliakoff, *Shooting the Past* (DVD, BBC, London, 1999).

[6]   C. Cochrane, The collection, preservation and use of moving images in the United Kingdom, *Audiovisual Librarian* 20(2) (1994) 122–130.

[7]   TASI (Technical Advisory Service for Images), *Putting Things in Order: Links to Metadata Schemas and Related Standards (2006)*. Available at: http://www.tasi.ac.uk/resources/schemas.html (accessed 31 December 2007).

[8]   H. Greisdorf and B. O'Connor, Modelling what users see when they look at images: a cognitive viewpoint, *Journal of Documentation* 58(1) (2002) 6–29.

[9]   B.C. O'Connor and M.K. O'Connor, Categories, photographs and predicaments: exploratory research on representing pictures for access, *Bulletin of the American Society for Information Science* 25(6) (1999) 17–20.

[10]  E.M. Rasmussen, Indexing images. In: M.E. Williams (ed.), *Annual Review of Information Science and Technology 32*, (Information Today, Inc., Medford, NJ, 1997) 169–196.

[11]  P.G.B. Enser, Visual image retrieval. In: B. Cronin (ed.) *Annual Review of Information Science and Technology 42*, (Information Today, Inc., Medford, NJ, 2008) 3–42.

[12]  K. Markey, Interindexer consistency tests: a literature review and report of a test of consistency in indexing visual materials, *Library and Information Science Research* 6, (1984) 155–177.

[13]  S. Shatford, Describing a picture: a thousand words are seldom cost effective, *Cataloging & Classification Quarterly* 4(4) (1984) 13–30.

[14]  S. Shatford, Analyzing the subject of a picture: a theoretical approach, *Cataloguing & Classification Quarterly* 5(3) (1986) 39–61.

[15]  A.E. Cawkell, *Indexing collections of electronic images: a review* (British Library Research Review 15, British Library, London, 1993).

[16]  S. Shatford Layne, Some issues in the indexing of images, *Journal of the American Society for Information Science* 45(8) (1994) 583–588.

[17]  E. Svenonius, Access to nonbook materials: the limits of subject indexing for visual and aural languages, *Journal of the American Society for Information Science* 45(8) (1994) 600–606.

[18]  S. Ørnager, The newspaper image database: empirical supported analysis of users' typology and word association clusters. In: E. Fox, P. Ingwersen and R. Fidel (eds), *Proceedings of the 18th Annual Special Interest Group Conference on Research and Development in Information Retrieval (ACM SIGIR '95)*, (ACM Press, New York, 1995) 212–218.

[19]  P.G.B. Enser, Progress in documentation: pictorial information retrieval, *Journal of Documentation* 51(2) (1995) 126–170.

[20] P.G.B. Enser, Visual image retrieval: seeking the alliance of concept-based and content-based paradigms, *Journal of Information Science* 26(4) (2000) 199–210.

[21] R. Hidderley, P. Brown, M. Menzies, D. Rankine, S. Rollason and M. Wilding, Capturing iconology: a study in retrieval modelling and image indexing. In: M. Collier and K. Arnold (eds), *Proceedings of the Third International Conference on Electronic Library and Visual Information Research (ELVIRA3)*, (Aslib, London, 1995) 79–91.

[22] P.G.B. Enser, C.J. Sandom, J.S. Hare and P.H. Lewis, Facing the reality of semantic image retrieval, *Journal of Documentation* 63(4) (2007) 465–481.

[23] R. Fidel, The image retrieval task: implications for the design and evaluation of image databases, *The New Review of Hypermedia and Multimedia* 3 (1997). 181–199.

[24] M.C. Krause, Intellectual problems of indexing picture collections, *Audiovisual Librarian* 14(2) (1998) 73–81.

[25] F.W. Lancaster, *Indexing and Abstracting in Theory and Practice (3rd edn)* (Facet, London, 2003).

[26] J.P. Eakins and M.E. Graham, *Content-based image retrieval: a report to the JISC Technology Applications Programme.* Available at: http://www.jisc.ac.uk/uploaded_documents/jtap-039.doc (accessed 31 December 2007).

[27] M. Markkula and E. Sormunen, End-user searching challenges indexing practices in the digital newspaper photo archive, *Information Retrieval* 1(4) (2000) 259–285.

[28] E. Panofsky, *Studies in Iconology* (Harper & Row, New York, 1962).

[29] A. Jaimes and S.-F. Chang, A conceptual framework for indexing visual information at multiple levels. In: G. Beretta & R. Schettini (eds), *Proceedings of the First IS&T/SPIE Internet Imaging Conference* (SPIE vol. 3964, SPIE, Bellingham, WA, 2000) 2–15.

[30] C. Jörgensen, A. Jaimes, A.B. Benitez and S-F. Chang, A conceptual framework and empirical research for classifying visual descriptors, *Journal of the American Society for Information Science and Technology* 52(11) (2001) 938–947.

[31] E. Rosch, C. Mervis, W. Gray, D. Johnson and P. Boyes-Braem, Basic objects in natural categories, *Cognitive Psychology* 8(3) (1976) 382–439.

[32] J.S. Hare, P.H. Lewis, P.G.B. Enser and C.J. Sandom, Semantic facets: an in-depth analysis of a semantic image retrieval system. In: N. Sebe and M. Worring (eds), *Proceedings of the Sixth ACM International Conference on Image and Video Retrieval* (ACM, New York, 2007)

[33] M. Hogan, C. Jörgensen and P. Jörgensen, The visual thesaurus in a hypermedia environment: a preliminary exploration of conceptual issues and applications. In: D. Bearman (ed.), *Hypermedia and Interactivity in Museums: Proceedings of an*

*International Conference* (Archives & Museum Informatics, Pittsburgh, PA, 1991) 202–221.

[34] H. Besser, Visual access to visual images: the UC Berkeley image database project, *Library Trends* 38(4) (1990) 787–798.

[35] J. Turner, Representing and accessing information in the stockshot database at the National Film Board of Canada, *Canadian Journal of Information Science* 15(4) (1990) 1–22.

[36] J. Yang and A.G. Hauptmann, Annotating news video with locations. In: H. Sundaram, M. Naphade, J.R. Smith and R.Yong (eds), *Proceedings of the Sixth International Conference on Image and Video Retrieval (CIVR 2006)* (Lecture Notes in Computer Science, Vol. 4071, Springer, Berlin, 2006) 153–162.

[37] J. Falconer, The cataloguing and indexing of the photographic collection of the Royal Commonwealth Society, *The Indexer* 14(1) (1984) 15–22.

[38] P.G.B. Enser, Query analysis in a visual information retrieval context, *Journal of Document and Text Management* 1(1) (1993) 25–52.

[39] S.K. Hastings, Query categories in a study of intellectual access to digitized art images. In: T. Kinney (ed.), *Proceedings of the 58th Annual Meeting of the American Society for Information Science (ASIS'95)* (ASIS, Silver Spring, MD 1995) 3–8.

[40] C. Gordon, Patterns of user queries in an ICONCLASS database, *Visual Resources* 12 (1996) 177–186.

[41] L.H. Armitage and P.G.B. Enser, Analysis of user need in image archives, *Journal of Information Science* 23(4) (1997) 287–299.

[42] H. Chen, An analysis of image queries in the field of art history, *Journal of the American Society for Information Science and Technology* 52(3) (2001) 260–273.

[43] L.H. Keister, User types and queries: impact on image access systems. In: R. Fidel, T.B. Hahn, E.M. Rasmussen and P.J. Smith (eds), *Challenges in Indexing Electronic Text and Images* (ASIS Monograph Series, Learned Information Inc., Medford, NJ, 1994) 7–22.

[44] C. Jörgensen, Image attributes in describing tasks: an investigation, *Information Processing and Management* 34(2/3) (1998) 161–174.

[45] C.O. Frost and A. Noakes, Browsing images using broad classification categories. In: E.K. Jacob (ed.), *Proceedings of the Ninth ASIS SIGCR Classification Research Workshop* (ASIS, Silver Spring, MD, 1998) 71–89.

[46] Y. Choi and E.M. Rasmussen, Users' relevance criteria in image retrieval in American history, *Information Processing and Management* 38(5) (2002) 695–726.

[47] L. Hollink, A.Th. Schreiber,.B.J. Wielinga and M. Worring, Classification of user image descriptions, *International Journal of Human Computer Studies* 61(5) (2004) 601–621.

[48]  C. Jörgensen and P. Jörgensen, Image querying by image professionals, *Journal of the American Society for Information Science and Technology* 56(12) (2005) 1346–1359.

[49]  A.E. Cawkell, Selected aspects of image processing and management: review and future prospects, *Journal of Information Science* 18(3) (1992) 179–192.

[50]  S. Santini and R.C. Jain, Do images mean anything? In: *Proceedings of the IEEE International Conference on Image Processing (ICIP-97)* (IEEE, New York, 1997) 564–567.

[51]  Y. Rui, T.S. Huang and S. Mehrotra, Relevance feedback techniques in interactive content-based image retrieval. In: I.K. Sethi and R.C. Jain (eds), *Proceedings of the Sixth SPIE Conference on Storage and Retrieval for Image and Video Databases* (SPIE vol. 3312, SPIE, Bellingham, WA, 1997) 25–36.

[52]  A. Goodrum and A. Spink, Image searching on the excite web search engine, *Information Processing and Management* 37(2) (2001) 295–311.

[53]  M.L. Kherfi, D. Ziou and A. Bernardi, Image retrieval from the World Wide Web: issues, techniques, and systems, *ACM Computing Surveys* 36(1) (2004) 35–67.

[54]  A.W.M. Smeulders, M. Worring, S. Santini, A. Gupta and R.C. Jain, Content-based retrieval at the end of the early years, *IEEE Transactions on Pattern Analysis and Machine Intelligence* 22(12) (2000) 1349–1380.

[55]  A. Goodrum, M. Bejune and A.C. Siochi, A state transition analysis of image search patterns on the Web. In: E.M. Bakker, T.S. Huang, M.S. Lew, N. Sebe and X. Zhou (eds.): *Proceedings of the Second International Conference on Image and Video Retrieval (CIVR 2003)* (Lecture Notes in Computer Science, Vol. 2728, Springer, Berlin, 2003) 281–290.

[56]  K. Roddy, Subject access to visual resources: what the 90s might portend, *Library Hi Tech* 9(1) (1991) 45–49.

[57]  C.J. Sandom and P.G.B. Enser, *VIRAMI: Visual Information Retrieval for Archival Moving Imagery* (Library and Information Commission Research Report 129, The Council for Museums, Archives and Libraries, London, 2002).

[58]  M. Hertzum, Requests for information from a film archive: a case study of multimedia retrieval, *Journal of Documentation* 59(2) (2003) 168–186.

[59]  A.E. Cawkell, Picture-queries and picture databases, *Journal of Information Science* 19(6) (1993) 409–423.

[60]  S.-K. Chang and T. Kunii, Pictorial database systems, *IEEE Computer Magazine Special Issue on Pictorial Information Systems* 14(11) (1981) 13–21.

[61]  S.-K. Chang and S.-H. Liu, Picture indexing and abstraction techniques for pictorial databases, *IEEE Transactions on Pattern Analysis and Machine Intelligence* 6(4) (1984) 475–484.

[62] H. Tamura and N.Yokoya, Image database systems: a survey, *Pattern recognition* 171(1) (1984) 29–43.

[63] G. Nagy, Image database, *Image and Vision Computing* 3(3) (1985) 111–117.

[64] T.L. Kunii (ed.), *Visual Database Systems* (Elsevier, Amsterdam, 1989).

[65] L.F. Lunin, An overview of electronic image information, *Optical Information Systems* 10(3) (1990) 114–130.

[66] C.H.C. Leung, Architecture of an image database system, *Information Services and Use* 10 (1990) 391–397.

[67] S.E. Arnold, The large data construct: a new frontier in database design, *Microcomputers for Information Management* 7(3) (1990) 185–203.

[68] H. Besser, Image databases: the first decade, the present, and the future. In: P.B. Heidorn and B. Sandore, (eds), *Digital Image Access and Retrieval: Papers presented at the 1996 Clinic on Library Applications of Data Processing* (Elsevier, Amsterdam, 1997) 11–28.

[69] G.A. Seloff, Automated access to the NASA-JSC image archives, *Library Trends* 38(4) (1990) 682–696.

[70] E. Hyvönen, A. Styrman and S. Saarela, *Ontology-based Image Retrieval* (HIIT Publications Number 2002–03, Helsinki Institute for Information Technology, Helsinki, Finland, 2002) 15–27.

[71] M.J. Swain and D.H. Ballard, Color indexing, *International Journal of Computer Vision* 7(1) (1991) 11–32.

[72] J.R. Smith and S.F. Chang, Querying by color regions using the VisualSEEK content-based visual query system. In: M.T. Maybury (ed.), *Intelligent Multimedia Information Retrieval* (AAAI Press, Menlo Park, CA, 1997) 23–41.

[73] T. Kato and T. Kurita, Visual interaction with electronic art gallery. In: A. Min Tjoa and R.Wagner (eds), *Proceedings of the International Conference in Database and Expert Systems Applications (DEXA'90)* (Springer, London, 1990) 234–240.

[74] F. Idris and S. Panchanathan, Review of image and video indexing techniques, *Journal of Visual Communication and Image Representation* 8(2) (1997) 146–166.

[75] D.A. Forsyth, Computer vision tools for finding images and video sequences, *Library Trends* 48(2) (1999) 326–355.

[76] B. Sandore (ed), *Library Trends* 48(2), 1999, 283–524.

[77] J.P. Eakins, Towards intelligent image retrieval, *Pattern Recognition* 35(1) (2002) 3–14.

[78] R. Datta, J. Li and J.Z. Wang, Content-based image retrieval – approaches and trends of the new age. In: H. Zhang, J. Smith and Q. Tian (eds), *Proceedings of the Seventh ACM SIGMM International Workshop on Multimedia Information Retrieval, (MIR 2005)* (ACM, New York, 2005) 253–262.

[79]  M. Flickner, H. Sawhney, W. Niblack, J. Ashley, Q. Huang, B. Dom, M. Gorkani, J. Hafner, D. Lee, D. Petkovic, D.Steele and P. Yanker, P., Query by image and video content: the QBIC system, *IEEE Computer Magazine* 28(9) (1995) 23–32.

[80]  B. Johansson, *A survey on: contents based search in image databases (2000)*. Available at: http://www.cvl.isy.liu.se/ScOut/TechRep/PaperInfo/bj2000.html (accessed 31 December 2007).

[81]  R.C. Veltkamp and M. Tanase, *Content-based Image Retrieval Systems: a Survey (2000)*. Available at: http://citeseer.ist.psu.edu/373932.html (accessed 6 January 2008).

[82]  H. Chu, Research in image indexing and retrieval as reflected in the literature, *Journal of the American Society for Information Science and Technology* 52(12) (2001) 1011–1018.

[83]  T. Huang, S. Mehrotra and K. Ramchandran, Multimedia Analysis and Retrieval System (MARS) Project. In: P.B. Heidorn and B. Sandore (eds), *Digital Image Access and Retrieval: Papers presented at the 1996 Clinic on Library Applications of Data Processing* (Elsevier, Amsterdam, 1997) 100–117.

[84]  S-F. Chang, J.R. Smith, M. Beigi and A. Benitez, Visual information retrieval from large distributed online repositories, *Communications of the ACM* 40(12) (1997) 63–71.

[85]  J.P. Eakins, Content-based image retrieval – what's holding it back? In: *Proceedings of the Eighth Annual Conference of the Advanced School for Computing and Imaging* (ASCI, Delft, 2002).

[86]  M.G. Christel and R.M. Conescu, Addressing the challenge of visual information access from digital image and video libraries. In: *Proceedings of the 5th ACM/IEEE-CS Joint Conference on Digital Libraries* (ACM, New York, 2005) 69–78.

[87]  V.N. Gudivada and V.V. Raghavan, Content-based image retrieval systems, *IEEE Computer Magazine* 28(9) (1995) 18–22.

[88]  P. Aigrain, H.-J. Zhang and D. Petkovic, Content-based representation and retrieval of visual media: a state of the art review, *Multimedia Tools and Applications* 3 (1996) 179–202.

[89]  D.A. Forsyth and M.M. Fleck, Automatic detection of human nudes, *International Journal of Computer Vision* 32(1) (1999) 63–77.

[90]  H. Müller, N. Michoux, D. Bandon and A. Geissbuhler, A review of content-based image retrieval systems in medical applications – clinical benefits and future directions, *International Journal of Medical Informatics* 73 (2004) 1–23.

[91]  J.S. Hare, P.H. Lewis, P.G.B. Enser and C.J. Sandom, Mind the gap: another look at the problem of the semantic gap in image retrieval. In: E.Y. Chang, A. Hanjalic and N. Sebe (eds), *Proceedings of the 2006 SPIE Conference on Multimedia Content*

*Analysis, Management and Retrieval* (SPIE Vol. 6073, SPIE, Bellingham, WA, 2006) 1–12.

[92] K. Barnard, P. Duygulu, D. Forsyth, N. de Freitas, D.M. Blei and M.I. Jordan, Matching words and pictures, *Journal of Machine Learning Research* 3 (2003) 1107–1135.

[93] G. Salton and M.J. McGill, *Introduction to Modern Information Retrieval* (McGraw-Hill, New York, 1983).

[94] S. Deerwester, S.T. Dumais, G.W. Furnas, T.K. Landauer and R. Harshman, Indexing by latent semantic analysis, *Journal of the American Society for Information Science* 41(6) (1990) 391–407.

[95] G. Schreiber, B. Dubbeldam, J. Wielemaker and B. Wielinga, Ontology-based photo annotation, *IEEE Intelligent Systems* 16(3) (2001) 2–10.

[96] B. Hu, S. Dasmahapatra, P. Lewis and N. Shadbolt, N., Ontology-based medical image annotation with description logics. In: *Proceedings of the 15th IEEE International Conference on Tools with Artificial Intelligence* (IEEE, New York, 2003) 77–82.

[97] L. Hollink, S. Little and J. Hunter, Evaluating the application of semantic inferencing rules to image annotation. In: *Proceedings of the 3rd International Conference on Knowledge Capture* (ACM, New York, 2005) 91–98.

[98] L. Hollink, A.Th. Schreiber, J. Wielemaker and B.J. Wielinga, Semantic annotation of image collections. In: S. Handschuh, M. Koivunen, R. Dieng and S. Staab (eds), *Proceedings of the K-Cap 2003 Workshop on Knowledge Markup and Semantic Annotation* (ACM, New York, 2003) 41–48.

[99] E. Hyvönen, M. Salminen, M. Junnila and S. Kettula, A content creation process for the semantic web. In: *Proceedings of the 2004 LREC Workshop on Ontologies and Lexical Resources in Distributed Environments* (2004). Available at: http://www.seco.tkk.fi/publications/2004/hyvonen-salminen-et-al-a-content-creation-process-2004.pdf (accessed 12 March 2008).

[100] M. J. Addis, K. Martinez, P. Lewis, J. Stevenson and F. Giorgini, New ways to search, navigate and use multimedia museum collections over the web. In: J. Trant and D. Bearman, (eds), *Proceedings of the 2005 Conference on Museums and the Web* (2005). Available at: http://www.archimuse.com/mw2005/papers/addis/addis.html (accessed on 31 December 2007).

[101] A. Amin, van M. Assem, de V. Boer, L. Hardamn, M. HildeBrand, L. Hollink, van J. Kersen, B. Omelayenko, van J. Ossenbruggen., A.B. Schreiber, R. Siebes, J. Taekema, J. Wielemaker and B. Wielinga, *MultimediaN E-Culture Demonstrator:*

*Objectives and Architecture* (Technical Report BSIK, MultimediaN Project, Subproject N9C "Pilot E-Culture", CWI, Amsterdam, DEN, The Hague, 2006).

[102] L. Hollink, *Semantic Annotation for Retrieval of Visual Resources* (SIKS Dissertation Series No. 2006–24, Vrije Universiteit, Amsterdam, 2006).

[103] N. Sebe, M.S. Lew, X. Zhou, T.S. Huang and E.M. Bakker, The state of the art in image and video retrieval. In: E.M. Bakker, T.S. Huang, M.S. Lew, N. Sebe and X. Zhou (eds), *Proceedings of the Second International Conference on Image and Video Retrieval* (Lecture Notes in Computer Science, Vol. 2728, Springer, Berlin, 2003) 7–12.

[104] M.R. Naphade and J.R. Smith, On the detection of semantic concepts at TRECVID. In: *Proceedings of the Twelfth Annual ACM International Conference on Multimedia* (ACM Press, New York, 2004) 660–667

[105] A.F. Smeaton, Indexing, browsing and searching of digital video. In: B. Cronin (ed.), *Annual Review of Information Science & Technology 38(1)* (Information Today, Inc., Medford, NJ, 2004) 371–407.

[106] A.G. Hauptmann, Lessons for the future from a decade of Informedia video analysis research. In: W-K. Leow, M.S. Lew, T-S.Chua, W-Y. Ma, L. Chaisorn and E.M. Bakker (eds), *Proceedings of the Fourth International Conference on Image and Video* (Lecture Notes in Computer Science, Vol. 3568, Springer, Berlin, 2005) 1–10.

[107] Carnegie Mellon University, *Informedia Digital Video Library (2006)*. Available at: http://www.informedia.cs.cmu.edu/ (accessed 31 December 2007).

[108] M.J. Whitbrock and A.G. Hauptmann, Speech recognition for a digital video library, *Journal of the American Society for Information Science* 49(7) (1998) 619–632.

[109] H. Lee, A.F. Smeaton, N.E. O'Connor and B. Smyth, User evaluation of Físchlár-News: an automatic broadcast news delivery system, *ACM Transactions on Information Systems* 24(2) (2006) 145–189.

[110] A. Hauptmann, R. Tan and W-H. Lin, How many high-level concepts will fill the semantic gap in news video retrieval? In: N. Sebe and M. Worring (eds), *Proceedings of the 2007 ACM International Conference on Image and Video Retrieval* (ACM, New York, 2007).

[111] A.F. Smeaton, Large scale evaluations of multimedia information retrieval: the TRECVid experience. In: W-K. Leow, M.S. Lew, T-S. Chua, W-Y. Ma, L. Chaisorn, L. and E.M. Bakker (eds), *Proceedings of the Fourth International Conference on Image and Video Retrieval* (Lecture Notes in Computer Science, Vol. 3568, Springer, Berlin, 2005) 11–17.

[112] M.G. Christel and R.M. Conescu, Mining novice user activity with TRECVID interactive retrieval tasks. In: H. Sundaram, M. Naphade, J.R. Smith and R. Yong

(eds), *Proceedings of the Fifth International Conference on Image and Video Retrieval* (Lecture Notes in Computer Science Vol. 4071, Springer Berlin, 2006) 21–30.

[113] A.F. Smeaton, P. Over and W. Kraaij, Evaluation campaigns and TRECVid. In: *Proceedings of the Eighth ACM International Workshop on Multimedia Information Retrieval*, (ACM, New York, 2006) 321–330.

[114] J.M. Martinez (ed.), *MPEG-7 Overview (version 10) (ISO/IEC JTC1/SC29/WG11) (2004)* (International Organisation for Standardisation, Palma, Mallorca, 2004). Available at: http://www.chiariglione.org/MPEG/standards/mpeg-7/mpeg-7.htm (accessed 31 December 2007).

[115] H. Sundaram, M. Naphade, J.R. Smith and R.Yong (eds), *Proceedings of the Fifth International Conference on Image and Video Retrieval* (Lecture Notes in Computer Science Vol. 4071, Springer Berlin, 2006).

[116] M.S. Lew, N. Sebe, C. Djeraba and R. Jain, Content-based multimedia information retrieval: state of the art and challenges, *ACM Transactions on Multimedia Computing, Communications and Applications* 2(1) (2006) 1–19.

# 11

# Information policies: yesterday, today, tomorrow

ELIZABETH ORNA

## Abstract

This article presents a brief history of the development of ideas about national and organizational information policies, from the first establishment of a UK Ministry of Information in the First World War to the present day. The issues and tensions that have characterized attempts to develop and implement policies on the national and organizational scale are discussed, with particular reference to: the power relations between the parties to them; the relative significance accorded to information technology and information content; the transition from formulating policy to acting on it; and the threats to the survival of those policies that get as far as implementation. In conclusion, the contribution to date of information science to the theory and practice of information policies is assessed, and suggestions are offered on directions for future efforts, in the light of the past of this interesting field.

## Introduction

I have to begin this article with a confession: up till now, I have always avoided writing about national information policies. Over the years, I have read much of what others have written on the subject and admired a good deal of it; but in my own work I have concentrated on trying to help organizations to develop information policies for themselves, by working with them and writing for them. It offers some chance of producing at least some visible effect within a reasonable time, while observation suggests that governments do not take much notice of what information scientists write about national information policies, even on those rare occasions when they actually invite their advice on the subject.

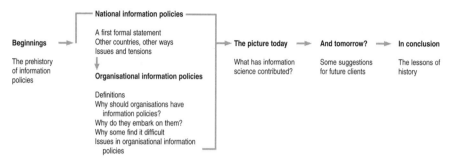

**Figure 1** The shape of the story

So when I was invited to contribute a paper on information policies to this special issue, my first inclination was to write only on organizational policies. But when I started re-reading the literature and thinking about the article, it became clear that national information policy was the essential context for organizational policies and strategies, which could not be properly understood without it.

Tackling the subject I had tried to avoid turned out to be worthwhile, because I began to see a coherent story, with some dominant themes that relate these two aspects of information policy. The next problem was how to tell the story: it was obvious that it had to be a chronological account, but within that, was it possible to intertwine the two strands within a single narrative, or would there have to be two separate stories, with the links between them made clear during the telling of each? For clarity, it had to be the latter, and this is how the article is organized (see Figure 1).

There is one other thing to explain before I leave readers to get on with it. This special issue seeks to review the development of the whole information science field, so the individual contributions cannot be exhaustive surveys; they are articles, not definitive comprehensive works on their subjects. This article has certainly had to omit some topics that would find a place in a comprehensive study and to deal with many others in summary form. I hope that the references to other sources go some way towards making up for this.

## Beginnings: the pre-history of information policy

Governments first began to be concerned with the idea of 'information policy', in the modern sense of the term, some time around the late 1970s and the early 1980s (e.g. Moore and Steel [1]; Rowlands [2]). The earliest use of the term 'Information policy' in relation to governments, however, goes back to activities that began under the name of propaganda in the First World War.[1]

The UK Government set up a Ministry of Information in 1917; it was dissolved in 1918, but re-established the day after the Second World War broke out in 1939 (National Archives [3]; Clark [4]). Its role in that war covered news and press censorship and home and overseas 'publicity'. Wound up in 1946, it was replaced by the Central Office of Information (COI)[5] which today defines itself as 'the Government's centre of excellence in marketing and communications'.

In the USA, a parallel body – the Office of War Information – was set up in 1942 (US National Archives and Records Administration [6]). It established a Joint Committee on War Information Policy with the UK, which was dissolved at the end of the war.

After that point, developments in the two countries diverged in an interesting way. While in the UK the COI continued to be the government's instrument for telling the home and overseas world what it wanted them to know, by the early 1960s thinking in the USA had moved to topics that have become central to national information policies as defined today: in particular, access for the public to government information it wants, rather than what government thinks it ought to have; and protection of personal data gathered for state purposes.

On the first, Rourke [7] writes of executive officials concealing information from elected representatives and the public, and of some Congress complicity in the practice. He concludes that 'the tradition of disclosure might wither in the shade of administrative evasion or inertia were it not for the continued exercise of outside vigilance' [7, p. 694) (a lesson that is being re-learned in the UK since its Freedom of Information Act of 2005 nearly 40 years after the US Act of 1966).

And on the second, Dunn [8] contributes prescient and still relevant reflections on the inevitable tensions between the collection of statistical data about the population for policy decision-making, and the protection of individual privacy (this was in the context of alarmist press and public response to his 1965 proposals for a National Data Center). He explains the distinction between statistical information systems that are concerned with the 'public face of the individual' and intelligence systems that seek information about individuals as individuals. It is an oversimplification to see the former as a contest between government and individuals: 'the conflict is between conflicting aspects of our own individual personal interests [...]

Information is power, but both information and power are morally neutral – each has the ability to enslave and to release, and the important thing is what standards serve as our guide as we attempt to strike the balances and re-strike them every year' [8, p. 26] (Dunn also disposes in this article of already prevalent myths about the power of computers to perform wonders 'at the touch of a button').

One other element in the earlier history of ideas about information policy should be mentioned here: the strand concerned with scientific and technical information, which contributed both to the concept of information policy and to the development of information science. The name of J.D. Bernal, crystallographer and Marxist, is particularly associated with it, as described by Muddiman [9].

While Bernal's ideas on 'planned science' dedicated to peace, welfare and the benefit of humanity, as set out in his 1939 book on *The Social Function of Science* [10], did not prosper in the climate of the Cold War, his perception of the importance of scientific communication, supported by user-centred systems of information management, did take root. That aspect of his ideas found a welcome among the professional information community in the 1950s and 1960s, when he was a respected member of Aslib Council.

Muddiman sums up his achievement as a 'Red information scientist': 'He inaugurated the serious discussion of science policy in Britain, anticipating the development of policy studies in the information sphere … Throughout his information career, Bernal insisted that documentation and communication were at root social, rather than technological, phenomena. Of all the early pioneers of information science, it was thus perhaps Bernal who ensured that the new profession recognized the social dimensions of its discipline' (see also Vickery [11] for an informative and sympathetic account of Bernal's views).

The end of the 1960s marks the transition to the characteristic modern concerns of national information policies. They are outlined in the next section.

## National information policies

By 1970 most of the elements that make up the contemporary idea of national information policy had emerged: what governments tell their own population and those of other countries for their own policy purposes; protection of personal data and freedom of information; collection of statistical data for policy-making;[2] and the use of ICT to manage and analyse information.[3]

From that time on, it has received progressively more attention, with a variety of approaches, in the USA and the UK and elsewhere: from governments; and from researchers, in the LIS and other academic communities, and in the ICT industries.

Researchers have proposed retrospectively various reasons for the attention paid to national information. Rowlands [2, 13] puts it down to the challenge to established policy and regulatory order posed by large-scale electronic data-processing that affects civil liberties, confidentiality, access to government information and national security. Moore and Steel [1] explain it in terms of a response to pressures of competition and constraints on resources. Maceviciute and Wilson [14] write of information being recognized as a national resource that requires management, and Rowlands too refers to the perception that it is a national resource, which can bring economic, social, and cultural benefits [2].

## A first formal statement

In 1976, a first formal statement of National Information Policy (the Rockefeller Report [15]) appeared in the USA, in response to a Presidential Directive (from Richard Nixon, though by the time it appeared he had been replaced by Jimmy Carter). Published by the National Commission on Libraries and Information Science, which had been closely involved in its preparation, it recommended that the USA should develop a coordinated National Information Policy, managed centrally and supported by an advisory committee representing the private sector, local government, and the academic and professional disciplines concerned with the issues discussed in it. The report gave a clear and comprehensive statement of those issues, from the impact of ICT and its potential for shaping the quality of decisions, to post-industrial society and its influence on the economy and employment, and existing legislation on freedom of information (1966) and privacy (1974).

The scope of the Rockefeller Report matches well with Oppenheim's [16] definition in 1994 of national information policy as a series of decisions taken by a national government, which are designed to encourage a better information infrastructure. But by the time that definition was published, things had changed in the USA, and Oppenheim continues: 'Some countries [...] have explicit information policies; others, including the USA and the UK, do not. Often (as in the UK) the policy is to have no formal policy and to leave it to the marketplace [...] several countries without clearly stated information policies – the UK, the Netherlands, the USA – have strong information industries. This raises the question whether such a policy is needed' [16, p. 143]. Hill [17] summarizes the situation on similar lines – and indeed explicitly contrasts the mid-1990s situation with that in which the Rockefeller report was published.

Those observations point in two directions: to the range of approaches in different countries, and to issues and tensions characteristic of national information policies – especially those which are not explicit and not formalized.

## Other countries, other ways

While the goals of information policy are similar in many countries, the mechanisms chosen to achieve them, as Moore [18] observes, vary widely. Moore [19], like Oppenheim, identifies two broad models of national information policy: 'laissez faire', in which the state leaves most responsibility to the market; and 'dirigiste' which places more emphasis on the role of the state as participant.

Writing specifically of East Asia, Moore [18] describes its governments as relying on partnership between the state and the private sector, and argues that the 'evidence seems to suggest' that this model is more likely to be successful, especially for small countries, whose ICT infrastructure can be viable only if it occupies a monopoly position. For this reason, in East Asia, the state retains ownership of infrastructure but encourages competition in construction and operation.

The same author [20] also points to different national approaches that cut across the East/West division, citing: policy development by the executive branch of government (Scandinavia, Japan, Singapore); delegation to an advisory body of experts from the sectors that will be most affected by changes (Sweden, Canada, Australia); and a combination of these two, leaving the executive responsible for developing policy (European Union, USA). On this analysis, the UK differs from all these, by relying on informal and piecemeal 'muddling through', which makes it impossible to point to a single document that describes what British national information policy encompasses.

Muir and Oppenheim [21–23] make similar points in a series of articles on worldwide developments in national information policy.

## Issues and tensions in national information policies

Governments of all kinds encounter inherent problems in the field of national information policy. Those problems interact with political, economic, social and cultural factors, which influence how governments respond to them, and the response changes over time. The main issues relate to: the nature of information itself, power relations, and the economic issue of market orientation vs public good.

### The nature of information itself

Oppenheim [16, p. 141] suggests that governments find it difficult to get to grips with information policy because they have a problem with defining information, which arises from the fact that it is dynamic and innovative, and has social and economic implications – all of which make it hard to handle. That difficulty is not limited to governments.

### Power relations

Information policies, on both the national and organizational scale, entail relations between groups of people who are parties to them in some way. There are differences in the relative power enjoyed by the various groups, as between, for example: individuals/organizations subject to legislation which is part of the policy, and the government which determines the policy; vendors of ICT solutions, and those who have to use them in the organizations that purchase them; industries with a commercial interest in exploiting scientific research, and supporters of free access to it.

As we have seen, one approach open to governments is to hand much of the power of policy making to the market, which is what the British Government has done fairly consistently for many years. Oppenheim [24], in evidence to the House of Lords Enquiry into the Information Superhighway, characterized the UK government approach as a 'consistent policy that competition in the open marketplace' and the de-regulation of telecommunications will deliver the technology which will create 'lasting, highly paid jobs'.[4] As against that, Oppenheim argues that any UK government policy for developing the 'information society' should make a single cabinet minister responsible; there should be agreed policies for government websites across all departments, and means to allow all citizens and communities access; and copyright law should be revised to achieve a consistent balance between the needs of creators, owners and users, and fair dealing with machine-readable data. Copyright law should not extend to materials produced by government.

Brown [25] describes Australian government responses since information policy became an issue in the late 1960s as 'piecemeal, sporadic' and reactive rather than systematic. She identifies a significant change in government thinking at the time of writing as a 'growing realization that powerful stakeholders have stolen a march on the citizens at large …', creating rising anxiety about privacy and security and the increasing influence of ICT in daily lives. In a continuation of the article [26] she observes that 'so-called Information Society politics'[5] are 'not concerned with […] the needs of individual users'. Information is a means to an end; a tool to be used for government purposes.

Oppenheim wrote in 1994, 'While in theory IT is a benign technology offering rewards to all in society, in practice the implementation of information technology tools tends to exacerbate the difference between the information rich and the information poor' [16, p. 134].

Horner and Day [27] provide a rare example in the LIS literature of the response of trades unions to the microelectronics revolution of the 1970s and 1980s. Attempts to negotiate new technology agreements were submerged in the Thatcher government's assault on unions in the 1980s. The authors' view is that 'In the longer term, the need is to deconstruct the assumption of ICTs' neutrality and to see them as inherently designed around management strategies. Such strategies are themselves set in the context of essentially antagonistic relations of production.' They accurately foresaw 'increasing casualization of the workforce' [27, p. 334]. This industrial relations story is still being played out today, with the unions in a weaker position than when the article was written.

Marcella and Baxter [29] in a report on the findings from a citizenship information research project conclude that there is a real danger of class-based exclusion from access to information, from the technology used to access it, and from awareness of what the exclusion deprives them of.

The Institute for Public Policy Research manifesto for Digital Britain (Davies [30]) repeats the earlier examples of power inequalities. It warns of the dangers inherent in 'overemphasis on micro-delivery challenges in areas such as e-government' in which the political nature of policy choices goes under-appreciated. The UK's enviable ICT infrastructure is not matched by 'skills or imagination to use it effectively', while emphasis on the 'knowledge economy' and generalized claims about the 'impact of ICT' have both 'outlived their usefulness'.

Government awareness of Web 2.0, which seems to have dawned in spring 2007, may possibly have brought a change of heart. An independent review on *The Power of Information* (Mayo and Steinberg [31]) commissioned by the British Government, sets out opportunities for co-operation between government and citizens in generating and using information now that people who were formerly limited to the receiving end are becoming skilled in using, re-using and creating information in new ways. The review recommends that government should work with user communities whose goals 'align closely with those of different parts of government' for common social and economic objectives; provide innovators who re-use government-held information with the information they need; and prepare citizens for a world of plentiful (and sometimes unreliable) information and help excluded groups to take advantage of it.

The Government response [32] was unusually positive; it accepted most of the report's recommendations, including:

- Developing experimental partnerships between major departments and user-generated sites in key policy areas.
- Consulting operators/users of existing user-generated sites before building its own versions, and modifying government services to complement citizen-led endeavours.
- Promoting publication of regulatory information, and encouraging its publication in open formats under licences permitting re-use.

### Market orientation vs public good

There is what Koenig [33] describes as an 'under-recognized' tension between those two views of information. On one hand, information 'doesn't exist in any meaningful sense in a wild state' so ownership should be vested in the creators, distributors, etc. who added the value by putting it into products/services. But on the public-good side, its unique characteristic is that it can be replicated or disseminated at costs that are marginal compared with those of creating it; and that leads to the argument that 'society would be daft' not to encourage the widest/cheapest distribution possible. He observes that changes in IT, from the early 1990s on, both strengthen the argument for the public-good view, and drive forward competition in using IT to create and manipulate information, with tension among stakeholders fiercer than ever before. An accurate prediction; and the tension is still with us.

Moore [34] examines the contradictory goals of de-regulating the telecommunications market and universal access to high-quality telecoms services. He attacks the implicit assumption that 'Information provided free at the point of use represents a distortion of the real market' as an oversimplification; and argues that we need to understand better how markets for information work, appreciate their limitations, and develop policies to support free provision of information at the point of use where appropriate, 'while using conventional market mechanisms elsewhere'.

The British Government response [32] to *The Power of Information*, described above, recognizes these arguments and partially accepts the recommendations on changing the current charging model for re-use of public sector information and regulation of the public-sector information market, which, however, require 'further consideration'.

### Technology- or information-led

From the time when the potential of IT for handling and manipulating information became evident, it has exerted an irresistible attraction on the thinking of governments about information policy, which has all too often relegated actual information to a lowly supporting role.

In the UK the disproportion has been commented on and complained of from the start, and still is today; de Saulles [35] for example objects to 'e-government' policies biased towards IT and 'communication' aspects rather than actual information. Current aspirations to shepherd the 'customer' population towards electronic interaction with government information are under the rubric of 'transformational government'. The relevant publications do not actually say who or what is to be transformed, but the stated aim is to rationalize the use of the web by government departments in order to deliver 'customer-centric' services (Cabinet Office [36]). There is much ground to make up in respect of both parts of that aim. Deficiencies in the necessary professional skills in IT procurement and project management, compounded by 'ten or more years of uncoordinated growth of government websites' are recognized by the National Audit Office (NAO) [37]. Steps to rectify the situation include a Government IT academy and establishment of the Chief Information Officer as a 'board-level position' (Cabinet Office [36]).

Less detail is available on how the actual information content presented on rationalized websites is to become more customer-centric. While the NAO reports that focus-group participants have found the websites of government departments and agencies 'complex [...] with information useful to them hard to find amongst large amounts of policy material and official documentation', dealing with those difficulties is discussed primarily in aspirational terms: the vision in the *Service Transformation Agreement* (HM Treasury [38]), for example, is of future services that will be 'better for customers [...] simpler, more streamlined and intuitive, more accessible and convenient'.

The NAO's recognition that not everyone can use the internet, and that exclusion is highest among elderly people and those on means-tested benefits, is welcome, but they are likely to have a long wait before they benefit from 'money released from improved efficiency'. The task described as 're-ordering information to make it easily findable; re-presenting [it] so that it is clearer and makes sense for citizens or businesses' and 'joining [it] up effectively' is as demanding as rectifying past neglect of essential IT expertise; but there is no indication of comparable investment in it, and apparently no recognition of the professional skills and knowledge it requires. It would be interesting to have an update of the survey of internet and intranet use in 23 government departments made in 1999 by the Committee of Departmental Librarians (Cumming and Cuthbertson, [39]). At that date, in 68 percent of the organizations surveyed 'libraries had no input at all into the websites, even information management and indexing were usually left to IT or other sections', and the authors note the 'predominance of press and publicity sections in managing government websites' in contrast with academic institutions.

Although the British government seems now to be moving towards a better understanding of how human beings (including civil servants) and ICT can work together in generating and using qualitative as well as quantitative information, the transformation should probably not be expected any time soon, and it certainly will not be of the kind achieved at the wave of a wand.

## Government and research

In the light of this short history there is little reason to be surprised by the way governments treat research they themselves have commissioned (including non-use and non-publication); by the 'difference between the information, advice and research that policy makers seek and that upon which they act' (Strachan and Rowlands [40]); or by Oppenheim's [16] observation that there is virtually no input from information professionals into government policy-making. It is a pity none the less that governments have not taken the view of information-policy making proposed by Rowlands [2], as a process of negotiation, 'bringing together competing value frames and resolving conflicts'.

### From formulating the policy to managing action

The transition from formulating policy to implementing it is another can of worms (as the UK Government has found, for example, with its Freedom of Information Act, which has created similar problems to those that arose in the USA 40 years earlier). The forte of politicians is in issuing policies, or directives to establish policies. In the nature of things they can have little conception of the work of the real human beings who have to wrestle with putting into practice the stream of policies and initiatives. Here are two examples of what it entails.

The first comes from a government department (the Department of Trade and Industry (DTI)). MacLachlan [41] writes from long experience of developing information management in the Department, starting in 1989, when the Cabinet Office recommended government departments to develop an information policy and audit their information resources. A first version was written in that year, and it was revised in the light of experience in 1993. By the late 1990s existing systems for managing internal information were under strain; and a new initiative on modernizing government from the Cabinet Office, with the then fashionable key theme of sharing information and knowledge, required all records to be made available electronically by 2004. This led to setting up a DTI working group on information architecture; as well as taxonomy, metadata standards, thesaurus, procedures etc., its programme included another revision of information policy. The revised policy set out seven principles governing how the Department would manage information; defined the types of information it covered, and the policies for security, versioning, modification and disposal, intellectual property, information management responsibilities etc.; and set out explicitly how information should be managed and by whom. At the time of writing (in 2004) MacLachlan was able to state that they had 'begun to develop both a recognition of the relevance of information management and some skills in the

DTI user population'. A modest claim, and it had taken consistent work by committed people over 15 years to reach that point.

The second example comes from the CRM (customer relationship management) National Project, a £4.275m initiative led by the London borough of Tower Hamlets, launched in 2003 to 'bring clarity and definition to the role of customer relationship management in local government'. The project, which was embedded in an initiative from the Office of the Deputy Prime Minister for a National Strategy for local e-government [42], included as one element among many a model information management policy for local authorities. While CRM was described in an introductory presentation to 'e-champions' in 2002 as 'More than IT – a philosophy and approach [...] – A fundamental change (transformation) to put the customer at the focus rather than the product or service', IT and the introduction of e-government seem to have been the main message that local authorities got.

A search for the model information management policy for purposes of this article led into quite a labyrinth. One of the participating councils, Salford [43], described on its website (last updated April 2004) the 'tremendous progress' made by that date, including 'clear standards and guidelines for [...] information management'.

Salford was also involved in setting up a 'CRM Academy' to offer independent advice. A search of its site [44] for information management policy produced only entries from vendors recommending their CRM systems.

Websites quoted by a participant in the development of the policy model (Budzak [45]) can no longer be accessed. The Local e-Government Programme [46] officially closed in April 2006, though the site continues to offer advice; a search for information management policy provided only two results, both referring to a protocol for establishing a consistent approach to management of Freedom of Information Act requests.

Another participating council, Brent, refers in its IT Strategy 2007 v1.4 [47] to 'A new Information Management policy [which] will bring structure and clarity to the wealth of information we hold so that all staff have access to a deep and resource-rich pool of knowledge.'

But that is as far as I could take the search in the time available; I am sorry it did not lead to the model policy on which Brent's path to its deep pool of knowledge is presumably based.

## Organizational information policies

This is a shorter story than national information policies, and its telling is based in part on personal experience. Organizational information policies seem to date back only to the early 1980s, and they have received less attention than national from both researchers and practitioners. As observed by participants in a 1996 British Library workshop on information policies (Rowlands [48]), this was a key area of information policy that had not been explored to any depth. I became aware that this was so in 1980, when embarking on my first attempt to articulate the idea and to design a policy for an organization (Orna and Hall [49]).

Brown [25], like the participants in the British Library workshop on information policies, argues that the definition should cover both national and organizational forms, and that organizational information policy merits study – though a distinction should still be made between the public and corporate spheres. She considers, however, that it should be studied, 'not with reference to the organization itself but in the way it interacts with, and influences direction in, public policy.'

That interaction is indeed important, but the emphasis here will be rather different. It is based on the reflection that the task of putting national information policies into practice has to be carried out by government departments, and what are they but organizations of a specific kind? As such they are a point of intersection between national and organizational information policies, and in my view, the specific context of 'the organization itself' is the most appropriate way into organizational information policy.

### Definition

Orna [50] and [51] defines organizational information policy as a policy 'founded on an organization's overall objectives and the priorities within them', which 'defines, at a general level: the objectives of information use in the organization, what "information" means for it in the context of whatever it is in business for', and the principles on which it will manage information, employ human resources and technology in using it, and assign a value to it.

An information policy is 'a dynamic tool', which can be used as the basis for developing an organizational information strategy; and which can 'relate everything that is done with information to the organization's overall objectives; enable effective decisions on resource allocation; promote interaction, communication and mutual support between all parts of the organization, and between it and its "customers" or public; provide objective criteria for assessing the results of information-based activities; {and] give feedback to the process of developing corporate policies.'

## Why should organizations have information policies?

On that definition organizational information policies and strategies are meant to be used, and not as objects of contemplation but as a basis for action. They have been commended to organizations both for avoiding risks (financial losses from incomplete and uncoordinated exploitation of information, wasted time, failures of innovation, and reputation loss); and for positive benefits, including negotiation and openness among those responsible for different aspects of information management, productive use of IT in supporting staff in their use of information, and ability to initiate change to take advantage of changing environments (Orna [50]). These reasons have similarities with the ideas advanced by Itami [52], Nonaka and Takeuchi [53], Davenport and Prusak [54, 55], and Marchand et al. [56], and are much influenced by their thinking.[6]

## Why do they embark on them?

Different organizations have embarked on information policies from various situations. Many were forced into it by external economic pressures; Moore and Steel [1] are among those who describe the recession of the late 1970s and early 1980s as causing businesses to change their view of information services, and see them not as overheads but as important corporate resources with potential for helping them to survive economic storms.

Others came to it on the basis of thinking about their existing experience of information use, with the aim of bringing greater coherence to things they were already doing, benefiting from experience, dealing successfully with changes on the horizon and achieving desired innovations, and with clear ideas of how to use the information policy and who would be involved in the process. (This was certainly the case with at least one major company in the pharmaceutical industry, which, as described in Orna [57], gave a lead in developing information policies.)

The outcomes differed accordingly. Van Mesdag [58] for example describes firms under economic pressure, without an integrated approach to information, responding by buying tools to 'collect, process, store, retrieve and present information' but without having thought about where to get information to put in the store or the objectives of outputting it. Neyland and Surridge [59] tell of the uncomprehending response of some British universities to the JISC requirement to develop an information strategy. One British university had a five-year-old information strategy document that had never been acted on, another an Information Strategy Committee of the same age that had never produced a strategy.

Surveys of business over the period from the mid-1990s to the present suggest a similar picture of points not quite grasped. A telephone survey of a random sample of nearly 1000 chief executives in the UK (Baxter [60]) showed that while 60 percent claimed their company had a strategy/policy for information management, only 20 percent were aware of the company having an overall information budget; half had no formal information provision; and the majority did not know who was responsible for the information resource.

Nearly 10 years later, information professionals showed up little better. In 2005, Documation-UK, supported by Vignette (vendors of integrated document-management systems) surveyed 119 information management and IT professionals. Over 44 percent of respondents reported that their company was without a document and information-management strategy. While nearly all respondents thought information management was important to their organization only 42 percent of them were aware of any regulations or legislation relating to business information management that affected their work directly [61].

More encouraging examples come from organizations in both public and private sectors that are concerned with managing information by the nature of their business;[7] have worked they way towards it from first principles over a long time;[8] or have benefited from initiatives by experienced and energetic information professionals and key information users, supported by 'management champions'.[9] They have not only developed information policies and strategies but have succeeded in bringing them into beneficial operation over time. Some continue to be used successfully in meeting external challenges and initiating innovatory change from within; some have fallen victims to hazards described later.

## Why some find it difficult

While organizations realize that information is an important resource, as Oppenheim [16] says, they do not find it easy to handle.

A major stumbling block is understanding that each individual organization has to define for itself what constitutes information for it, in the light of what it is in business for. It is rare to find one that has done so. There is little awareness of the full range 'that emerges once one starts unpacking the meaning of mission statements or corporate objectives' [50, p. 31], or that information as a resource benefits the organization only when it forms part of human knowledge and is applied effectively in action.

## Issues in organizational information policies

Organizations, like national governments, encounter issues and tensions in trying to develop information policy, and, like them, respond in different ways.

### Human beings or technology first?

A major point of division is how they envisage the interaction between human beings and technologies for using information, and which they think of first when they consider information policy. The reasons, like those of governments, go back to the people who make the decisions (the amount of power they exert in the organization; their professional background; and their understanding of the technology, of the term 'information' and of how people in the organization need to use it), and to the relations between them and the people who sell them ICT solutions.

Early examples of the alternatives can be seen in Karni [62], who writes from the point of view of the IT professional, and defines information policy solely in terms of IT and systems; and in Weitzel [63], who insists that it must extend its range from IT management to the management of information content and use.

Blackler [64] takes an approach related to the thinking about ICT and information management of such researchers as Ken Eason [65] at HUSAT and Enid Mumford [66] at Manchester Business School. He contrasts two planning styles: task/technology centred, and organization and end-user centred. The priority in recent years, he says, has been to 'make the technologies work'; few forums exist in the UK for multi-disciplinary debate on IT issues and 'ergonomists and cognitive scientists [have predominated] in those that have existed'; and too much emphasis has been placed on rational thinking.

Monk [67] claims a dominant role for IT as 'the very means by which markets and other economic mechanisms operate'; its role is not just to profit its corporate owners; its primary significance is in the 'operation of the economy as a whole'. He concludes that 'the IT industries have in effect got their hand on the tiller of the economy but appear not to realize it yet, or perhaps they do and that is why they are keeping quiet about it', and one may reasonably suspect that the last phrase represents his opinion on the matter.

There are reports too in the early 1990s of disingenuous behaviour within companies in decisions about buying new IT systems. Gauthier and Sifonis [68] write of the need to 'dispel [...] truisms that became gospel in many countries' that IT solves business problems. The high cost of IT staff and equipment is accompanied by nebulous benefits, and non-IT staff dissociate from it. Technologists are not 'innocent victims' – 'the position of CIO [Chief Information Officer] was created by technologists for technologists' to give them a management status consistent with the rising role of IT.

Farbey et al. [69] describe an investigation, commissioned by a vendor, of how clients decided to acquire new systems. Case studies showed less than half claimed to have an IT strategy, decisions were made piecemeal, and uses proposed were all far from current thinking on the subject – they did not, for example, include reconfiguring how work was done, connecting to customers, or supporting co-operative work. The benefits mentioned were all short-term and quantitative. Powell [70] observes that 'often, mere lip service is paid to the strategic nature of IT'; strategic justification has become a tool for securing investment in IT by circumventing established organizational policy on investments. Labelling what you want as strategic ensures that you will get it!

The dominance of IT-centred policies was challenged in practice in the 1990s. Two examples come from the museum world; Nunn [71] describes how the Natural History Museum moved towards a corporate information strategy, from an initial focus on the technology to realizing that full value from it was attainable only if systems meet the needs of users and are integrated organization-wide. At the Tate, a similar process took place, which I was fortunate enough to be able to observe over several years. Beard et al. [72] describe a progression from IS strategy to information policy. The digital strategy which the gallery is developing has been 'framed within a developing information policy which sets out why the organization's information resources [...] need to be treated with as much care as the works themselves.' This was a long-term evolution/revolution driven by an alliance of strategists, systems and LIS professionals and top management (documented in Orna [51, 73]).

## Top-down or middle-up-down?

Another long-running issue concerns whether the initiative for information policy should proceed top-down, or middle-up-down as advocated by Nonaka and Takeuchi [53]. The best-known UK attempt to encourage top-down action is probably the IMPACT Programme, which began in 1995, when the Hawley Committee, a group of Chief Executives with an interest in maximizing the return from corporate information, produced a 10-point *Board Agenda* [74] addressed to directors. Ward and Ward [75] describe it as a simple check-list and supporting guidance, couched in language which they tactfully call 'appropriate at Board level', and as a successful attempt to engage senior management in information governance issues and reach beyond the pre-occupation with technology and IT investment – but without explicitly addressing either knowledge issues or exploitation of information or knowledge in any detail. It is not clear whether the success has been long-lasting. The *Agenda* gave no direct indication of 'where shortcomings may exist or how gaps might be plugged'. It was followed by the *Information Health Index* (KPMG IMPACT Programme Ltd [76]), which was designed to give a quick picture of information governance in companies, with 'potential to guide information strategy and policy'.

The idea of 'middle-up-down' management as an essential enabler of knowledge creation, along with a strategy for knowledge and information, is described by Nonaka and Takeuchi [53]. It refers to the autonomy given by top management to groups entrusted with responsibility for new developments, which allows original ideas to develop and spread through 'a spiral conversion process involving both the top and the front-line employees', a process which 'puts middle managers at the very center of knowledge management' [53, p. 127]. Examples of the process in operation are presented in their book; others are described in Orna [51] and [73]. (In the first of these references, there is also an extensive discussion of the relation between knowledge management and information management and of the significance of both for information strategy.)

*Information culture*

A third major issue in organizational information policy is the influence of the organization's 'culture', especially in respect of information. The key questions are whether it is recognized or unacknowledged; and whether or not the policy takes account of it and aims to change it. Ginman [77] reports on research in Finland on the relationship between information culture and business performance, which indicates links between the CEO's information culture, company culture, its 'life cycle' stage, and business performance.

Davenport et al. [78] introduced the idea of organization politics in relation to power structures into the discussion of the subject. They identify five political models, from feudalism to technocratic utopianism, and conclude that the wrong political structure can sink efforts to create information-based organizations. Their advice is: recognize the politics of information and their effect on organizational culture, and aim where necessary to change them, to achieve a more information-friendly political system. These ideas are followed up in Davenport and Prusak [54] and [55].

Literature reviews of organizational and information culture and business performance by Abell and Winterman [79] suggest that an adaptive 'empowering' culture is seen as necessary for good long-term performance, and that human knowledge and interpretation of data confer a competitive edge.

A Reuters study, in 1994, of information sources and their use in business [80] recognizes, however, that:

> today the giving and withholding of information is inextricably linked with organizational politics and, as a result, the knowledge-based organization where free-flow of information contributes to the general good is still largely a fantasy.

The authors ask what will happen to organizations that are unable, because of information politics, to capitalize on coming innovations in multimedia information diffusion to homes and businesses. Today, when the promised innovations and more have arrived, it is doubtful whether organizations have become any better at managing the politics of information. Kristiansson [81] observes that information politics still affect the way organizations are structured and vice versa; he considers that since an organic type of structure has proved most suitable for handling the complexity and unpredictability that still surround organizations, they should seek to develop their information politics to support that form and counteract hierarchical and 'mechanic' structures, a counsel that like much good advice, is easier to give than to follow.

## Valuing information

The ability to assign a reliable, and preferably monetary, value to information would be a winner in gaining and keeping the attention of senior management; most organizations, however, have been reluctant to approach it, because they could not see how to do it. The difficulty arises partly from mistrust of qualitative measures and partly from the intellectual demands of methods for converting qualitative to quantitative. It is compounded by imperfect understanding of the unique qualities of information, which affect its value crucially: as Taylor [82] points out, the value of information 'cannot be measured in precise terms prior to its use […] it is given value by its user'; when information is exchanged and traded, its value in use can increase for all parties; its value is not reduced by use, it can be used many times to add value to many activities by many users; as an 'asset' or 'intellectual capital' it has value only when it is being put to productive use (see Orna [51, 83]).

Support for qualitative measures of information value comes from research by Oppenheim et al. [84] and Marchand et al. [56]. Oppenheim and his colleagues, on the basis of research with a sample of UK organizations, concluded that 'arriving at a value of information or knowledge is not an objective exercise' because its value is 'by its very nature […] subjective, dependent on the interpretation [of those] who employ information in particular situations for particular purposes.' Marchand and his colleagues, working with a large international sample of senior managers, make a strong case for qualitative, and statistically reliable, measures of the value of information in relation to business performance. The metric they developed for their research depends on the relation between senior managers' judgment of their own company's business performance, and the extent to which the company combines effective management of information and IT with appropriate information and knowledge behaviour (its 'information orientation').

M'Pherson [85], who is unusual in approaching the subject from a background of systems engineering, has over a number of years tackled the problem of measuring intangible value, in order to ensure that 'the intangibles of a company are valued rigorously, to the extent that Intellectual Capital value becomes an accounting number.' His 'Inclusive Value Accounting

Framework', developed through action-research applications in a number of companies, achieves this on the basis of knowledgeable judgments by responsible managers. He acknowledges that the intellectual effort they need to make in coming to terms with the concepts involved is a major barrier; it can probably be overcome only in large corporations.

Ryan [86] describes a less exact and exacting method (in use at the European Bank of Reconstruction and Development) for determining the value of the information provided by an information unit; it depends on 'time-saved tariffs' agreed between the unit and its users – i.e. the time that the unit's services saved the users, converted to an agreed pounds-per-hour figure.

That concludes this necessarily brief account of organizational information policies. It now remains to draw the strands of this article together, in a brief picture of what our discipline and profession have contributed in the field of information policy up to the present; and to look ahead to the future – not with anything so portentous as a prediction, only a suggestion, in the light of yesterday and today, of tasks for tomorrow.

## The picture today

Looking back over the years since the IIS was founded, on the basis of direct observation from inside the information world for many of them, gives something of the sense of seeing the same bits of luggage coming round time and again on the carousel. There has been some progress over time, but the same tensions and misunderstandings repeat themselves, which suggests that not much learning goes on.

In the UK, leaving national information policy to the market has not paid off as well as expected. The ICT industry has dominated, its power not balanced by sufficient knowledge on the government side to control it. Government talk of the empowerment of users and of 'transparency' has therefore been perceived as empty, naive, or disingenuous. In practice, IT-led national information policies have shown up dangerous weak points in human/ICT relations (mostly recently in the stories of disappearing disks of sensitive data, caused by human errors and failures to appreciate security risks [87–89]), and technical failures of promised large and complex systems for integrating data, most notably for the National Health Service [90] and national ID cards [91].

The interface between policy directives and formulation and implementation has not been a happy scene either. Frequent policy initiatives have rolled out after too little thinking and too little study of past history, and too little time has been devoted to supporting those who have to carry them out.

To set against that, however, is the recent apparent change in government thinking in its response [32] to *The Power of Information* [31]; though, given the number of more pressing concerns the government faces at present, it seems unlikely to be expressed in action any time soon.

So far as organizational information policies are concerned, there is comparatively little to show in the way of actual working information policies and strategies that have survived for a long time. It seems, in the recent words of a colleague in search of examples of information policies in organizations, that 'once they have ticked the FoIA and DPA boxes, and have a website and a CMS in place (whatever they may or may not be doing with them) that's it'. TOTO (the top of the organization) for the most part still has undue faith in technology, and weak understanding of what information means and of what LIS professionals know. On the other hand, however, there are more examples of mutual understanding and co-operation between information managers and IT/systems; and of information management and knowledge management working together on an equal footing.

Like any other policy, information policies are vulnerable to change. Following up the fate of soundly established policies that were working well, in organizations where I had either made case studies or undertaken consultancy assignments, suggests the main threats to survival are: change in power structures at the top, especially loss of the original sponsor; and external pressures, in the form of financial imperatives, the general economic climate or specific market conditions; and legislative changes requiring compliance – all compounded by the corporate amnesia so prevalent at board and senior management level.

## The contribution of information science to information policies

Over the years covered by this brief history, the discipline of information science, and its practitioners, have contributed a body of information policy research both theoretical and practical, much of it based on study of how organizations think and behave. Their research has built up a strong case for information policies, and has provided evidence of how to achieve and use them, on both a national and organizational scale.

They have recognized, from the earliest days, the potential and risks of what is now called the digital revolution; and the thinking of those whom the brief for this issue calls 'founding players' and their successors has played a leading part in efforts to narrow the gap between ICT and information content, between 'socio-' and technical approaches.

There are today many well-established LIS professionals at work, whose education and training have been influenced by the information science discipline. They have deep knowledge of their organizations and shrewd ability to make use of their power structures. Good opportunists, they use their knowledge to exert middle-up-down leadership and educate TOTO, and they work as initiators, bridge builders and 'translators' between groups who use different language to talk about similar things.

And in spite of the difficulty that decision-makers, in government and in organizations, have in grasping their message and retaining it, researchers and practitioners have persevered.

## And tomorrow?

Will information policies/strategies still be needed, and is it worth going on trying?

The short answer is yes, above all to try to sort out the consequences of power imbalance, which become graver and more dangerous as the dependence of information transactions on the ICT industry increases.

It will be clear from what has gone before that I hold no undue hopes, because understanding at the top is so often both narrow and shallow, and because of the hazards to which that exposes information policies. But that is not to say that it is time to abandon future efforts. Here are my suggestions for what they should be addressed to.

## National

- Controlling the power of the information industries; making national information policy in the UK less market-driven and more dirigiste, to use Moore's word [19].
- Encouraging the British Government to follow up the lead it gave in commissioning in 2007 *The Power of Information* [31] (see above) and in responding to it.

- Imposing a 'due diligence' requirement throughout government that before introducing any initiative/policy/legislation, the history of previous attempts in the same line must be investigated and taken into account.[10]

## Organizational

- Helping organizations to: get value from social computing without endangering the integrity of their information resources; being aware of how easily it can be subverted; remembering that the 'wisdom of crowds' depends on who is in the crowd, and the 'collective intelligence of employees' on how minded they are to put it at the disposal of their employers and colleagues.
- Educating all users, from TOTO down, in information management that goes beyond using IT tools and systems, and relates information to what they need to do with it.

## Both national and organizational

- Getting the best rather than the worst from Web 2.0 developments nationally and in organizations.
- Paying more attention to the socio- aspect of socio-technical systems; seeking forms of human/technology co-operation that take a realistic view of human nature. In particular, on the technical side, search development to match the capability of the technology (see e.g. Dutra [92]) and on the socio- side, more attention to the psychology and sociology of organizations in order to make it worth people's while to use the technology to contribute and exchange their knowledge.
- Securing preservation of digital content, nationally (through the recently launched plan for a government-wide service managed by the National Archives [93]) and in organizations.
- Bringing information products[11] within the scope of information policy/strategy. As the definition in the note makes clear, this term covers the whole range from traditional print on paper to all kinds of web-based products, and the information policies of all organizations, including government departments should take an integrated view of whatever in that line they offer to their own staff and the outside world. Without information products, 'information content' could not

exist in any accessible form, and they are the main embodiment of the knowledge that would otherwise remain locked in individual minds. To get full value from them, they need – but seldom get – the combined skills and knowledge of many professions, in particular LIS, ITC and information design, and the collaboration of those who will need to use them in their work. (The full arguments are developed in Orna [73, 94].)

- Respecting all users, including those who are not able to use electronically presented information.
- Making thinking time respectable.

## In conclusion

History should teach us to accept that progress will continue to resemble those medieval circle dances which advance so many steps, go back the same number, then forward again, making slow progress onwards because the forward steps are slightly longer than the backward. It will give us a more realistic view than believing that technology and the market will take us forward with giant strides. It is better to join the dance and use knowledge from our history to make the forward steps longer.

## Acknowledgements

I am grateful to the referees and to Alan Gilchrist for their helpful comments.

## Notes

1  Recently discovered sound recordings and research on the history of propaganda reveal some disreputable origins of British propaganda, from privately produced recordings of patriotic (and fanciful) 'docu-dramas' of life at the front to highly organized official concealment and falsification of news for home and overseas consumption, to manufacture and planting of atrocity stories. By the end of the First World War, government propaganda seems to have embodied most of the activities that the Ministry of Information and later the Central Office of Information became responsible for at a more respectable level (programme: The Sound of Flanders, The Archive Hour, presented by Frank Gardner, BBC R4, 24 November 2007).

2  The long history of how UK governments have dealt with this is set out in the National Archives website [12]; prefaced with the melancholy statement that

'Statistical Departments does not have a parent', a piece of archive-speak which characterizes in other senses the collection of statistics in the UK. Not until the Second World War, at the insistence of Churchill, was a Central Statistical Office established (1941). Growth continued postwar under Claus Moser, but its functions and resources were reduced after Sir Derek Rayner's review in 1980. Erosion continued until 1991 when the direction changed, with a series of reforms culminating in the Office of Population Censuses and Surveys and CSO merging to form today's Office of National Statistics.

3  It is interesting that the modern scope of national information policy pays comparatively little attention to the aspects under which the concept first appeared – dissemination, presentation, communication and the audience to which they are addressed.

4  Rowlands [2] describes politicians as using the information society portmanteau of modernizing the telecoms infrastructure, promoting competitiveness, re-skilling the workforce, social cohesion, extending democracy, and open/accountable government, to 'create a warm feeling in audiences'.

5  George et al. [28] describe the information society as a 'fuzzy social concept' which leaders of many countries think a desirable state 'whatever it is'. Their analysis suggests that the information society 'seems to be used as a rallying concept for the mobilization of bias within a country […] a rallying image of an electronic utopia that may have little to do with what actually evolves'.

6  Itami [52] describes people as the embodiment of 'invisible assets' who 'carry and exchange the information necessary for strategic fit'. Davenport and Prusak [55] assert that knowledge creation 'remains largely an act of individuals or groups and their brains', and Nonaka and Takeuchi [53, p. 74] give first place to a strategy for knowledge and information in their list of conditions for the creation of knowledge in companies.

7  For example the British Library, the subject of two case studies covering the period from 1989 to 1998–9, the year after it was handed over (Orna [50, 57]).

8  Examples are the Tate, the Victoria and Albert Museum, and Surrey Police; see case studies in Orna [50].

9  For a number of case studies from the UK and other countries, see Orna [50].

10  It might enable them to follow Gerry Robinson's succinct advice (BBC2, 12 December 2007) in connection with NHS policies: 'Don't keep introducing ruddy policies – manage it!'

11  'The products, print on paper or electronic, through which information is presented for use. They embody the results of the transformation of knowledge into information […] and are an integral blend of content and container' [73].

# References

[1]     N. Moore and J. Steel, *Information-Intensive Britain. British Library R & D Report No. 6038* (The Policy Studies Institute/British Library Board, London, 1991).

[2]     I. Rowlands, Some compass bearings for information policy orienteering, *Aslib Proceedings* 50(8) (1998) 230–37.

[3]     National Archives. Available at: www.nationalarchives.gov.uk (accessed 9 January 2008).

[4]     T.F. Clark, Do we need government information services? *Public Administration* 35(4) (1957) 335–46.

[5]     Central Office of Information. Available at: www.coi.gov.uk (accessed 10 January 2008).

[6]     US National Archives and Records Administration. Available at: www.archives.gov/research/ (accessed 10 January 2008).

[7]     F.E. Rourke, Administrative secrecy: a Congressional dilemma, *The American Political Science Review* 54 (1960) 684–94.

[8]     E.S. Dunn Jr, The idea of a National Data Center and the issue of personal privacy, *The American Statistician* 21(1) (1967) 21–7.

[9]     D. Muddiman, Red information scientist: the information career of J.D. Bernal, *Journal of Documentation* 59(4) (2003) 387–409.

[10]    J.D. Bernal, *The Social Function of Science*. (Routledge, London, 1939).

[11]    B. Vickery, *J.D. Bernal: science and social development* (2006). Available at: www.lucis.me.uk/bernal.htm/ (accessed 28 February 2008).

[12]    National Archives, *The National Digital Archive of Datasets* (2007). Available at: www.ndad.nationalarchives.gov.uk/AH/5/detail.html (accessed 10 January 2008).

[13]    I. Rowlands, Understanding information policy: concepts, frameworks and research tools, *Journal of Information Science* 22(1) (1996) 13–25.

[14]    E. Maceviciute and T.D. Wilson, The development of the information management research area, *Information Research* 7(3) (2002). Available at: http://informationr.net/ir/7-3/paper133.html (accessed 5 April 2008).

[15]    Domestic Council Committee on the Right of Privacy, *Rockefeller Report, National Information Policy* (National Commission on Libraries and Information Science, Washington, DC, 1976).

[16]    C. Oppenheim, Are national information plans useful? *Alexandria* 6(2) (1994) 133–43.

[17]    M.W. Hill, *National Information Policies and Strategies. An Overview and Bibliographic Survey*. British Library Research: Information Policy Issues (Bowker Saur, London, 1994).

[18]    N. Moore, The information policy agenda in East Asia, *Journal of Information Science* 23(2) (1997) 139–47.

[19]    N. Moore, Policies for an information society, *Aslib Proceedings* 50(1) (1998) 20–24.

[20]    N. Moore, The British national information strategy, *Journal of Information Science* 24(5) (1998) 337–44.

[21]    A. Muir and C. Oppenheim, National Information Policy: developments worldwide. I: Electronic government, *Journal of Information Science* 28(3) (2002) 173–86.

[22]    A. Muir and C. Oppenheim, National Information Policy: developments worldwide. II: Universal access – addressing the digital divide, *Journal of Information Science* 28(4) (2002) 263–73.

[23]    A. Muir and C. Oppenheim, National Information Policy: developments worldwide. IV: Copyright, freedom of information and data protection, *Journal of Information Science* 28(6) (2002) 467–81.

[24]    C. Oppenheim, An agenda for action to achieve the information society in the UK, *Journal of Information Science* 22(6) (1996) 407–42.

[25]    M. Brown, The field of information policy. 1: Fundamental concepts, *Journal of Information Science* 23(4) (1997) 261–75.

[26]    M. Brown, The field of information policy. 2: Redefining the boundaries and methodologies, *Journal of Information Science* 23(5) (1997) 339–51.

[27]    D. Horner and P. Day, Labour and the information society: trade union policies for teleworking, *Journal of Information Science* 21(5) (1995) 333–41.

[28]    J.F. George et al., The information society: image versus reality in national computer plans. *Information Infrastructure and Policy* 4, (1995) 181–92.

[29]    R. Marcella and G. Baxter, The impact of social class and status on citizenship information need: the results of two national surveys in the UK, Journal of Information Science 26(4) (2000) 239–54.

[30]    W. Davies, *Modernising with Purpose: a Manifesto for a Digital Britain* (Institute for Public Policy Research, London, 2005).

[31]    E. Mayo and T. Steinberg, The power of information: an independent review. Available at: www.cabinetoffice.gov.uk/upload/assets/www.cabinetoffice.gov.uk/strategy/power_information.pdf (accessed 10 January 2008).

[32]    *The Government's Response to The Power of Information: an Independent Review by Ed Mayo and Tom Steinberg* (2007) Presented to Parliament by the Chancellor of the Duchy of Lancaster, June 2007, Cmd 7157.

[33]   M. Koenig, Information policy – the mounting tension (value additive versus uniquely distributable public good), *Journal of Information Science* 21(3) (1995) 229–31.

[34]   N. Moore, Policy issues in the multimedia age, *Journal of Information Science* 22(3) (1996) 213–18.

[35]   M. de Saulles, Information literacy amongst UK SMEs: an information policy gap, *Aslib Proceedings* 59(1) (2007) 68–79.

[36]   Cabinet Office, *Transformational Government Enabled by Technology: Annual Report 2006.* Cmnd 6970 (2007).

[37]   National Audit Office, *Government on the Internet: Progress in Delivering Information Services Online* (2007). HC259 Session 2006–7. Available at: www.nao.org.uk/publications/nao_reports/06–07/0607529es.htm (accessed 10 January 2008).

[38]   HM Treasury, *Service Transformation Agreement* (2007). Available at: www.hm-treasury.gov.uk/media/B/9/pbr_csr07_service.pdf (accessed 10 January 2008).

[39]   M. Cumming and L. Cuthbertson, Wired in Whitehall: a survey of internet and intranet use in government, *Aslib Proceedings* 53(1) (2001) 32–8.

[40]   J. Strachan and I. Rowlands, Information for policy making. In: I. Rowlands (ed.) *Understanding Information Policy: Proceedings of a British Library Workshop, July 1996* (Bowker-Saur, London, 1997).

[41]   L. MacLachlan, From architecture to construction: the electronic records management programme at the DTI. In: A. Gilchrist and B. Mahon (eds), *Information Architecture: Designing Information Environments for Purpose* (Facet, London, 2004).

[42]   Office of the Deputy Prime Minister, *The National Strategy for Local e–Government* (2002). Available at: http://archive.cabinetoffice.gov.uk/e-envoy/ (accessed 10 January 2008).

[43]   Salford Council, *CRM National Project* (2004). Available at: www.salford.gov.uk/council/corporate/e-government/crmnp.htm (accessed 10 January 2008).

[44]   Salford Council, *CRM Academy* (2003-). Available at: www.crmacademy.org/ (accessed 10 January 2008).

[45]   D. Budzak, Developing an information management policy – is too much attention paid to the technology? *Information Management and Technology* 39(2) (2006) 89–93.

[46]   Department of Communities and Local Government, *Local e-Government Programme.* Available at:

www.communities.gov.uk/localgovernment/efficiencybetter/localegovernment/ (accessed 10 January 2008).

[47]   Brent Council, *IT Strategy 2007* (2007). Available at: www.brent.gov.uk/ (accessed 10 January 2008).

[48]   I. Rowlands (ed.), *Understanding Information Policy: Proceedings of a British Library Workshop, July 1996* (Bowker-Saur, London, 1997).

[49]   E. Orna and G. Hall, Developing an information policy, *Aslib Proceedings* 33(1) (1981) 15–20.

[50]   E. Orna, *Practical Information Policies*, 2nd Edition (Gower, Aldershot, 1999).

[51]   E. Orna, *Information Strategy in Practice* (Gower, Aldershot, 2004).

[52]   H. Itami, with T.W. Roehl, *Mobilizing Invisible Assets* (Harvard University Press, Boston, MA, 1987).

[53]   I. Nonaka and H. Takeuchi, *The Knowledge-Creating Company* (Oxford University Press, New York/Oxford, 1995).

[54]   T.H. Davenport and L. Prusak, *Information Ecology* (Oxford University Press, New York/Oxford, 1997).

[55]   T.H. Davenport and L. Prusak, *Working Knowledge* (Harvard Business School Press, Boston, MA, 1998).

[56]   D.A. Marchand, W.J. Kettinger and J.D. Rollins, *Information Orientation* (Oxford University Press, Oxford, 2002).

[57]   E.Orna, *Practical Information Policies*, 1st Edition (Gower, Aldershot, 1990).

[58]   M. van Mesdag, Information: the resource, *Managing Information* (London) August [1(2) (1981)] 3–38.

[59]   D. Neyland and C. Surridge, Information strategy stories: ideas for evolving a dynamic strategic process, *Perspectives, Policy and Practice in Higher Education*, 7(1) (2003) 9–13.

[60]   J. Baxter, *Management Summary of LA Survey for the Information for Business Campaign* (Information Research Network/Library Association, London, 1996).

[61]   *Over 44% of Companies without Information Management Strategy* (2005.) Available at: http://managinginformation.com/newsletters/previous/issue187.htm 9 September 2005 (accessed 10 January 2008).

[62]   R. Karni, A methodological framework for formulating information policy, *Information and Management* 6 (1983) 269–80.

[63]   J.R. Weitzel, Strategic information management: targeting information for organizational performance, *Information Management Review* 3(1) (1987) 9–19.

[64]   F. Blackler, Information systems design and planned organization change: applying Unger's theory of social reconstruction, *Behaviour and Information Technology* 11(3) (1992) 175–83.

[65]   K. Eason, *Information Technology and Organisational Change* (Taylor and Francis, London, 1988).

[66]   E. Mumford, From bank teller to office worker: the pursuit of systems designed for people in practice and research, *International Journal of Information Management* 6 (1986) 59–73.

[67]   P. Monk, The economic significance of infrastructural IT systems, *Journal of Information Technology* 8 (1993) 14–21.

[68]   M.R. Gauthier and J.G. Sifonis, Managing information technology investments in the 1990s, *Bulletin of the American Society for Information Science*, June/July (1990) 16–19.

[69]   B. Farbey et al., Evaluating business information systems: reflections on an empirical study, *Information Systems Journal* 5, (1995) 235–52.

[70]   P. Powell, Causality in the alignment of IT and business strategy, *Journal of Strategic Information Systems* 2(4) (1993) 320–34.

[71]   L. Nunn, A corporate information strategy for the Natural History Museum, *MDA Information* 1(2) (1994) 2–3.

[72]   A. Beard et al., Towards a broader strategy. In: *MDA Annual Report 1999/2000* (Museum Documentation Association, Cambridge, 2001) 12–15.

[73]   E. Orna, *Making Knowledge Visible* (Gower, Aldershot, 2005).

[74]   Hawley Committee, KPMG IMPACT Programme Ltd, *Information as an Asset: the Board Agenda* (KPMG, London,1995).

[75]   S.D. Ward and B.K. Ward, Information and knowledge management: business opportunity or corporate risk. In: *Proceedings of the 2005 Online Information Conference* (Learned Information, Oxford, 2005). 83–9.

[76]   KPMG IMPACT Programme Ltd, *Information as an Asset: the Information Health Index* (KPMG, London, 1995).

[77]   M. Ginman, Information culture and business performance, *IATUL Quarterly* 2(2) (1987) 93–106.

[78]   T.H. Davenport et al., Information politics, *Sloan Management Review* Fall (1992) 53–65.

[79]   A. Abell and V. Winterman, *Information Use and Business Success: a Review of Recent Research on Effective Information Delivery*, Information Policy Briefings No. 4 (British Library, London, 1993).

[80]   Reuters, *To Know or Not to Know: the Politics of Information* (Reuters Business information, London, 1994).

[81]   M.R. Kristiansson, Re-thinking strategic planning, Nord I&D, *Knowledge and Change* 181–94. Available at: www2.db.dk/NIOD/kristiansson.pdf (accessed 2 April 2008).

[82]   R.S. Taylor, *Value-Added Processes in Information Services* (Ablex, Norwood, NJ, 1986).

[83]   E. Orna, Valuing information: problems and opportunities. In: D. Best (ed.), *The Fourth Resource: Information and its Management* (Aslib/Gower, Aldershot, 1996).

[84]   C. Oppenheim, J. Stenson and R.M.S. Wilson, A new approach to valuing information assets. In: *Proceedings of the 26th Online Information Conference* (Learned Information, Oxford, 2002).

[85]   P.K. M'Pherson, *Rigorous measurement of IC value: what it means and what the benefits and costs might be*. Paper presented at the 5th International Conference on Theory and Practice in Performance Measurement and Management, London (2006).

[86]   F. Ryan, Surviving and thriving in a harsh world, *Library and Information Update* 4(5) (2005) 26–9.

[87]   H. Osborne, HMRC: a catalogue of data losses, *Guardian* 17 December 2007.

[88]   L. Smith, Security in tatters as more data goes AWOL, *Information World Review* January (2008) 1.

[89]   L. Smith, Data bombshell engulfs MoD, *Information World Review* February (2008) 1.

[90]   J. Carvel, Family doctors to shun national database of patients' records, *Guardian* 20 November 2007.

[91]   J. Ashley, The national ID register will leak like a battered bucket, *Guardian* 21 January 2008.

[92]   J. Dutra, Enterprise search: rethinking it in a Web 2.0 world, *FreePint* 29 November 2007. Available at: www.freepint.com/issues/291107.htm 2005 (accessed 10 January 2008).

[93]   *Government Commits to Finding a Solution to Preserving Its Digital Information* (14 June 2007). Available at: www.nationalarchives.gov.uk/news/stories/161.htm (accessed 10 January 2008).

[94]   E. Orna, Collaboration between LIS and information design disciplines: on what? why? potential benefits? *Information Research* 12(4) (2007). *CoLIS 6 Conference Proceedings Supplement*. Available at: http://informationr.net/ir/12-4/colis/colis02.html (accessed 5 April 2008).

# 12

# The disparity in professional qualifications and progress in information handling: a European perspective

BARRY MAHON

## Abstract

This paper is a personal view of the development of the role(s) of information professionals in the 50 years since IIS was founded. One of the justifications for the formation of IIS was that the then current professional bodies were not relevant to the needs of those employed in industrial information services. This paper reviews briefly the situation when IIS was formed, from the viewpoint of professional requirements and the developments since. The conclusion is drawn that today's information world, very different from that of 50 years ago, faces similar problems of a lack of suitable qualifications and a confusion in the roles of different actors in the field.

## Introduction

The suggested brief I received from the Editor of this compilation marking 50 years since the foundation of the Institute of Information Scientists was to cover the European aspects of the IIS, such as they were. I have added the last phrase because I am not certain that any professional aspect of the role of IIS outside the UK was considered at the foundation. I was, at a time shortly after the foundation, a student at the institution where Jason Farradane, a founding father, taught his brand of information science. One did not discuss the politics of professional bodies within the course, one listened to the opinions on certain aspects of the way information systems and services were created, managed, researched and used and took note of the opinions. The more committed of the students actually joined IIS, although there was no pressure to do so.

I have drawn upon my experiences as a member of the IIS in 'Europe' for a number of years, as a resident consultant to the European Commission and subsequently as the Director of the European Society for Information Dissemination in Chemistry (EUSIDIC) and the International Council for Scientific and Technical Information (ICSTI), in creating this contribution on certain aspects of the way the information sector has developed over the last 50 years, from the almost exclusive domain of librarianship to a regular topic on the front pages of newspapers, TV and radio, driven by a global availability and distribution system.

## Fifty years ago, did Europe exist?

It most certainly did. The technological base of the major industrial powers in Europe was chemistry, engineering, pharmaceuticals, etc., all of which were major generators and consumers of information. In 1957 a new political structure for Europe was created, reflected by the Treaty of Rome. Essentially, it created three bodies, one political and two industrial, to develop the future of Europe or, at that time, a part of geographical Europe. The industrial bodies, the European Coal and Steel Community (ECSC) and Euratom, represented the old and the new of European industry. Coal and steel had been at the root of the political difficulties of the previous 50 years, while nuclear science represented a hope that a military weapon could be developed into a cheap alternative to coal, amongst other ideas. The idealism and foresight of those who created the ECSC and Euratom is now recognized even if, politically, some aspects of the EU, as it is now referred to, are not universally accepted.

In terms of the information sector, the information raw materials of industrial Europe were primarily the results of scientific endeavour, as published in scientific journals. What the founders of IIS foresaw was that there was a need to recognize that material of this nature needed a different treatment, which was not recognized by the majority of information-related professional bodies extant at that time. For example, one of the founders of IIS was a specialist in patent information, an area where 'normal' publication *per se* was not an option, but where information was a critical component. Patent information was and is an international activity, which has been recognized since the inception of the patent system. Apart from being recognized as a specialized niche, in information terms, patents and their associated legal partners, trademarks, were not part of mainstream information, as recognized by professional bodies. The creation of a European industrial/political entity predicated the need to create a wider information environment.

In the creation of the EU, to use the modern acronym as a shorthand for what it has become, some topics were off-limits. Education was one, it was, and is still to all intents and purposes, a national responsibility, in EU terms. Any effort to deal with professional training at a European level came up against this reality, even if there was a willingness to consider the potential of a wider baseline of professional training as an important element of the development of a European environment.

This perhaps explains why the creation of a European LIS Curriculum project has taken until 2006 to see the light of day [1]. It is ironic that its creation coincides with the 50th anniversary of a body created to open up professional activity in the information sector. The acronym LIS, meaning library and information science, as much as the creation of the European curriculum as a project, represents a step forward which is to be welcomed, even if its development has taken such a long time.

However, reference to the European LIS curriculum is moving forward too quickly in the time line of the development of an international information environment. It will be dealt with again later in this communication.

## The international nature of information, a brief history

This history will concentrate on the implementation of new technologies to provide solutions to information issues, but it is recognized that information systems and services, especially those in science and technology, have a long history of being international. Chemical Abstracts Service (CAS) of the American Chemical Society started in 1907, and similar services in engineering and physics started at earlier dates. This indicates the international nature of the subject matters as well as the necessity to broadcast results as widely as possible using the means available at the time. Libraries of course pre-date the availability of abstracting and indexing facilities and these materials were treated in the same way as books and other literature. In some ways the advent of new professional bodies mirrors the application of new technologies to dealing with increases in the volume and complexity of what came to be described as scientific and technical information (STI).

In addition to the well known services and the publication programmes of the science-based international bodies publishing in English there is a long history of publication of STI in languages other than English: German and

French being primary examples, but Russian, Japanese and Chinese have also made significant contributions. Various political developments in the first half of the twentieth century have ensured that English became the de facto language of science and technology, although other languages were active. Much of the development of technologies applied to information originated in the USA and later moved to Europe, but knowledge of English was a requirement in order to keep up to date with developments.

Therefore many of the applications which have given rise to the widespread use of computing in dealing with the management of information have their origins in the USA and the UK, where the common language facilitated the transfer of know-how.

A remarkable piece of work by Noyer and Serres at the University of Rennes (France) provides us with a time line of the history of the handling of information, as the working title says, *From Paul Otlet to the Internet by way of Hypertext* [2]. The text is in French but the names are immediately recognizable by those with even a passing interest in the developments. The period covered is 1885 to 1979, since the latter was the year when one of the authors submitted the thesis which was the object of the work.

It is perhaps interesting that the time line does not have a specific linked reference point for STI until 1970, although there are references to 'documentation' from the outset and STI is first mentioned in the time line in 1958. This may well be due to the fact that the work is reported in French, but they do mention that the first recorded use of the phrase 'information retrieval' is in 1950, by Calvin Mooers. Coincidentally, the first issue of *American Documentation* (later to become the *Journal of the American Society of Information Science*) was also in 1950. Parenthetically, the American Documentation Institute, which had been created in 1937, did not change its title to the American Society for Information Science (ASIS) until 1968, nor add the 'T' standing for technology (ASIS&T) until 2000.

By 1955 Eugene Garfield had described the *Citation Index for Science*, while 1957 brings the Dorking conference on Classification for Information Retrieval and the first publication by Luhn on 'mechanized encoding and searching of literature information' using early IBM equipment. The year 1961 brings the first specification of MEDLARS by the National Library of Medicine. In 1962 Euratom publishes its *Thesaurus* and in 1963 what might be described as the French version of IIS, the Association des professionnels de l'information et de la documentation (ADBS, formerly the Association française des documentalistes et des bibliothécaires specialisés), is formed. In

1964 CAS begins the distribution of magnetic tape containing the bibliographic descriptions from the printed editions and in late 1965 the first telecommunications connection between computers is noted. In 1969 the first telecommunications network dedicated to information retrieval in Europe is opened by the European Space Agency (ESA) and, coincidentally, two UN institutions, the Organization for Economic Co-operation and Development (OECD), the International Committee for Social Science Documentation and the German institute for development (Deutsche Stiftung für Entwicklungsländer) publish their trilingual 'list of aligned descriptors'.

This highly selective chronology illustrates that the creation and early years of the IIS straddled some of the most significant developments which might be said to mark a movement from librarianship to information management. The characterization of the change in this manner may be contentious but it would seem from anecdotal remarks by Farradane that this was the principal justification for the creation of the IIS.

## The development of modern information services in Europe

As mentioned earlier, Europe was already a highly developed information environment before 1957, but it might be argued that in the post-1945 period the country that had earlier been at the forefront of technological development, Germany, had other priorities and in very general terms Europe had slipped behind the US and Japan in its economic progress.

After the formation of the EU in 1957 one of the priorities for the new grouping was technical development, in particular through the Euratom vehicle. Research centres were set up in a number of locations and ancillary services to serve them, including information services, were started. Obviously the emphasis was on nuclear technologies but this involved such a wide range of interests that many subject areas were covered.

As the time line has shown, the majority of the developments in information management using new technologies had taken place in the USA in the period 1950–70, but European institutions had been partners in certain areas. The Chemical Abstracts Service, as one example, had a programme of internships in their development areas and a number of Europeans spent periods in the USA learning about, and using, the new information products. The expectation was that they would bring this knowledge back to Europe.

It is interesting to note that almost all the pioneers who took part in the CAS programme and others who spent time in the USA at that period were not librarians or documentation experts. They were for the most part scientists who had come to information by way of the then embryonic computer science route or through an almost accidental coincidence of their interests with computers and information. The latter was the route of probably the best known pioneer, Dr Tony Kent, originally of Nottingham University in the UK and later with the Royal Chemical Society. He came to information via work on his PhD thesis which involved using a computer to classify the nesting habits of birds.

The first international grouping of 'modern' information people was created, mostly from former interns at Chemical Abstracts, in 1970. This was EUSIDIC (now called the European Association of Information Services). EUSIDIC was responsible for bringing together the work on information handling by computer pioneers from the non-library/documentation world with pioneers from that world who were interested in the new developments that the computer could create. Over the years EUSIDIC widened its interests beyond chemistry, as evidenced by the change of name, and became representative of almost all the interests in the information sector, librarians, documentation managers, publishers, consultancies, etc. The list of chairpersons of EUSIDIC is a 'who's who' of European information personalities, including Arnoud de Kemp from Springer, Robert Kimberly, then of the Institute for Scientific Information (ISI) and Nigel Oxbrow of TFPL, to name but a very few.

Almost in parallel the EU was creating a committee to examine the role that that institution could play in information services development. This was called the Committee for Information and Documentation in Science and Technology (CIDST). It consisted of personnel nominated by the then Member States, with responsibilities in the area of technical information. Again, they were, for the most part, not from a librarianship background.

It is of historical interest to extract some of the terminology from the original EU resolution on STI and documentation:

> [...] in order to achieve economic, scientific and technical progress it is important that scientific, technical, economic and social documentation and data should be made available by the most modern methods to all persons needing to use such information, under the most favourable conditions as regards speed and expense [...] In order to encourage progress in scientific

and technical information and documentation and gradually to establish a European documentation and information network, the Member States shall coordinate their action regarding:

the encouragement of initiatives of whatever origin for the creation and rational development of scientific and technical information and documentation systems, so that through their permanent association a European network will be established; [...]

the encouragement of the training of specialists and the education of users; [...].[3]

The resolution was agreed in June 1971, presumably based on discussions that took place in the late 1960s, not long after the first information products and services using new technologies began to appear. It aligns well with the thinking process that gave rise to the IIS, namely the need to upgrade the methods by which information was to be managed.

CIDST's activities were slow to start, partly because the European Commission was going through a significant reorganization, but also because some of the activities of Euratom were being run down and three new member states were introduced in 1973, Denmark, Ireland and the UK.

A programme of work was agreed and funded in 1975 which was far sighted, given the technical, organizational and political situation of the time. It foresaw the creation of a network to connect electronic databases in such a way as to allow users throughout the EU to access the data and perform searches on it. It is hard to appreciate today just how radical this proposal was. Telecommunications supply in Europe was in the hands of government owned monopolies, only a few databases existed in a form which might allow remote access and very few if any potential users had the equipment (or the financial resources) to use such a facility.

This was the first step in the formalization of the international nature of information at a European political level. The programme recognized the need to co-ordinate the work under way in the member states of the time and to set in place ancillary facilities which would enable resources to be shared.

Amongst the work groups created under the 1971 resolution was one to examine the requirements for training of specialists in STI. This brought up the questions of equivalence of qualifications and even wider questions on the type of training that would be required.

## The role of professional bodies in the development of information professionals

A review of the potential role of European institutions in harmonization of qualifications was undertaken by Schur, published in 1974 [4]. Some of his comments make interesting reading after the passage of time:

> It is fairly clear from the above account of the activities of the Commission and Council that the results achieved over the past seventeen years [since 1957, in the area of harmonization] have not been commensurate with the efforts expended.

> If no action is taken now by the [UK] professional institutions [to work together on recognition of qualifications], Lord Bowden's prediction made on 5 January 1973 may yet come true. He said, in somewhat less than diplomatic language, 'Following the enlargement negotiations in Brussels, the European Commissioners are attempting to frame regulations which, if they are implemented, will effectively take over the whole English educational system [...].

These extracts are not representative of the tone of the extremely learned analysis undertaken in the paper of the legal basis and attempts to implement policy on harmonization undertaken by the EU up to that time. They probably indicate a certain frustration with the professional bodies that they had not taken up the matter of 'upgrading' qualifications to meet possible future requirements, likely to be brought about by membership of the EU.

Compare Schur's words in 1974/75 with those of Marshall [5] in 1997:

> Things may change only when pressure from within the European community forces the Italian library system to align itself with those in the rest of Europe, when it will then become necessary to ensure that the same standards are attained by all. It is already possible for Europeans to find employment outside their native country as qualifications are increasingly recognized within all of Europe. However, if Italian qualifications fail to compete with those of others because of the inadequate professional training

and a lack of standardization in Italy itself Italians may well suffer. The Italian library system ought to be in preparation for future changes if it is to keep up with those of its European neighbours. But first things first, the Italian system will have to undergo huge reforms before anything else can change.

While in no way wishing to pick on the situation in one country in 1997 the quotation shows that in the 25 years following an agreement at European level on attempting to harmonize qualifications in the fields which would be expected to manage information resources, there had been little progress, as Schur had already noted in more general terms, for the 17 years since the foundation of the EU.

As part of a commentary [6] on the build up to a set of actions designed to move forward the development of the EU in 1992 the then Chief Executive of the UK Library Association said:

There are major differences between the composition, structure and habits of library and information professional bodies in the 12 countries of the Community.

An article in 2005 [7] by a staff member of the Chartered Institute of Library and Information Professionals (CILIP – the body created in 2002 by a merger of the Library Association and IIS in the UK) states:

The framework has been closely mapped to the new National Qualifications Framework in the UK and to the new CPD Framework for the Health Service. CILIP is now working with other European partners to ensure that there is equivalence between the British model and the European CERTIDoc.

This reference is to an agreed framework created by CILIP for admission to the various grades of membership. CERTIDoc is a consortium of five organizations and a number of 'associates' (which does not include CILIP) with the objective described here:

[…] objective of the CERTIDoc project is to ensure consistency between all the mechanisms for certifying information-documentation professionals at the European level. These all use a common Guide, one of the major achievements of the CERTIDoc project, which was supported by the [EU]

Leonardo da Vinci programme. CERTIDoc will also bring greater visibility, a better image and increased professional mobility to this professional sector requiring specific and rapidly changing competencies. [8]

The European LIS Curriculum Project, referred to earlier, is a process which was started in 2002 and culminated in the publication of an e-book in December 2005 [9] under the aegis of the EU education programme SOCRATES and EUCLID (the European Association for Library and Information Education and Research). It is not at all clear, despite the considerable effort involved in the creation of the e-book, what are the next steps. Kajberg [10], reviewing the process which lead to the e-book, says:

> Virtual conferences and other web-based communication packages furthering interpersonal communication, either formal or informal, between European LIS school academics are fine, but why not think more largely and more ambitiously and go for more far-reaching solutions?

Which would seem to indicate that there is no agreed pathway for the implementation of the outcomes of the work.

What does this review of the various developments in qualification equivalence and education co-ordination say about the role of professional bodies? Perhaps it is not them but the individuals who undertake the professional work who should be asked. Information, an international good, has a unique economic value, in that it is not, generally speaking, diminished by use. It is surprising that the professional bodies have not found it necessary to co-ordinate more closely the educational basis of the professionals who deal with it. In some professional areas, such as cataloguing, there has been active and close international co-operation and co-ordination, presumably because there are economic advantages, while in others, such as training course content and even the level of qualification to fulfil the same tasks, there has been little or no co-operation, until recently.

## Is it already too late?

The programme description for a EUSIDIC conference (www.eusidic.net) to be held in early 2008 asks the following questions about the situation that information suppliers face:

Libraries, Information Services, ILS vendors and Information Providers are increasingly confronted by end-users whose expectations have been raised by the proliferation of easy, reliable – and limited – systems like Amazon and Google. The professionals are thus faced with the need to find ways to open the eyes of those who have never learned how much more there is to this experience. While information-gathering is a science, the art lies in knowing where to locate the critical added value, and how to apply it, beyond the retrieval and the discovery.

Are information professionals, services, vendors and information providers ready for this challenge? Can they help to equip and develop the coming Google-raised generation of baby Einsteins who will soon be snapping at their heels?

While 'baby Einsteins' may be an exaggeration as a description of those who use Google and other tools for their information retrieval, the question is valid.

It is interesting to examine the text in more detail and ask why the phrase 'and limited' is included after 'easy' and 'reliable' as descriptions of the systems? Limited in what sense? They are limited in that they deliver results based on the occurrence of the search term(s) but is that much different from the methodology offered by a library catalogue? The issue that arises from this 'defensive' approach to new methods of delivering information is that it may be already too late to rescue the role of an information professional, as conceived by the founders of the IIS, from the wide range of personnel who would now describe themselves and their work as being concerned with managing information.

What the EUSIDIC question really addresses is: have the developments in the handling of information brought about by the internet left the traditional information professionals behind? Are the present day information professionals sufficiently involved in information systems design?

A recent paper by Orna [11] has a useful illustration (Figure 1) which puts the newer concepts of information management into context. She describes the area in the middle of her diagram as 'where collaboration between LIS professionals and information designers is needed'. She goes on to specify some of the contributions that information professionals can make to information products, based on their training and experience. She uses the

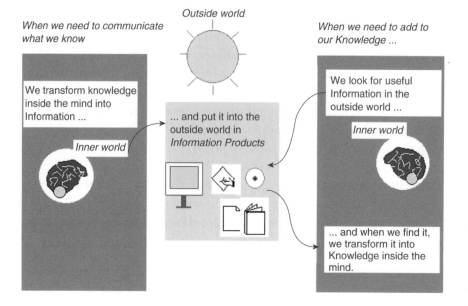

© Liz Orna 2007 - based on an illustration by Graham Stevens in Making Knowledge Visible (Orna, 2005)

**Figure 1** Transformations: information to knowledge, knowledge to information

phrase 'knowledge and information managers' to describe the personnel who could make the contribution. In this imprecision of description between LIS and knowledge/information managers there lies perhaps a clue to the issues that the IIS and associated professional bodies have not yet addressed, namely that the work being undertaken and the job titles used vary to such an extent that common ground is hard to identify.

As Orna points out, '[Information designers'] knowledge of what the other professionals are up to is uneven. Between them and in-house 'traditional' ICT [information and communication technology] professionals, there can be deep hostility; many [information] designers can justly claim much deeper knowledge of technology tools relevant to design in all media than many ICT professionals who hold a lot of power within their organizations.'

This is a situation which will be familiar to many of us, but we would have difficulty in defining an information designer, as indeed Orna has, preferring to quote three different options and expressing the view that their job extends far beyond making [information] products look impressive, concluding that 'LIS professionals who know what information designers do are few and far between'. Orna's masterly analysis is supported in the paper by a number of case studies which serve to illustrate, often with serious consequences, the lack of understanding between the various professions tasked with information delivery.

Loasby [12] in a short analysis of the history of indexing the BBC's website brings in a plethora of terminology to describe the various processes – CVs (controlled vocabularies), CMS (content management systems), folksonomies, tag clouds; all under the umbrella term metadata, which has become a default term for what information scientists would recognize as the whole range of activities and processes designed to make information retrievable. Loasby concludes:

> We [the BBC?] are still not really tapping into end user language, and we will have to do so for the more subjective facets such as mood and style. Users will have to want to gather up and describe assets, so program AV [audio-visual content] may end up being folksonomy's saviour, too.

> More and more we expect to break the back of the work with automation while using human brainpower to perfect the results. We will have to harness the power of folksonomies while remembering there is stuff our audience will demand we know about our own content. Most of all, we have to ensure our choices of metadata systems are made with the user in mind.

The shorthand nature of these conclusions may be due to the brief nature of the communication but leaves an interesting set of questions unanswered. The holy grail of information system design has always been user satisfaction, more often honoured in the breach than in the practice. Refreshingly, Loasby's communication recognizes the shortcomings of even the most up to date tools while striving to satisfy almost unspecifiable user requirements such as mood and style.

Loasby's job description is 'information architecture team leader' thereby introducing, in this paper, a term this author has felt for some time best describes the role that the IIS was created for. An information architect is someone who does for information what a conventional architect does for the spaces we use every day, namely making them useful, usable and encouraging us to benefit from them. As with conventional architects, information architects do not always succeed in achieving their objectives, but attempt to make the best use of the tools and materials at their disposal. In addition, both are normally constrained by financial resources, leading to compromises.

## After 50 years, an ongoing problem

This paper has selected certain actions which have had the effect of extending the international nature of information, looked at the work undertaken to co-ordinate the training of information professionals and examined, by examples of the work being undertaken by information professionals, whether these have had any effect on their activities.

The examples chosen would seem to indicate that information professionals are not able to keep pace with the expectations of users, despite the wide range of new tools at their disposal. There is also an indication that users make assumptions about information products and services based on claims which information professionals would consider to be exaggerated. The reaction of the professionals, in some cases, is to dismiss the products as inadequate and/or to suggest that there is a lack of understanding of the role of the LIS professional in the organization. In parallel with this there is little indication that LIS training has broadened its scope to deal with the new requirements.

The IIS was created to provide a meeting place for those who, at that time, felt the professional bodies did not fully represent their professional activities. Despite the enormous changes in the range and coverage of information products and services and the progress of the information management technologies, the method of handling the content, the information, is still the topic which gives rise to contentious opinions. The issues that to-day's information professionals face in fitting in to the increasingly complex mix of skills required to satisfy the information requirements of their audiences are similar to those faced by the Institute's founders. The complexity has led to a demand for tools and skills which are being delivered by personnel and organizations from a wide range of backgrounds. As such this represents the same situation as was perceived in the late 1950s, the challenges were identified but the methods of dealing with them were not agreed at a professional level.

It is unfortunate that despite the universal nature of the information product and the means of delivery, the 50th anniversary of the IIS, a pioneering body in identifying the professional requirements, is not coincident with an overall agreement on the skills and training required. Only a few of the commentators on the wider information sector in the general media are recognizable as information professionals in the mould of those who founded the IIS. While this might be a matter for regret it should be seen as an opportunity, the input of new ideas was one of the reasons why the IIS was founded. It remains to be seen if the current professional bodies recognize the benefits to be gained by embracing the ideas created by the newcomers to the information sector.

## References

[1] European LIS Curriculum Project, *ASIST Bulletin*, December 2006/January 2007. Available at: www.asis.org/Bulletin/Dec-06/EuropeanLIS.html (accessed 19 January 2008).

[2] J.-M. Noyer and A. Serres, *De Paul Otlet à Internet en passant par Hypertexte: quelques repères et fragments* (URFIST, Rennes, 1997). Available at: www.uhb.fr/urfist/HistInt/Cadres.htm (accessed 19 January 2008).

[3] Resolution of the Council and of the Representatives of the Member States, meeting in the Council, with a view to co-ordinating the action of the Member States regarding scientific and technical information and documentation (STID), adopted at the 157th Council meeting held on 24 June 1971. *Official Journal of the EC* Part C 122 10/12/1971 P. 0007–0008. Available at: http://eur-lex.europa.eu/LexUriServ/LexUriServ.do?uri=CELEX:41971X1210:EN:HTML (accessed 19 January 2008)

[4] H. Schur, The European Communities and the harmonization of educational and professional qualifications, *Journal of Librarianship and Information Science* 7(1) (1975) 49–65.

[5] J. Marshall, Librarianship as a profession in Italy, *Journal of Librarianship and Information Science* 29(1) (1997) 29–37.

[6] G. Cunningham, Libraries, information and Europe, *Journal of Librarianship and Information Science* 22(2) (1990) 63–70.

[7] M. Watson, Professional qualifications: a CILIP perspective, *AIDAInformazioni* 23(4) (2005) 24–30. Available in English at: http://eprints.rclis.org/archive/00011663/01/watson23(4).pdf (accessed 19 January 2008).

[8] CERTIDoc, European system of certification of information professionals. Available at: www.certidoc.net/en/all.php (accessed 19 January 2008).

[9]    L. Kajberg and L. Lørring: European curriculum: reflections on library and information science education. Available at: http://biblis.db.dk/uhtbin/hyperion.exe/db.leikaj05 (accessed 19 January 2008).

[10]   L. Kajberg, Developing an e-book as an integrated process among 100 academic colleagues, *ASIST Bulletin* December 2006/January 2007. Available at: www.asis.org/Bulletin/Dec-06/kajberg.html (accessed 19 January 2008).

[11]   L. Orna, Collaboration between library and information science and information design disciplines: on what? Why? Potential benefits? *Information research* 12(4) (2007). Available at: http://informationr.net/ir/12-4/colis/colis02.html (accessed 19 January 2008).

[12]   K. Loasby, Changing Approaches to Metadata at bbc.co.uk: From Chaos to Control and Then Letting Go Again, *ASIST Bulletin* 25(October/November) (2006). Available at: www.asist.org/Bulletin/Oct-06/loasby.html (accessed 19 January 2008).

# 13

# Electronic scholarly publishing and open access

CHARLES OPPENHEIM

## Abstract

A review of recent developments in electronic publishing, with a focus on Open Access (OA) is provided. It describes the two main types of OA, i.e. the 'gold' OA journal route and the 'green' repository route, highlighting the advantages and disadvantages of the two, and the reactions of the publishing industry to these developments. Quality, cost and copyright issues are explored, as well as some of the business models of OA. It is noted that whilst so far there is no evidence that a shift to OA will lead to libraries cancelling subscriptions to toll-access journals, this may happen in the future, and that despite the apparently compelling reasons for authors to move to OA, so far few have shown themselves willing to do so. Conclusions about the future of scholarly publications are drawn.

## Introduction

The scholarly publishing industry has been greatly affected by the digital era, because 'the very content of the publishing business is, at the end of the day, a digitizable asset' [1]. Scholarly publishers realized soon after the development of electronic databases in the early 1970s that 'the content they acquire is an asset that can be manipulated and stored in digital form' [1, p. 10] and, led by various experimental projects such as Quartet, a study of electronic journals funded by the British Library in the 1980s, they gradually over the next 30 years made the move from printed format to digital format, seeing it as a cheaper, faster and more effective method of getting their titles to their readers. Thus emerged the electronic journal, with one of the earliest launched in September 1990 (*Electronic Journal of Communication*). It was an early, free, online, peer-reviewed journal [2].

In this article, rather than looking back at the last 50 years of the scholarly publishing industry, some recent developments in the electronic scholarly publishing arena are considered. The focus is on the publication of primary scholarly information, i.e. publications that report original research findings (typically peer-reviewed), rather than on electronic abstracting and indexing databases (whose history has been well reviewed in [3, 4] and whose current situation can be gleaned from news items and comments in journals such as *Online*). There is also an emphasis in this article on electronic journals rather than e-books, as the e-book scholarly monograph market is very small at the moment. Finally, the article does not focus on one key aspect of scholarly publishing, i.e. its function for determining priority for the exposition of an idea or results, but rather on the role of scholarly publishing in disseminating ideas and results to the wider community.

During the second half of the twentieth century, there was an 'explosion of scientific, technical and medical (STM) publishing with a consequent impact on libraries and the research process' [5]. Academics supported this expansion because of its capacity to report rapidly the latest scholarship and research [6]. From the 1970s, there was an interest in the use of electronic publishing not only because the traditional role of the scholarly publication – both to report results quickly so that an author could stake a claim to that research output before his or her rivals, and as a formal record of peer-reviewed scholarly achievement – was under stress in the print world, but also because the two functions could be achieved better in the electronic environment. Scholars also realized in the 1990s that the use of the world wide web would 'accelerate research, enrich education, share the learning of the rich with the poor and the poor with the rich, make this literature as useful as it can be, and lay the foundation for uniting humanity in a common intellectual conversation and quest for knowledge' [7]. Authors would submit 'their papers electronically to a computer which could be accessed by their editor' [8, p. 97]. Then: 'The editor read the paper in this form, and perhaps sent it to a referee's computer; the referee's comments were returned electronically to the editor, who transmitted them to the authors. In other words, the traditional process was simply replicated in electronic form' [8, p. 97].

There is no question that the scholarly publishing industry is currently undergoing a period of major change. It is surprising that in the many reviews of this process (see e.g. [9]) no one has drawn attention to the fact that the abstracting and indexing industry went through a similar change in the 1970s, i.e. the move from printed abstracting services to online databases. This change was accompanied by great fears amongst the publishers of these services regarding the business models to adopt. There were understandable fears of cannibalization and loss of revenues. The influential Barwise Report [10] reassured these publishers that there was little to fear from the online revolution, and indeed, so it turned out. There may be a need for another Barwise Report to address the fears of the scholarly publishing industry in the face of both dramatic changes to delivery of scholarly information and the threat of free competitive services, a challenge the abstracting and indexing services did not have to face.

At present, the electronic scholarly communication market is dominated by the USA. A few years ago, it was estimated that the USA accounts for 58% of STM literature, Europe 26% and the rest of the world a mere 16% [11]. Scholarly journal production growth has been variable since the beginning of the twentieth century. From 1900 to 1945, the average annual rate of increase in the number of journals published was 3.3%. The rate increased to 4.7% per year in the period from 1945 to 1979 [6]. However, after 1980, 'the rate of increase reverted to 3.3 per cent a year' [6] and it is unclear now whether the number of scholarly journals continues to grow. Morris [12] has written an authoritative review of the available data. What is clear is that the number of electronic journals is growing. The Association of Learned and Professional Society Publishers (ALPSP) has showed that 174 publishers had launched a total of 1048 new journal titles in the five-year period 2001–5 – an average of 6.02 per publisher [6]. A problem these days in evaluating statistics of e-journal production is the question of whether the journal is electronic only, or parallel published with a print journal, and, if it is parallel published, whether the e-journal is identical in content to that of its print counterpart. Furthermore, many e-journals may exist in theory, but in practice have added no articles for months or years and may well be moribund. The days when authors such as de Solla Price [13] could reasonably reliably count the number of journals in existence are no more.

Scholarly journal prices are rising much faster than libraries' budgets, and this is a major concern for many authors, librarians and institutions. In the UK, it has been estimated that between 1998 and 2003 the average price of an academic journal rose by 58%, while the UK retail price index rose by 11% in the same period [5]. It is this concern that has caused many academics and librarians to consider other means of providing research output at a lower cost, or even for free. This is one (but by no means the only) reason why there is so much interest in a new publishing model – open access (OA) – that offers a vision of research outputs freely and widely available throughout the world. The term OA covers two different approaches – that of institutional repositories and open access journals, which are explained in Section 3 below. Currently, OA outputs form a relatively small part of the scholarly electronic articles market, and their penetration by subject is variable; it is well known that, for example, there is particularly low penetration in the social sciences and the humanities.

Though still a relatively small area of scholarly journal publishing, OA in principle offers free of charge access worldwide to primary scholarly research outputs. In fact, this claim is somewhat simplistic, as access to OA requires reliable networked computers and reliable telecoms and power supplies to be in place – not something that is universally available. However, an increase in the number of OA journals (and indeed, the other major form of OA publishing – repositories, which are discussed further below) is potentially not good news for many STM publishers, both commercial and not for profit. Their fear of loss of revenue and profit due to subscribers cancelling subscriptions to toll-access (i.e. subscription-based) journals in favour of access to materials in OA format, whether in institutional repositories or in the form of OA journals, is understandable, despite the lack of any hard evidence as yet of such cancellations taking place because of OA. Some major publishers, in an attempt not to lose their authors, have announced the launches of their own partial or full OA journals. This development is discussed further below.

## Some drivers of change

Several developments have created pressure for change in the formal system of scholarly communication. The most important of these are developments in technology. The emergence of the internet and networked technology has given the scholarly community the tools to bring to reality large-scale, barrier-free access to research and scholarly writings, without the necessity of utilizing commercial publishers. The internet has enabled scholars with access to a computer and the internet to communicate worldwide the fruits of their intellectual work [9]. In particular, the new technologies offer publishers (and that means anyone who publishes, not just the organizations traditionally thought of as publishers) the opportunity to overcome key limitations of traditional print media, such as: size limitations in content storage and delivery, the cost of printing and the time-consuming and expensive delivery of product [14].

A second major driver has been the recognition that taxpayers fund much research directly or indirectly. Therefore, there is an ethical argument that the outputs of such taxpayers' expenditure should be made available free of charge to those taxpayers. This principle, which was the subject of fierce debate in the UK in the 1990s and beyond regarding the dissemination of government statistics and reports (again, funded by the taxpayer and up until that time in the UK charged for), has resulted in a complete about turn by the UK Government. It now offers the vast bulk of its information electronically to the public at no charge [16], i.e. outputs from research carried out by Government in order to ensure the efficiency of its operations are available to taxpayers free of charge. However, this approach is not applied by governments to other types of research directly or indirectly funded by the taxpayer. For example, in the UK, the National Health Service (NHS) foots the bill for a great deal of research. Despite the fact that about 90% of the findings are published on the internet, the NHS must pay subscriptions to journals to read many of the results of the research it has funded.

## What is open access?

It is important to distinguish the two forms of OA that have gained the widest support – the so-called green and gold routes. Green OA refers to so-called self-archiving, whereby an author places a copy of the scholarly output in one or more OA repositories (these may be an institutional repository (IR), a subject-based repository, or a combination of them). The same item may well also appear in a traditional journal (which may be print, parallel published or electronic only). The business model for green OA publishing is simply that the body maintaining the repository pays for the ingest of materials, addition of metadata and other technical and administrative requirements.

Gold OA, in contrast, is publishing the article in an OA journal, i.e. an electronic or parallel-published journal that allows free of charge access to the articles within it. The business models for such gold OA journals are discussed further below; however, it is worth stressing that the concept of (the incorrectly named) 'author pays', which has received such wide publicity, is by no means the only possible business model, and indeed, the majority of gold OA journals receive modest or no income from any source. It is also a misnomer to call the business model 'author pays' because in practice, it is the author's employer or funder who pays, not the author him or herself. One of the more depressing things about current debates on OA is that it is so focussed on a minority of OA outputs (gold, author pays) and even for these, a misleading name is given.

It is natural to assume that because digitization has allowed for the easy and cost-effective distribution of content instantaneously, costs are dramatically lowered. However, a large proportion of the costs of scholarly journal publishing are fixed costs such as review and refereeing, the provision of outline submission and review systems, editorial and illustrative work and typesetting, as well as indirect costs such as subscription maintenance, marketing and author administration. [6]

It is, for example, claimed that the cost of preparing information remains significant – even when articles and editorial services are provided at no charge, the remaining costs of preparing information for publication are considerable – and may actually increase when a journal moves from print to online [16]. Thus, moving from print to electronic involves more costs for publishers than many realize.

Researchers have little interest in making money from their research outputs, and regard toll-based access-barriers as restricting their potential impact to only those who can and do pay the access-tolls [17]. Institutions cannot afford the access tolls to all the refereed research journals to which they would like access; this means that some researchers cannot access some research papers; just how serious a problem this is remains contentious. Many surveys indicate that scholars are not merely satisfied with their current access to scholarly materials they want, but feel access has improved (no doubt thanks in part to 'Big Deals', discussed further below) in recent years.

Nonetheless, just as publishers' concerns about the growth of OA are understandable and may or may not be justified, concerns that researchers are not getting the access to scholarly materials they need is understandable, even if again, the evidence is mixed at present. What is clear is that the use of (the less convenient) method of document supply to obtain access to full-text scholarly materials is declining. This might imply there is an increasing local availability of desired resources. At the same time, because price rises have gone up faster than their spending power, many libraries have been forced to cancel a number of journal subscriptions. Libraries have implicitly expressed their dissatisfaction with the pricing situation by forming consortia and pooling their purchasing power in order to negotiate lower pricing and better terms of use in respect of online journals [6]. Because many libraries have been forced to cancel their subscriptions, publishers have had no choice but to further increase the subscription prices of their journals to cover their costs for supply to a smaller number of customers. The idea of charging all or some of the costs against the author is attractive. For the sake of citation and peer-review, authors and scholars may be willing to accept such costs if funding can be found from, for example, funding agencies or their employer. Hitherto, page charges have been employed for costly items, such as colour photos, but they have generally not been used widely by scholarly publishers.

Whilst it is misleading to over-play the influence of the serials pricing crisis in the development of OA, the new business model for academic journals, i.e. author-pays journals, was without doubt developed in part in response to the crisis. In contrast to a traditional journal, which generates most of its revenue with subscription fees, the author-pays journal makes its articles freely available on the internet, generating revenue from fees supplied by the author (rarely), the author's employer (sometimes) or the author's funder (usually).

Author-pays journals essentially shift the cost of publication, including peer review, from the institutional subscriber to the author's funder or employer, by charging the author a submission fee, a publication fee, or a combination of the two. The fee will cover the cost of operating the publication, including the cost of processing and reviewing papers that are rejected [11]. Gold journals reduce the concerns of institutions that are unwilling to pay for subscriptions they can barely afford, though, of course, some costs remain for the library, e.g. cataloguing. Authors have concerns that not only do they have to rely on funding from grants and their institutions to conduct their research, but also '56% of OA authors are concerned about the cost to their institution of traditional journals' [18]. A solution to this problem is self-archiving into IRs – the 'green' OA route. Harnad [17] claims that 'there will be no need for a second wave of help once the palpable benefits (access and impact) of freeing the literature begin to be felt by the research community'. However, all the evidence indicates that the use of mandates, i.e. forcing staff to self-archive, is the only way to achieve high levels of self-archiving. It is indeed curious that for all its benefits to authors in the form of higher citation counts [19–24] and the fact that to self-archive requires little effort, so few authors voluntarily do so.

In their 2004 study [18], Swan and Brown claimed that more than half the OA authors they surveyed had not paid to publish their work in open access journals. One of the main reasons for this may be that a large number of institutions (around 400) are now 'members' of BioMed Central (BMC), as a result of which authors at those institutions are not required to pay a fee to publish in BMC, and biomedical articles dominate the OA market. Also, OA publishers will waive fees in the case of financial hardship.

Whilst OA diminishes costs of production and distribution, other costs remain. As Anderson notes [16], for information to be made freely and permanently available to the public, the costs of creation, publication, and distribution must be absorbed by someone other than those who wish to use it. The internet eliminates most distribution costs, but not all of them.

Many readers of scholarly journals work in commercial organizations. They are often overlooked in discussions on OA, but can have an important influence on the debate. They consume far more in terms of journal subscriptions than they contribute in the form of articles. They would therefore welcome the development of OA but would provide much less income into the scholarly publishing market than they do at present by means of toll-access subscriptions.

If author-pays OA were adopted on a wide scale, the revenue stream would then come from fewer institutions than those that subscribe to toll access today, leading to higher education institutions carrying a bigger proportion of the costs to maintain the market [25]. It has also been claimed [26] that on a like for like basis, open access publishing will have a lower cost base, and as it will transfer some of the payments from industry users to the authors, so is likely to lead to higher costs for universities and research institutes.

Harnad, the most energetic advocate for open access, has frequently pointed out in his postings on discussion lists that scholarly authors do not want to get paid royalties based on usage of their output; what they want is that other researchers read and use their work. As Owens [27] put it, 'the driving force behind most scientists' careers is to achieve the maximum visibility for their research', whether it is OA or not. Harnad goes further than this and argues that the trend towards OA has acquired unstoppable momentum, and that the quickest and most appropriate way forward is by self-archiving ('the green route') rather than by the use of OA journals (the 'gold route'). In addition, Blackwell Publishing's President, Robert Campbell, has claimed in unpublished conference papers that the Gold route is not popular among authors, less well-funded institutes, or in developing countries, where even a 10-dollar charge to an author would seem excessive.

Some publishers, most notably Reed Elsevier and Banks Publishing, have extended their criticisms of OA to claims along the lines of 'The last thing that medical professionals want are people with illnesses reading this information, marching into surgeries and asking things.' However, this is a line of argument that is most unlikely to influence politicians and decision-makers in an age where society's expectations are of increasing transparency.

It is worth stressing that OA is not necessarily appropriate for all disciplines. In particular, the fields of social science and humanities research are characterized by relatively modest or zero external funding, so researchers do not have the capacity to pay under an author-pays model. Except for economics, there is also less of a culture of exchanging preprints in these subject areas, so the concept of IRs may have less obvious appeal than to those in the hard sciences.

A crucial piece of the cost jigsaw puzzle is the question whether OA offers savings for those who both create and purchase scholarly information (typically universities and research institutions, and to a lesser extent private sector organizations such as in the pharmaceutical industry). The seminal work by Houghton and co-workers [28], which demonstrated the potential for massive cost savings for universities in the case of large-scale IR adoption, and more modest, but still significant savings if there is wide-scale adoption of author-pays OA journals, has not been challenged to date, and unless it is, remains the last word on this particular topic.

## Quality issues

There is a widely held suspicion (certainly amongst commercial publishers and to a lesser extent amongst authors) that articles in gold OA journals are less well peer-reviewed than their counterparts in toll-access journals. This perception has two roots; firstly, as gold OA journals are new, they have not yet had a chance to attain high status, and secondly, there is a feeling that because income depends on the number of accepted articles, the editors will be under pressure to accept poor quality manuscripts to keep the income stream up. Whilst there is no evidence that weaker papers appear more often in Gold OA journals than in toll-access journals (and indeed, citation evidence indicates the reverse may be true), this perception, noted by Swan and Brown [18] amongst others, deters some authors from submitting to gold OA journals.

A related concern is whether OA really does, as it has been claimed, increase citation counts (and, by implication, impact) of an article. The matter has been reviewed in [29]. There does seem to be clear evidence of increased citation counts for OA materials, which refutes the second charge, noted above, that OA journal editors are under pressure to accept lower-quality articles.

## Copyright issues

The well-known 'Faustian bargain' occurs when authors assign copyright in their scholarly output to a publisher in return for the publisher improving, delivering and marketing the output. For many years, this bargain was accepted as equitable by authors, but this is no longer the case because of the advent of OA. Ownership of copyright gives the owner the right to authorize, or prevent, a number of so-called 'restricted acts', including to reproduce the work, to modify the work, to distribute the work, e.g. through the internet, to perform the work in public or to broadcast the work.

In the case of scholarly publications, the ownership position is somewhat complex. In UK law, the first owner is the creator unless the material has been created in the course of an individual's employee duties. For many authors, it is arguable whether creating scholarly output is part of their employee duties, but, particularly with the increase in research assessment, there is a strong argument that it is an employee's duty to produce scholarly output. In addition, many employers lay claim to the copyright in their employee's outputs by means of a contract of employment. However, balanced against this is the custom and practice, long established, that employers have not intervened when authors have willingly signed copyright in their articles and monographs to a publisher. A court would probably conclude that although on paper the employer may have rights, it has waived those rights by its custom and practice. Indeed, some contracts of employment explicitly state that employees retain copyright in scholarly output.

Protecting rights is in the interest of both parties; publishers want to prevent their digital content from being used, duplicated and distributed without permission or compensation, whilst authors of scholarly works want to ensure their moral right to be identified as the creator is upheld.

OA poses some possible risks. Some may take advantage of OA output for inappropriate purposes, e.g. piracy. In this regard, publishers and authors are on the same side. However, in other regards their position has polarized, because their primary motivations for wanting to protect the content are different.

The situation is confused because many authors do not know who owns the copyright in their work. A study by Swan and Brown [30] showed that when asked 'who retains the copyright to the last article they self-archived; over a third (35%) said it was themselves; 37% said it remained with the publisher and 6% that it remained with another party (e.g. the employer). People working in industry or in non-commercial research institutions were most likely to say that copyright remains with their employer. Almost one quarter (22%) don't know who retains the copyright.' Similar results have been found in other research [31, 32]. With this level of confusion (or indifference) to copyright ownership, it is likely that campaigns, such as those developed by JISC in the UK and SURF in the Netherlands, to persuade authors to retain copyright in their scholarly output will face an uphill struggle.

Some, but by no means all, publishers wish to retain copyright as a means of profiting from authors' work and preventing unlawful distribution of the work's contents. Authors' financial incentives lie in the cash value of reputation, which translates into salary increases, promotions, bonuses, paid speaking engagements, consulting contracts, etc.

Publishers want to limit access to the information to those who pay for the privilege and, if authors choose to place their output into OA journals or repositories, then there is the risk that the resulting easy access will lead to loss of reputation, piracy and plagiarism, as well as lost revenues. The worry about losing revenues is the major reason why publishers see OA as an issue, despite the claims, made by organizations such as the Partnership for Research Integrity in Science and Medicine (PRISM), funded by the Association of American Publishers, that their primary concern regarding OA is the quality of peer review. PRISM's nominal concern, to protect the quality of scientific research, is believed by few observers. It would be more honest if it acknowledged that publishers' primary concern is financial, together with the fact that some publishers believe authors should be grateful as they add value to the publication, therefore they deserve exclusive rights in it. Suber, however, notes [33] that publishers offer 'less' value to the final product than authors, and adds that 'publishers deserve to be paid for the value they add. But it doesn't follow that they deserve to control access or that they deserve a package of exclusive rights'.

Whilst OA journals allow authors to retain the copyright, it comes at a price, i.e. it is up to the author to police copyright infringement, rather than the publisher. Another factor is that whilst OA publishing is entirely compatible with copyright law, in that it gives the copyright holder the right to make access open or restricted, it excludes the publisher [11]. Thus, publishers, who are more experienced in chasing copyright infringers, are replaced in OA by authors, who have little or no experience in such matters.

Can publishers and authors agree on copyright issues and OA? This might be possible since for authors to provide open access to their own work, they do not need to retain full copyright, and in order for publishers to publish, they do not need to acquire full copyright. This raises hope that we might find a balance giving each side all it needs [33]. Unfortunately, the current level of rhetoric as demonstrated by some OA evangelists in discussion list postings and PRISM in its press releases does not give much hope that this will be achieved in the near future.

A key role for libraries is their preservation function. Libraries have the mandate not only to ensure equity of access and availability to the present generation of users, but also have the responsibility of ensuring that access and availability for future users [34]. Digital preservation is frequently prevented by copyright law [35]. Libraries are concerned that publishers, driven by market and profit forces, are not the right agencies to be entrusted with the responsibility of preservation [34]. Libraries are looking for a way of preserving information whilst still allowing access to electronic resources and ideally not being dependent on publishers' goodwill. OA gives much more control to libraries to achieve those ends than does traditional scholarly publishing. We are a long way from resolving this particular issue.

## Technical protection measures

A key development in the electronic publishing marketplace has been the growth in importance of so-called technical protection measures (TPMs), sometimes misleadingly called digital rights management systems.[1] TPMs are methods adopted by rightsholders that prevent unauthorized access to, or copying of, electronic materials. The problem that arises is that TPMs often prevent a bona fide user from accessing or copying material that in law would not be an infringing activity. Thus, in effect, the delicate balance between rights owners and users achieved in copyright law, with its array of checks and balances (the exceptions to copyright) to prevent monopoly abuse is being bypassed. The issues raised are explored in variable depth in [36–38].

Up until now, much of the digital content that reaches libraries has not been heavily restricted by TPM, but equally, publishers do not plan to publish special non-TPM-protected copies for specific use by libraries [39]. This has given libraries cause for concern. The report [39] noted that TPM could 'limit librarians' ability to preserve or archive a work, e.g. by preventing a work from being moved from more perishable to more permanent storage media'.

Although TPMs are viewed by the commercial electronic publishing industry (amongst many others) as a method for the prevention of piracy and copyright abuse and a way to track consumer usage, they are viewed by librarians and users as a means of restricting access. Whilst libraries are keen to respect copyright, publishers have concerns about such library users. TPMs prevent bona fide users from carrying out actions that they consider to be their *right*,[2] e.g. to copy a small proportion of a copyright work for non-commercial research or private study, and therefore are extremely controversial with librarians and users.

## Impact of OA on publishers

A recent UK survey of publishers [40] found (unsurprisingly) that some publishers believed the OA movement would have a negative impact on their journals and on scholarly publishing overall. The reasons for this included the potential for loss of revenue, inability of authors to pay and concern that OA might be mandated (i.e. in practical terms, enforced) by various institutions' governing bodies and funding agencies. The same study stated [40] that 'only a few felt that the OA movement might have a positive impact, potentially increasing visibility and therefore attracting more advertising. Some commented that the movement had pushed them to experiment and they embraced that experimentation.'

The most interesting recent market development has been the take-up by many large commercial publishers of OA experiments. In some cases, established publishers have launched new OA journals; in other cases existing journals have been transformed into partial (often called hybrid) or fully OA forms. Whilst many of the publishers have not made public the impact such moves have had on income or on submission of manuscripts, Oxford University Press has been notable in funding research to evaluate these impacts [41].

Springer's Open Choice model was the first to provide a roughly proportionate reduction in the cost following an increase in author-financed articles. In consequence, if enough authors take advantage of Open Choice, the subscription prices will go down. Open Choice offers authors the opportunity to have their journal articles made available with full open access in exchange for payment of a basic fee. Such authors are not required to transfer their copyright to Springer. The result is that Springer journals contain a mixture of Springer Open Choice articles, and articles published under the traditional subscription-based model. So far, there appears to have been relatively little take-up of the OA option by authors, but arguably it is early days.

In 2006, Taylor & Francis developed its open access initiative, called *iOpenAccess*. Taylor & Francis make an author's work freely available for a one-off fee of US$3100. To date, 194 of its journals are part of the initiative. One benefit for authors is that there are no embargo restrictions on posting their version of the published article to any institutional or subject repository. However, and in contrast to Springer, authors are still required to assign copyright, which some authors may not wish to do. Similarly, in June 2006, Elsevier announced an open access option for its authors. As long as the author pays the publisher a fee, then the article will be made freely available.

Blackwell has a long standing interest in OA, monitoring the evolving issues, and contributing to government and industry evaluation initiatives. The company offers a service called *Online Open*, similarly to Elsevier, offering the author the opportunity to freely disseminate the research in return for a publication fee.

Many of the major electronic scholarly publishers are involved in the World Health Organization's HINARI, the Food and Agricultural Organization's AGORA and the United Nations Environment Programme's OARE initiatives. These services offer free or low cost access to a range of electronic scientific journals to various developing countries. Of course, OA has also allowed developing countries the chance to access research at a relatively low cost. Previously (before the OA movement began), developing countries simply did not have the budgets to subscribe to scholarly journals, and it might be argued that, at least in part, the HINARI and similar initiatives occurred in response to the OA movement gaining the moral high ground on this issue.

Finally, it is worth noting that in general, not for profit and learned society publishers have often been in the forefront of innovative reactions to the onset of OA, and the recent trend of publishers working closely with funding agencies, such as the Wellcome Trust, in order to develop a coherent approach to both copyright and OA.

## The role of funding agencies

Funding agencies, including Governments and their agencies, and charities, provide a large proportion of the funds that lead to scholarly research. As such, they can potentially influence policy towards OA, and thereby affect the electronic scholarly publishing industry. The argument is that funding agencies have it in their power to make it a condition of grant that outputs from the research they fund must appear in an OA vehicle (possibly with an embargo period if the research is also to be published using a commercial or learned society scholarly publisher). One charity that adopted this idea early on was the Wellcome Trust, one of the most important funders of life sciences research in the world: The Trust was the first UK research funder to introduce a grant condition that requires grantees to make their research papers freely available to all [42].

Wellcome has stated that once its funded research is available 'it will be possible to examine the effectiveness of our funding strategy and realign it as appropriate' [42]. The outputs from all Wellcome Trust research funded since it made its policy decision can be found in PubMed Central (the US National Library of Medicine's online archive) or UK PubMed Central, but no study regarding the effectiveness of the Wellcome policy appears to have yet been undertaken.

Research Councils UK (RCUK) is a strategic partnership between the eight UK Research Councils. Between them, they disburse public money for scholarly research in all subject areas. RCUK was established in 2002 to enable the Councils to work together more effectively to enhance the overall impact and effectiveness of their research. With such a remit, one might expect RCUK to take an active interest in the dissemination of the outputs of research, but for many years it showed no such interest. This is reflected in the fact that for a long period, RCUK prevaricated regarding recommending to its members such conditions of funding. In the end it left the decision to the individual Research Councils, the majority of which have gone some way towards the Wellcome position.

In the USA, the situation is more politicized, with a series of bills before Congress attempting to enforce publication of outputs from government-funded research (most notably research funded by the National Institutes of Health). Finally, at the end of 2007, President Bush signed into law the Consolidated Appropriations Act of 2007 (H.R. 2764), which included a provision directing the National Institutes of Health (NIH) to provide the public with open online access to findings from its funded research. This is the first time the US Government has mandated public access to research funded by a major agency.

The provision directs the NIH to change its existing public access policy, implemented as a voluntary measure in 2005. Researchers will now be *required* to deposit electronic copies of their peer-reviewed manuscripts in PubMed Central. Full texts of the articles will then be publicly available and searchable online in PubMed Central no later than 12 months after publication in a journal. This is the most important OA policy development in recent months, and it will be interesting to see how publishers respond to it.

## Institutional policies

Many research institutions are setting up IRs. These IRs typically are created following the development of an institutional policy stating the purpose of the repository and outlining the institution's stance on OA. The managerial and cultural issues associated with IRs are considered in [43]. Typically, institutional policies state that the employees are encouraged to deposit a copy of all published refereed articles in the host IR. This falls short of a full compulsory mandate, which some consider would be difficult to implement in a single institution without the full backing of the wider academic community, including research councils and learned societies [43]. Some publishers have argued that the need for mandates indicates that academics are not persuaded by the virtues of OA and therefore have to be forced to self-archive. However, surveys and anecdotal evidence indicate that the real issue is not that scholars are not convinced by OA, but rather they do not have the time to convert their materials into a format suitable for an IR, and the matter simply is not a high enough priority for them. Concerns about copyright issues are also a factor, even though these concerns are often based on misunderstandings of the legal position. Services such as OpenDOAR, which provide lists of IRs, their subject areas and policies, and ROAR, which provides information about the size of repositories and their development over time, are useful for tracking IR developments over time.

As well as an IR involving a significant start up cost (estimates vary wildly and depend on accounting policies), the repository, once established, remains an additional cost that the library or some other part of the institution must incur. Nonetheless, Houghton's research [28], as noted earlier, has indicated that the cost–benefit of establishing IRs is extremely favourable, and so even if costs are higher than some published estimates, the overall benefit is significant.

## Publisher approaches

Publishers active in OA can be divided into born open access publishers and conventional publishers.

*Born OA publishers* are recently founded publishers that *only* publish OA journals (i.e. do not sell subscription-based journals). There are a number of possible funding models for such journal publishers. The first relies on volunteer effort by editorial staff together with some small costs on behalf of the sponsoring organization for maintaining the archive of articles. A slight variation on this theme is where the editorial staff are given an honorarium for their efforts, this being provided by an external sponsor. The third method, and the best known (but, as noted above, in practice a small minority) are author-pays OA journals. Even here, there are variations on the theme, with some journals charging the author a submission fee when the manuscript is provided, some demanding a fee when the manuscript is accepted for publication, and some combining the two. Some OA publishers offer institutions subscriptions, whereby any employee of that institution can then submit items to that OA journal for nothing, or for a very low fee. In practical terms, this is little different from the institution's library subscribing to a toll-access journal. Individual article fees are sometimes waived if the author can demonstrate they do not have the necessary funds. There is, of course, no reason why one cannot make profits from 'author pays' journals, but in many cases they are published on a not for profit basis.

The Public Library of Science (PLoS) is arguably the most important born open access publisher because it was one of the first in the field and because some of its journals are now amongst those with the highest impact factors in their respective fields. The PLoS website states: 'everything we publish is freely available online throughout the world, for you to read, download, copy, distribute, and use any way you wish, no permission required. Published research results and ideas are the foundation for future progress in science and medicine' [44]. PLoS specializes in journals in the life sciences.

*Conventional publishers* started life as subscription-based publishers but have since experimented with OA. A number of examples have been noted above. The Springer Open Choice model is a typical example. Such a programme typically results in a given journal having a mix of open access and restricted or toll-access articles, but an alternative scenario is a publisher that owns some titles that are OA only, some that are subscription only and perhaps some that combine the two. Where a given journal issue has a mixture of OA and toll-access articles, subscribers can see all the full text of all the articles, but non-subscribers can only view the OA articles.

Hindawi Publishing is an excellent example of a publishing corporation that has undergone a transition to an OA model, transforming its complete journal collection to open access format. Hindawi states, 'OA journals are run in essentially the same way as their subscription based counterparts [...] when we began converting journals to OA, and developing new Open Access titles, we started to look more closely at a number of questions regarding the value that we, as publishers, can provide to the researchers that we serve' [45]. This Egypt-based company is able to take advantage of its access to well qualified, motivated, but relatively low paid editorial staff based in Egypt. Its success provides an important clue to the future of scholarly electronic publishing; it is likely that operational centres for OA journal publishing will move to countries such as Egypt, Israel, India and China, with a large number of well qualified editorial staff available.

There seems to be a consensus that OA journal publishing offers lower margins than subscription-based publishing. This is understandably a matter of concern to many scholarly publishers, some of whom have enjoyed very high profit margins over many years. The approach publishers have taken to this challenge to their well established and profitable business model can be broadly divided into three. There are some, such as Hindawi, that have adopted the OA model with enthusiasm. There are others, such as Springer, Taylor & Francis and Oxford University Press that have taken a more cautious approach, making a few journals OA or offering authors the choice of OA or not for a given title. Finally, there are those publishers that are resisting OA and, in a few cases, trying actively to hold back its advance by, for example, refusing to let their authors submit materials to an IR after it has been published in one of their titles. Some publishers are facing both ways at once, in that they are experimenting with OA and at the same time support the vigorously anti-OA approach adopted by PRISM.

## The new environment and libraries

In recent years, libraries have adapted to the challenges posed by the so-called hybrid library [46], i.e. a library comprising a balance of print and electronic resources, without too much difficulty. Traditionally, the academic or corporate library's principal role has been to acquire scholarly material. Even as late as the early 1990s, it could be argued that this was still the prime focus of a university or corporate library, although the diversity of formats had clearly increased. The emphasis has shifted from the access and storage of material to the creation and distribution of electronic scholarly publications [47]. In addition, fewer users seem to be visiting the physical buildings [48].

Even taking into account librarians' concerns about possible disintermediation, it might be thought that librarians would be enthusiastic about OA because of the potential cost savings and because it makes access to scholarly materials that much more universal. However, librarians have concerns regarding OA. In particular, the expansion of 'gold' journals means that further cataloguing work is required to draw users' attention to these new sources of peer-reviewed information, the administration of IRs typically falls on the library's shoulders, and more advice has to be given to patrons regarding the sensible use of the many new OA sources. Nonetheless, Chang stated, 'because of the benefits of open access, libraries could provide direct access to scholarly publications via these repositories instead of via serials publishers and vendors. The serials crisis that has long impeded library operations of all sizes would be relieved to a great extent. Libraries would consequently spend less time dealing with subscription issues.' [48]

A number of high profile cases over the years have shown that, perhaps because of the development of OA, libraries have become more robust in their approach to publishers. Cancellations of site licence deals with Elsevier and Springer by major libraries have been reported, and the activities of library consortia have led to tougher negotiations before a publisher can be sure of a major sale.

## Conclusions

It may be intuitively reasonable to assume that a move by authors to self-archive will reduce the profits of publishers, but as yet there is no clear evidence of such an impact. Equally, the evidence for the claim that authors are deeply unhappy about access to materials is tenuous. Gold OA is a new business model for the publishing industry, and publishers should evaluate, and if appropriate, embrace this new business opportunity. In contrast, green OA is a situation (some might say a threat) to which they must respond. There are a number of recommendations that can be made to ensure that the changes in the business model run smoothly. Firstly, libraries and publishers need to work with, not against each other. In that regard, the stance taken by PRISM is divisive and counter-productive and should be dropped as soon as possible. Libraries will increasingly switch to OA sources, leading to libraries gaining a more prominent role in scholarly publishing with activity in both the preservation and distribution of scholarly research. Libraries will need to move from being passive to active players in the scholarly communication chain. Scholars need to understand their rights, and become more concerned with getting their work published by whatever means are best. I predict we will see a number of the less important toll-access journals disappear, to be replaced by OA journals and by increasing use of IRs. However, I do not see OA leading to the demise of the major 'must have' commercial scholarly journals.

It seems that the numerous changes in the electronic scholarly publishing scene in the last 10 years will not slow down. We will see further rationalization of what is a very fragmented industry, with the larger conglomerates continuing to acquire smaller publishers. We can expect continued lobbying by the industry to ensure that governments do not interfere with the current market conditions. We can expect to see further publishers similar to Hindawi developing rapidly by offering a mixture of relatively low editorial costs and carrying no baggage from a previous generation of business models and delivery systems; and finally, we can expect funders to continue to move towards requiring OA outputs from the recipients of their funding, and institutions to move steadily towards mandating OA. It will be an interesting time.

## Acknowledgements

I would like to thank Emma Marijewycz and Faye Louise Hodges for their help in literature searching for this article. I would also like to thank the anonymous referees for their helpful comments.

## Notes

1   The term 'DRM' refers to an entire process of identifying who the rights owner is, expressing that ownership in some fashion, ensuring such expressions are searchable and displayable through to enforcing control of access to the materials through

TPMs. Thus, TPMs are a small sub-set of the entire DRM universe, and it is misleading to use the terms synonymously.

2   Strictly speaking, users do not have the right to enjoy an exception to copyright, such as copying for research or private study, as these are permissions or exceptions under the law. However, many users do consider that it is their right to make such copies.

## References

[1]   J.B. Thompson, *Books in the Digital Age* (Polity Press, Cambridge, 2005).

[2]   P. Suber, *Timeline of the Open Access Movement* (2007). Available at: www.earlham.edu/~peters/fos/timeline.htm (accessed 27 November 2007).

[3]   C.P. Bourne and T.B. Hahn, *A History of Online Information Systems 1963–1976* (MIT Press, Cambridge, 2003).

[4]   D.I. Raitt *Online Information Systems* (Learned Information, London, 1984).

[5]   C. Steele, The library's perspective on scholarly publishing in the 21st century. In: G.E. Gorman (ed.) *Scholarly Publishing in an Electronic Era* (Facet, London, 2005).

[6]   J. Cox, *Scholarly Publishing Practice: the ALPSP Report on Academic Publishers' Policies in Online Publishing* (ALPSP, Worthing, 2003).

[7]   J. Willinsky, *Copyright Contradictions in Scholarly Publishing* (no date). Available at: http://research2.csci.educ.ubc.ca/eprints/archive/00000006/01/index.html (accessed 21 August 2007).

[8]   J. Feather, *The Information Society: a Study of Continuity and Change* (Facet, London, 2004).

[9]   S.S. Bergman, The scholarly communication movement: highlights and recent developments, *Collection Building* 25(4) (2006) 108–28.

[10]  T.P. Barwise, *Online Searching: the Impact on User Charges of the Extended Use of Online Information Services* (Commission of the European Communities, Luxembourg, 1979).

[11]  J. Cox, Evolution or revolution in scholarly publishing: challenges to the publisher. In: G.E. Gorman (ed.) *Scholarly Publishing in an Electronic Era* (Facet, London, 2005).

[12]  S. Morris, Mapping the journal publishing landscape: how much do we know? *Learned Publishing* 20(4) 2007, 299–310.

[13]  D.J. de Solla Price, *Little Science, Big Science* (Columbia University Press, New York, 1963).

[14]  B. Blunden and M. Blunden (eds), *Electronic Publishing Strategies* (Pira, Leatherhead, 1997).

[15]   S. Saxby, Information access policy and crown copyright regulation in the electronic age: which way forward? *International Journal of Law and Information Technology* 6(1) (1998) 1–33.

[16]   R. Anderson, Open access in the real world: confronting economic and legal reality, *C&RL News* 65(4) (2004). Available at: http://dlist.sir.arizona.edu/351/02/SCHOLARLY%5FCOMMUNICATION.doc (accessed 16 August 2007).

[17]   S. Harnad, Open access to peer-reviewed research through author/institution self-archiving. In: J. Andrews and D. Law (eds) *Digital Libraries: Policy, Planning and Practice* (Ashgate, Aldershot, 2004).

[18]   A. Swan and S. Brown, Authors and open access publishing, *Learned Publishing* 17(3) (2004) 219–24.

[19]   K. Antelman, Do open access articles have a greater research impact? *College and Research Libraries* 65(5) (2005) 372–82.

[20]   G. Eysenbach, *Citation advantage of open access articles* (2006). Available at: http://dx.doi.org/10.1371/journal.pbio.0040157 (accessed 27 November 2007).

[21]   M.J. Kurtz et al., The effect of use and access on citations, *Information Processing and Management* 41(6) (2005) 1395–1402.

[22]   S. Lawrence, Online or invisible? *Nature* 411 (6837) (2001) 521.

[23]   H.F. Moed, The effect of open access on citation impact: an analysis of ArXiv's condensed matter section, *Journal of the American Society for Information Science and Technology* 58(13) (2007) 2047–54.

[24]   H. Sotudeh and A. Horri, The citation performance of open access journals, *Journal of the American Society for Information Science and Technology* 58(13) (2007) 2145–56.

[25]   D. Stern, Open access or differential pricing for journals: the road best traveled? *Online* 29(2) (2005) 30–36.

[26]   D. Sainsbury, Open access is not the only science publishing model, *The Financial Times* 10 November (2004) 16.

[27]   S.R. Owens, Revolution or evolution? A shift to an open access model of publishing would clearly benefit science, but who should pay? *EMBO Reports* 4(8) (2003) 741–3.

[28]   J.W. Houghton, C. Steele and P.J. Sheehan, *Research Communication Costs in Australia: Emerging Opportunities and Benefits* (Department of Education, Science and Training, Canberra, 2006).

[29]   I.D. Craig, A.M. Plume, M.E. McVeigh, J. Pringle and M. Amin, Do open access articles have greater citation impact? A critical review of the literature, *Journal of Informetrics* 1(3) (2006) 239–48.

[30]   A. Swan and S. Brown, *Open Access Self-Archiving: an Author Study* (Key Perspectives Ltd, Truro, 2005).

[31]   M. Bates, S. Loddington, S. Manuel and C. Oppenheim, Attitudes to the rights and rewards for author contributions to repositories for teaching and learning, *ALT-J Research in Learning Technology* 15(1) (2007) 67–82.

[32]   E. Gadd, S. Loddington and C. Oppenheim, A comparison of academics' attitudes towards the rights protection of their research and teaching materials, *Journal of Information Science* 33(6) (2007) 686–701.

[33]   P. Suber, *SPARC Open Access Newsletter*. Available at: www.earlham.edu/~peters/fos/newsletter/06–02–07.htm (accessed 21 August 2007].

[34]   S.R. Urs, Copyright, academic research and libraries: balancing the rights of stakeholders in the digital age, *Electronic Library and Information Systems* 38(3) (2004) 201–207.

[35]   A. Muir, Digital preservation: awareness, responsibilities and rights issues, *Journal of Information Science* 30(1) (2004) 73–92.

[36]   T. Gillespie, *Wired Shut: Copyright and the Shape of Digital Culture* (MIT Press, Cambridge, 2007).

[37]   C. May, *Digital Rights Management: the Problem of Expanding Ownership Rights* (Chandos, Oxford, 2007).

[38]   N. Lucchi, *Digital Media and Intellectual Property* (Springer, Heidelberg, 2006).

[39]   D. Penny and R. Cliffe, DRM: still a balancing act? (Electronic Publishing Services Ltd., London, 2006).

[40]   Kaufmann-Wills Group, *The Facts about Open Access: a Study of the Financial and Non-Financial Effects of Alternative Business Models on Scholarly Journals/Researchers* (ALPSP, Worthing, 2005).

[41]   Oxford Journals, *Assessing the Impact of Open Access* (2006) www.oxfordjournals.org/news/oa_report.pdf (accessed 10 March 2008].

[42]   N. Jacob (ed.) *Open Access: Key Strategic, Technical and Economic Aspects* (Chandos, Oxford, 2006).

[43]   R. Jones, T. Andrew and J. MacColl, *The Institutional Repository* (Chandos, Oxford, 2006).

[44]   Public Library of Science. Available at: www.plos.org/ (accessed 3 January 2008).

[45]   P. Peters, Going all the way: how Hindawi became an open access publisher, *Learned Publishing* 20(3) (2007) 191–5.

[46]   C. Oppenheim and D. Smithson, What is the hybrid library? *Journal of Information Science* 25(2) (1999) 97–112.

[47]   G.E. Gorman and F. Rowland (eds), *Scholarly publishing in an Electronic Era* (Facet, London, 2005).

[48] S.H. Chang, Institutional repositories: the library's new role, *OCLC Systems and Services* 19(3) (2003) 77–9.

# 14

## Social software: fun and games, or business tools?

WENDY A. WARR

## Abstract

This is the era of social networking, collective intelligence, participation, collaborative creation, and borderless distribution. Every day we are bombarded with more publicity about collaborative environments, news feeds, blogs, wikis, podcasting, webcasting, folksonomies, social bookmarking, social citations, collaborative filtering, recommender systems, media sharing, massive multiplayer online games, virtual worlds, and mash-ups. This sort of anarchic environment appeals to the digital natives, but which of these so-called 'Web 2.0' technologies are going to have a real business impact? This paper addresses the impact that issues such as quality control, security, privacy and bandwidth may have on the implementation of social networking in hide-bound, large organizations.

## Introduction[1]

Fifty years ago information was stored on punch cards. SDI services appeared about 10 years later and databases were available online from about 1978. In 1988 PCs were in common use and by 1998 the web was being used as a business tool. The web of the 1990s might be thought of as 'Web 1.0', for now in 2008 there is much hype about Web 2.0, but what does that mean? Web 2.0 is an umbrella term for a number of new internet services that are not necessarily closely related. Indeed, some people feel that Web 2.0 is not a valid overall title for these technologies. A reductionist view is that of a read–write web and lots of people using it. Tim O'Reilly and colleagues [1] introduced the term in 2004 and later produced a report refining the concept [2].

O'Reilly defines eight core patterns of Web 2.0:

1. Harnessing collective intelligence
2. Data as the next 'Intel Inside'
3. Innovation in assembly
4. Rich user experiences
5. Software above the level of a single device
6. Perpetual beta
7. Leveraging [sic] the long tail
8. Lightweight software and business models and cost effective scalability.

He expands on these patterns as follows. Harnessing collective intelligence is sometimes described as *the* core pattern of Web 2.0; it describes *architectures of participation* [3] that embrace the effective use of network effects and feedback loops to create systems that get better the more that people use them. The second core pattern above is jargon for the fact that information has become as important as, or more important than software, since software itself has become a commodity.

The web, says O'Reilly, has become a massive source of small pieces of data and services, loosely joined, increasing the recombinant possibilities and unintended uses of systems and information. The web page has evolved to become far more than HTML markup and now embodies 'full software experiences' that enable interaction and immersion in innovative new ways. This relates also to pattern 5 above: software such as the horizontally federated 'blogosphere' (hundreds of blog platforms and aggregators) or the vertically integrated iTunes (server farm plus online store plus iTunes client plus iPods) are changing the software landscape. Indeed, the concept of a software 'release' is disappearing. Software is continuously changing: eBay, for example, deploys a new version of its service approximately every two weeks. Hence the phrase 'perpetual beta' that is commonly heard in connection with Web 2.0. The idea of the 'long tail' is that 80% of the internet's resources might be useful to only about 20% of users; Web 2.0 allows the mass servicing of micromarkets cost effectively. Finally, O'Reilly claims that lightweight software and new business models are changing the economics of online software development fundamentally, providing new players with powerful new weapons against established players and even entire industries.

Other parties have not been slow to capitalize upon the '2.0' brand: Web 2.0 has led to Library 2.0 [4, 5], Office 2.0 (backed by an annual conference in San Francisco), Enterprise 2.0 (with a conference in Boston) and probably other 'twos'. Andrew McAfee [6] defines Enterprise 2.0 (for getting the most out of

Web 2.0 applications in the enterprise) using the acronym SLATES for some features that do not seem very different from those of Web 2.0:

- Search (information must be searchable)
- Linking (links must connect and cross-reference blog posts, wikis etc. into an interactive and interdependent community)
- Authoring (simple tools must be provided to allow everyone to contribute and edit content)
- Tagging (users must be able to assign their own terms and descriptions, which allows content to be structured in a way that is meaningful for users)
- Extensions (applications should include a suggestion and recommendation system such as that found on Amazon [7] or StumbleUpon [8] – 'if you liked X, you'll like Y')
- Signals (technology, such as RSS, that tells users when new content of interest appears).

The current article briefly outlines a number of Web 2.0 concepts, without discussing details of the technologies or software involved in implementing them. The strengths and weaknesses of specific IT companies, marketing issues, 'monetization' [9], and market economics [10] are also beyond the scope of this study. Some of the drawbacks of Web 2.0 technologies are discussed, but the main focus of the article is on Web 2.0 technology adoption in the publishing, chemical and pharmaceutical industries. The semantic web and Web 2.0 may be related in certain ways but the semantic web is outside the scope of this article.

## Social software

Social software includes a large number of tools used for online communication, e.g. instant messaging, text chat, internet fora, weblogs (or blogs for short), wikis, social network services, social guides, social bookmarking, social citations, social libraries and virtual worlds. These are discussed in more detail in the sections that immediately follow this one. Most of us are familiar with applications such as instant messaging (e.g. MSN Messenger, Yahoo Messenger, AOL Instant Messenger, Skype), text chat (e.g. Internet Relay Chat, IRC), internet fora, blogs and wikis. Skype [11] is a well-known example of the use of Voice-over-Internet protocol (VoIP). In 2005

Skype was bought by eBay for $2.6 billion, a price that many analysts now consider excessive. By 2007 as many as 220 million people had registered with Skype. A study by Ofcom in the UK [12] in September 2007 found that 17% of adults with broadband have used Skype or the Tesco VoIP service at least once. In the UK only 14% of those who said that they were users professed to use these services every day, but penetration is 27% of households in France and the Netherlands.

## Wikis

One of the best known wikis is Wikipedia [13]. As of September 2007 it boasted 8.2 million articles in 253 languages. It is one of the 10 most visited sites on the web. Specialized Wikipedia projects also exist. A Wikipedia WikiProject in chemistry [14], for example, strives to incorporate the collaborative efforts of those with interests within chemistry and related areas into the articles and therefore improve the overall quality of the Wikipedia.

Much has been written about the possible inaccuracy of an encyclopaedia multi-authored by anonymous and perhaps unreliable 'experts' but proponents argue that there are so many people reading and editing Wikipedia that errors should be edited out sooner rather than later. This is an example of the concept of 'wisdom of crowds' [15], a term introduced by James Surowiecki to describe the aggregation of information in groups, resulting in decisions that, he argues, are often better than could have been made by any single member of the group.

## Blogs and feeds

Blogs are now in such common use that engines (e.g. Google blogsearch [16] and Technorati [17]) have been developed specifically to search them. Most of us are also familiar with web feeds such as RSS and Atom. RSS (Really Simple Syndication or Rich Site Summary) is a family of web feed formats used to publish frequently updated content such as blog entries, news headlines or podcasts. An RSS document, which is called a 'feed', 'web feed' or 'channel', contains either a summary of content from an associated web site or the full text. The name Atom applies to a pair of related standards. The Atom Syndication Format is an XML language used for web feeds, while the Atom Publishing Protocol (APP or 'AtomPub') is a simple HTTP-based protocol for creating and updating web resources.

A podcast is a digital media file, or a series of such files, that is distributed over the internet using syndication feeds for playback on portable media players and personal computers. The term 'podcast' is a portmanteau of the words 'iPod' and 'broadcast'. A podcast is distinguished from other digital media formats by its ability to be syndicated, subscribed to, and downloaded automatically when new content is added, using an aggregator or feed reader capable of reading feed formats such as RSS or Atom. (It seemed appropriate to use the definitions of all these terms given in Wikipedia [13].)

Social networking tools such as blogs, wikis and podcasts are becoming very popular in academia [18]; one expert claims that the most popular platform for viewing lectures at the University of California, Berkeley will soon be by podcast [19]. The American Chemical Society (ACS) has a digital presence on YouTube [20] where viewers can watch videos from the most recent ACS National Meeting and video clips originally released as part of press releases [21].

## Social networks and guides

User-generated content and virtual communities [22] are not new phenomena. Virtual communities have been used since the 1980s. The ChemWeb.com community in the 1990s had virtual lectures and discussion groups but the technology of the time was not capable of supporting the visionary features it wanted to offer [23]. A number of cultural factors were also involved in its decline. The discussion groups were never well used; even in the 2000s chemists in industry are reluctant to broadcast their views openly.

With Web 2.0 the community's contributions are foremost: the site exists only to create and serve those contributions; the result of user-generated content is 'collective intelligence'. YouTube [20] would not exist without the videos contributed by community members. YouTube is not just a site where teenagers share shots of interest only to a minority; in 2007 the world at large learned of the protests by monks in Burma because dissidents were able to broadcast videos through services such as YouTube. YouTube is just one of very many social network services. Another well-known example is Flickr (for sharing photographs) [24].

Social guides such as WikiTravel [25] and TripAdvisor [26] cater for specific interests, in this case travel. WikiTravel is a project to create a free, complete, up-to-date and reliable worldwide travel guide (with the appearance on screen of Wikipedia). TripAdvisor carries over 10 million reviews and opinions of hotels, vacations etc. supplied by travellers. The various Web 2.0 applications do not operate in isolation. They can be joined together in 'mash-ups', web applications that combine data and/or functionality from more than one source. A mash-up example is TripAdvisor maps, which combines the TripAdvisor hotel popularity index and Google maps. Mash-ups are a newer content aggregation technology than 'portals'. A web portal (e.g. Yahoo) is a site that provides a single function through a web page or site.

Facebook [27] and MySpace [28] are hugely popular consumer networking sites. Facebook claims that it has 66 million active users (as of March 2008) with about 250,000 new registrations every day since January 2007. Facebook advertises such statistics on its web site. MySpace figures are more elusive: the press office supplies them by telephone to accredited representatives of the media. In January MySpace apparently claimed more than 110 million monthly active users worldwide, with on average 300,000 new people signing up every day [29]; the UK press office told this author in March 2008 that there are nearly 110 million users worldwide. Even though such social networking sites are ostensibly for consumers, they have been used by universities and commercial employers to check up on the activities of students or the validity of *curricula vitae*.

Social networks such as LinkedIn [30], Ryze [31] and XING [32] for business and professional use are also growing in popularity. In March 2008 LinkedIn claimed more than 19 million registered users, up from 14 million in August 2007. It is a contact network with user profiles and recommendations. Users are connected by direct connections, second degree connections (i.e. the contacts of one of your primary contacts are your own secondary contacts) and third degree connections. This author's 202 connections (February 2008) supposedly link her to more than 684,900 professionals.

LinkedIn is used to find jobs, people, and business opportunities. Employers can list jobs and seek employees; job seekers can view profiles of hirers and get introduced. The 'gated access' approach is used in the hope of ensuring that users only accept contacts whom they trust and would recommend. Newer services are the 'LinkedIn Answers' service (members broadcast questions and hope that experts will provide useful answers), groups, and news ('discover articles that your colleagues are reading'). New services will doubtless continue to be added.

One of the problems with social networks is that it might be necessary to belong to more than one in order to communicate with all one's friends.

Presumably some people are registered with both MySpace and with Facebook, and find time to participate actively in both communities, but this author currently has no intention of indulging in multiple professional networks.

A quick look at Alexa [33] reveals the most popular (most visited) web sites (listed below). The names of the top 10 sites are unchanged on 4 March 2008 compared with 7 October 2007, but their precise rankings differ. Alexa computes traffic rankings by analysing the web usage of millions of Alexa Toolbar users. Other free rankings services survey fewer users or are biased by country or type of site, according to a quick check in March 2008, but they confirm that Google and Yahoo are in the top three, that YouTube is in the top five, that msn.com is in the top six and that MySpace is in the top nine.

The most popular web sites on 7 October 2007, according to Alexa, were:

1. Yahoo.com
2. Google.com
3. MSN.com
4. YouTube.com
5. Live.com
6. MySpace.com
7. Orkut.com
8. Facebook.com
9. Wikipedia.com
10. Hi5.com.

The most popular web sites on 4 March 2008, according to Alexa, were:

1. Yahoo.com
2. YouTube.com
3. Live.com
4. Google.com
5. MySpace.com
6. MSN.com
7. Facebook.com
8. Hi5.com
9. Wikipedia.com
10. Orkut.com.

## Social bookmarking

Social bookmarking sites [34,35], such as del.icio.us [36] and furl [37] allow people to share bookmarks for internet pages, assigning keywords ('tags') of their own choice to describe the sites that have appealed to them. Bookmark lists organized by tag, date, owner, etc. can be communicated using RSS feeds. 'Tag clouds' draw sites into clusters and tagging is used to create an informal taxonomy dubbed a 'folksonomy'. (The term 'folksonomy' is attributed to Thomas vander Wal [38] by anecdote and by Wikipedia.)

Standard knowledge management systems, information portals, intranets and workflow applications are usually highly structured (and thus somewhat inflexible) from the start [6]. Users have little opportunity to influence the structure. Wikis and blogs, however, start as blank pages, and the highly flexible folksonomies start to grow as users enter tags. A discussion of the advantages and disadvantages of taxonomies and folksonomies [39] is beyond the scope of this article.

Sites such as Digg [40] and Reddit [41] are, strictly speaking, methods for social news distribution rather than social networking sites. They use the same sharing, tagging and voting technologies as social networking sites but they apply them to news stories rather than web pages per se [34]. The popularity of such facilities is in no doubt. One expert reports: 'Just two years ago social bookmarking was a new animal. Today it's folksonomy and it's studied in graduate school.' [19].

Tagging is also used in a more 'academic' way in freely accessible sites such as CiteULike [42], Connotea [43, 44], and BibSonomy [45]. Problems he encountered in his own research led Richard Cameron to create the free service CiteULike which enables the sharing and discovery of links to scholarly literature. CiteULike aims to make it easier for groups of researchers to communicate and collaborate online and it is offered in multiple languages. Connotea was conceived by Nature Publishing Group in 2004, on seeing the possibilities offered by del.icio.us. BibSonomy is offered by the Knowledge and Data Engineering Group of the University of Kassel, Germany; it is available in both German and English versions.

## Virtual worlds

At the other extreme, perhaps, from the basic and practical uses of Web 2.0 are virtual worlds such as massively multiplayer online (role-playing) games: MMO(RP)Gs such as World of Warcraft [46] and non-game worlds such as Second Life [47], and The Sims [48]. Second Life is an internet-based virtual world launched in 2003, developed by Linden Lab. A downloadable client program called the Second Life Viewer enables its users, called 'residents', to interact with each other through motional avatars. Residents (more than 20 million are registered) can explore, meet other residents, socialize, participate in individual and group activities, and create and trade items (virtual property) and services from one another. This virtual world even has its own economy and its own currency. The Sims is a strategic life-simulation computer game created by Will Wright, published by Maxis, and distributed by Electronic Arts. It is a simulation of the daily activities of one or more virtual characters ('Sims') in a suburban household near SimCity.

Those who think that virtual worlds are esoteric and impractical for industrial and academic pursuits might consider this statement by an analyst [49]: 'By the end of 2011, 80 percent of active internet users (and Fortune 500 enterprises) will have a "second life", but not necessarily in Second Life [...] enterprise clients [...] should investigate and experiment [...] but limit substantial financial investments until the environments stabilize and mature.'

As well as for entertainment, Second Life has been used by business (e.g. Adidas, Dell, Calvin Klein, Warner Brothers, Nature and Harvey Nash), universities (e.g. the Open University, Ohio University, Harvard Law School, and Princeton University), cultural organizations (e.g. Virtual Rome, Louvre, and the Alliance of Second Life Librarians), politicians (e.g. Hillary Clinton, John Edwards, and Antonio di Pietro), banks (e.g. ING, Saxo, and ABN Amro) and even by countries (Sweden, for example, has an embassy on Second Life).

Some specific usage examples are discussed later, but a few related to the above users are worth mentioning here. Harvey Nash has a job board in Second Life. Princeton University's island includes a conference area, a museum of the arts, a performance hall, and an information centre. There are several places designed for teaching and learning. A wilderness and activity area and a science museum are planned for the future. Roma is a virtual Rome re-creation and Second Louvre Museum is a Second Life video. Antonio di Pietro, founder of Italy's Italia de Valori party and Italy's Minister of Infrastructure conducted a live press conference in Second Life in July 2007 with leading members of the Italian press to discuss and demonstrate the power of Second Life as a tool for political and social organizing. John Edwards was the first presidential candidate to have an official second life and Hillary Clinton and Barack Obama have campaign headquarters in the virtual world. Saxo uses Second Life to build its company culture across different offices around the world. It also has a basement in Second Life where employees can play a game of pool and it designed its new, real-world headquarters in Copenhagen in Second Life. It has also created an interface in the virtual world allowing investors to win Second Life currency (Linden dollars) and try trading.

## Statistics

The world of Web 2.0 is fast changing and a lot can happen in just six months. The well publicized studies outlined in this section are a snapshot of 2006–2007 Web 2.0 usage and they are likely to have been out of date even when the current article was prepared late in 2007.

Booz Allen Hamilton [50] interviewed 2400 consumers in the UK, Germany and the USA between August and October 2006 about their attitude to Web 2.0, and what it offers in the broad sense, and about their actual user behaviour. The survey found that 41% of internet users in the UK use Web 2.0 sites to interact and participate with others in a massive worldwide community of users, and Web 2.0 usage is prevalent across all age groups and both sexes. Users share information without privacy concerns and rely on recommendations from anonymous peers. Although newer sites still have predominantly young user communities (50% of MySpace users are under the age of 25), a significant proportion (24%) fall into the older 35–49 age bracket. The more established the site, the more balanced the age group using it: 25% of Amazon users are over the age of 50.

Two contradictory studies of Web 2.0 business usage were published in 2007. On 20 March 2007, Forrester released some results from a December 2006 survey [51] of 119 chief information officers (CIOs) at mid-size and larger companies. It indicated that Web 2.0 is being broadly and rapidly brought into enterprises: 89% of the CIOs said they had adopted at least one of six prominent Web 2.0 tools, blogs, wikis, podcasts, RSS, social networking, and content tagging, and 35% said they were already using all six of the tools. Although Forrester did not break down the adoption rates by tool, it did say that CIOs saw relatively high business value in RSS, wikis, and tagging and relatively low value in social networking and blogging.

On 22 March 2007 McKinsey released the results of a broader survey of Web 2.0 adoption [52], and the results are quite different. In January 2007 McKinsey surveyed 2847 executives (not just CIOs) from around the world. The survey found strong interest in many Web 2.0 technologies but much less widespread adoption. McKinsey looked at six Web 2.0 tools: blogs, wikis, podcasts, RSS, social networking, and mash-ups. (It did not include tagging.) It found that social networking was actually the most popular tool, with 19% of companies having invested in it, followed by podcasts (17%), blogs (16%), RSS (14%), wikis (13%), and mash-ups (4%). After adding in companies planning to invest in the tools, the percentages are as follows: social networking (37%), RSS (35%), podcasts (35%), wikis (33%), blogs (32%), and mash-ups (21%). It seems that American companies may not be the leaders in embracing Web 2.0 in coming years. Leading the way are Indian firms, 80% of which plan to increase their investments in Web 2.0 over the next three years, compared with 69% of Asia-Pacific firms, 65% of European firms, 64% of Chinese firms, 64% of North American firms, and 62% of Latin American firms.

Why do the McKinsey numbers differ from those of Forrester? Perhaps it is all a question of whom you ask: anecdotal evidence shows that top management and workers at the coal face have very different perspectives on which technologies are actually in use in an organization. In some organizations management bans the use of social networking sites. For example, in an exchange of views on the UK Electronic Information Group (UKeIG) listserver [53], someone from English Heritage said that English Heritage does not allow use of Facebook while someone else (Phil Bradley) pointed out that that there is a Facebook group for English Heritage staff, albeit with only 14 members at that time.

In June 2007, Forrester [54] studied the reaction of 275 IT decision makers to the term 'Web 2.0': 44% reacted positively, 20% were strongly positive, 29% were neutral, 3% reacted negatively and 3% had never heard of Web 2.0, but, significantly, out of 268 familiar with Web 2.0, 53% were somewhat concerned, and 25% were very concerned, about the risks of employee-driven, unsanctioned use of Web 2.0 technologies. This leads us on to consider some of the negative aspects of Web 2.0.

## Issues

The problem of malicious or inappropriate use is not confined to new *internet* technologies (junk mail comes through the letterbox and the fax machine, for example) but the misuse of Web 2.0 could lead to many problems, which do need consideration:

- spam, spim, spit, skam, splog
- breach of security
- breach of privacy
- clogging of bandwidth
- leak of company secrets
- lack of control (by management or by community rules)
- the need to set rules
- fear of 'shadow IT'
- user addiction
- waste of employees' time
- virtual crime.

Web 2.0 leads to new types of spam including 'spim', 'spit', 'skam', and 'splog'. 'Spim' is spam sent to a mobile phone or by instant messenger. 'Skam' covers spam such as reception of strange messages from total strangers in Skype. 'Spit' is spam over mobile telephony in general. A 'splog' is a spam blog. Neologisms are not the only feature of verbal communication in the age of the digital native (someone born in the internet era or just before); 'If U Cn Rd Ths' you will be familiar with the impact of mobile telephony on usage of written English.

At least one highly visible example of a breach of security has been reported [55]. In September 2007, a Microsoft staffer by the name of Jason Langridge posted an entry to his blog that detailed an upgrade to the Windows Mobile operating system, and he included a link to a page where the upgrade could be downloaded. Unfortunately for his employer, the upgrade, Windows Mobile 6.1 (to solve an incompatibility issue that left Windows Mobile 6.0 users unable to read Office 2007 file formats) was not supposed to be made publicly available for at least two more weeks.

This is just one of the sorts of risk that IT departments fear. They are suspicious of intellectual property leaks, of silos of information, and of users operating their own insecure servers. They fear 'shadow IT': unlicensed copies of software are unearthed or some system breaks and IT staff discover hardware or software in the organization that they did not know existed. Some large organizations have banned instant messaging and social sites not just on the grounds of security but also because they can consume vast amounts of bandwidth. Control is a debatable issue. Corporate wikis are not free-for-alls: they have rules. Wikipedia is now 'controlled', although there are those who object to censorship by anonymous experts, who do not advertise a fair procedure for appeals. Corporate wikis, behind a firewall, are said to be most effective when the number of users is small and the content is focused.

This author was sent a private e-mail message by a pharmaceutical industry researcher who wishes to remain anonymous, in which he revealed the message that his company displayed when he tried to access Gerry McKiernan's entries on Facebook [56]:

> The following URL is blocked by [Company X] policy because of its content categorization by our subscription service: 'Social Networking' http://iastate.facebook.com/group.php?gid=3D5055907636. Please read [Company X] Web Content Filter Policy for more information. If you feel there is a valid business reason to access this site, please submit the Web Content Filter Override Request Form which will be reviewed by appropriate management. Exception requests may require approval from a Vice-President or above.

He remarked that he had little hope getting an exception approved: the firewall in the same company used to block the translation function in Google and it took months to get the decision reversed.

In a discussion on the UKeIG listserver [53], Phil Bradley stated 'If you can't trust your staff to use resources sensibly perhaps you shouldn't let them have computers. A technical support department should ensure that they understand what the issues are and how to deal with them rather than attempt a blanket policy of hiding behind the word "no".' Another subscriber to the list replied that students spend an increasingly disproportionate amount of time poking and writing on walls, to which Bradley replied that in his student days he used to spend too much time playing pool. Euan Semple [57, and quoted in 58] feels that these arguments will eventually become a recruitment issue as the digital natives refuse jobs at organizations that will not allow staff to keep up with their online networks. How would you feel if your employer took away your cell phone or BlackBerry?

A virtual crime is a virtual criminal act that takes place in a massively multiplayer online game, and as such is beyond the scope of this article. South Korea, a country where such games are extremely popular, has a special police investigation unit for virtual crimes.

## Adoption
### Information professionals

Information professionals were early adopters of Web 2.0 technologies [4, 59, 60]. In June 2007 LexisNexis announced the results of a nationwide survey [61] showing that 39% of information professionals access blogs at least weekly and 34% access wikis. Video or audio podcasts were used less: 16% access video podcasts and 15% audio podcasts.

The pros and cons of email, listservers, blogs, wikis and social networks have doubtless been discussed on many listservers popular with information professionals; this author can cite examples from UKeIG and an even more specialized group, the chemical information listserver, chminf-l [62]. The large number of messages appearing on chminf-l and the UKeIG list about Gerry McKiernan's activities on Facebook [56] have provoked lively discussion. When key workers leave an organization, their 'email' does not leave with them if it is on a blog or wiki. The newer systems also allow for extensive commenting, recommending and tagging. Despite all that, many information professionals still use email (and the chminf-l list) much more than they use Web 2.0 social software.

The UK National Archives organization has a wiki, called Your Archives [63], with the look and feel of Wikipedia. Facebook has a Library 2.0 interest group and a UKeIG group. The Chartered Institute of Library and Information Professionals (CILIP) has held virtual meetings in Second Life and it held a virtual seminar in connection with the Umbrella meeting in 2007 through Second Life [64].

There is more than one library 'in-world' in Second Life. The Alliance Library System of Illinois has a library project in which a number of librarians from all over the world are taking second lives and jobs in Second Life [65]. The 'residents' apparently appreciate having an in-world access to these library services and materials. Another Second Life library project has a blog [66] located on the InfoIsland.

Library of Congress is funding preservation of Second Life material [67, 68]. Through its National Digital Information Infrastructure and Preservation

Program (NDIIPP), it has eight partnerships as part of its new Preserving Creative America initiative to address the long-term preservation of creative content in digital form. These partners will target preservation issues across a broad range of creative works, including digital photographs, cartoons, motion pictures, sound recordings and even video games. The work will be conducted by a combination of industry trade associations, private sector companies and not-for-profit organizations, and cultural heritage institutions. One of these projects includes Second Life.

One of the Library of Congress partners, the University of Illinois at Urbana-Champaign [68], has launched a Preserving Virtual Worlds project to explore methods for preserving digital games and interactive fiction. Major activities will include developing basic standards for metadata and content representation and conducting a series of archiving case studies for early video games, electronic literature and Second Life. Second Life content participants include Life to the Second Power, Democracy Island and the International Spaceflight Museum. Partners are the University of Maryland, Stanford University, Rochester Institute of Technology, and Linden Lab.

The Department of Information Studies, University of Sheffield has launched the Centre for Information Literacy with Sheila Webber as Director. The centre has offices on the Eduserv island in Second Life. Webber herself has a Second Life blog, 'Adventures of Yoshikawa' [69].

## Publishers

Publishers have also embraced Web 2.0. *USA Today* has reportedly switched on all the social functionality of Facebook and MySpace. *The Economist* now publishes almost all its letters online, using a blog content management system enabled for comments. Nature Publishing Group has three islands on Second Life, dubbed 'Second Nature' [70, 71]. Nature Network [70–72] is designed as a professional toolkit for scientists and has been described as 'somewhere between Facebook and LinkedIn'.

Some recently launched learned publications now offer collaborative features. *ACS Chemical Biology*, for example, has a wiki, podcasts and 'Ask the Expert'; *ACS Nano* has a free online resource, ACS Nanotation, that enables nanoscientists to save time by reading reviews that identify the most significant new research [73]. In addition, researchers can get answers to their questions from top scientists. Other tools available to registered users include a wiki and multimedia networking opportunities. Members can upload photos to the image gallery and share videos at NanoTube, and enjoy free podcasts.

Elsevier has launched 2collab [74], a free web application that provides researchers with a platform to share resources with networks of peers and specialists in an online community. It allows researchers to add, share and rate bookmarks, tag resources, and to add comments and create topical groups. Each user is encouraged to create a personal profile, which everyone can view to ensure the authenticity of fellow users. Elsevier's Scirus Topic Pages (still in a beta-test version) [75] is a free, wiki-like service for the scientific community, where scientific experts summarize specific scientific topics, and where links to the latest, most relevant journal literature and web sources are presented on one page.

## Pharmaceutical and chemical industries

A Forrester survey [76] has indicated that 71% of CIOs are more interested in Web 2.0 technologies if they are offered as a 'suite'; 91% of those using the six Web 2.0 technologies (blogs, wikis, podcasts, RSS, social networking, and content tagging) prefer suites. Large vendors, such as Microsoft, IBM and Oracle, are preferred over smaller, 'pure play' firms such as Socialtext, NewsGator and MindTouch. Typical suites are Microsoft Office SharePoint Server ('SharePoint'), SuiteTwo from Intel and IBM Lotus Connections. Such applications promote the notion of 'software as a service' (SaaS). When it comes to SaaS, CIOs look at the smaller vendors and ask if they will be in business in two to three years' time, whereas they see IBM as having a lot of stability.

SharePoint is a competitor to classical enterprise content management programs such as FileNet, Documentum and Open Text. SuiteTwo currently offers wiki, blog, RSS and portal technology. Phase two release may include podcasting, social networking, VoIP and instant messaging. IBM Lotus Connections includes software for blogs and bookmarking (in a program called Dogear), plus Activities, a user-friendly repository for groups to share and collaborate on a project. This last option, a departure from more complex, traditional document management systems, is used by the Federal Aviation Administration where it is claimed that IBM's tools are very collaborative and give the end-users more control over how they communicate with their colleagues, but these tools are on-site, and server-based behind the firewall. Here the *intranet* rather than the internet is harnessed as the platform. For businesses, Web 2.0 often becomes entwined with service-oriented architectures and other web services technologies.

The pharmaceutical and chemical industries are using Web 2.0 technologies behind firewalls but most have said little about this in public. Some AstraZeneca scientists have used Documentum eRoom as a secure, web-based workspace for efficient collaboration among distributed workers. Pfizer's Research Information Factory, and the use of wikis, blogs, tagging and Pfizerpedia [77] were described at a recent conference [78].

Whether you believe that pharmaceutical companies use Web 2.0 extensively depends (as with all surveys) on whom exactly you ask. A colleague of this author, at another pharmaceutical company, allows this comment to be printed anonymously:

> There are pockets of wiki-madness inside our research group, much of it well thought out and perhaps even useful, albeit nascent and little-used and poorly advertised, but the environment and IT infrastructure is not terribly supportive, even if the current senior management is. One idea was to use a wiki to host a gene/target annotation system, so anyone and everyone could provide material on their favourite genes, pathways and systems, connect it somehow to well curated reference databases, and use the wiki concept to capture proprietary and personal additions.

Another anonymous comment is as follows. 'We've started to use SharePoint to establish a group-wide "MySite" dialogue, blog and "social site" for our internal chemistry colleagues [...] it has the look and feel of some of the web's social sites, just internalized and supportive of proprietary Q&A.'

Martin Leach of Merck & Co. allowed his comments to be attributed in *Chemical & Engineering News* [79]:

> drug industry IT is trending toward highly configurable architectures that employ web-based search functions such as the semantic web and open-source programs like wikis.

Workers at three different chemical companies have also shared anonymous comments with this author. At one company SharePoint is proving popular, while management encourages standard knowledge management systems because they have security, records retention policies etc., but wikis are growing up everywhere as adjuncts. One colleague says that wikis are seen as a 'sexier' way of doing the help and support functions around their major knowledge management system. SharePoint is glossier and more professional but wikis are nice and simple to use. Wikis are used in help files at one company. Another colleague reports that the situation is not necessarily that wikis are frowned upon; in some cases management cannot see why anyone should need a wiki if a 'proper' tool is available.

## The future

Will hide-bound, large organizations be able to prevent social software from creeping in through the back door? Probably not. One courageous approach has been taken by the computer company Dell. It launched IdeaStorm, a Digg-like [40] community-driven web site. Users can submit ideas and product improvements, and vote them up or down. Dell thus risks having customer complaints exposed in public but the company claims that it has actually had success with customer suggestions. As the Deloitte Touche analyst John Hagel, cited in [80], has said: 'Remember that the watercooler conversations are going to happen whether you listen or not. The only choice you have is whether you will participate.' Of course, web sites of the type 'CompanyXSucks.com' were quite common even before the days of Web 2.0, but they were not interactive.

Blanket bans on social computing can be small-minded and may not prevail. Employers need to have some trust in the people they choose to employ. In the past they did not resort to banning telephones in case employees made private calls. It is, however, not unusual for companies to maintain procedures for monitoring access to pornography, gambling and other facilities on the web, and for preventing improper use of email, and most people would agree that an organization needs some guidelines about the use of social computing in the workplace. There are good arguments on both sides. It is likely that a happy medium can be achieved, as seems to have happened at Pfizer. Given the reluctance of pharmaceutical companies to reveal details of tools that might give them a competitive edge, management must have approved the public exposure given to Pfizerpedia and the like [77, 78].

Although some of the mistakes made with public virtual communities and e-commerce in the 1990s may well be repeated (e.g. users unwilling to share information, too many companies trying to take a share of the pie, unrealistic expectations, and erroneous estimates of usage and advertising revenues), after some experimentation, efficient tools behind the firewall will be established. The really useful technologies will rise to the top. People will eventually distinguish hype from practicality. It is also certain that there will be consolidation and among the many, many pure play companies (as happened with the virtual communities and e-commerce sites); some will not survive but the best will flourish. LinkedIn, for example, looks as if it is approaching the productivity phase.

Forrester Research [81] concludes that social computing has radically changed the way people interact with both information and one another on the internet, giving people the ability to generate, self-publish, and find information more efficiently, and share expertise in an approach that is much easier and cheaper than that of earlier knowledge management systems. Web 2.0 will not go away, however much IT and legal departments might wish that it would. The analysts advise, however, that before implementing Web 2.0 technologies, potential users must balance the risks (in reliability, security, governance, compliance, and privacy) against the opportunities Web 2.0 represents. They also suggest that lessons learned from earlier instant messaging deployments might be relevant in evaluating Web 2.0.

As with many expensive surveys and studies, the conclusions of the Forrester report seem fairly obvious. What is not so clear is where we are on the 'S-curve' and how long it will be before the use of Web 2.0 technologies in business is routine and the next wave of disruptive technology is getting daily exposure in the press. Some people are already using the term Web 3.0, usually without any clear definitions or strategy. No doubt, in about five years' time something new on the web will be making an impact, whether it be Web 3.0, the semantic web, or something completely different.

## Acknowledgements

The author is grateful to Professor Peter Willett for reading a draft of this paper and making many useful comments.

## Note

1   This paper is based on a presentation given at ICIC, the International Conference on Trends for Scientific Information Professionals, Sitges (Barcelona), Spain, 21–24 October 2007.

# References

[1]     T. O'Reilly, *What is Web 2.0? Design Patterns and Business Models for the Next Generation of Software* (2005). Available at: www.oreillynet.com/lpt/a/6228 (accessed 3 March 2008).

[2]     J. Musser and T. O'Reilly, *Web 2.0 Principles and Best Practices* [O'Reilly Radar Report] (O'Reilly Media, Sebastopol, 2006).

[3]     *Dion Hinchcliffe's Web 2.0 blog.* Available at: web2.socialcomputingmagazine.com (accessed 2 March 2008).

[4]     M.E. Casey and L.C. Savastinuk, *Library 2.0: a Guide to Participatory Library Service* (Information Today, Medford, 2007).

[5]     *Second Life Library 2.0.* Available at: infoisland.org/feed/ (accessed 3 March 2008).

[6]     A.P. McAfee, Enterprise 2.0: the dawn of emergent collaboration, *MIT Sloan Management* Review 47(3) (2006) 21–8.

[7]     *Amazon.* Available at www.amazon.com (accessed 3 March 2008).

[8]     *Stumbleupon.* Available at: www.stumbleupon.com/ (accessed 3 March 2008).

[9]     K. Weide, *Social Networking Services in the United States: Popular, Yes, But How to Monetize Them?* (IDC, Framingham, 2007).

[10]    R.E. Happe, *U.S. Social Networking Application 2007–2012 Forecast and Analysis* (IDC, Framingham, 2007).

[11]    *Skype.* Available at: www.skype.com (accessed 4 March 2008).

[12]    E. Judge, Offers of free calls over the internet fail to switch on phone users, *The Times* 3 September 2007. Available at: business.timesonline.co.uk/tol/business/industry_sectors/telecoms/article2373509.ece (accessed 3 March 2008).

[13]    *Wikipedia.* Available at: www.wikipedia.com (accessed 3 March 2008).

[14]    *Wikipedia: WikiProject Chemistry.* Available at: en.wikipedia.org/wiki/Wikipedia:WikiProject_Chemistry (accessed 3 March 2008).

[15]    J. Surowiecki, *The Wisdom of Crowds* (Random House/Anchor Books, New York, 2005).

[16]    *Google Blogsearch.* Available at: blogsearch.google.com/ (accessed 3 March 2008).

[17]    *Technorati.* Available at: www.technorati.com/ (accessed 3 March 2008).

[18]    R. Petkewich, New education tools, *Chemical & Engineering News* 85(17) (2007) 44–5.

[19]    T.K. Huwe, Surfing the Library 2.0 wave, *Computers in Libraries* 27(1) (2007) 36–8.

[20]    *YouTube.* Available at: www.youtube.com (accessed 3 March 2008).

[21]    *ACS podcasts.* Available at: www.youtube.com/user/AmeriChemSoc (accessed 4 March 2008).

[22] J. Hagel and A.G. Armstrong, *Net.gain* (Harvard Business School Press, Boston, 1997).

[23] W.A. Warr, Communication and communities of chemists, *Journal of Chemical Information and Computer Sciences* 38(6) (1998) 966–75.

[24] *Flickr*. Available at: www.flickr.com (accessed 3 March 2008).

[25] *WikiTravel*. Available at: www.wikitravel.com (accessed 3 March 2008).

[26] *TripAdvisor*. Available at: www.tripadvisor.com (accessed 3 March 2008).

[27] *Facebook*. Available at: www.facebook.com (accessed 3 March 2008).

[28] *MySpace*. Available at: www.myspace.com (accessed 3 March 2008).

[29] J. Owyang, *Social Network Stats: Facebook, MySpace, Reunion* (2008). Available at: www.web-strategist.com/blog/2008/01/09/social-network-stats-facebook-myspace-reunion-jan-2008/ (accessed 4 March 2008).

[30] *LinkedIn*. Available at: www.linkedin.com (accessed 3 March 2008).

[31] *Ryze*. Available at: www.ryze.com (accessed 3 March 2008).

[32] *XING*. Available at: www.xing.com (accessed 3 March 2008).

[33] *Alexa*. Available at www.alexa.com (accessed 4 March 2008).

[34] D. Winder, Back to basics: social bookmarking, *Information World Review* (November 2007) 29–31.

[35] T. Hammond, T. Hannay, B. Lund and J. Scott, Social bookmarking tools (I): a general review, *D-Lib Magazine* 11(4) (2005). Available at: www.dlib.org/dlib/april05/hammond/04hammond.html (accessed 4 March 2008).

[36] *Del.icio.us*. Available at: del.icio.us (accessed 4 March 2008).

[37] *Furl*. Available at: www.furl.net (accessed 4 March 2008).

[38] *Thomas Vander Wal's vanderwal.net*. Available at: www.vanderwal.net/ (accessed 4 March 2008).

[39] E. Peterson, Beneath the metadata: some philosophical problems with folksonomy, *D-Lib MagazineI* 12(11) (2006). Available at: www.dlib.org/dlib/november06/peterson/11peterson.html (accessed 4 March 2008).

[40] *Digg*. Available at: digg.com/ (accessed 4 March 2008).

[41] *Reddit*. Available at: reddit.com/ (accessed 4 March 2008).

[42] *CiteULike*. Available at: www.citeulike.org (accessed 4 March 2008).

[43] *Connotea*. Available at: www.connotea.com (accessed 4 March 2008).

[44] B. Lund, T. Hammond, M. Flack and T. Hannay, Social bookmarking tools (II): a case study – Connotea, *D-Lib Magazine* 11(4) (2005). Available at: www.dlib.org/dlib/april05/lund/04lund.html (accessed 4 March 2008).

[45] *Bibsonomy*. Available at: www.bibsonomy.org (accessed 4 March 2008).

[46] *World of Warcraft*. Available at: www.worldofwarcraft.com (accessed 4 March 2008).

[47] *Second Life*. Available at: www.secondlife.com (accessed 4 March 2008).

[48]   *The Sims*. Available at: thesims.ea.com/ (accessed 4 March 2008).

[49]   *Gartner, Inc. Press Release* (2007). Available at:
       www.gartner.com/it/page.jsp?id=503861 (accessed 4 March 2008).

[50]   Booz Allen Hamilton, *Urgent Need for Companies To Adapt to the Web 2.0 Model of
       Consumer Interaction and Participation* (2006). Available at:
       www.boozallen.com/capabilities/Industries/industries_
       article/26060199?lpid=827466 (accessed 4 March 2008).

[51]   G.O. Young, E. Daley, H. Lo and A. Lawson, *Efficiency Gains and Competitive
       Pressures Drive Enterprise Web 2.0 Adoption* (Forrester Research, Cambridge, MA,
       2007).

[52]   J. Bughin and J. Manyika, *How Businesses Are Using Web 2.0.* (McKinsey, Brussels,
       2007). Available at:
       www.mckinseyquarterly.com/Marketing/Digital_Marketing/How_businesses_are_
       using_Web_20_A_McKinsey_Global_Survey_1913?gp=1 (accessed 4 March
       2008).

[53]   *Archives of UKEIG-INTRANETS-FORUM@JISCMAIL.AC.UK*. Available at:
       www.jiscmail.ac.uk/archives/ukeig-intranets-forum.html (accessed 4 March 2008).

[54]   G.O. Young, B.J. Holmes and A. Lawson, *IT Will Measure Web 2.0 Tools Like Any
       Other App.* (Forrester Research, Cambridge, MA, 2007).

[55]   N. Gohring, Microsoft blogger accidentally leaks office mobile upgrade, *PCWorld*,
       September 28, 2007 Available at: www.pcworld.com/article/id,137812-
       c,windows/article.html (accessed 4 March 2008).

[56]   *Gerry McKiernan's Entries on Facebook*. Available at:
       www.facebook.com/p/Gerry_McKiernan/16926735 (accessed 4 March 2008).

[57]   Euansemple.com, *Social Computing for the Business World*. Available at:
       www.euansemple.com (accessed 4 March 2008).

[58]   Anon, Become trusted guides, *Update* (July/August 2007) 5.

[59]   J. Klobas (ed.), *Wikis: Tools for Information Work and Collaboration* (Chandos
       Publishing, Oxford, 2006).

[60]   P. Bradley, *How to Use Web 2.0 in Your Library* (Facet Publishing, London, 2007).

[61]   *Lexis Nexis Releases Survey on Information Professionals' Use of Web 2.0 and Knowledge
       Management to Add Value to Their Organizations*. Press release available at:
       www.lexisnexis.com/about/releases/0980.asp (accessed 4 March 2008).

[62]   *Archives of Chminf-l*. Available at: listserv.indiana.edu/cgi-bin/wa-
       iub.exe?A0=CHMINF-L (accessed 4 March 2008).

[63]   *Your Archives*. Available at: yourarchives.nationalarchives.gov.uk (accessed 4 March
       2008).

[64] *CILIP Virtual Members Day Allowed Members to Chat with Each Other and CILIP Staff* (2007). Available at: tinyurl.com/3yrvfp (accessed 4 March 2008).

[65] L. Bell, T. Peters and K. Pope, Get a (Second) Life! Prospecting for Gold in a 3-D World, *Computers in Libraries* 27(1) (2007) 10–15.

[66] *Second Life Library Project Blog.* Available at: infoisland.org/feed/ (accessed 3 March 2008).

[67] *Library of Congress News Item.* Available at: www.loc.gov/loc/lcib/0709/preserve.html (accessed 4 March 2008).

[68] *Library of Congress News Item.* Available at: www.loc.gov/today/pr/2007/07–156.html (accessed 4 March 2008).

[69] *Adventures of Yoshikawa.* Available at: adventuresofyoshikawa.blogspot.com (accessed 4 March 2008).

[70] S. Everts, Second Life science, *Chemical and Engineering News* 85(26) (2007) 49.

[71] G. Baynes, Personalisation and collaboration, *Research Information* 34 (2008) 16–17.

[72] *Nature Network.* Available at: network.nature.com (accessed 4 March 2008).

[73] *ACS Publications.* Available at: pubs.acs.org (accessed 4 March 2008).

[74] *2collab.* Available at: www.2collab.com (accessed 4 March 2008).

[75] *Elsevier Topic Pages.* Available at: topics.scirus.com/TestTopicPages/index.jsp (accessed 3 March 2008).

[76] G.O. Young, E. Daley and A.L. Baer, *CIOs Want Suites for Web 2.0* (Forrester Research, Cambridge, MA, 2007).

[77] R. Mullin, Seeing the forest at Pfizer, *Chemical and Engineering News* 85(36) (2007) 29.

[78] B. Gardner, *Approaches to Information Integration.* Paper presented at ICIC, the International Conference on Trends for Scientific Information Professionals, Sitges (Barcelona), Spain, 21–4 October 2007. Slides available at: www.infonortics.com/chemical/ch07/slides/gardner.pdf (accessed 4 March 2008).

[79] R. Mullin, The big picture: drug firms forge an information management architecture to take on the research data glut. *Chemical & Engineering News* 85(40) (2007) 13–17, 37.

[80] D. Daniel, Five tips for bringing Web 2.0 into the enterprise, *CIO Magazine* (1 June 2007). Available at: www.cio.com/article/print/115300 (accessed 4 March 2008).

[81] R. Koplowitz, G.O. Young, C. Moore and S. Semmes, *Web 2.0. Social Computing Dresses up for Business* (Forrester Research, Cambridge, MA, 2007).

# 15

# Bibliometrics to webometrics

MIKE THELWALL

## Abstract

Bibliometrics has changed out of all recognition since 1958; becoming established as a field, being taught widely in library and information science schools, and being at the core of a number of science evaluation research groups around the world. This was all made possible by the work of Eugene Garfield and his Science Citation Index. This article reviews the distance that bibliometrics has travelled since 1958 by comparing early bibliometrics with current practice, and by giving an overview of a range of recent developments, such as patent analysis, national research evaluation exercises, visualization techniques, new applications, online citation indexes, and the creation of digital libraries. Webometrics, a modern, fast-growing offshoot of bibliometrics, is reviewed in detail. Finally, future prospects are discussed with regard to both bibliometrics and webometrics.

## Introduction

The last 50 years have seen two major technological changes in scholarly publishing and two major changes in the way research can be quantitatively analysed, alongside numerous less significant developments. The two publishing changes are the computerization of the printing process, reducing costs significantly and allowing more journals and books to appear in print; and the conversion of the entire publishing cycle (submission of articles, refereeing and publication) to the internet, allowing faster and possibly cheaper communication throughout. Historically, the first major change for the development of quantitative analysis of academic publishing (bibliometrics) was the creation of the Institute for Scientific Information

(ISI, now Thomson Scientific) citation database, which began functioning in 1962 [1, 2] together with associated post-war sociological theory allowing it to be used to assess the impact of scientific work [3]. Since then there has been a continuous increase in the computing power available in universities, which has helped to make increasing numbers of bibliometric analyses possible. The second major development for bibliometrics was the web publishing of an increasingly broad range of research-related documents, from articles to email discussion lists, allowing the creation of a range of new metrics relating to their access and use.

In this article, the focus is on the measurement of science. Conveniently for this special issue, the two significant changes fall just after the beginning and just before the end of the period in question, although in between bibliometrics has arisen as a recognized scientific specialism: taught in universities as part of information science courses, with a substantial body of techniques, some theories, and an international group of specialist science evaluators. This review article has a dual focus: general bibliometric issues and the field of webometrics, a new research area that has grown out of bibliometrics. The next section discusses bibliometrics originating within the first half of 1958–2008 and the following section discusses a selection of more recent developments. A further section then focuses exclusively on webometrics.

## Bibliometrics

Bibliometrics encompasses the measurement of 'properties of documents, and of document-related processes' [4]. The range of bibliometric techniques includes word frequency analysis [5], citation analysis [6], co-word analysis [7] and simple document counting, such as the number of publications by an author, research group or country. In practice, however, bibliometrics is primarily applied to science-related documents and hence has considerable overlap with scientometrics, the science measurement field.

Although recognizably bibliometric techniques have been applied for at least a century, the emergence of bibliometrics as a scientific field was triggered (in the 1960s) by the development of the Institute for Scientific Information (ISI) Science Citation Index (SCI) by Eugene Garfield [2], as a logical continuation of his drive to support scientific literature searching. The SCI was created as a database of the references made by authors, to earlier articles, in their articles published in the top scientific journals, originally focusing on general science and genetics. The underlying idea, still highly relevant today, is that if a scientist reads an article, then s/he would benefit from knowing which articles cited it, since they may cover a similar topic and might update or correct the original article. The importance of the SCI is also consistent with Bradford's [8] law of scattering: although a scientist may keep up-to-date with a research specialism by reading all relevant journals when they appear, a minority of relevant articles will be scattered throughout other journals. Hence citation searching protects researchers from missing relevant articles in non-core journals.

Almost a by-product of the SCI, and later also the Social Sciences Citation Index (SSCI) and the Arts and Humanities Citation Index (AHCI), was the ability to generate easily a range of new statistics: not just the number of citations to any given article but also, using other fields in the SCI database, aggregated publication and citation counts. These aggregated statistics include the number of citations to all articles in a journal or all articles by an author, research group, or country. Some were further developed into named indicators with supporting theories and reasonably well accepted standard interpretations. Perhaps the most well known is the journal impact factor (JIF), defined below.

Since the publication of the SCI, two types of bibliometric application have arisen: evaluative and relational [4]. Evaluative bibliometrics seeks to assess the impact of scholarly work, usually to compare the relative scientific contributions of two or more individuals or groups. These evaluations are sometimes used to inform research policy and to help direct research funding [6]. In contrast, relational bibliometrics seeks to illuminate relationships within research, such as the cognitive structure of research fields, the emergence of new research fronts, or national and international co-authorship patterns.

## Evaluative bibliometrics

Most evaluative bibliometric techniques use citations as their raw data. The theory for this stems from Robert Merton's [3] sociology of science, which postulates that citations are the way in which scholars acknowledge influential prior work. On this basis, citation counting could be used as an indicator of scientific value because more influential work would tend to be more frequently cited. In fact the term 'impact' is now accepted as appropriate for that which citations measure or indicate. Subsequent research has shown that

Merton's perspective is a simplification of reality: there are many different reasons to cite articles as well as many influences on which articles to select, when multiple options are available [9, 10]. From an alternative perspective, de Solla Price [11] showed that a cumulative advantage process could be at work for highly cited papers, where papers that are initially well cited then tend to continue to be cited partly because they have been cited rather than for their intrinsic worth. This is similar to Merton's [12] 'Matthew effect' in science, whereby recognized scholars tend to be awarded a disproportionate credit for their research. Despite complications such as these, indicators based upon citation counts have been widely adopted.

The journal impact factor, introduced in the early 1960s [13–15] is the number of citations from ISI-indexed articles published in the year X to articles in the journal published in years X − 1 and X − 2, divided by the number of (citable) items published in the journal in the years X − 1 and X − 2. On the basis of Merton [3], journals with higher JIFs tend to publish higher impact research and hence tend to be better regarded. Nevertheless, there seems to be general agreement that, even within discrete subject fields, ranking journals based upon JIFs is problematic [4, 6]. Moreover, as the JIF has gained in popularity, there seem to have been attempts by journal editors to recommend authors to cite other articles in the same journal to improve its JIF.

A second common application is tenure and promotion decisions which may take into account the JIFs of the journals in which an academic has published, or the citation counts of their publications. This is not recommended by many bibliometricians, however, since citation counts at the level of individual authors are unreliable and those making the decisions may be unaware of field differences [6].

A third application, usually conducted by expert bibliometricians, is comparing academic departments through citations to their publications. Even carefully constructed bibliometric indicators, which are reasonably robust because of aggregation over the publications of entire departments, need to be combined with other sources of evidence (e.g. funding, sources of esteem, peer review, narrative) in order to give solid evidence for major decisions, such as those involving funding.

## Relational bibliometrics

There were several early attempts to develop bibliometric methods to examine relations within science through ISI data, although the growth of relational analysis methods was probably constrained by the lack of sufficient computing power in the early days, especially for visualizations. Nevertheless, early relational analyses produced interesting insights into the structure of science through simple means, such as network diagrams of the flow of citations between key sets of articles [16]. This idea was apparently invented by the geneticist Dr Gordon Allen in 1960, who sent his citation diagram to an enthusiastic Garfield [16]. Journal citation diagrams were another early invention: these can illustrate the connections between journals within a field, detect journals that cross field boundaries and identify central or peripheral journals.

One important relational method, sometimes attributed to Garfield, is co-citation as a measure of similarity [17, 18]. The basis of this is that pairs of documents that often appear together in reference lists (i.e. are co-cited) are likely to be similar in some way. This means that if collections of documents are arranged according to their co-citation counts then this should produce a pattern reflecting cognitive scientific relationships. Author co-citation analysis (ACA) is a similar technique in that it measures the similarity of pairs of authors through the frequency with which their work is co-cited [19]. ACA operates at a high enough level of aggregation to be a practical tool for mapping the structures of fields [20].

## Bibliometrics today

Mainstream bibliometrics has evolved rather than undergone revolutionary change in response to the web and web-related developments. The core citation-based impact measures are still in place, but are now supplemented by a range of complementary techniques. In addition, there is now a body of theory and case studies to draw upon so that an experienced bibliometrician can be reasonably sure of finding good ways to generate indicators from citations for any common task and also of how to interpret the results. In particular there has been an ongoing debate about the validity of using citations to measure impact, in parallel with the development of theories of citer motivations, which have recently been extensively reviewed [21].

Aside from the core citation analysis methods, the biggest change in bibliometrics stems from the availability of new significant sources of information about scholarly communication, such as patents, web pages, and digital library usage statistics. Of course, the wider field of scientometrics has never been exclusively interested in academic papers and has also used other data such as funding as well as qualitative indicators, such as peer review judgments.

There are perhaps three main trends in the recent history of bibliometrics, and citation analysis in particular. These are to improve the quality of results through improved metrics and careful data cleaning, to develop metrics for new tasks, and to apply bibliometrics to an increasing range of problems, particularly in descriptive relational contexts (see the knowledge domain visualization section below for examples of the latter).

## The h-index and current bibliometric indicators

Perhaps the most significant new evaluative metric is the *h*-index [22] which, for a scientist, is the largest number *h* such that s/he has at least *h* publications cited at least *h* times. A high *h* index indicates that a scientist has published a considerable body of highly cited work. It is a metric that is easily calculated and intuitive to understand, and hence its appeal. There have been a number of studies of the *h*-index, evaluating it, proposing new versions or applying it to sets of scholars. For example, ranked lists of the *h*-indexes of UK and US LIS professors [23, 24] may be of interest to researchers in the field.

Apart from the *h*-index, the most important evaluative bibliometric indicators seem to have evolved gradually. For example, because there are widely differing field-based citation norms, comparing citation counts is inappropriate across multiple fields. Hence, it is now best practice to field-normalize citation indicators [6] when using them to evaluate an academic department. Even if a set of departments in the same discipline are to be compared, raw citation counts, or average citations per researcher, would not be an accurate reflection of their citation impact because the departments might specialize in fields with different average citation rates. Hence, departments engaging in research in fields with high average citation counts would have an unfair advantage unless the indicators were normalized, for example through dividing each department's citations by the field average. Hence the evaluative citation analysis goal has shifted from evaluating the impact of research to evaluating its impact relative to a field.

## National research evaluation exercises

Systematic research assessment exercises seem set to become an important but still controversial application area for bibliometrics. Four countries now have periodic national research evaluation exercises that help to direct a significant proportion of their research funding. The UK's Research Assessment Exercise (RAE, see www.rae.ac.uk) was the first and has taken place in 1986, 1989, 1992, 1996, 2001 and in 2008. It is primarily based upon peer review, with small panels of subject experts awarding ratings to relevant groups from each university. In addition to peer review, normally based on the top four publications of each researcher, the panels take into account other factors, such as funding, PhD completions and a narrative. Although bibliometrics have not yet played a formal role, they can be included in the narrative part of the submission and the panels may also use them as part of their decision making process. Anecdotal evidence suggests that many disciplines have also developed informal publication guidelines and lists of target journals that are influenced by JIFs. The 2008 RAE was set to be conducted in parallel with bibliometrics, however, and subsequent RAEs may have a much heavier bibliometric component [25], something that has been argued for on the basis that academic publications are already peer reviewed, e.g. [26]. The rationale behind a shift towards bibliometrics is that bibliometric indicators such as citations and JIFs are transparent and cheap compared to peer review. Nevertheless, bibliometrics is inadequate on its own and so RAEs are likely to always contain a range of other inputs, probably including peer review as a final criterion.

New Zealand's Performance Based Research Fund,[1] which started in 2003, ran again partially in 2006 and is set to run again in 2012. It is quite similar to the RAE except that it has always given grades to individual academics rather than whole submissions. The UK RAE converted to individual grades rather than group grades in 2008, but in the New Zealand system every academic submits an evidence portfolio, rather than a fixed number of publications, although for most academics the heart of their portfolio would probably have been the component of up to four 'nominated research outputs' [27].

In Australia, the Institutional Grants Scheme (IGS), which predominantly replaced the earlier Research Quantum, is effectively a national evaluation exercise. Australian assessment has never included a significant element of peer review but has always been based primarily upon external funding for research. Starting in 2002, the funding was based upon 'success in attracting research students (30% of funding), in attracting research income (60%) and in the quality and output of its research publications (10%)' [28].

The world's largest science system, that of the USA, does not have a national science evaluation exercise. Instead, US research funding is allocated competitively on a grant-by-grant basis, with ex-ante evaluations being of secondary importance and carried out by the funding agencies [29]. The Netherlands' research evaluation process is a different type again, comprising a 'patchwork' of evaluations by different funding agencies and stakeholders [30]. Different again is the evaluation system of the former Foundation for Research Development (FRD), now superseded by the National Research Foundation (NRF) in South Africa, which combined the New Zealand style retrospective evaluation of individual researchers with a second stage, the evaluation of the researchers' future plans, before awarding funding grants [31]. The current NRF system is similar, with a preliminary stage of rating individual researchers by peer review,[2] with rated researchers allowed to apply for grant funding. Finally, and despite the above descriptions, probably the majority of countries conduct ad-hoc evaluations rather than a systematic exercise, with Italy being an example of this [32].

How effective and useful are these research evaluation systems? This is clearly a controversial issue and one that does not have a simple answer. In Australia, however, there is evidence of the problems of a simplistic scheme: a negative impact of counting publications but not evaluating their quality seems to be an increased volume of lower quality journal articles [33]. The UK's RAE has been congratulated for its success, based upon bibliometric evidence of UK performance relative to the world [34], but it is not clear whether this assessment is widely believed.

## New bibliometric databases: Google Scholar and Scopus

In 1992 the ISI was sold by Garfield and other shareholders to a company that later became Thomson Scientific, and which continued the citation indexes. Recent years have seen the emergence of significant challengers to the ISI indexes in the form of alternative large-scale online scholarly article databases like Google Scholar and Scopus (Elsevier), which contain embedded citation information. In addition, there are smaller-scale field-specific digital libraries and archives that contain citation indexes, such as CiteSeer for Computer Science, and the CiteBase initiative[3] to index the citations of free online scholarly publications, including those in archives like arXiv[4] (physics, mathematics, computer science and quantitative biology).

One article has compared the Web of Science (with ISI data), Google Scholar and Scopus with the explicit objective of assessing the extent to which the results of a citation analysis depend upon the data source used, using the task of ranking the faculty in a single library and information science school. The findings showed that Google Scholar was probably too difficult to use for a large-scale citation analysis and that the other two gave similar results overall [35]. Nevertheless, weaknesses in the coverage of certain fields resulted in significant disadvantages to some faculty members, depending upon the database used. Hence the use of both in conjunction with each other would give the fairest results. In addition, the poor coverage of conferences by both in comparison to Google Scholar illustrates that neither gives fair results to academics who publish in fields which emphasize conferences, such as computer science and computational linguistics [35]. Another investigation compared different databases for coverage of social sciences research, finding Scopus to offer particularly good coverage [36]. Other studies with wider disciplinary coverage have also shown that the coverage of Google Scholar is variable and can be low or particularly unreliable for some disciplines [37, 38].

Despite the limitations of all current citation sources, hopefully the existence of challengers to the ISI will make it easier than ever before to critically assess the extent of ISI coverage and to identify national and other biases.

## Knowledge domain visualization

The increasing use of sophisticated visualizations is probably the most significant development in relational bibliometrics and has led to the creation of a new field: knowledge domain visualization (KDViz), within the information visualization research area [39]. This involves significant computing resources and is part of a wider 'eResearch' trend to harness computers for social science research goals. In addition to Chen's [39] three dimensional information-rich visualizations of individual research fields, others have implemented ambitious plans to map large areas of science via citations in the ISI database [40, 41].

Whilst early relational bibliometric analyses might have produced simple hand-drawn diagrams of citations between authors, journals or articles, later researchers developed software to automate this process. For example, Olle

Persson's Bibexcel[5] can be fed citation data from the ISI and used to produce a range of two-dimensional diagrams, such as an ego network (a term borrowed from social network analysis) of researchers with the strongest citation relationship with a given author. Similarly, Loet Leydesdorff has a set of programs[6] that can convert ISI data into a format that can produce diagrams, especially to illustrate the citation relationships between individual journals [42]. Eugene Garfield's HistCite[7] produces timeline visualisations for citations within a collection of articles. It is unusual that it is aimed at supporting literature searches rather than bibliometrics.

There are several sets of visualization software with significant inputs from computer scientists that are free to use and can easily process ISI data to produce three dimensional visualizations. Katy Borner's InfoViz Cyberinfrastructure[8] is a general purpose suite of open source software with many algorithms to process and display the data. A particular advantage is its ability to process massive amounts of data. For example Boyack [41] produced a combined science and technology map using bibliometric coupling on the references from over a million papers in the Science Citation Index. Chaomei Chen's CiteSpace[9] software focuses exclusively on bibliometric analysis and can produce beautiful three dimensional visualizations of citation networks. One of the interesting features of some of Chen's networks is the ability to include not just the basic structure but also many layers of additional information chosen by the researcher through the use of colour and other features. For example a circle representing an article in a network of articles may reveal the article's annual citation counts by representing them with differently coloured layers [43].

## Patents

A patent is a set of time-limited exclusive rights to an invention, normally granted by a government patent office. The term patent is also used for the officially registered invention descriptions. These documents are similar in some ways to academic papers, for example through the inclusion of a set of references. The adoption of patents as an indicator of scientific value stems from a recognition that academic researchers can be, and perhaps sometimes should be, directly involved in the development of useful technologies [44].

Patent indicators can be direct, in the sense of counting researchers' patent awards to reward those with novel research with potential commercial value. Patent indicators can also be indirect by using patent references to identify the cited academic work which is thereby endorsed as having applicable value [45]. Patent analyses have also been used to evaluate the performance of a country's technology and to identify flows of knowledge transfer between science and technology [46]. For example, one empirical study of patents relative to the Netherlands concluded that the results did not fit the existing theoretical models of university–industry relationships, which therefore needed to be reconsidered [47].

## Usage data from digital libraries

Perhaps the most significant challenge for bibliometrics in the long run is that the new digital libraries are producing large-scale evidence of the usage patterns of academic articles for the first time [48]. Editors are already receiving usage statistics in addition to impact factors from publishers in some cases and it seems likely that the two give useful complementary information [49, 50]. Research into log files may also be able to connect usage patterns to user demographics in some cases, which may give additional insights into users [51] and information seeking patterns [52].

Two important questions concern the impact of open access publishing upon the visibility of articles and publishers' revenues. One study of mathematics articles in ArXiv addressed both questions and suggested that open access articles tend to be cited more often but that more citable articles tend to be deposited in ArXiv, rather than necessarily attracting more citations because of being deposited there. In addition, there was some evidence that open access articles that were subsequently published were less frequently downloaded (a reduction of 23%) from publishers' web sites [53].

Digital library usage data can correlate with citation counts. For instance, early readership data seems to be moderately good at predicting future citation counts for an article [54]. Nevertheless, there will be many articles for which citations and usage statistics differ greatly. This raises the possibility that usage data may be used as evidence of a different kind of impact. For example, it may be seen as valuable in some subjects that research is used in undergraduate teaching and usage statistics would be more valuable than citations to assess this. Perhaps in the future we will have 'usage classics' as well as 'citation classics'. Publishers already often distribute lists of the most downloaded articles to editorial boards of journals but the lack of standardization of usage statistics seems to have prevented the creation of universal lists, say for physics or information science. Moreover, the currently available usage statistics are not unproblematic: for example publishers have already noticed that individual articles can pick up high usage rates through being set as compulsory reading by the instructor of a large class.

## Webometrics

Webometrics is the quantitative analysis of web phenomena, drawing upon informetric methods [55], and typically addressing problems related to bibliometrics. Webometrics was triggered by the realization that the web is an enormous document repository with many of these documents being academic-related [56]. Moreover, the web has its own citation indexes in the form of commercial search engines, and so it is ready for researchers to exploit. In fact, several major search engines can also deliver their results automatically to investigators' computer programs, allowing large-scale investigations [57]. One of the most visible outputs of webometrics is the ranking of world universities based upon their web sites and online impact [58].

Webometrics includes link analysis, web citation analysis, search engine evaluation and purely descriptive studies of the web. These are reviewed below, in addition to one recent application: the analysis of Web 2.0 phenomena. Note that there is also some research into developing web-based metrics for web sites to evaluate various aspects of their construction, such as usability and information content, but this will not be reviewed here.

### Link analysis

Link analysis is the quantitative study of hyperlinks between web pages. The use of links in bibliometrics was triggered by Ingwersen's [59] web impact factor (WIF), created through analogy to the JIF, and the potential that hyperlinks might be usable by bibliometricians in ways analogous to citations, e.g. [60]. The standard WIF measures the average number of links per page to a web space (e.g. a web site or a whole country) from external pages. The hypothesis underlying early link analysis was that the number of links targeting an academic web site might be proportional to the research productivity of the owning organization, at the level of universities [61], departments [62], research groups [63], or individual scientists [64]. Essentially the two are related because more productive researchers seem to produce more web content, on average, although this content does not attract more links per page [65]. Nevertheless, the pattern is likely to be obscured in all except large-scale studies because of the often indirect relationship between research productivity and web visibility. For example, some researchers produce highly visible web resources as the main output of their research, whilst others with equally high quality offline research attract less online attention.

Subsequent hyperlink research has introduced new metrics and applications as well as improved counting methods, such as the alternative document models [66]. In most cases this research has focused on method development or case studies. The wide variety of reasons why links are created and the fact that, unlike citing, linking is not central to any areas of science, has led to hyperlinks rarely being used in an evaluative role. Nevertheless, they can be useful in describing the evolution or connectivity of research groups within a field, especially in comparison with other sources of similar information, such as citations or patents [67]. Links are also valuable to gain insights into web use in a variety of contexts, such as by departments in different fields [68, 69].

A generic problem with link analysis is that the web is continually changing and seems to be constantly expanding so that webometric findings might become rapidly obsolete. A series of longitudinal investigations into university web sites in Australia, New Zealand and the UK have addressed this issue. These university web sites seem to have stabilized in size from 2001, after several years of rapid growth [70]. A comparison of links between the web sites from year to year found that this site size stabilization concealed changes in the individual links, but concluded that typical quantitative studies could nevertheless have a shelf life of many years [71].

## Web citation analysis

A number of webometric investigations have focused not on web sites but on academic publications; using the web to count how often journal articles are cited. The rationale behind this is partly to give a second opinion for the traditional ISI data, and partly to see if the web can produce evidence of wider use of research, including informal scholarly communication and for commercial applications. A number of studies have shown that the results of web-based citation counting correlates significantly with ISI citation counts across a range of disciplines, with web citations being typically more numerous [37, 72–74]. Nevertheless, many of the online citations are relatively trivial, for example appearing in journal contents lists rather than in the reference sections of academic articles. If this can be automated then it would give an interesting alternative to the ISI citation indexes.

## Search engines

A significant amount of webometrics research has evaluated commercial search engines [75]. The two main investigation topics have been the extent of the coverage of the web and the accuracy of the reported results. Research into developing search engine algorithms (information retrieval), and into how search engines are used (information seeking) are not part of webometrics. The two audiences for webometrics search engine research are researchers who use the engines for data gathering (e.g. the link counts above) and web searchers wanting to understand their results.

Search engines have been a main portal to the web for most users since the early years. Hence, it has been logical to assess how much of the web they cover. In 1999, a survey of the main search engines estimated that none covered more than 17.5% of the 'indexable' web and that the overlap between search engines was surprisingly low [76]. Here the 'indexable' web is roughly the set of pages that a perfect search engine could be expected to find if it found all web site home pages and followed links to find the remainder of pages in the sites. The absence of comparable figures after 1999 is due to three factors: first, an obscure Hypertext Transfer Protocol technology, the virtual server, has rendered the sampling method of Lawrence and Giles ineffective; second, the rise of dynamic pages means that it is no longer reasonable to talk in terms of the 'total number of web pages'; finally, given that search engine coverage of the web is only partial, the exact percentage is not particularly relevant, unless it has substantially changed. One outcome of this research, however, was clear evidence that meta-search engines could give more results through combining multiple engines. Nevertheless, these have lost out to Google, presumably because the key task of a search engine is to deliver relevant results in the first results page, rather than a comprehensive list of pages.

Given that web coverage is partial, is it biased in any important ways? This is important because the key role of search engines as intermediaries between web users and content gives them considerable economic power in the new online economy [77, 78]. In fact, coverage is biased internationally in favour of countries that were early adopters of the web [79]. This is a side effect of the way search engines find pages rather than a policy decision.

The issue of accuracy of search engine results is multifaceted, relating to the extent to which a search engine correctly reports its own knowledge of the web. Bar-Ilan and Peritz [80] have shown that search engines are not internally consistent in the way they report results to users. Through a longitudinal analysis of the results of the query 'Informetric OR Informetrics' in Google they showed that search engines reported only a fraction of the pages in their database. Although some of the omitted pages duplicated other returned results, this was not always the case and so some information would be lost to the user. A related analysis with Microsoft Live Search [81] suggested that one reason for lost information could be the search engine policy of returning a maximum of two pages per site.

Many webometric studies have used the hit count estimates provided by search engines on their results pages (e.g. the '50,000' in 'Results 1–10 of about 50,000') rather than the list of matching URLs. For example, Ingwersen [59] used these to estimate the number of hyperlinks between pairs of countries. The problem with using these estimates is that they can be unreliable and can even lead to inconsistencies [82–84], such as expanded queries giving fewer results. In the infancy of webometrics these estimates could be highly variable and so techniques were proposed to smooth out the inconsistencies [85], although the estimates subsequently became much more stable.

A recent analysis of the accuracy of hit count estimates for Live Search found a surprising pattern. The estimates tended to be stable for large numbers ($>8000$) and small numbers ($<300$) but unstable for mid-range numbers. The reason seems to be that the high estimates were of the total number of matches known to the search engine, whereas the low estimates were of the number of matches after the elimination of duplicate pages, near-duplicate matches and multiple pages from the same site. The instability in the middle of the results was due to the transition between these two types of estimate [81]. The different nature of the estimates is a problem for webometrics investigations that use queries with both high and low hit counts.

## Describing the web

Given the importance of the web, some webometrics research has been purely descriptive. A wide variety of statistics have been reported using various survey methods. These include: the average web page size; average number and type of meta-tags used and the average use of technologies like Java and JavaScript [86, 87]. In addition, many commercial web intelligence companies have reported basic statistics such as the number of users, pages and web servers, broken down by country. Here only two types of descriptive analysis are reported, however: link structure characterizations and longitudinal studies.

There are two separate key findings about web links, concerning the overall web structure and how the links evolve. Researchers at AltaVista used a copy of a web crawl to construct a holistic picture of the link structure of the web [88]. They found a bow tie model (Figure 1), with a core 'strongly connected component' (SCC) of 28% of pages that could all reach each other by clicking on one or more links. This seems to be the heart of the web, being relatively easy to navigate and containing the well-linked portal sites like Yahoo! Directory and the Dmoz Open Source Directory. In addition 21% of pages could be reached by clicking on one or more links, starting at any SCC page, but could not 'get back' to the SCC by following chains of links. This 'OUT' component includes many web sites that are linked to by Yahoo! or other SCC pages but do not contain any links to pages outside of the site. In contrast, the 'IN' component is the 21% of pages that link to the SCC directly or by following links. These seem to be pages or sites that are unknown to the core of the web. Finally, some groups of pages do not link to the rest of the web in any way (8%, DISCONNECTED) and a substantial proportion has more exotic connections (22%, TENDRILS).

The bow tie model was later recast as a corona model by Björneborn [89], in order to emphasize the centrality of the SCC and the often close

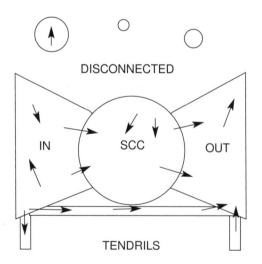

**Figure 1** The bow tie model of the web

connection between IN and SCC, and between SCC and OUT. For example, the core of a site could be in the SCC but with many pages deeper inside the site being in OUT. Björneborn [90] also investigated shortest link paths between subsites of UK university web sites, finding that computer science often connects otherwise disparate research fields.

Web dynamics research, in contrast to the structural analysis described above, is concerned with measuring, characterizing and modelling changes in the web. A key finding is that the cumulative advantage/Matthew effect phenomenon of bibliometrics (and elsewhere) applies to web links [91]. On the web, a few pages attract millions of links whereas hundreds of millions of pages attract one or none. This imbalance can be accounted for on the basis that when a new link is created it is more likely to target pages that already have many links. Of course nobody counts links to pages before deciding where their link should target, but the mediating factor is search engines. People are most likely to know about pages that have many links to them because search engines use links to find pages and to rank them [92]. Hence pages with many links to them are more visible online.

A study of the distribution of links to pages found that this cumulative advantage phenomenon fitted some types of pages, such as company home pages, but not others, like university home pages. In the latter case a second factor must have been at work, such as pre-knowledge of the existence of the page [93]. A consequence of either case is that a page with no links to it is unlikely to attract many more. Hence web site owners should initiate the creation of a few links to their site to help attract more. An implication for webometrics is that counts of links to a page are not reliable as indicators of the quality of the page's contents: pages may have many links because they became highly visible at some time in the past.

Finally, a different type of web dynamics is the analysis of changes in online information. Koehler [94] tracked a set of web pages from 1996, finding that they initially disappeared regularly, but there was then a period of stabilization, during which the surviving pages stopped disappearing. Koehler also claims that the survival rate of web pages will differ according to specialism. A differently organized study analysed 738 web sites in 1997 and 2004, finding a sevenfold growth in size during this period [95]. There were significant increases in some types of web content, such as dynamic pages and internal web site links, although the number of site outlinks (pointing to pages outside a site) did not grow as fast as the number of pages inside the site. The study found that only 25% of the site outlinks from 1997 still existed in the same place in 2004.

In summary, the web is clearly a complex, evolving entity that, despite its unregulated nature, exhibits strong patterns when analysed on a large scale.

## Measuring Web 2.0

Web 2.0 is a term coined by the publisher Tim O'Reilly mainly to refer to web sites that are driven by consumer content, such as blogs, Wikipedia and social network sites. The growth in volume of web content created by ordinary users has spawned a market intelligence industry and much measurement research. The idea behind these is data mining: since so many people have recorded informal thoughts online in various formats, such as blogs, chatrooms, bulletin boards and social network sites, it should be possible to extract patterns such as consumer reactions to products or world events. In order to address issues like these, new software has been developed by large companies like IBM's Web Fountain [96] and Microsoft's Pulse [97]. In addition, specialist web intelligence companies like Nielsen BuzzMetrics and Market Sentinel have been created or adapted.

A good example of a research initiative to harness consumer generated media (CGM) is an attempt to predict sales patterns for books based upon the volume of blog discussions of them [98]. The predictions had only limited success, however, perhaps because people often blogged about books after reading them, when it would be too late to predict a purchase. Other similar research has had less commercial goals. Gruhl et al. [99] analysed the volume of discussion for a selection of topics in blogspace, finding several different patterns. For example, some topics were discussed for one short period of time only, whereas others were discussed continuously, with or without occasional bursts of extra debate. A social sciences-oriented study sought to build retrospective timelines for major events from blog and news discussions, finding this to be possible to a limited extent [100, 101]. Problems occurred, for example, when a long running series of similar relatively minor events received little discussion but omitting them all from a timeline would omit an important aspect of the overall event.

In addition to the data mining style of research, there have been many studies of Web 2.0 sites in order to describe their contents and explain user behaviour in them. Here, research into social network sites is reviewed. A large-scale study of the early years of Facebook provides the most comprehensive overview of user activities. The data came from February 2004 to March 2006, when Facebook was a social network site exclusively for US college students [102].

Users seemed to fit their Facebooking with their normal pattern of computer use whilst studying, rather than allocating separate times. In terms of the geography of friendship, members mainly used Facebook to communicate with other students at the same college rather than school friends at distant universities. This suggests that social networking is an extension of offline communication rather than promoting radically new geographies of communication, although the latter is enabled by the technology of Facebook. This conclusion is supported by qualitative research into another popular site, MySpace [103, 104].

A webometric study of MySpace has indirectly investigated activity levels but focused on member profiles [105]. Amongst other findings, this showed that about a third of registered members accessed the site weekly and the average reported age was 21. Although other research found that MySpace close friends tended to reflect offline friendships [103], both male and female users preferred to have a majority of female friends [105]. Another study looked at the geography of friendship, finding that the majority of friends tended to live within a hundred miles, although a minority lived in the same town or city [106].

Finally, many statistics about Web 2.0 have been published by market research companies. Despite the uncertain provenance of this data, the results sometimes seem reasonable and also, because of the cost of obtaining the data, seem unlikely to be duplicated by academic researchers. An example is the announcement by HitWise that MySpace had supplanted Google as the most visited web site by US users by December 2007 [107]. The data for this was reported to come from two million US web users via an agreement between HitWise and the users' internet service providers. Making the results of overview analyses public gives useful publicity to HitWise and valuable insights to web researchers.

## Conclusions and future prospects
### Bibliometrics

Bibliometrics has changed out of all recognition since 1958, when it did not exist as a field or even as a coordinated group of researchers. Today it is taught widely in library and information science schools, and is at the core of a number of science evaluation research groups around the world, such as the Centre for Science and Technology Studies in the Netherlands. A number of bibliometric indicators are now internationally well known, principally the JIF, and bibliometrics are at least taken into account in a number of countries when making important policy decisions about the future of government funded research. At the same time the state of the art for bibliometrics indicators has moved on so that most of the indicators that are well known and easy to calculate also have significant flaws in which practitioners will be well versed, but casual users may overlook. Hence one important task for bibliometric practitioners seems to be to convince policy makers of the importance of commissioning high quality robust indicators, as well as ensuring that no indicator is taken at face value.

Bibliometrics has also changed in the sense of expanding the number of data sources that can be drawn upon. Currently, Scopus and Google Scholar are the most important international bibliometric databases to challenge those of Thomson Scientific. More importantly, large-scale patent analysis is now much easier than before with the digitization and indexing of patent databases. This opens up an aspect of the commercial value of scientific research for bibliometric study.

Finally, bibliometrics has also changed by expanding the range of tasks investigated. In particular, the current wide range of relational bibliometric studies opens up new ways of understanding the scholarly communication process and the structure of science through citation relationships between journals, between scholars and between papers. Moreover, citation analysis in conjunction with visualization also helps to understand the structure of individual fields, and is particularly useful for emerging and rapidly developing important research areas, such as nanotechnology and biotechnology [42].

## Webometrics

Webometrics research has been conducted by both information scientists and computer scientists, with different motivations. Within information science, webometrics has expanded from its initial focus on bibliometric-style investigations to more descriptive and social science-oriented research. It seems likely that webometric techniques will continue to evolve in response to new web developments, seeking to provide valuable descriptive results and perhaps also commercially applicable data mining techniques.

There are three main appeals of webometrics in contrast to traditional bibliometrics. First, the web can be timelier than the ISI databases. A typical research project might get funded, conduct research, report findings and then submit articles to journals. The time lag between the start of the project and the publication of the results in a journal is likely to be at least two years. Hence ISI-based bibliometrics is inevitably always retrospective, describing the research of years ago. In contrast, a research project might start by publishing a web site and could therefore be analysed with webometrics long before its research is published. The second advantage of the web is that it contains a wide range of scholarly-related artefacts, including presentations, patents, data, software and general web sites. Hence webometrics is potentially able to gather a wide range of evidence of research impact or connections. Finally, the web is free to access for all web users and so it potentially opens bibliometric-style analyses to those who could not access or afford ISI data.

Research into webometrics has also revealed many shortcomings, some of which are related to its advantages. First, the web is not quality controlled, unlike the ISI publication lists. Hence web data tends to be of lower quality, which means that webometric results are normally indicative rather than providing robust evidence. Second, web data is not standardized and so it is difficult to extract all except the simplest data (e.g. link counts). In particular, it is difficult to separate out the different types of publication. For example, there does not seem to be a simple way to separate out web citations in online journal articles from those in online course reading lists. Hence webometric results (e.g. link counts, web citation counts) tend to be the total of a mix of sources with variable value [e.g. 68, 108]. Third, although web data can be very timely, it can be impossible to find the publication date of a web page and so webometric results typically combine new and old web pages into one data set. Finally, web data is incomplete in several senses and in arbitrary ways. Although some academic articles are freely available online, the majority probably are not. Similarly, some researchers and research groups maintain extensive and comprehensive web sites but others do not. Hence the results reflect the web, which in turn is a very partial reflection of the activities of research.

Comparing the advantages and disadvantages of webometrics, it seems that it is unlikely to replace traditional bibliometrics but can be useful for several other purposes. First, it can be used for fast pilot studies to identify areas for follow-up systematic bibliometric analyses, e.g. [109]. Second, it can be used to assess the extent to which researchers are successful in publicizing their work online, given that this is an important activity. Third, it can be used for relational analyses of communication in disciplinary or geographic areas of science. Finally, its methods can help the analysis of Web 2.0 and online repositories for social sciences and humanities research goals.

## Notes

1  PBRF, see www.tec.govt.nz
2  results published at http://evaluation.nrf.ac.za/Content/Facts/ratings.aspx
3  www.citebase.org
4  www.arXiv.org
5  www.umu.se/inforsk/Bibexcel/
6  http://users.fmg.uva.nl/lleydesdorff/software.htm
7  http://www.histcite.com
8  http://iv.slis.indiana.edu/sw/
9  http://cluster.cis.drexel.edu/~cchen/citespace/

## References

[1]  B. Thackray and H.B. Brock, Eugene Garfield: history, scientific information and chemical endeavour. In: B. Cronin and H.B. Atkins (eds) *The Web of Knowledge: a Festschrift in Honor of Eugene Garfield* (Information Today, Medford, NJ, 2000) 11–23. [ASIS Monograph Series]

[2]  E. Garfield, *Citation Indexing: Its Theory and Applications in Science, Technology and the Humanities* (Wiley Interscience, New York, 1979).

[3]  R.K. Merton, *The Sociology of Science: Theoretical and Empirical Investigations* (University of Chicago Press, Chicago, 1973).

[4]  C.L. Borgman and J. Furner, Scholarly communication and bibliometrics, *Annual Review of Information Science and Technology* 36 (2002) 3–72.

[5]  G.K. Zipf, *Human Behavior and the Principle of Least Effort: an Introduction to Human Ecology* (Addison-Wesley, Cambridge, MA, 1949)

[6]  H.F. Moed, *Citation Analysis in Research Evaluation (Information Science and Knowledge Management)* (Springer, New York, 2005).

[7]  L. Leydesdorff, Why words and co-words cannot map the development of the sciences. *Journal of the American Society for Information Science* 48(5) (1997) 418–27.

[8]  S.C. Bradford, Sources of information on specific subjects. *Engineering: an Illustrated Weekly Journal* 137(26 January) (1934) 85–6.

[9]  C. Oppenheim and S. Renn, Highly cited old papers and the reasons why they continue to be cited, *Journal of the American Society for Information Science* 29(5) (1978) 225–31.

[10] B. Cronin, The *Citation Process: the Role and Significance of Citations in Scientific Communication* (Taylor Graham, London, 1984).

[11] D. de Solla Price, A general theory of bibliometric and other cumulative advantage processes, *Journal of the American Society for Information Science* 27(4) (1976) 292–306.

[12] R.K. Merton, The Matthew effect in science, *Science* 159(3810) (1968) 56–63.

[13] E. Garfield, Citation analysis as a tool in journal evaluation, *Science* 178(4060) (1972) 471–9.

[14] E. Garfield, *The Agony and the Ecstasy: the History and the Meaning of the Journal Impact Factor* (2005). Paper presented at the Fifth International Congress on Peer Review in Biomedical Publication, in Chicago, USA, 2005. Available at: http://garfield.library.upenn.edu/papers/jifchicago2005.pdf (accessed 27 September 2007)

[15] S.J. Bensman, Garfield and the impact factor, *Annual Review of Information Science and Technology* 41 (2007) 93–155.

[16] A. Cawkell, Visualizing citation connections. In: B. Cronin and H.B. Atkins (eds) *The Web of Knowledge: a Festschrift in Honor of Eugene Garfield* (Information Today, Medford, NJ, 2000) 177–94. [ASIS Monograph Series]

[17] H. Small, Co-citation in the scientific literature: a new measure of the relationship between two documents, *Journal of the American Society for Information Science* 24(4) (1973) 265–9.

[18] I.V. Marshakova, System of document connections based on references, *Nauchno-Tekhnicheskaia Informatsiia* 2(1) (1973) 3–8.

[19] H.D. White and B.C. Griffith, Author co-citation: a literature measure of intellectual structure, *Journal of the American Society for Information Science* 32(3) (1982) 163–72.

[20] H.D. White, Pathfinder networks and author cocitation analysis: a remapping of paradigmatic information scientists, *Journal of the American Society for Information Science* 54(5) (2003) 423–34.

[21] J. Nicolaisen, Citation analysis, *Annual Review of Information Science and Technology* 41 (2007) 609–41.

[22] J.E. Hirsch, An index to quantify an individual's scientific research output, *Proceedings of the National Academy of Sciences* 102(46) (2005) 16569–72.

[23] C. Oppenheim, Using the *h*-index to rank influential British researchers in information science and librarianship, *Journal of the American Society for Information Science and Technology* 58(2) (2007) 297–301.

[24] B. Cronin and L.I. Meho, Using the *h*-index to rank influential information scientists, *Journal of the American Society for Information Science and Technology* 57(9) (2006) 1275–8.

[25] S. Harnad, Open access scientometrics and the UK Research Assessment Exercise. In: D. Torres-Salinas and H.F. Moed (eds) *Proceedings of 11th Annual Meeting of the International Society for Scientometrics and Informetrics* (CINDOC, Madrid, Spain, 2007) 27–33.

[26] V. Bence and C. Oppenheim, The influence of peer review on the Research Assessment Exercise, *Journal of Information Science* 30(4) (2004) 347–68.

[27] Tertiary Education Commission, *Performance-Based Research Fund – a Guideline for 2003* (2003). Available at: www.tec.govt.nz/upload/downloads/pbrffinal-july03.pdf (accessed 7 September 2007).

[28] DEST, *Institutional Grants Scheme* (n.d.) Available at: www.dest.gov.au/sectors/higher_education/programmes_funding/general_funding/ operating_grants/institutional_grants_scheme.htm (accessed 12 September 2007).

[29] S.E. Cozzens, Assessing federally-supported academic research in the United States, *Research Evaluation* 9(1) (2000) 5–10.

[30] B. van der Meulen and A. Rip, Evaluation of societal quality of public sector research in the Netherlands, *Research Evaluation* 9(1) (2000) 11–25.

[31] M. Pienaar et al., The South African system of evaluating and rating individual researchers: its merits, shortcomings, impact and future, *Research Evaluation* 9(1) (2000) 27–36.

[32] A. Silvani, G. Sirilli and F. Tuzi, R&D evaluation in Italy: more needs to be done, *Research Evaluation* 14(3) (2005) 207–15.

[33] L. Butler, Explaining Australia's increased share of ISI publications – the effects of a funding formula based on publication counts, *Research Policy* 32(1) (2003) 143–55.

[34] J. Adams, Research assessment in the UK, *Science* 296(5569) (2002) 805.

[35] L.I. Meho and K. Yang, Impact of data sources on citation counts and rankings of LIS faculty: Web of Science vs. Scopus and Google Scholar, *Journal of the American Society for Information Science and Technology* 58(13) (2007) 2105–25.

[36] M. Norris and C. Oppenheim, Comparing alternatives to the Web of Science for coverage of the social sciences literature, *Journal of Informetrics* 1(1) (2007) 161–9.

[37] K. Kousha and M. Thelwall, Google Scholar citations and Google Web/URL citations: a multi-discipline exploratory analysis, *Journal of the American Society for Information Science and Technology* 58(7) (2007) 1055–65.

[38] P. Jacsó, Google Scholar: the pros and the cons, *Online Information Review* 29(2) (2005) 208–14.

[39]  C. Chen, *Information Visualization: Beyond the Horizon*, 2nd Edition (Springer, New York, 2004).

[40]  H. Small, Visualising science through citation mapping, *Journal of American Society for Information Science* 50(9) (1999) 799–813.

[41]  K. Boyack, Using detailed maps of science to identify potential collaborations. In: D. Torres-Salinas and H.F. Moed (eds), *Proceedings of ISSI 2007 Volume 1* (CSIC, Madrid, 2007) 124–35.

[42]  L. Leydesdorff, Betweenness centrality as an indicator of the interdisciplinarity of scientific journals, *Journal of the American Society for Information Science & Technology* 58(9) (2007) 1303–19.

[43]  C. Chen, CiteSpace II: detecting and visualizing emerging trends and transient patterns in scientific literature, *Journal of the American Society for Information Science and Technology* 57(3) (2006) 359–77.

[44]  M. Gibbons et al., *The New Production of Knowledge* (Sage, London, 1994).

[45]  M. Meyer, Academic patents as an indicator of useful research? A new approach to measure academic inventiveness, *Research Evaluation* 12(1) (2003) 17–27.

[46]  C. Oppenheim, Do patent citations count? In: B. Cronin and H.B. Atkins (eds) *The Web of Knowledge: a Festschrift in Honor of Eugene Garfield* (Information Today, Medford, NJ, 2000) 405–32. [ASIS Monograph Series]

[47]  L. Leydesdorff, The university-industry knowledge relationship: analyzing patents and the science base of technologies, *Journal of the American Society for Information Science and Technology* 54(11) (2004) 991–1001.

[48]  H.-R. Ke et al., Exploring behavior of e-journal users in science and technology: transaction log analysis of Elsevier's ScienceDirect OnSite in Taiwan, *Library & Information Science Research* 24(3) (2002) 265–91.

[49]  K. Marek and E.J. Valauskas, Web logs as indices of electronic journal use: tools for identifying a 'classic' article, *Libri* 52(4) (2002) 220–30.

[50]  M.J. Kurtz et al., The bibliometric properties of article readership information, *Journal of the American Society for Information Science & Technology* 56(2) (2005) 111–28.

[51]  S. Jones et al., A transaction log analysis of a digital library, *International Journal on Digital Libraries* 3(2) (2000) 152–69.

[52]  P. Huntington, D. Nicholas and H.R. Jamali, Site navigation and its impact on content viewed by the virtual scholar: a deep log analysis, *Journal of Information Science* 33(5) (2007) 598–610.

[53]  P.M. Davis and M.J. Fromerth, Does the arXiv lead to higher citations and reduced publisher downloads for mathematics articles? *Scientometrics* 71(2) (2007) 203–15.

[54] T.S. Brody, S. Harnad and L. Carr, Earlier web usage statistics as predictors of later citation impact, *Journal of the American Society for Information Science and Technology* 57(8) (2006) 1060–72.

[55] L. Björneborn and P. Ingwersen, Toward a basic framework for webometrics, *Journal of the American Society for Information Science and Technology* 55(14) (2004) 1216–27.

[56] T.C. Almind and P. Ingwersen, Informetric analyses on the World Wide Web: methodological approaches to 'Webometrics', Journal of Documentation 53(4) (1997) 404–26.

[57] P. Mayr and F. Tosques, *Google Web APIs: an Instrument for Webometric Analyses?* (2005) Available at: www.ib.hu-berlin.de/%7Emayr/arbeiten/ISSI2005_Mayr_Toques.pdf (accessed 7 January 2008).

[58] I.F. Aguillo et al., Scientific research activity and communication measured with cybermetrics indicators, *Journal of the American Society for Information Science and Technology* 57(10) (2006) 1296–1302.

[59] P. Ingwersen, The calculation of Web Impact Factors, *Journal of Documentation* 54(2) (1998) 236–43.

[60] B. Cronin, Bibliometrics and beyond: some thoughts on web-based citation analysis, *Journal of Information Science* 27(1) (2001) 1–7.

[61] M. Thelwall, Extracting macroscopic information from web links, *Journal of the American Society for Information Science and Technology* 52(13) (2001) 1157–68.

[62] O. Thomas and P. Willet, Webometric analysis of departments of librarianship and information science, *Journal of Information Science* 26(6) (2000) 421–8.

[63] F. Barjak and M. Thelwall, A statistical analysis of the web presences of European life sciences research teams, *Journal of the American Society for Information Science and Technology* 59(4) (2008) 628–43.

[64] F. Barjak, X. Li and M. Thelwall, Which factors explain the web impact of scientists' personal home pages? *Journal of the American Society for Information Science and Technology* 58(2) (2007) 200–211.

[65] M. Thelwall and G. Harries, Do better scholars' Web publications have significantly higher online impact? *Journal of American Society for Information Science and Technology* 55(2) (2004) 149–59.

[66] M. Thelwall, *Link Analysis: an Information Science Approach* (Academic Press, San Diego, 2004).

[67] G. Heimeriks, M. Hörlesberger and P. van den Besselaar, Mapping communication and collaboration in heterogeneous research networks, *Scientometrics* 58(2) (2003) 391–413.

[68] G. Harries et al., Hyperlinks as a data source for science mapping, *Journal of Information Science* 30(5) (2004) 436–47.

[69] X. Li et al., National and international university departmental web site interlinking, part 2: link patterns, *Scientometrics* 64(2) (2005) 187–208.

[70] N. Payne and M. Thelwall, A longitudinal study of academic webs: growth and stabilisation, *Scientometrics* 71(3) (2007) 523–39.

[71] N. Payne, *A Longitudinal Study of Academic Web Links: Identifying and Explaining Change* (University of Wolverhampton, Wolverhampton, 2007)

[72] L. Vaughan and D. Shaw, Bibliographic and web citations: what is the difference? *Journal of the American Society for Information Science and Technology* 54(14) (2003) 1313–22.

[73] L. Vaughan and D. Shaw, Web citation data for impact assessment: a comparison of four science disciplines, *Journal of the American Society for Information Science & Technology* 56(10) (2005) 1075–87.

[74] K. Kousha and M. Thelwall, Motivations for URL citations to open access library and information science articles, *Scientometrics* 68(3) (2006) 501–17.

[75] J.Bar-Ilan, The use of Web search engines in information science research. *Annual Review of Information Science and Technology* 38 (2004) 231–88.

[76] S. Lawrence and C.L. Giles, Accessibility of information on the web, *Nature* 400(6740) (1999) 107–9.

[77] L. Introna and H. Nissenbaum, Shaping the web: why the politics of search engines matters, *The Information Society* 16(3) (2000) 1–17.

[78] E. Van Couvering, New media? The political economy of Internet search engines. In: *Annual Conference of the International Association of Media & Communications Researchers* (Porto Alegre, Brazil, 2004). Available at: http://personal.lse.ac.uk/vancouve/IAMCR-CTP_SearchEnginePoliticalEconomy_EVC_2004-07-14.pdf (accessed 7 January 2008).

[79] L. Vaughan and M. Thelwall, Search engine coverage bias: evidence and possible causes, *Information Processing and Management* 40(4) (2004) 693–707.

[80] J. Bar-Ilan and B.C. Peritz, Evolution, continuity, and disappearance of documents on a specific topic on the Web: a longitudinal study of 'informetrics', *Journal of the American Society for Information Science and Technology* 55(11) (2004) 980 –90.

[81] M. Thelwall, Extracting accurate and complete results from search engines: case study Windows Live, *Journal of the American Society for Information Science and Technology* 59(1) (2008) 38–50. Available at: www.scit.wlv.ac.uk/%7Ecm1993/papers/2007_Accurate_Complete_preprint.doc (accessed 22 May 2007).

[82] H.W. Snyder and H. Rosenbaum, Can search engines be used for Web-link analysis? A critical review, *Journal of Documentation* 55(4) (1999) 375–84.

[83] J. Bar-Ilan, Search engine results over time – a case study on search engine stability, *Cybermetrics* (1999). Available at: www.cindoc.csic.es/cybermetrics/articles/v2i1p1.html (accessed 7 January 2008).

[84] W. Mettrop and P. Nieuwenhuysen, Internet search engines – fluctuations in document accessibility, *Journal of Documentation* 57(5) (2001) 623–51.

[85] R. Rousseau, Daily time series of common single word searches in AltaVista and NorthernLight, *Cybermetrics* 2/3 (1999). Available at: www.cindoc.csic.es/cybermetrics/articles/v2i1p2.html (accessed 25 July 2006).

[86] A.G. Smith, Does metadata count? A Webometric investigation. In: M. Tegelaars (ed.), *Proceedings of DC-2002, Florence, 14–17 October 2002* (Firenze University Press, Firenze, 2002) 133–8.

[87] T. Craven, Variations in use of meta tag keywords by web pages in different languages, *Journal of Information Science* 30(3) (2004) 268–79.

[88] A. Broder et al., Graph structure in the web, *Journal of Computer Networks* 33(1/6) (2000) 309–20.

[89] L. Björneborn, *Small-world link structures across an academic web space – a library and information science approach*. PhD thesis, Department of Information Studies (Royal School of Library and Information Science, Copenhagen, Denmark, 2004).

[90] L. Björneborn, 'Mini small worlds' of shortest link paths crossing domain boundaries in an academic Web space, *Scientometrics* 68(3) (2006) 395–414.

[91] A.L. Barabási and R. Albert, Emergence of scaling in random networks, *Science* 286(5439) (1999) 509–12.

[92] S. Brin and L. Page, The anatomy of a large scale hypertextual Web search engine, *Computer Networks and ISDN Systems* 30(1/7) (1998) 107–17.

[93] D. Pennock et al., Winners don't take all: characterizing the competition for links on the web, *Proceedings of the National Academy of Sciences* 99(8) (2002) 5207–11.

[94] W. Koehler, A longitudinal study of Web pages continued: a report after six years, *Information Research* 9(2). Available at: http://informationr.net/ir/9–2/paper174.html (accessed 20 September 2007).

[95] J.L. Ortega, I. Aguillo and J.A. Prieto, Longitudinal study of content and elements in the scientific web environment, *Journal of Information Science* 32(4) (2006) 344–51.

[96] D. Gruhl et al., How to build a WebFountain: an architecture for very large-scale text analytics, *IBM Systems Journal* 43(1) (2004) 64–77.

[97] M. Gamon et al., Pulse: mining customer opinions from free text (IDA 2005), *Lecture Notes in Computer Science* 3646 (2005) 121–32.

[98]  D. Gruhl et al., The predictive power of online chatter. In: R.L. Grossman et al. (eds), *KDD '05: Proceedings of the Eleventh ACM SIGKDD International Conference on Knowledge Discovery in Data Mining* (ACM Press, New York, 2005) 78–87.

[99]  D. Gruhl et al. Information diffusion through Blogspace. In: *WWW2004, New York*. (2004). Available at: www2004.org/proceedings/docs/1p491.pdf (accessed 10 July 2006).

[100]  M. Thelwall, R. Prabowo and R. Fairclough, Are raw RSS feeds suitable for broad issue scanning? A science concern case study, *Journal of the American Society for Information Science and Technology* 57(12) (2006) 1644–54.

[101]  M. Thelwall and R. Prabowo, Identifying and characterizing public science-related concerns from RSS feeds, *Journal of the American Society for Information Science & Technology* 58(3) (2007) 379–90.

[102]  S.A. Golder, D. Wilkinson and B.A. Huberman, Rhythms of social interaction: messaging within a massive online network. In: *3rd International Conference on Communities and Technologies (CT2007), East Lansing, MI*, (2007) Available at: www.hpl.hp.com/research/idl/papers/facebook/facebook.pd (accessed 7 January 2008).

[103]  d. boyd, Friendster and publicly articulated social networks. In: *Conference on Human Factors and Computing Systems (CHI 2004, Vienna: April 24–29)* (ACM Press, New York, 2004). Available at: www.danah.org/papers/CHI2004Friendster.pdf (accessed 3 July 2007).

[104]  d. boyd, Friends, Friendsters, and MySpace Top 8: writing community into being on social network sites, *First Monday* 11(2) (2006). Available at: www.firstmonday.org/issues/issue11_12/boyd/index.html (accessed 23 June 2007).

[105]  M. Thelwall, Social networks, gender and friending: an analysis of MySpace member profiles. *Journal of the American Society for Information Science and Technology*, 59(8) (2008), 1321–30.

[106]  T. Escher, *The Geography of (Online) Social Networks (Web 2.0, York University)* (2007). Available at: http://people.oii.ox.ac.uk/escher/wp-content/uploads/2007/09/Escher_York_presentation.pdf (accessed 18 September 2007).

[107]  L. Prescott, *Hitwise US Consumer Generated Media Report* (2007). Available at: www.hitwise.com/ (accessed 19 March 2007).

[108]  D. Wilkinson et al., Motivations for academic Web site interlinking: evidence for the Web as a novel source of information on informal scholarly communication, *Journal of Information Science* 29(1) (2003) 49–56.

[109] S. Robinson et al., *The Role of Networking in Research Activities (NetReAct D4.1)* (Empirica Gesellschaft für Kommunikations- und Technologieforschung mbH, Bonn, Germany, 2006).

# 16

# How I learned to love the Brits

EUGENE GARFIELD

As a child I grew up in awe of an English accent. That was not unusual for an American because so many movie stars spoke with an English accent. All during my high school and college days I instinctively believed that anyone who spoke with an Oxford or BBC accent was an authority. And I even held professors and intellectuals who adopted the Harvard version of an English accent in awe. Several of my professors at Columbia University deserved that sort of adulation since they were indeed experts in their respective fields. However, that all changed when I reached Johns Hopkins University in 1951, when I audited a course in statistics with Professor W.G. Cochran. The student who sat next to me was a Brit who spoke with great authority but after a few weeks I began to realize that most of what he said was nonsense.

For the next few years I had little contact with Englishmen during my stay at Johns Hopkins but my boss at the Welch Medical Library Indexing Project reminded me regularly that he had studied Elizabethan medicine at Oxford.

My next encounter with the English occurred after leaving the Welch Project. I was impressed by the performance of the editor of the *Journal of Documentation,* who stood up to the harassment from my then former boss. He was angry at me for submitting a paper to the *Journal of Documentation* without his permission. So much so that he asked the attorney for the university to write a 'cease and desist' letter but the editor did not buckle to his threats. So I can honestly say that my first published paper appeared in an English publication [1]. These stressful events occurred while I was enrolled at Columbia University School of Library Service.

Of course, even during my two years in Baltimore the British influence on my career was felt strongly. My 'bible', so to speak, at that time was the one-volume, 700+ page *Proceedings of the 1948 Royal Society Scientific Information*

*Conference* [2]. I mentioned the key role played by John Desmond Bernal in that meeting when I spoke about his impact on science policy studies and the field of information science at the recent symposium held at University College in Dublin in September 2007 [3]. Hopefully the Royal Society will soon post the full text of the *Royal Society Proceedings* to their website. A few years ago I was able to convince the National Academy of Sciences Press to post the full text of the two volumes of the 1958 *Proceedings of the International Conference on Scientific Information* sponsored by the National Science Foundation [4].

The English connection picked up again in the spring of 1957 when much to my surprise I received an invitation to attend the Dorking Conference on Classification. My brief recollection of that conference follows, with thanks to Robert V. Williams (the co-coordinator of the *Pioneers of Information Science Scrapbook* [5], which includes my account titled *Memories of the 1957 Dorking Conference*, also at [6]). William's 'scrapbook' contains the reflections and comments of many of the 'pioneers' of information science who were invited to a dinner in their honor at the 1998 Conference on the History and Heritage of Science Information Systems, held in Pittsburgh, PA, October 23–25. These web pages contain their brief reflections as well as interesting photographs.

(The relevant text of my remarks at Dorking is available at [7] taken from the *Proceedings of the International Study Conference on Classification for Information Retrieval* held at Beatrice Webb House, Dorking, England, May 13–17, 1957 and published by ASLIB, at the Pergamon Press, in 1957.)

At Dorking my awe of the English was not only restored but reinforced. The group of friends I made there affected the course of my career. Within one year the Institute for Information Scientists was founded. One of the crowning moments of my life occurred when I was invited to become an Honorary Fellow in 1966.

Alan Gilchrist has briefly described to me the origins of the *Journal of Information Science* and its predecessors. To help celebrate this 50th anniversary occasion we have compiled a *HistCite*$^{TM}$ bibliographical record of JIS from its official inception in 1979 [8, 9]. *HistCite*$^{TM}$ is a system designed to help selectively identify the significant (most cited) papers retrieved in topical searches of the Web of Science (SCI, SSCI and/or AHCI). Once a marked list of papers has been created, the resulting export file is processed to create tables ordered by author, year, or citation frequency as well as historiographs which include a small percentage of the most-cited papers and their citation links. Time and space do not permit me to report in detail on the two previous decades during which time I first met and came under the stimulating influence of Anthony E. Cawkell and his family. Tony and I were associated for more than 30 years until his death a few years ago. Initially he was our man in London and then Director of Research. During that time I visited England about four times each year and enjoyed the pleasures of London and the stimulation of dozens of colleagues in science publishing and the library and information worlds. I then came to realize that the 'English' connection also included the Welsh, the Scots and the Irish.

The formation of the Institute of Information Scientists in 1958 had a great influence on its US counterpart at the time, the American Documentation Institute. The name of the IIS stimulated me and others to push for a name change of ADI to the American Society for Information Science (ASIS). The ADI officially changed its name to ASIS on 1 January 1968 just 10 years after the founding of the IIS. ADI's journal, *American Documentation,* retained its title until the end of 1969 when it became the *Journal of the American Society for Information Science.* When I became President of ASIS in 2000 I was able to convince the membership it was time to become the American Society for Information Science & Technology (ASIS&T).

However, it may interest and amuse some of my English colleagues to know how I became an information scientist. Upon graduation from library school in New York, I began my career as a documentation consultant. My first client was Smith, Kline & French Laboratories in Philadelphia, now Glaxo SmithKline. However, in order to give the impression that I was not just a lone self-employed person I adopted the business name Eugene Garfield Associates – Information Engineers. Having started as an engineering major when I was 17, and recognizing my affinity for engineering approaches to problems, that seemed a more appropriate appellation for my expertise in scientific documentation and especially IBM punched card machines and calculators.

I subsequently received a letter from the Pennsylvania Board of Professional Engineers stating that I was not allowed to call myself an information engineer unless I had a degree from an accredited engineering school or the equivalent thereof. Rather than fight City Hall, as we say in the USA, I decided to become an information scientist. Then in 1960 I changed the name of my company to the Institute for Scientific Information. That move proved to be quite important, I believe, in the exponential growth of ISI's activities over the next few decades. I must say that the British influence and connection was a factor. Non-profit, academic or government enterprises were more highly regarded in the library world than private ventures. It was many decades later that for-profit enterprises achieved equal regard in the USA and the UK. The Information Industry Association was founded by me and four other individual entrepreneurs because in those days the National Federation of Abstracting and Indexing Services limited membership to non-profit and governmental information organizations.

In the Spring of 1957, I temporarily shared an office in Washington, DC, at Thomas Circle with my new partner Harry Brager, a public relations man. He wisely recommended changing the title of 'Management's DocuMation Preview' to *Current Contents*®. A few weeks later, I received an unexpected invitation to discuss CC® and citation indexing (based on my papers in *Science* [10] and the *Journal of the Patent Office Society* [11]) at the International Conference on Classification for Information Retrieval mentioned earlier. The conference was only a few weeks off and I was nearly broke. Using TWA's instalment plan, I bought a round-trip ticket to London at a cost of $489 – a small fortune for me in those days. The plane from New York stopped in Newfoundland en route to Scotland and the greenest land I had ever seen. After a visit to relatives in Manchester, I went straight to Dorking in Surrey and my first personal encounter with British information scientists. I would meet J.D. Bernal one year later at the International Conference on Scientific Information in Washington, DC.

It is quite possible that Jesse Shera, editor of *American Documentation* had suggested I be invited to Dorking. In 1953 he had invited me to become Associate Editor. Other participants included Robert Fairthorne, D.J. Foskett, Jason Farradane, Eric J. Coates, Cyril Cleverdon, Brian C. Vickery, D.J. Campbell, N.T. Ball, Jack Wells, Barbara Kyle, John Mills, and last, but not least, S.R. Ranganathan. I spoke at length with Mills and Ranganathan about my personal encounter with Henry Evelyn Bliss in 1954 [12]. The Bliss classification was better known in the UK than in the USA thanks to Jack Mills.

Forty years later, FID publication #7146 commemorated the 40th anniversary of Dorking. Unfortunately, I was unaware of this 1997 meeting, so I missed the opportunity to catch up with old friends, many of whom I had not seen for decades. In that reminiscence of the Dorking conference, Robert Fairthorne mentioned my 'surprise' at the British members 'disagreeing without being disagreeable', unlike the rancor frequently encountered at the early meetings of the American Documentation Institute. On the other hand, Cyril Cleverdon recalled the evening when 'Gene Garfield defended his proposals for a citation index against a group of very skeptical and outspoken critics', including Cyril himself! Jean Aitchison recalled me as 'a young man vigorously marketing his ideas of journal contents lists, at an extra evening session'. Indeed, 1957 was the year that the Life Sciences edition of *Current Contents* was introduced to the pharmaceutical industry.

The 1957 Dorking *Proceedings* volume, page 98, contains a concise account of citation indexes covered in the evening session on 14 May.

On the second day, I realized that if I attended Wednesday's session, I would not see London. So I took an early morning train to Victoria Station. During the next 15 hours, I visited everything from the Tower of London to Parliament and the British Museum. I arrived at Victoria Station about midnight and was shocked to learn that it was closed. The only transportation to Dorking was a taxi. When I chaired the morning session the next day, the audience gasped when I said that I had taxied from London. I didn't mention that it used most of my remaining cash.

This remarkable meeting eventually led to my joining the UK Institute of Information Scientists which, as mentioned above, awarded me an Honorary Fellowship in 1966. Through IIS, I made the friendship of researchers like John Martyn, Alan Gilchrist, Charles Oppenheim, Blaise Cronin and others too numerous to mention.

As a postscript to the remarks on the early days of *JIS* and the IIS, I would like to add that my role as science communicator, intertwined with my activities in information science, were in another world which led me to friendships with British journalists like John Maddox, Bernard Dixon, Maurice Goldsmith, Anthony Michaelis, Steven Lock – editor of the *British Medical Journal*, Richard Horton, editor of *Lancet*, Maeve O'Connor – medical editor, and John Ziman, former editor of *Philosophical Magazine*. Other colleagues not to be forgotten include D.J. Urquhart, Maurice B. Line and the many friends at the British Lending Library. Last but not the least are my British 'émigré' friends – Derek J. deSolla Price, Norman Horrocks, Arnold Thackray, Michael Lynch. Peter Willett, Monty Hyams and Wendy Warr were also among my many friends in the chemical information world. I'm sure many others have been inadvertently omitted. In my numerous dealings with publishers, those who stood out in the British pantheon are Per Saugman, Robert Campbell, Gunther Hayden and Gillian Page. And last but not least, my present partner at *The Scientist*, Vitek Tracz.

Every family and profession also has its rogues and adversaries. Unique in the history of scientific publishing is Robert Maxwell whose exploits have been described in great detail by others. But it is not often known that the founder of Pergamon was known to me from the 1950s when I was a consultant to *Biological Abstracts* and he attempted to take them over by one means or another including setting up a competitive service. For over three decades Maxwell tried to recruit me as his director of research after first threatening me with copyright violation when we included some of his journals in *Current Contents*. Much to his dismay he found that in spite of his histrionics he was no match for my intellectual property attorney Arthur H. Seidel and his partner Edward Gonda.

Maxwell's relentless pursuit of ISI kept up until the time of his untimely death shortly after he had acquired a small percentage of shares in the company just before it was sold to JPT and then Thomson. The full story needs to be told in another venue at another time.

## References

[1]   E. Garfield, The preparation of subject heading lists by punched card methods, *Journal of Documentation* 10(1) (1954). Reprinted in *Essays of an Information Scientist*, Volume 6 (1983) 444–53. Available at: www.garfield.library.upenn.edu/essays/v6p444y1983.pdf (accessed 1 February 2008).

[2]   B. Vickery, The Royal Society Scientific Information Conference of 1948, *Journal of Documentation* 54(3) (1998) 281–3.

[3]   E. Garfield, *Tracing the Influence of J.D. Bernal on the World of Science through Citation Analysis, paper presented at the British Association for Crystal Growth/Irish Association for Crystal Growth Conference & Bernal Symposium on Protein Crystallization, University College Dublin, Belfield, Ireland, 3–4, September 2007* (2007). Available at: http://garfield.library.upenn.edu/papers/bernaldublin0907.pdf (accessed 1 February 2008).

[4]   *Proceedings of the International Conference on Scientific Information, sponsored by the National Science Foundation, National Academy of Sciences, American Documentation Institute, and National Research Council, 1959.* Available at: www.nap.edu/catalog/10866.html (accessed 1 February 2008).

[5]   R.V. Williams, *Pioneers of Information Science Scrapbook* (?1999). Available at: www.libsci.sc.edu/Bob/ISP/scrapbook.htm (accessed 1 February 2008).

[6]   E. Garfield, *Memories of the 1957 Dorking Conference, held at Beatrice Webb House, Dorking, England, 13–17 May, 1957.* Available at:

http://garfield.library.upenn.edu/papers/memoriesofdorkingconference1957.html (accessed 1 February 2008).

[7]     Available at: www.garfield.library.upenn.edu/papers/proc_35may1957.pdf (accessed 1 February 2008).

[8]     *HistCite Compilation for Journal of Information Science*. Available at: http://garfield.library.upenn.edu/histcomp/j_info_sci/index-tl.html (accessed 1 February 2008).

[9]     *HistCite Compilation for Journal of Information Science (with Citing Papers)*. Available at: http://garfield.library.upenn.edu/histcomp/j_info_sci_citing/index-tl.html (accessed 1 February 2008).

[10]   E. Garfield, Citation indexes for science: a new dimension in documentation through association of ideas, *Science* 122(3159) (1955) 108–11. Available at: http://garfield.library.upenn.edu/papers/science1955.pdf (accessed 1 February 2008).

[11]   E. Garfield, Breaking the subject index barrier – a citation index for chemical patents, *Journal of the Patent Office Society* 39(8) (1957) 583–95. Available at: www.garfield.library.upenn.edu/essays/v6p472y1983.pdf (accessed 1 February 2008).

[12]   E. Garfield, The 'Other' Immortal: a memorable day with Henry E. Bliss, *Wilson Library Bulletin* 49(4) (1974) 288–92. Reprinted in *Essays of an Information Scientist*, Volume 2 (1974–76) 250–51; and in *Current Contents* 15 (1975) 7–8. Available at: www.garfield.library.upenn.edu/essays/v2p250y1974-76.pdf (accessed 1 February 2008).

# Index